GOLF IN EUROPE

*A Traveler's Guide to 200
of Europe's Best Golf Courses*

By SAUL GALIN

HAWTHORN BOOKS, INC.   Publishers   New York

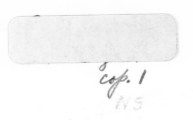

First edition: 1967

Roo249 72407

PREFACE

Golfing in Europe can be fun. Part of the fun is the ease with which you can combine it with your other activities. Wherever you are in western Europe, you are almost certain to have an excellent course within an hour's traveling time, or at most two hours'. Often you will find clusters of courses, especially around capital cities and other places popular with American visitors.

Thus, if you plan to visit London or Paris, there are numerous courses listed for the areas around these cities; or if you are on the Riviera, you will find several listings there. If you know where you are going—whether to a particular city, region, or general area—look at the table of contents for that country, and there you are, an excellent course where you know you will be welcome.

Incidentally, if you know your itinerary, it is always a good idea to write or call ahead to reserve the course. This is especially true if you are traveling in the prime summer months and want to play on a weekend. European courses, like American, can be crowded, but a reservation will hold your place—and also help you obtain a caddie. Wherever a reservation seems absolutely necessary, I have indicated it for that course.

My basis for selection of courses has been threefold: first, the excellence of the course and the beauty of its surroundings; second, its accessibility by normal means of transportation (bus, car or train) and, third, the very important fact that you will be welcome. There are, surely, many fine courses that you might have heard of but which you don't find listed here. In most cases these courses place severe restrictions on visitors or else are altogether closed to nonmembers who cannot be introduced by a member. Also, I have chosen courses where some English is spoken—I know, because I spoke English to all of the club secretaries.

What will surely surprise you is the low cost of golf in Europe. Green fees, caddies, instruction by the professional, the rental of equipment—all of these are extremely reasonable, often as little as $1 for green fees on a celebrated links. Such fees will surely rise slowly year by year, but you can always count on the general range listed here.

Another particularly attractive feature is that you can rent a set of clubs at most courses—but that is obviously up to you. Many golfers wouldn't think of playing with any but their own clubs, but you may wish to travel light. In fact, the only item you should bring with you is a letter of introduction from your local golf club, if you belong to one; also your handicap, if you have one. Such a letter, normally, is the sole document that a Euro-

5

pean club secretary will be interested in, and even that is not required on most courses. For further details, check my section on "other information" for each club.

Also keep in mind the fact that golf in most of Europe is played all year round. European weather lacks the extremes of American heat and cold and stays close to a range of 30°–75° F. much of the time, making golf playable for four seasons. In fact, many courses are even more attractive off-season— fewer crowds, more attention from the professional, unlimited Sunday play, and a terrain that remains springy and playable.

In the section on accommodations, I have indicated hotels, large and small, that I think you will find comfortable and that I personally like. I have not visited all of them, but they come with high recommendations from people in the area—club secretaries, club professionals, tourist people for the region. Whenever a hotel offers a pension (room and all meals) or half pension (room and one or two meals), I have so indicated. Some golfers may want to remain for three or more days in a particular spot, and a pension eliminates the restaurant problem. This is, obviously, an individual matter. The listings exist for your convenience.

I hope that this guide proves to be exactly that—that it guides you to new golfing experiences. Whether golf becomes merely a sideline on your trip, or whether it is the sole object of your tour, you can be assured that golf in Europe is a great experience—for the high quality of the courses, the beauty of the surroundings, and the general standard of excellence you will find. If your expectations are high, you will not be disappointed.

CONTENTS

GOLF
IN EUROPE

AUSTRIA

Nearly all the most popular Austrian cities and regions contain courses that welcome visitors. Although most of these courses are nine-holers, they offer sufficient variety and interest to attract nearly every type of player. Also, the scenery is usually so fine that even the most experienced golfer won't mind only nine holes. Incidentally, it is the mountainous terrain that explains the relative shortness of most Austrian courses.

It is fitting that the championship course of the country should be in Vienna, a city almost everyone will want to visit. It is an excellent 18 holes—perhaps not equal to the best in England and Scotland, but surely up to most on the continent.

After Vienna, Salzburg, with its numerous festivals and other attractions, will draw most visitors; it offers three good courses of varying difficulty. Start perhaps with *Salzkammergut*, which has the added advantage of being near the famous spa of Bad Ischl; then try *Salzburg-Klessheim*, in the city of Salzburg itself; and finish with *Kitzbühel-Mittersill*, set in the heart of the famous Tirol, where excellent skiing also awaits you. All are within 1 to 1½ hours of Salzburg by car.

For the visitor to Innsbruck or that general area, two courses will provide excellent practice for more difficult ones in Austria and the rest of Europe. Start with either *Innsbruck-Igls* or *Achensee*. Neither should give the average player much trouble, but both will give you a good idea of a mountain course.

For further resort areas try *Semmering* in the southern Alps and *Kärntner* in Dellach, on lovely Lake Wörth. If you wish, you can combine your golf with skiing in the first or with water sports in the second.

Austria is one of the most inexpensive countries in Europe, and its tourist facilities promise comfort, beauty and personal satisfaction.

Golf-Club Wien

The Vienna Golf Course is the championship course of Austria. Although only moderately long, it has excellent overall balance, with 4 long holes at par 5 and 5 short ones at par 3. These shorts are really short. The remainder of the holes are in the middle range of 350 yards. This kind of variety and balance should satisfy everyone, possibly giving the nod to the moderately long to long hitter. The terrain is gently undulating, and several greens are situated on elevated plateaus or in valleys. The greens are well trapped, and the many majestic old trees are always a hazard to anyone off line. In all, this is a course to delight every type of player, and there is the added incentive of having Vienna almost at one's elbow for the evenings.

LOCATION: The course is in the Vienna Prater, an enormous park about a ten-minute drive or bus ride north of the center of Vienna.

OTHER INFORMATION: The course is open to nonmembers, unlimited, but guests must be a member of a local golf club. It is open for the entire season (April-December). Professionals are always on hand. Practice ground is available.

Number of holes: 18. *Par:* 71. *Length:* 6055 yards.

Green fees: weekdays, $2; weekends, $3/day. *Lessons:* $4/hour. *Caddies:* $1.75/18 holes. *Equipment and caddie carts:* clubs $1/day, carts $0.50/day.

OTHER SPORTS FACILITIES: Tennis, riding and swimming.

ACCOMMODATIONS: No living space in the club house, but bar and restaurant are available.

In Vienna: *Ambassador* (Neuer Markt 5, Tel. 527511). A luxury hotel of international standing, open all year. Rooms from $10 to $14 for best single; $18 to $26 for best double; private bath, central heating; taxes and services not included. *Bristol* (Kärntner Ring 1, Tel. 529552). A luxury hotel of international standing, open all year. Rooms from $10 to $15 for best single; $18 to $27 for best double; private bath, central heating; taxes and services not included. *France* (Schottenring 3, Tel. 343540). A first-class hotel, open all year. Rooms from $8 to $10 for best single; $15.75 to $17.50 for best double; private bath, central heating, continental breakfast; taxes and services included. *Royal* (Singerstrasse 3, Tel. 524631). A first-class hotel, open all year. Rooms from $9.75 to $13.75 for best single; $13:50 to $19.50 for best double; private bath, central heating; taxes and services included. *Astoria* (Kärntner Strasse 32, Tel. 526585). A very good, comfortable hotel, open all year. Rooms from $8 to $8.75 for best single; $14 to $14.50 for best double; private bath, central heating; taxes and services not included.

TOURIST ATTRACTIONS: Vienna is one of the most sophisticated and charming capitals in the world. Try to see the Spanish Riding School, the Art History Museum (with paintings by Rembrandt, Breughel, Tintoretto and Velasquez), the Cathedral of St. Stephen, the Opera House and the Schönbrunn Palace. Whatever you do, visit that famous Viennese institution, the café (the Mozart Café is a good one to start with). A tip to the women: Don't leave Vienna without looking at knitwear, leather goods, petit-point and fine jewelry.

FOR FURTHER INFORMATION: Write to: Secretary, Golf-Club Wien, Freudenau 65A, 1020 Wien 2, Austria. Telephone: 55.14.62.

Kärntner Golf Club Dellach

The Kärntner Golf Club Dellach is in south central Austria, tucked away in the Alps and sheltered from winds and the cold. Summers are hot but attractive because of the picturesque countryside and the many water sports offered by Lake Wörth. The course is a good one, flat, with an interesting variety of holes, many overlooking the lake. The long driver has a decided advantage here, although the careful, accurate player may also do well. It is a good course for the relatively experienced golfer.

LOCATION: The course is in Dellach on Lake Wörth, 6 miles E of Velden, 12 miles W of Klagenfurt, 205 miles SW of Vienna, 170 miles SE of Salzburg, 194 miles E of Innsbruck, 176 miles SW of Wiener Neustadt. It is accessible by car.

OTHER INFORMATION: The course is open to nonmembers, unlimited, for the entire season (April-October), with a professional always on hand. The most crowded months are July and August, with weather best May-September. Practice ground is available.
Number of holes: 9. *Par:* 70 (for twice around). *Length:* 6066 yards. *Green fees:* $2.25/day. *Lessons:* $3/hour. *Caddies:* $0.75/9 holes. *Equipment and caddie carts:* clubs $1.75/day, carts $0.75/day.

OTHER SPORTS FACILITIES: Swimming, fishing, water-skiing, tennis, sailing.

ACCOMMODATIONS: No living space in the club house, but restaurant and bar are available.
In Dellach am Wörther See: *Golf-Hotel Velden* (Dellach am Wörther See, Tel. Velden 821). A very good, comfortable hotel, open spring, summer, autumn. Rooms from $7.50 to $10 for best single; $8 to $11.50 for

best double; private bath, central heating; full pension from $8/day; taxes and services included.

In Velden am Wörther See: *See-Hotel Mösslacher* (Velden am Wörther See, Tel. 218). A very good, comfortable hotel, open all year. Rooms from $3.50 to $8.50 for best single; $5.50 to $13.50 for best double; private bath and shower, central heating; full pension from $6/day; taxes and services not included.

In Klagenfurt: *Moser-Verdino* (Klagenfurt, Tel. 3431). A very good, comfortable hotel, open all year. Rooms from $6 to $7 for best single; $8.50 to $12 for best double; private bath, central heating; taxes and services included.

TOURIST ATTRACTIONS: Some fabulous old mansions, walking tours along Lake Wörth and historic sites.

FOR FURTHER INFORMATION: Write to: Secretary, Kärntner Golf Club, Dellach am Wörther See, Austria. Telephone: Velden 357.

Golf Club Murhof

In Styria near the Mur Valley, close to the last foothills of the Alps in hilly southeast Austria and surrounded by mountains with rich forests, this attractive course is made for the long driver, with most of the holes well over 400 yards and a few over 500. If you play it twice around, its length may seem even greater because of the hilly terrain. Not an easy course, Murhof will give even the expert player a good workout. But if the course makes you wince, the surrounding area is pleasant and remote, rich in historical and cultural sites and charming old world villages with winding streets and shops that often resemble Renaissance wine cellars.

LOCATION: The course is in Frohnleiten, 16 miles S of Bruck, 15 miles N of Graz, 286 miles E of Innsbruck, 185 miles E of Salzburg, 142 miles SW of Vienna. It is accessible by car.

OTHER INFORMATION: The course is open to nonmembers, unlimited, for the entire season (April-November), with a professional always on hand. The weather is best from June through September. Practice ground available.

Number of holes: 9. *Par:* 72 (for twice around). *Length:* 6550 yards. *Green fees:* weekdays $1.75, weekends, $2/day. *Lessons:* $2.50/hour. *Caddies:* $0.75/9 holes, $1.25/18 holes. *Golfing equipment and caddie carts:* clubs $2/day, carts $0.50/day.

OTHER SPORTS FACILITIES: Fishing, shooting, swimming and mountain-climbing.

ACCOMMODATIONS: In the club house: single room with shower, $3.50; double room with shower, $7; double room with bath, $8.50. The club house also has a restaurant and bar.

In Graz: *Daniel* (Bahnhofplatz 6, Tel. 96181). A first-class hotel, open all year: Rooms from $5 to $6 for best single; $10 to $11.25 for best double; private bath and shower, central heating; full pension from $9.75/day; taxes and services included. *Erzherzog Johann* (Graz, Tel. 97112). A very good, comfortable hotel, open all year. Rooms from $4.50 to $5.50 for best single; $7 to $8.25 for best double; private bath and shower, central heating; full pension from $8/day; taxes and services included.

In Bruck an der Mur: *Bauer* (Bruck an der Mur, Tel. 51331). A very good, comfortable hotel, open all year. Rooms from $4.50 to $5.50 for best single; $7 to $10 for best double; private bath and shower, central heating; full pension from $7/day; taxes and services included. *Schreiner* (Bruck an der Mur, Tel. 51220). A good, comfortable hotel, open all year. Rooms from $3.50 to $4.50 for best single; $5.25 to $6.50 for best double; bath and shower, central heating; full pension from $5.75/day; taxes and services included.

TOURIST ATTRACTIONS: Graz and Bruck an der Mur are attractive old world towns with houses and streets dating back to the fifteenth century. Be sure to see the Schloss Eggenberg with its famous hunting museum. Also noteworthy are a fifteenth-century cathedral built by Emperor Frederick III and St. Paul's Gate, the remains of a sixteenth-century fortification. The local tourist office will also arrange excursions to various historical and cultural sights.

FOR FURTHER INFORMATION: Write to: Golf Club Murhof, Frohnleiten, Steiermark, Austria. Telephone: (Peggau) 03127-228.

Golf Club Achensee

Set in the woods against the background of the Achensee, largest lake in the Tyrol and one of the loveliest in Austria, and at the foot of the snow-capped Alps, this course is one of the most pleasant and enjoyable in Austria as well as the shortest in the country. It is slightly hilly, demands careful and accurate driving and putting and is a paradise for the short driver. It is a good tune-up course if you find yourself in the Innsbruck area, preparatory to trying some of the fiercer 18-holers in France, Switzerland or Italy. And if you plan to go on to the British Isles, this is an especially good place to begin.

LOCATION: The course is in Pertisau in NW Austria, about 30 miles E of Innsbruck, 83 miles W of Salzburg, 164 miles SW of Linz, 272 miles W of Vienna. It is accessible by car.

OTHER INFORMATION: The course is open to nonmembers, unlimited, for the entire season (June-September), with a professional always on hand. Most crowded months are July and August, and the weather is best in August. Practice ground is available.

Number of holes: 9. *Par:* 63 (for twice around). *Length:* 4030 yards (for twice around).
Green fees: $1.50/day. *Lessons:* $2.50/hour. *Caddies:* $0.75/9 holes, $1.25/18 holes. *Golfing equipment and caddie carts:* none available.

OTHER SPORTS FACILITIES: Tennis.
ACCOMMODATIONS: No living space in the club house.
In Pertisau-Achensee: *Pfandler* (Pertisau-Achensee, Tel. Maurach 223). A good, comfortable hotel, open April-October. Rooms from $3 to $4 for best single; $6.50 to $7.50 for best double; private bath and shower, central heating; full pension from $6/day; taxes and services included. *Strand* (Pertisau-Achensee, Tel. Maurach 259). A good, comfortable hotel, open May-October. Rooms from $2.50 to $3.50 for best single; $7 to $8 for best double; private bath, central heating; taxes and services not included.

TOURIST ATTRACTIONS: Some good walking tours and beautiful panoramic views. For more detailed information, see this section for *Golf Club Innsbruck-Igls,* p. 17.

FOR FURTHER INFORMATION: Write to: Secretary, Golf Club Achensee, Pertisau/Tirol, Austria. Telephone: 05243/206.

Golf Club Innsbruck-Igls

On the outskirts of Innsbruck, site of the 1964 Winter Olympics, this course is set against a background of thick forests and picturesque mountains. As a golf course of medium length, it is for the short as well as the long driver. The fairways are soft, the greens in very good condition, the roughs short. The terrain is gently sloping, full of interesting natural hazards, but not overtiring. This is a perfect course for the average golfer, particularly the player new to European courses. Innsbruck itself (meaning bridge over the Inn) is one of the loveliest towns in Austria and a wonderful tourist center. Most of it still retains the charm and ease of old Austria with good restaurants, pleasant cafes and gracious, helpful people.

LOCATION: The course is in Igls, about 12 miles S of Innsbruck, 47 miles S of Garmisch-Partenkirchen, Germany, 104 miles S of Munich, 103 miles SW of Salzburg, 301 miles W of Vienna. It is accessible by car.

OTHER INFORMATION: The course is open to nonmembers, unlimited, for the entire season (April-October), with a professional always on hand. The most crowded season is from June 15 to September 15, with the weather best in September and October. Practice ground is available.
Number of holes: 9 with 18 different tees. *Par:* 68 (for twice around). *Length:* 5091 yards.
Green fees: weekdays $2.50, weekends $3/day. *Lessons:* $3.50/hour.

Caddies: $0.75 for 9 holes. *Golfing equipment and caddie carts:* clubs $0.75/day, carts $1.75/day.

OTHER SPORTS FACILITIES: Riding and swimming.

ACCOMMODATIONS: No living space in the club house, but a restaurant and bar are available.

In Igls: *Ägidihof* (Bilgeristrasse 1, Tel. 7108). A good, comfortable hotel, open all year. Rooms from $4.50 to $6.50 for best single; $7.50 to $12 for best double; private bath and shower, central heating; full pension from $6.50/day; taxes and services included. *Sport Hotel* (Igls, Tel. 7241). A very good, comfortable hotel, open summer and winter. Rooms from $7.50 to $11 for best single; $14 to 16.50 for best double; private bath and shower, central heating; full pension from $10/day; taxes and services included.

In Innsbruck: *Europa* (Südtirolerplatz 2, Tel. 25771). A first-class hotel, open all year. Rooms from $7 to $11 for best single; $9 to $17 for best double; private bath and shower, central heating; full pension from $11.75/day; taxes and services not included. *Goldener Adler* (Herzog-Friedrichstrasse 6, Tel. 26334). A very good, comfortable hotel, open all year. Rooms from $4.50 to $7.50 for best single; $9 to $15 for best double; private bath and shower, central heating, continental breakfast; full pension from $8/day; taxes and services included.

TOURIST ATTRACTIONS: Innsbruck is the cultural and touristic capital of the Old Tyrol. If you like palaces, don't miss the Hofburg, built by the Empress Maria Theresa. There is also a beautiful church, the Hofkirche, where you can see the Emperor Maximilian's tomb. Don't fail to see the Renaissance furnishings of the chancel and the church.

Innsbruck is also noted for its historic inns, especially the Goldener Adler, and its festivals and fine gardens.

FOR FURTHER INFORMATION: Write to: Secretary, Golf Club Innsbruck-Igls, Tyrol, Austria. Telephone: 7165.

Golf Club Linz

Known as the capital of Northern Austria, Linz is built on both sides of the Danube. It is one of Austria's great industrial cities as well as one of the most important cultural centers. The surrounding area, especially to the north, is hilly, with thick forests and wide valleys, and has an atmosphere of brooding melancholy. The course is in the suburbs, at the foothills of the Alps, so the scenery includes both mountains and water (the Danube). It is made for the short as well as the long driver (the holes run from 140 to 520 yards) and requires careful, accurate play. It should present few difficulties for the average golfer, but the bunkering is tricky and not to be taken for granted.

LOCATION: The course is in Puchenau bei Linz, about 3 miles from Linz, 80 miles NE of Salzburg, 184 miles NE of Innsbruck, 178 miles E of Munich, 105 miles W of Vienna. It is accessible by car.

OTHER INFORMATION: The course is open to nonmembers, unlimited, for the entire season (April-November), with a professional always on hand. The most crowded months are July and August; the weather is best from June to September. Practice ground is available.
Number of holes: 9. *Par:* 70 (for twice around). *Length:* 3033 yards. *Green fees:* weekdays $1.75, weekends $2/day. *Lessons:* $2/half hour. *Caddies:* $1.25/18 holes. *Golfing equipment and caddie carts:* clubs $1.50/day, carts $0.50/day.

OTHER SPORTS FACILITIES: Swimming and tennis.

ACCOMMODATIONS: No living space in the club house, but restaurant and bar are available.
In Linz: *Park* (Christian Coulinstrasse 16-18, Tel. 28931). A first-class hotel, open all year. Rooms from $7 to $11 for best single; $13 to $20 for best double; private bath and shower, central heating; full pension from $13.50/day; taxes and services included. *Scharmüller* (Linz, Tel. 21761). A very good, comfortable hotel, open all year. Rooms from $4 to $5 for best single; $7 to $8.50 for best double; private bath, central heating; taxes and services not included. *Schwechaterhof* (Landstrasse 18, Tel. 23583). A very good, comfortable hotel, open all year. Rooms from $5.50 to $6.75 for single; $7 to $8.50 for best double; private bath and shower, central heating; full pension from $10/day; taxes and services included.

TOURIST ATTRACTIONS: Two good museums here, especially the New Gallery, are devoted to nineteenth- and twentieth-century Austrian and German art. There is also the castle of Emperor Frederick III, built in the fifteenth century, as well as some interesting buildings and the Hauptplatz.

FOR FURTHER INFORMATION: Write to: Secretary, Golf Club Linz, Linz/Donau, Austria. Telephone 27234.

Golf Club Kitzbühel-Mittersill

Here is a good Alpine course in the heart of one of the oldest and most important ski centers in Austria. Kitzbühel itself has preserved the atmosphere of the old Tyrolean villages. Set against the massive Kitzbühel Alps, it looks like a fairy-tale village come to life. The course is a fairly long one and somewhat tricky, favoring the power hitter. The difference in elevation of some holes—as one would expect in a mountain course—may give trouble. Some added hazards are rough crossroads, water supply lids and wire netting. A good course for the experienced player, troublesome for the beginner.

LOCATION: The course is in Kitzbühel-Mittersill, 100 miles S of Munich, 62 miles E of Innsbruck, 50 miles W of Salzburg, 235 miles W of Vienna. It is easily accessible by air, train and bus from Munich, and by train and car from Innsbruck and Salzburg.

OTHER INFORMATION: The course is open to nonmembers, unlimited, for the entire season (May-October), with a professional always on hand. The most crowded season is from mid-July to the end of August, with the weather best in August and September. Practice ground is available. *Number of holes:* 18 (9 holes & different tees for second 9). *Par:* 72. *Length:* 6280 yards. *Green fees:* weekdays $2.50, weekends $3/day. *Lessons:* $3/hour. *Caddies:* $1/9 holes, $1.50/18 holes. *Golfing equipment and caddie carts:* clubs $1/day, carts $0.50/day.

OTHER SPORTS FACILITIES: Tennis, swimming, water-skiing, mountain-climbing and riding.

ACCOMMODATIONS: No living space in the club house, but restaurant and bar are available.
In Kitzbühel: *Die Postkutsche* (Kitzbühel, Tel. 3013). A first-class hotel, open all year. Single room $10; double room $14; private bath, central heating; full pension from $16/day; taxes and services included. *Klausner* (Bahnhofstrasse, Tel. 2136). A very good, comfortable hotel, open all year. Rooms from $5 to $6 for best single; $10 to $11 for best double; private bath, central heating; full pension from $7.50/day; taxes and services not included. *Kurhaus Bellevue* (Kitzbühel, Tel. 2766). A good, comfortable hotel, open all year. Rooms from $3.50 to $4.50 for best single; $8 to $9.50 for best double; private bath, central heating; full pension from $7.50; taxes and services not included. *Pension Hinterseer* (Kitzbühel, Tel. 2920). A good, comfortable pension, open all year. Rooms from $4 to $5 for best single; $7 to $8 for best double; private bath and shower, central heating; taxes and services included.

TOURIST ATTRACTIONS: The visitor will enjoy tours in the Alps, walks and excellent shopping (knitted goods and sportswear from the area). The scenery is magnificent.

FOR FURTHER INFORMATION: Write to: Secretary, Golf Club Kitzbühel-Mittersill, Kitzbühel, Austria. Telephone: (05356) 3007, 2276.

Golf and Country Club Salzburg-Klesheim

Salzburg is probably one of the most charming ciites in Europe and a delightful place to golf. It is Mozart's city, gay, festive, simple and yet sophisticated in the tradition of a world long since gone. The city still has old picturesque streets with wrought-iron signs, Medieval and Renaissance houses, spacious squares and beautiful fountains. Surrounding it are bright-blue lakes, majestic mountains and small operetta-like villages famous for graciousness and hospitality. Against this attractve background, the course is interesting and challenging because the fairways are narrow and run through the woods, both with doglegs. The natural hazards may be lovely to look at, but they will make the indifferent player unhappy. This course favors the long driver, but a close, careful game will also be repaid. Try it at least once around.

LOCATION: The course is about 2 miles from downtown Salzburg, 85 miles E of Munich, 101 miles NE of Innsbruck, 82 miles SW of Linz, 142 miles NW of Klagenfurt, 184 miles W of Vienna. It is accessible by car.

OTHER INFORMATION: The course is open to members of registered golf clubs, unlimited, for the entire season (April-November), with a professional on hand from May to November. The weather is best from August to September. Practice ground is available.

Number of holes: 9. Par: 69 (for twice around). Length: 2789 yards. Green fees: weekdays $2, weekends $3/day. Lessons: $3.50/hour. Caddies: $0.75/9 holes. Golfing equipment and caddie carts: none for rent.

OTHER SPORTS FACILITIES: Tennis and swimming.

ACCOMMODATIONS: No living space in the club house, but restaurant is available.

In Salzburg: Gastschloss Mönchstein (Monchsberg 26, Tel. 81363). A luxury hotel of the highest international standing, open spring, summer and autumn. Rooms from $11.75 to $15 for the best single; $17.50 to $35 for the best double; private bath, central heating; taxes and services not included. Goldener Hirsch (Getreidegasse 37, Tel. 2019). A first-class hotel with night and day service, open all year. Rooms from $15.50 to $21 for best single; $21.50 to $24.50 for best double; private bath, central heating; taxes and services included. Europa-Hotel (Rainerstrasse 31, Tel. 73391). A very good, comfortable hotel with night and day service, open all year. Rooms from $6.50 to $11 for best single; $11.75 to $20 for best double; private bath and shower, central heating, continental breakfast; full pension from $10/day; taxes and services included.

TOURIST ATTRACTIONS: Salzburg was made for tourists, especially music lovers. In January there is the Mozart festival week; in April, concerts in the Salzburg castle, and in July and August, the famous Salzburg festival devoted to drama and music. Mozart's birthplace is at 9 Getreidegasse. For those interested in architecture, there is the Salzburg Cathedral, modeled after St. Peter's (be sure to see the hand-operated barrel organ), and the fortress palace of Hohensalzburg. In the outskirts visit Schloss Hellbrunn and see the famous fountains and mechanical theater, where 113 figures are set in motion by organ music. There is also good shopping.

FOR FURTHER INFORMATION: Write to: Secretary, Golf and Country Club Salzburg-Klesheim, Salzburg, Austria. Telephone: 32625 and 31414.

Salzkammergut Golf Club

The Salzkammergut Golf Club is in the very center of Salzkammergut and on the outskirts of Bad Ischl, one of the most fashionable and historically important summer resorts in Austria. It is also a famous spa, known throughout Europe for its therapeutic waters. Before World War I it was the favorite resort of the Austrian royal family as well as of the composers Anton Bruckner, Johann Strauss, Brahms and Franz Lehár. The course is slightly hilly, strongly favors the long accurate driver, and has good fairways and greens. The layout is somewhat tricky and therefore might give trouble, especially where the hilly terrain hides hazards or creates optical illusions. This is an enjoyable course for the golfer who takes his game seriously.

LOCATION: The course is about 3 miles from Bad Ischl, 32 miles E of Salzburg, 135 miles NE of Innsbruck, 135 miles E of Munich, 172 miles SW of Vienna. It is accessible by car.

OTHER INFORMATION: The course is open to nonmembers, unlimited, for the entire season (April-November), with a professional on hand from May through October. The most crowded months are July and August; the weather is best in August and September. Practice ground is available.
Number of holes: 9. *Par:* 35. *Length:* 2835 yards.
Green fees: weekdays $2, weekends $2.50/day. *Lessons:* $3/hour. *Caddies:* available at $0.75/9 holes. *Golfing equipment and caddie carts:* clubs $0.75/day, carts $0.25/day.

OTHER SPORTS FACILITIES: Sailing, water-skiing, riding, fishing, mountain-climbing, and tennis.

ACCOMMODATIONS: No living space in the club house, but restaurant and bar are available.
In Bad Ischl: *Post* (Bad Ischl, Tel. 3441). A very good, comfortable hotel, open summer and winter. Rooms from $5 to $6 for best single; $8.50 to $12.50 for best double; private bath, central heating; full pension from $8/day; taxes and services not included.
In Strobl: *Grandhotel am See* (Strobl, Tel. 341). A very good, comfortable hotel, open summer and winter. Rooms from $7.50 to $8.50 for best single; $12.50 to $14 for best double; private bath, central heating; full pension from $12/day; taxes and services included.
In St. Wolfgang: *Weisses Rössl* (St. Wolfgang, Tel 306). A very good, comfortable hotel, open summer and winter. Rooms from $4.50 to $7.50 for best single; $7.50 to $13 for best double; private bath and shower, central heating; full pension from $7.50/day; taxes and services included.

TOURIST ATTRACTIONS: The Salzkammergut area is old Austria at its best, thoroughly charming and gracious. For seventy years Bad Ischl was one of the great fashionable centers of Europe, attracting kings and emperors, composers and painters. Be sure to see the Imperial Villa and gardens, and the Franz Lehár Museum. In St. Wolfgang you should have lunch or dinner at the White Horse Inn, one of the famous old inns in Austria. For those interested in church architecture, there is the altar of Michael Pacher, an outstanding example of Gothic construction. There are also numerous tours and excursions.

FOR FURTHER INFORMATION: Write to: Secretary, Salzkammergut Golf Club, Pfarrgasse 11, Bad Ischl, Austria. Telephone: 3341.

Golf-Club Semmering

The course is on the outskirts of Semmering, a famous mountain spa and winter sports center in lower Austria, built on terraces at altitudes of 3200 to 4325 feet. The town is well sheltered from the cold winds of the north and east, has almost no fog and promises plenty of clear, sunny days. The course itself is hilly, favors the short driver and calls for careful, accurate play. The nature of the terrain may cause trouble for the inexperienced golfer, but the average player who plays a close game will like this course. Don't let its short length fool you—the bunkering and hazards are tricky.

LOCATION: The course is about 2 miles from Semmering, 70 miles SW of Vienna, 34 miles SW of Wiener Neustadt, 175 miles E of Salzburg, 276 miles E of Innsbruck, 137 miles SE of Linz. It is accessible by car.

OTHER INFORMATION: The course is open to nonmembers, unlimited, for the entire season (May-October), with a professional always on hand. The most crowded month is August; weather is best from June to August.
Number of holes: 9. *Par:* 62 (for twice around). *Length:* 4171 yards (for twice around).
Green fees: $2.50/day. *Lessons:* $3/half hour. *Caddies:* $1.50/9 holes. *Golfing equipment and caddie carts:* clubs $2/day, carts $0.50/day.

OTHER SPORTS FACILITIES: Tennis, swimming and fishing.

ACCOMMODATIONS: No living space in this club house but restaurant and bar are available.
In Semmering: *Grandhotel Panhans* (Hochstrasse 32, Tel. 366). A first-class hotel, open all year. Rooms from $9.50 to $10 for the best single; $10 to $11.50 for best double; private bath and shower, central heating, continental breakfast; full pension from $15.50/day; taxes and services included. *Südbahnhotel* (Semmering, Tel. 455). A first-class hotel, open all year. Rooms from $6.50 to $8.50 for best single; $12 to $16.50 for best double; private bath, central heating; full pension from $9.75/day; taxes

and services not included. *Stefanie* (Semmering, Tel. 308). A good, comfortable hotel, open all year. Rooms from $2.75 to $3.50 for best single; $4.75 to $6 for best double; private bath and shower, central heating; full pension from $5/day; taxes and services not included.

TOURIST ATTRACTIONS: Mountain walks and Alpine excursions.

FOR FURTHER INFORMATION: Write to: Manager, Südbahnhotel, Semmering, Austria. Telephone: 02664/456.

BRITISH ISLES—ENGLAND

One of the great advantages of golfiing in England—in addition to the great golf—is the relative closeness of the courses to major cities. You can golf in beautiful country surroundings and still be within easy reach of a sophisticated city in the evening. Furthermore, the narrow shape of England puts many courses within short distances of each other. In the London area, for example, I have listed twelve that can be combined with the four in Sussex (the south) and the two in Kent (the west) to give you a holiday choice of eighteen courses—all within 15 to 60 miles of London. Similar groupings for the Midlands and the north put seven courses at your disposal there, all no more than two hours from each other. I have done the same with Cornwall and Devonshire, giving you five courses within driving distance.

Most green fees in England, even on the most famous courses, are very reasonable, and lessons with the ablest professionals are usually no more than $2.50 an hour. If you like a particular course and wish to return for several days, then your expenses are proportionally reduced. Several English clubs have a "dormy house," or small dormitory, for the visitor who wishes to rent a room and stay on. Or you can lodge in a nearby hotel; many courses provide hotels that are within a quarter or half a mile.

If you are touring London, there are so many good courses to choose from that you might let a good one slip. Two excellent holiday courses are *Moor Park* and *Thorndon Park*, with *Effingham, Huntercombe, Selsdon Park* and *Temple* not far behind. At Selsdon Park you can stay at the local hotel and enjoy good accommodations as well as good golf. Once your game has found its level, you might move on to *Royal Blackheath, Stoke Poges, Berkshire* and *Walton Heath*—all grand and all tough and all within 15 to 20 miles of central London.

If you enter England from France, then try *Prince's* at Sandwich (practice on the Red Course before trying the Blue), then go on to *Royal St. George's*, almost within walking distance. And if you enter England from the south, try *Dyke* or *Ham Manor* first, then follow with *Crowborough Beacon* and *Royal Ashdown Forest*. If you have sufficient leisure time around London, mix them up—play the easier courses near London, in the south, and in Kent, and then try the tougher ones as your game becomes accustomed to English golf.

In the Liverpool area on the Lancashire coast you have one of the great golfing regions in the British Isles, comparable to the Ayr coast and Fife in

Scotland. Here they are all tough, and it is impossible to indicate which you should play first. Make your own decisions with the knowledge that first-rate golf awaits you at any one or at all of these courses.

The inland courses in the Midlands and in Yorkshire are only slightly less demanding than the best of the seaside links and are often more interesting; but that depends on what you want. Whether you like seaside or inland golf, an average or a championship course, you will find excellent examples of each on your trip to England.

Addington Palace Golf Club

A notable links within a short distance of London is the Addington Palace Golf Course, which is scenically as well as professionally exciting. When Addington Palace was designed, many trees were uprooted, but enough were kept to line the entire course. The result is a scenic effect, especially in the spring and autumn, that will impress the most golf-directed of players. The course itself is full of unpredictable spots, from the first "short" hole, through the long 2nd, and on from one surprise to another. The 7th should be of particular interest, a par 3 152-yarder that calls for precision and good nerves. This goes for the entire course; it is a test of accuracy amid rolling fairways that charm the eye.

LOCATION: Addington Palace is 3 miles from the center of Croydon and 15 miles S of London. From the Main Line London Stations, there is train service to East Croydon Station, and then taxi service to the course, or else No. 130 bus from the station to the club house. Also accessible by car from London—about 30 minutes.

OTHER INFORMATION: The course is open to nonmembers during the week, but on weekends or holidays they must play with a member. Course is playable all year except when snow covers the links. A professional or his assistant is in daily attendance. The most crowded time is May through October, which is also the time of best weather. Practice ground is available.

Number of holes: 18. *Par:* 72 (Bogey, 76). *Length:* 6424 yards.

Green fees: weekdays $1.40/round, $2.80/day; half price with a member; no weekend or holiday play without a member. *Lessons:* $2.10/½ hour. *Caddies:* $7/day, including lunch money; reserve in advance. *Golfing equipment and caddie carts:* no clubs for rent, but trolleys for hire at $.28/round.

OTHER SPORTS FACILITIES: Tennis, swimming, bowling in the immediate area; full facilities in nearby London.

ACCOMMODATIONS: No living space in the club house, but coffee, lunch and afternoon tea are available in the dining room; also 3 bars. While most visitors will prefer to live in London, there are three reasonable comfortable hotels in Croydon: *The Aerodrome* (Tel. 5185), the *Elgin*

(Tel. Addiscombe 1000), the *Quendale Lodge* (Tel. 2839). Singles from $4.50, doubles from $8.50, with breakfast. No private baths, but the *Elgin* has numerous public baths. Central heating at the *Aerodrome*. For all add service tax, 10% or more.

OTHER TOURIST ATTRACTIONS: Croydon offers many historical sites, including the building where James I of Scotland was held prisoner; also a good shopping area. London, of course, offers everything to the visitor.

FOR FURTHER INFORMATION: Write to: Club Secretary, Addington Palace Golf Club Ltd., Addington Park, Surrey, England. Telephone: Addiscombe 3061.

Berkshire Golf Club

Berkshire is another of the fine courses ringing London, close enough for you to return to town in the evening and yet far enough out to convey a sense of the English countryside. Actually, Berkshire has two courses, the Red and the Blue. The Red is somewhat longer, but not much; the chief difference is in the degree of difficulty. Even here the margin is in small things—tighter fairways, more persistent hazards, more testing approaches. But the Blue compares favorably and should not be sold short. The Red is a course of marvelous balance, with 9 holes at 400 yards or over, and fully 6 par 3's, a superb test of the shorter game. Each of these 6 has its own interest, especially in the 190-yard 10th and the 230-yard 16th; each requires accuracy with both long-iron and putter. And as a change of pace, you begin with a 521-yard par 5 hole—a solid par 5 that nevertheless might become a birdie 4 for the very good player. Berkshire offers solid golf played on excellent heathland turf that has spring in it all year, with height and hills on both courses.

LOCATION: The course is 3 miles from Ascot and 2 from Bagshot, both accessible by rail from London; from the station, take car or taxi. Ascot is 26 miles SE of London.

OTHER INFORMATION: The course is open all year, but weekend play is restricted: the visitor must play with a member. During the week the nonmember is welcome, but he should have a letter of introduction from his own golf club and an official handicap. The professional is in daily attendance. The most crowded time is during the summer months, when the weather—always unpredictable—might be at its best. Practice ground is available.

Number of holes: 18 (for Red and Blue). *Par:* Red: 74 (S.S.S.); Blue: 73 (S.S.S.). *Length:* Red: 6379 yards; Blue: 6244 yards.

Green fees: $2.80/day. *Lessons:* $2.80/hour. *Caddies:* a few available through arrangement with the professional. *Golfing equipment and caddie carts:* by arrangement with the professional.

OTHER SPORTS FACILITIES: The area is full of good golf courses, at Sunningdale, Wentworth, and Swinley Forest. For the spectator, there are the Ascot races in June. The heath makes for good walking tours. And London offers all the rest.

ACCOMMODATIONS: No living space in the club house, but bar and restaurant are available. No service, however, on Mondays. Most visitors will probably prefer to live in London and drive or take the train to the course, but there are several comfortable hotels in the immediate area.

In Ascot: the *Berystede* (Tel. 888). Rooms with private bath; singles from $6.50 to $8; doubles from $11.20; full pension, from $60/week. Add 10% service. Central heating, garage. *Royal Foresters* (Tel. Winkfield Row 2556). Singles (with breakfast) from $4.20; doubles from $8.40; full pension, from $44/week. No private baths; central heating, garage.

In Bagshot: *The Cricketers'* (Tel. 3196). Singles at $5; doubles at $9; breakfast included; no private baths or central heating.

In Camberley (4 miles): the *Cambridge* (Tel. 5127) and *Frimley Hall* (Tel. 5502). Singles from $4.50, doubles from $8; full pension from $44/week at *Cambridge*. No private baths; central heating.

TOURIST ATTRACTIONS: This entire region is attractive for tours— Staines, Egham, Bagshot, Ascot, Bracknell. Windsor Park itself is only a few miles north. Ascot, of course, offers its famous races in the third week in June. And nearby London is obviously the main attraction.

FOR FURTHER INFORMATION: Write to: Club Secretary, Berkshire Golf Club, Ascot, Berkshire, England. Telephone: Ascot 495.

Effingham Golf Club

The Effingham Golf Club lies in the heart of rural England. The view from the club house and the course gives an uninterrupted vista of miles and miles of unspoiled woodland and green. Aside from the club, the general area offers the tourist a remarkable experience—a look at a part of England that most visitors never see. Effingham is known as a long driver's paradise, for many of its holes allow the hitter to open up. Even so, less powerful hitters will find plenty of shorter holes to their liking. As a conse- ,quence, this course is suitable for every type of golfer—the average player as well as the long driver.

LOCATION: Only 45 minutes S of London (25 miles), Effingham can be reached by train to Effingham Junction; from there by car or bus to the club. Buses (Green Line) also leave London for Leatherhead, where a change to No. 408 bus takes you to the club. By car, A246 running be- tween Leatherhead and Guildford.

OTHER INFORMATION: The course is open to nonmembers; member- ship in an American golf course will be honored, and the visitor should have

proof. The season is all year round, with two professionals on hand during the summer months for the aid of the beginner and the advanced golfer. Summer is most crowded. Practice ground is available.
Number of holes: 18. *Par:* 71 (Bogey, 74). *Length:* 6486 yards. *Green fees:* weekdays $2.80, weekends and holidays $4.20/day (half price with a member), weekly $8.40. *Lessons:* $2.80/hour. *Caddies:* $5.60/day (should be booked in advance). *Golfing equipment and caddie carts:* clubs $1.40/round but not available in great quantity; carts $.35/day.

OTHER SPORTS FACILITIES: At the club: tennis (two grass and two hard courts) and squash, at nominal cost, but the visitor must be introduced by a member.

ACCOMMODATIONS: The club house is a Georgian mansion facing south over the spacious lawn leading to the course. It contains several lounge rooms, a dining room, a bar and 16 rooms for visitors. All rooms have wash basins, and there are several bathroom facilities in the hallways. For reservations, write to the club secretary far in advance, particularly for the summer months. Bed and breakfast (3 days or less) cost $3 to $3.50/day, full pension, $35 to $39/week.
In Guildford: the *Angel* (Tel. 4280). Singles with private bath from $5.50 (with breakfast), doubles from $10. No central heating. For additional accommodations in the general area, see *Walton Heath Golf Club,* p. 40.

TOURIST ATTRACTIONS: Surrey is noted for its spendid moors, tracts of open land covered with heather, wild and lovely. Guildford has a long historical past, going back to King Alfred. Lewis Carroll lived there and is buried in the Mount Cemetery. A few miles SW is Loseley House, a large Elizabethan mansion where Elizabeth and James I used to visit. Walks through the local villages are recommended.

FOR FURTHER INFORMATION: Write to: Club Secretary, Effingham Golf Club, near Effingham Junction, Surrey, England. Telephone: Bookham 203.

Huntercombe Golf Club

Huntercombe is the oldest course in Oxfordshire and perhaps the most famous. It provides an excellent test of every golfer's technique, from beginner to expert. It has the added advantage of being both close to London and far enough away to provide the typical peace and quiet of the English countryside. Huntercombe itself was constructed on modern golf principles. It has a naturally sandy soil and downland turf and plenty of finely wooded and varied terrain. There are numerous hollows awaiting the golfer who closes his eyes and swings. The good putter, I should add, will have an advantage, for there are several outsize greens even though they have been reduced in size from the original bounty. Now the approach shots are normal.

LOCATION: The course is 7 miles from Henley-on-Thames, which is on the Oxford Road, 36 miles W of London. Henley-on-Thames can be reached by bus or train, and from there by car or taxi to the Club. Oxford is 20 miles to the NW, Reading 5 S.

OTHER INFORMATION: The course is open to nonmembers, unlimited, on weekdays. On some weekends they need an introduction from a member; check with the secretary about weekend play. The course is playable all year. A professional is on hand. The most crowded time is the summer. No practice ground is available.
Number of holes: 18. *Par:* 69. *Length:* 6144 yards.
Green fees: weekdays $2.10, weekends $2.80/day. *Lessons:* $2.10/hour. *Caddies:* $2.80/round. *Golfing equipment and caddie carts:* $1.40/round, carts $.35/round.

OTHER SPORTS FACILITIES: Tennis at Phyllis Court nearby; rowing and angling in Henley-on-Thames, which is famous for these activities.

ACCOMMODATIONS: No living space in the club house. A country hotel nearby has a bar and restaurant.
In Henley-on-Thames: The *Red Lion* (Tel. 135). Offers very comfortable quarters with private baths, central heating, garage; singles from $4.20, doubles from $8.40, with breakfast; 10% service charge. Also, more modest lodgings at the following hotels, without private baths: *Little White Hart, Sydney House, Two Brewers.*
In Maidenhead (9 miles): The *Skindles* (Tel. 25115). Private baths, central heating; singles from $5.50, doubles from $8.40, with breakfast; 10% service charge.
In Windsor (15 miles): The following have rooms with private baths, central heating and most comforts: the *Castle* (Tel. 61891), *Old House* (Tel. 61354) and *White Hart* (Tel. 63426), singles from $5.50, doubles from $10, with breakfast; 10% service charge.
In Oxford (20 miles): The *Randolph, Mitre* and *Royal Oxford Park* offer accommodations similar to those listed for Windsor above.

TOURIST ATTRACTIONS: Henley-on-Thames is situated on a beautiful section of the Thames River, the section from Maidenhead on. The towns and houses along the way, including Clivedon House, Cookham, Marlow and Medmenham, are of historic interest as well as attractive in themselves. Henley is famous as the site of the Henley Regatta and for rowing in general. Nearby, Reading (5 miles) is the center for the Thames Valley, a site full of prehistoric remains; see the Museum. Henley is only 20 miles from Oxford, which no visitor should miss.

FOR FURTHER INFORMATION: Write to: Club Secretary, Huntercombe Golf Club Henley-on-Thames, Oxfordshire, England. Telephone: Nettlebed 207.

Moor Park Golf Club

Moor Park is another fine inland course only a short distance from London, about 30 minutes by car or train. There are, in fact, two courses, one considerably longer than the other; but both have their attractions. The setting is beautiful, especially in the spring, when the beeches and pines almost close out the world. The park surrounding the course is itself worth a visit. The High Course was designed to favor the long driver, with 11 holes in the 400-yard class and many in the upper 400s. In addition to length, many of the holes have narrow approaches that call for precision. The short holes all require care. The West Course is some 600 yards shorter, but it is by no means easy. With some of the length cut off, the average player will soon discover what a test some of the holes really are. For the less experienced player, this is the course to try; there are several holes where he can come close to par and possibly even break it. Then move on to the High Course or move out to the seaside links, which are a true test of one's game.

LOCATION: The course is about 1 mile from the railroad station of Moor Park and Sandy Lodge in Rickmansworth. The latter is 18 miles NW of London in the direction of Aylesbury. The course is accessible by car or taxi from the railroad station.

Moor Park Golf Club, Ltd.

Entrance to the Moor Park Golf Club, one of the many fine courses near London.

OTHER INFORMATION: The course is open all year, weather permitting, to nonmembers with no restrictions or limitations. The professional is in daily attendance. Moor Park is most crowded during the summer months, especially August, when the best weather can also be expected. Practice ground is available.

Number of holes: 18 (for High and West Courses). *Par:* High: 73; West: 71. *Length:* High: 6602 yards; West: 6013 yards.

Green fees: weekdays $2.10, weekends and holidays $4.20/day. *Lessons:* $2.80/hour. *Caddies:* $2.10/18 holes. *Golfing equipment and caddie carts:* through arrangement with the professional.

OTHER SPORTS FACILITIES: In the immediate area, tennis and horseback riding. In London, the visitor will find all types of sporting events and facilities.

ACCOMMODATIONS: No living space in the club house, but bar and restaurant are available.

Most visitors will probably prefer to live in London (18 miles), but there are several comfortable hotels near the course.

In Rickmansworth: the *Park View* (Tel. 73165). Several rooms with private baths; singles from $4.50 to $7, doubles from $9; full pension from $42/week; 10% service charge. No central heating; garage.

In Harrow: The following hotels offer similar lodgings, singles from $4.20, doubles from $8.40; no private baths, no pension: the *Cumberland* (Tel. 8176), *Gayton Hall* (Tel. 3360), *King's Head* (Tel. Byron 5541). Harrow is in Middlesex, about 12 miles from London.

TOURIST ATTRACTIONS: London will be the chief attraction for most visitors. But the immediate area of Rickmansworth holds some interest; it makes an excellent base for excursions, especially to the valley of the Chess and around the surrounding lakes. Around Beaconsfield (10 miles) there are several historic sites of interest, including an old Quaker meeting house, a museum (at Chalfont St. Giles) of John Milton relics and the house in which Benjamin Disraeli lived, now also a museum.

FOR FURTHER INFORMATION: Write to: Club Secretary, Moor Park Golf Club, Rickmansworth, Hertfordshire, England. Telephone: Rickmansworth 3146.

Royal Blackheath Golf Club

Blackheath was one of the earliest centers of golf in England, and it has remained a fine place to play; it is all the more attractive because of its proximity to London. It was remodeled by James Braid, and that alone would insure a good game. The course as it is presently situated favors the precise player. Braid was interested in well-designed holes, and the course follows his prescription. The terrain and the many old trees provide natural obstacles that will defeat the player who relies on power at every turn. Even the short holes require some imagination, especially the 16th with its lake in the background and the cross bunkers in front of the green. To play golf at Royal Blackheath is to play amidst the finest traditions England offers.

LOCATION: The club is at Eltham, a suburb SE of London. It is just off the main Dover Road (A20) and an eight-minute walk from Nottingham Station, with frequent train service to Charing Cross and Waterloo stations.

OTHER INFORMATION: The course is open to nonmembers all year, but every visitor should carry a letter of introduction from his home club secretary. A professional is in daily attendance. The most crowded season is the summer months, when the weather is usually best. Practice ground is available.
Number of holes: 18. *Par:* 71. *Length:* 6148 yards.
Green fees: weekdays $2.10/day, $1.40/round; weekends and holidays $4.20/day ($1.40 with a member); monthly $7.50. *Lessons:* by arrangement with the professional. *Caddies:* by arrangement. *Golfing equipment and caddie carts:* by arrangement with the professional.

OTHER SPORTS FACILITIES: In the immediate area, horseback riding and tennis; in London, the entire range of sports facilities, active and spectator.

ACCOMMODATIONS: No living space in the club house, but bar and catering facilities available.
There are numerous guest houses in the area, but most visitors will probably prefer to live in London, where there is a vast variety of accommodations for every purse.

TOURIST ATTRACTIONS: Nearby London will, of course, provide the visitor with every kind of entertainment or cultural attraction he may wish.

FOR FURTHER INFORMATION: Write to: Club Secretary, The Club House, Court Road, Eltham, London, SE 9, England. Telephone: Eltham 1042.

Sandy Lodge Golf Club

Less than 30 minutes from Hyde Park Corner in London, the inland Sandy Lodge Golf Club nevertheless presents a striking seaside appearance. The course has an open aspect and lies on a bed of fine sand. Marram grass, originally imported from seaside courses, grows in the numerous sand mounds and bunkers. The turf of the greens and fairways is light and springy, and the course is dry in winter. Sandy Lodge suits both long and short drivers as there are four holes of 500 yards or more and several short holes. The course should prove a challenge for every type of player;

every kind of hole is there, from the 105-yard 8th to the 547-yard 11th.

LOCATION: You will find frequent train service from Baker Street Station in London to Moor Park Station, near the club house. By car the trip is about 15 miles, less than 30 minutes, to the NE. The club is nearest Rickmansworth (2 miles) and Northwood (1 mile) and is 3 miles from Watford, the biggest nearby town.

OTHER INFORMATION: The course is privately owned but is open to nonmembers, who should bring a letter of introduction from a member or obtain permission to play in advance; a letter to the secretary should do that. The course is open all year round and has a resident professional. The busiest seasons are spring and autumn, when the weather is usually best for golf. Large practice ground is available.
   Number of holes: 18. *Par:* 71. *Length:* 6430 yards.
   Green fees: weekdays $1.40/round, $2.10/day; Saturdays $3.50/round or day; Sundays $4.20/round or day. With member, cost is half. *Lessons:* $2.80/hour, $1.40/½ hour. *Caddies:* $5.60/day; should be reserved in advance. *Golfing equipment and caddie carts:* limited amount of equipment for rent, but professional has a well-stocked shop for sale; carts $0.25/round.

OTHER SPORTS FACILITIES: In Rickmansworth (2 miles) there are fine lakes for swimming, boating and excursions as well as fishing. International football (soccer) matches are played at Wembley Stadium, which is not far.

ACCOMMODATIONS: No living space in the club house, but several bars and a dining room are available.
   Nearby towns, Northwood, Watford, Rickmansworth, provide lodgings, but since London is so easily accessible, most visitors will seek accommodations there.
   In Rickmansworth: The *Park View* (Tel. 73165). Singles from $4.50 to $7, doubles from $9; private baths, breakfast. No central heating.

TOURIST ATTRACTIONS: There is good shopping in Watford as well as an interesting twelfth-century church. Walking excursions are also recommended in the immediate area.

FOR FURTHER INFORMATION: Write to: Club Secretary, Sandy Lodge Golf Club, Northwood, Middlesex, England. Telephone: Northwood 25429.

Selsdon Park Hotel Golf Club

The Selsdon Park Hotel Golf Club offers the visitor a very attractive sporting area only 30 minutes from London by bus or train. Set in a 200-acre park adjoining the Selsdon Park Hotel, the course is only one of many sports facilities open to hotel guests. At 6405 yards the course is suitable for all types of players, possibly favoring the medium and long hitter. There are several long holes—5 over 450 yards—but power will not be enough to insure a good score. The short, careful player can be assured that this finely tailored course requires precision as well.

LOCATION: The course is set on the Selsdon Park Hotel grounds in Sanderstead, 3 miles from Croydon and 12 from London. It is accessible by bus, train or car. Trains run frequently from Victoria, Charing Cross and London Bridge. Green Line buses (706 and 707) stop at the hotel. By car, take the London–Brighton Road (A23) or B271 from Croydon.

OTHER INFORMATION: The course is open all year to visitors, and the professional is in daily attendance. The course is most crowded on Sundays, especially during the summer months. The best weather can be expected during the summer. Practice ground is available.
  Number of holes: 18. *Par:* 73. *Length:* 6405 yards.
  Green fees: weekdays $1.50, weekends $2.80/day (free to residents of the Selsdon Park Hotel). *Lessons:* $5.60/½ hour with the professional; $2.80/½ hour with the assistant. *Caddies:* available if booked with the professional at $2.80/round. *Golfing equipment and caddie carts:* clubs $2.10/round, carts $0.35/round.

OTHER SPORTS FACILITIES: The hotel adjoining the course offers tennis (hard and grass courts), an open-air swimming pool, horseback riding, a croquet lawn. All except the riding are free to hotel guests.

ACCOMMODATIONS: The *Selsdon Park Hotel* (Tel. Sanderstead 2001) has more than 150 rooms, most of them with private baths; singles (with breakfast) from $9.50; full pension from $13/day, from $75/week. The hotel also has a large restaurant and lounge bar.
  The visitor staying in London will find accommodations of every kind.

TOURIST ATTRACTIONS: Croydon, 3 miles away, is a good shopping center; London, 30 minutes away, offers every kind of entertainment and attraction.

FOR FURTHER INFORMATION: About golf: write to: The Professional, Selsdon Park Hotel, Sanderstead, Surrey, England. Telephone: SAN 2001. About the hotel: write to: Selsdon Park Hotel, above address.

Stoke Poges Golf Club

Set in historic Buckinghamshire, only 5 miles from the Queen's country home in Windsor, Stoke Poges has for years attracted some of England's and the world's finest golfers. Although it is close to industrial Slough, the course leaves the city atmosphere far behind. The rolling woodland acres will give immediate relief to the visitor who wants to escape from an urban setting. Its greens are excellent, the bunkers have been renovated, and new teeing grounds have been made. The 7th hole is often considered to be among one of the great holes in golfing. The course suits both long and short drivers, but accuracy and precision, more than driving, will help the golfer who wants to make a good showing at Stoke Poges.

LOCATION: The course is accessible by car from Slough, 2 miles away. Taxis also are available. Trains leave London regularly for Slough and Windsor (5 miles S of Slough). London is 15 miles E.

OTHER INFORMATION: The course is open to nonmembers all year, with the exception of Sundays, when the visitor must be introduced by a member. Nonmembers should have proof of membership in a recognized home club. The green fee admits the visitor to all facilities. A professional is always on hand, and the most crowded season is summer, when the weather is also best.
Number of holes: 18. *Par:* 71. *Length:* 6600 yards.
Green fees: weekdays $2.80, Saturdays $3.50, Sundays guests must be introduced by a member. *Lessons:* $1.40/½ hour. *Caddies:* $7/day; request in advance if possible. *Golfing equipment and caddie carts:* equipment available; cost depends on type and quality; carts for rent by round or day.

OTHER SPORTS FACILITIES: In this area sports facilities are mostly golf courses; there are several within a radius of 10 miles.

ACCOMMODATIONS: No living space in the club house, but bar and restaurant are available.
For the visitor who does not wish to commute to Stoke Poges from London, there are many accommodations in Slough, Windsor, and Gerrards Cross.
In Slough: The *Royal* (Tel. 23024). Singles from $5, doubles from $8.50; breakfast included; some rooms with private baths; no central heating.
In Windsor: The *Castle* (Tel. 61891), the *Old House* (Tel. 61354), and the *White Hart* (Tel. 63426). Singles from $5.50, doubles from $11; breakfast included; many rooms with private baths; central heating except at *White Hart*.
In Gerrards Cross: The *Bull* (Tel. 2005) and the *Ethorpe* (Tel. 2039). Singles from $6.50, doubles from $12; with breakfast; central heating at the *Bull;* most rooms with private baths; full pension at the *Ethorpe* from $55/week.

TOURIST ATTRACTIONS: The entire area is full of historic interest. In the churchyard of Stoke Poges, Thomas Gray wrote "Elegy in a Country Churchyard." The present club house was built by the son of William Penn, the founder of Pennsylvania, and the original house was occupied by Sir John Coke, Lord Chief Justice to Queen Elizabeth I.
Nearby Windsor is, of course, a famous tourist site; it is the summer residence of English sovereigns since Norman times. Windsor Castle, the Great Park and the immediate area offer hours of interesting touring.

FOR FURTHER INFORMATION: Write to: Club Secretary, Stoke Poges Golf Club Ltd., Nr. Slough, Bucks, England. Telephone: 26385.

Temple Golf Club

The Temple Golf Club is easily accessible from London, and is situated in a fine unspoiled landscape near Maidenhead along the Thames River. Temple is especially suitable for the visiting player; it is challenging for the low and high handicapper without being too tiring or discouraging. With a length of just over 6000 yards, it has sufficient distance for the slugger— 2 holes over 500 yards, 5 over 400—without sacrificing the closer, possibly more interesting holes that give a course its character. This is a "dry" course, seemingly unaffected by the weather, even by rain or frost, with superbly kept greens and beautiful views, particularly from the 5th green. The popularity of any course is possibly best tested by the number of players who return, and visitors seem to come back to Temple year after year.

LOCATION: The course is accessible by car from Maidenhead (4 miles) or London (33 miles E), on the main road, M4. There is also train service to Maidenhead, which is 9 miles E of Henley-on-Thames, 38 SE of Oxford.

OTHER INFORMATION: The course is open all year to nonmembers; on Sundays a visitor must either be introduced by a member or have a letter of introduction from a recognized golf club. The professional or his assistant is in daily attendance. The most crowded times are spring and summer, with the best weather to be expected in April through October. Practice ground is available.
Number of holes: 18. *Par:* 70. *Length:* 6090 yards (can be lengthened). *Green fees:* weekdays $3.50, Saturdays $5; Sundays $5.60 (after 5 P.M., considerable reduction—about half). *Lessons:* $2.10 with the assistant; with the professional, Henry Cotton, by arrangement. *Caddies:* $3.50/round; should be reserved in advance. *Golfing equipment and caddie carts:* clubs $1.40/round, carts at nominal cost.

OTHER SPORTS FACILITIES: Squash racquets at the club; fishing and rowing in Henley-on-Thames. All facilities are available in London.

ACCOMMODATIONS: No living space in the club house, but bar and restaurant are available.
For hotels in the immediate area (Maidenhead, Henley-on-Thames, Oxford, Windsor), see this section for the *Huntercombe Golf Club,* p. 30.

TOURIST ATTRACTIONS: The immediate area is extremely attractive. The whole region beginning with Maidenhead is highly recommended for its scenic beauty as well as its historic interest. Follow the road to Henley, then on to Oxford; another road leads to Windsor and a third to Reading. For further details, see this section for the *Huntercombe Golf Club,* p. 30.

FOR FURTHER INFORMATION: Write to: Club Secretary, Temple Golf Club, Hurley, Nr. Maidenhead, Berkshire, England. Telephone: Hurley 248.

Thorndon Park Golf Club Ltd.

Thorndon is only a few miles from London, yet it is set in a picturesque old deer park. Most of the hazards are the natural ones of a beautiful lake and stream running through a small ravine, and the turf itself is a natural terrain excellent for golf. In many ways this is possibly the best course in the Essex area, and it is certainly a pleasure to play. There is plenty of space, a region that exudes tranquillity, and exciting golf. There is sufficient balance to keep every kind of player occupied and happy. And there is length—3 very long holes, 8 around 400 yards. The shorter holes are varied and interesting, for example, the 145-yard 5th over a ravine or the 182-yard 15th across the same ravine but with different angles and approaches. The 14th is particularly recommended for the testing quality of the hole as well as the beauty of the spot just beyond the green. Thorndon has few weak holes, possibly the drive-and-pitch 6th being the least exciting. The course provides excellent inland-golf only 30 to 35 minutes from London.

LOCATION: The course, 2½ miles from Brentwood, is accessible by car or taxi. Brentwood is on the rail line from London's Liverpool Street Station, about 20 miles W.

OTHER INFORMATION: The course is open all year, weather permitting, with nonmembers welcome at any time; all visitors, however, should have a letter of introduction from the secretary of their home club. The professional is always in attendance. The most crowded time is the summer, when the best weather can be expected. Weather is always unpredictable. Practice ground is available.

Number of holes: 18. *Par:* 72. *Length:* 6306 yards.

Green fees: weekdays $1.05/round, $1.40/day; Saturdays $2.10; Sundays and holidays $2.80. *Lessons:* $1.40/½ hour. *Caddies:* $1.40/18 holes. *Golfing equipment and caddie carts:* available by arrangement; carts $0.35/day.

OTHER SPORTS FACILITIES: In the immediate area: Tennis and horseback riding. London, to the west, offers all facilities; and the coast, to the east, provides water sports of all types.

ACCOMMODATIONS: No living space in the club house, but bar and restaurant are available.

Most visitors will prefer to live in London; for hotels there, consult any travel agent.

In Brentwood: *Lion and Lamb* (Tel. 6427). Very small hotel, singles from $4.50, doubles from $7; no private baths; central heating, garage.

In Chelmsford (9 miles): the *County* (Tel. 2414) and *Coval Lodge* (Tel. 2679). A few rooms with private baths; singles from $4.50, doubles from $8.50; central heating at *Coval Lodge*.

TOURIST ATTRACTIONS: Some of the small villages in the area are charming and worth a short visit. On the east coast, Southend is a big, noisy entertainment center and seaside resort, very popular during the summer months. To the west, London offers the visitor the entire range of tourist attractions.

FOR FURTHER INFORMATION: Write to: Club Secretary, Thorndon Park Golf Club Ltd., Brentwood, Essex, England. Telephone: Herongate 345.

Walton Heath Golf Club

Set in the High Heathland covered with heather, Walton Heath Golf Club offers a course that follows the natural undulations of the terrain. The links is laid out on the heath, about 600 to 700 feet above sea level and exposed to the breezes. The ground is fine and dry and playable even after a violent rain. Since Walton Heath lies open to the winds, it has the feel of a seaside links even though it is only 20 miles from London. It is not an easy course, as many expert golfers can testify. The greens are big and the shots longer, the bunkers deeper and steeper; it is golf on a grand scale, although it should not frighten away the less expert player. Golfing here will give him the feel of a large course, where each player is absolutely on his own to play as he sees fit. The accurate player will stand a better chance than the wild swinger who goes strictly for distance. This is true of most English championship courses. If scores are high here, there is no reason for embarrassment. Some of the finest medal play produces high scores. Late in August, annually, the Open Professional Match Play Championships are held here.

LOCATION: Twenty miles S of London, Walton Heath is about 5 miles from Epsom, Leatherhead, Dorking or Reigate. It can be reached easily by car from London, or you can take a bus to any of the above towns and then go by car to the course.

OTHER INFORMATION: The course is open all year to all visitors, except that on Sundays nonmembers must play with a member. A resident professional and three assistants are in attendance. April through September are the most crowded months. Practice ground is available.

Number of holes: Old course, 18; New Course, 18. *Par:* Old, 73; New, 72. *Length:* Old, 6830 yards; New, 6780 yards.

Green fees: weekdays and weekends $5.60/day. *Lessons:* up to $8.40/ hour with the professional, less with the assistant. *Caddies:* $7/day or $4.20/round. *Golfing equipment and caddie carts:* available by arrangement.

OTHER SPORTS FACILITIES: The main local sport is riding, and there are several livery stables nearby. There is tennis in the immediate area, and London is not too far away with all facilities.

ACCOMMODATIONS: No living space in the club house, but bar and restaurant are open from 9 A.M. to 9 P.M.

Local hotels are numerous and mostly good in Leatherhead, Epsom, Reigate, and Dorking—all within 4 to 8 miles of the course.

In Epsom: *Drift Bridge* (Tel. Burgh Heath 1663). Single with bath from $5, double from $9.50; full pension $55/week; no central heating.

Linden House and *Old Manor House*. No private baths; singles $4.20, doubles $8 up. Breakfast included.

In Leatherhead: The *New Bull* (Tel. 2153). Very small. Singles from $4.20, doubles from $8.40; some rooms with bath; no central heating; 10% service charge.

In Dorking: The *White House* (Tel. 2543). Singles from $5, doubles from $9.50; some private baths, central heating, garage.

In Reigate: *Monks Court* (Tel. 43883). Singles $3.50 to $5, doubles from $7; some private baths, no central heating, garage; 10% service charge.

London, of course, offers full accommodations of every type.

TOURIST ATTRACTIONS: Surrey is ideal for walking or car excursions. The landscape is particularly attractive, and the visitor will also find many local places of interest. Nearby Guildford offers several architectural sites, particularly inns, that date back many centuries; small towns and villages, like Godalming, Dorking, Wotton, Leatherhead offer the tourist many pleasant hours.

FOR FURTHER INFORMATION: Write to: Club Secretary, Walton Heath Golf Club, Tadworth, Surrey, England. Telephone: Tadworth 2380.

Knowle Golf Club Ltd.

The Knowle is an up-to-date course constructed on modern lines, consisting of two loops of 9 holes each. The architects took advantage of the natural contour of the land in the placing of the holes. They also took care to eliminate excessive or unnecessary fatigue. Many experts consider Knowle one of the best inland courses in England. The golfer who appreciates his surroundings will find scenic beauty as well as an excellent game. From several of the tees there are very fine views of the surrounding countryside. But the course is what really matters. There is not a single blind approach to the green, and the flag can be seen from almost every tee. This course was designed to please both the expert and the amateur. There is room for accuracy and precision, and there is room for the less ambitious player who wants to try out his game on an attractive course.

LOCATION: The Knowle Golf Club is within the city boundaries of Bristol. It can be reached by car or bus. Bristol itself is 116 miles W of

London (on A4), 13 NW of Bath, 35 S of Gloucester, 43 N of Taunton. It is on a main railroad line.

OTHER INFORMATION: The course welcomes nonmembers, unlimited, and a professional is always on hand. The most crowded time is during the summer months, especially on Saturday afternoons and Sunday mornings. The best weather can be expected in the summer. No practice ground is available.
Number of holes: 18. Par: 70 (S.S.S., 70). Length: 6208 yards.
Green fees: weekdays $1.05/round, $1.40/day; weekends and holidays $1.75/round, $2.80/day; $6 week; $9.60/month. Half price for women.
Lessons: $1.05/½ hour; $2.10/hour. Caddies: none available. Golfing equipment and caddie carts: both for rent by arrangement, at very nominal prices.

OTHER SPORTS FACILITIES: Bristol (with a population of almost 500,000) offers tennis, cricket, English football, greyhound racing and horseback riding.

ACCOMMODATIONS: No living space in the club house, but bar and restaurant are available.
In Bristol: The Grand (Tel. 21645) and the Grand Spa (Tel. 38955). Singles from $5, doubles from $10, plus 10% tax. All comforts, central heating, experienced staff. The Royal (Tel. 23591) and Hawthorn's (Tel. 38432). Less luxurious. Singles from $3.50, doubles $7, plus 10% tax.

TOURIST ATTRACTIONS: Bristol is an attractive city and makes a good base for the surrounding areas; you can visit such places as Bath, Stonehenge, Marlborough and Exeter. Bristol is itself full of picturesque and interesting buildings, many dating from its days as an important ancient seaport, a role it retains. Of particular interest are the old docks, the Church of St. Mary Redcliffe, Mary-le-Port Street, St. James' Church, the Cathedral. Don't miss a performance at the Royal Theatre, which dates back to 1766. There is also good shopping, and the surrounding countryside is full of fine views.

FOR FURTHER INFORMATION: Write to: Club Secretary, The Knowle Golf Club, Fairway, Bristol 4, England. Telephone: Bristol 76341.

Carlyon Bay Golf Club

The golfer who comes to the British Isles could hardly hope to find a more beautiful setting than the one provided by the Carlyon Bay Course. The course is situated on the cliffs overlooking Carlyon Bay, with the first 9 holes following the contours of the coastline over gentle undulating ground. From there you have magnificent views of the surrounding countryside and the English channel. Carlyon Bay itself is a brilliant blue, its color intensified by the reflection of light on quartz particles, which cover the seabed. Don't be fooled by the apparent easiness of the course. The par 3 holes are difficult, and some of the par 4s will prove trying even to the longest hitters. The deception is caused by clever bunkering and the use of natural hazards, which place a test of sharp judgment and skill on the player, especially on the newcomer. Added to this, there are several mine-shafts (not dangerous) dotted about the course, a throwback to the old mining days in Cornwall. Altogether, a challenging course in a superb setting.

LOCATION: The course is 3 miles from St. Austell, 14 miles E of Truro, 14 miles S of Newquay, 38 miles W of Plymouth. London is 250 miles E. By car, the main A30 road from London; by train, from Paddington Station in London on the London–Penzance line.

OTHER INFORMATION: Open all year. A nonmember must belong to a recognized golf club and possess an official handicap. There is a resident professional. The most crowded season is from June through September, with the best weather to be expected in May, September, October. Practice ground is available.
Number of holes: 18. *Par:* 69. *Length:* 5920 yards (for men), 5439 yards (for women).
Green fees: weekdays $1.40/day, weekends and holidays $2.10/day. *Lessons:* $1.40/½ hour. *Caddies:* available through prior arrangement with the professional at $1.40 to $1.75/round. *Golfing equipment and caddie carts:* clubs $1.40/round, carts $.28/round.

OTHER SPORTS FACILITIES: All water sports: swimming, sailing, water skiing, skin diving, shark fishing; also indoor and outdoor tennis, badminton.

ACCOMMODATIONS: No living space in the club house, but bar and restaurant are available.
The *Carlyon Bay Hotel,* 300 yards from the club house, offers accommodations, weekly terms at $51 to $75 during the summer season, less during the later fall and winter; most rooms without private bath. Daily terms can be arranged.
In Carlyon Bay: The *Cliff Head* (Tel. Par 2125). Provides rooms with private baths and breakfast. Singles from $5, doubles from $10. Weekly rates at a reduction; closed during winter months.
In St. Austell: The *White Hart* (Tel. 2100). Rooms with private baths; singles from $4.50, doubles $8.50.

TOURIST ATTRACTIONS: For the visitor who likes to explore new territory, the Cornish coast provides innumerable interesting sites. Fishing villages, Lands End, lovely inlets and bays, Tintagel Castle (seat of King Arthur and the Knights of the Round Table), and several other attractions are all within easy reach. Local products include China clay, pottery and ceramics.

FOR FURTHER INFORMATION: Write to: Club Secretary, Carlyon

Bay Golf Club, Carlyon Bay, St. Austell, Cornwall, England. Telephone: Par 2691.

Churston Golf Club

The Churston Golf Club is set on the south shore of Devonshire, part of the large peninsula that ends with Cornwall. It is picturesquely situated on the top of the cliffs overlooking Tor Bay, which affords the golfer a spectacular view while he enjoys the course. The ground is undulating, with plenty of natural features and much diversification. It is a course for the short driver, although not exclusively so, for three holes go over 480 yards. It is very suitable for the holiday visitor, since there isn't much rough and there are only a few blind carries off the tee. In all, Churston calls for a great variety of shots, without exhausting the visiting golfer.

LOCATION: The Churston Golf Club is 5 minutes by bus or car from the Churston station. It is 4 miles from Paignton, 3 from Brixham and 7 from Torquay. All of these are on the south coast of Devonshire 25 miles from Exeter (N), 20 from Plymouth (SW). Bristol is 110 miles N.

OTHER INFORMATION: The course is open all year to nonmembers who can show proof of membership in a golf club in the United Kingdom or abroad. A professional is in daily attendance. The most crowded time is July and August, with the best weather to be expected from May to June and September to October. Practice ground is available.
Number of holes: 18. *Par:* 70 (Bogey, 72). *Length:* 6238 yards.
Green fees: weekdays and weekends during summer $2/round, $2.80/day, $8 week, $13 two weeks. Winter rates about half. *Lessons:* $1.40/½ hour. *Caddies:* none available. *Golfing equipment and caddie carts:* clubs $1.05/round; carts $0.35/round.

OTHER SPORTS FACILITIES: Churston is a seaside links, so the visitor will find all types of water sports: yachting, fishing, beaches with safe swimming, water skiing. Also tennis and horseback riding.

ACCOMMODATIONS: No living space in the club house, but catering for light meals and a bar available. Many good restauraurants in the nearby towns.
In Paignton: The *Palace* (Tel. 57481) and the *Redcliffe* (Tel. 82228). Rooms with private baths; singles from $4; doubles from $8; plus service. The *Redcliffe* offers more comforts, central heating, etc. Pension from $45/week.
In Brixham: the *Combe Bank* (Tel. 2369) and the *Northcliffe* (Tel. 3225). Singles and doubles with private baths at about the same prices as the Palace.
In Torquay: the *Imperial* (Park Hill Road, Tel. 24301) and the *Palace* (Babbacombe Road, Tel. 22271). Singles with bath from $6 to $9; doubles from $12; with breakfast. Central heating, garage, experienced staff, all comforts.

TOURIST ATTRACTIONS: The coastal area is filled with much natural beauty, excellent for walking or car trips. There are also tours; good shopping in Plymouth and Exeter, within 30 to 40 minutes of the club house. In Dartmouth, a famous castle built during the reign of Edward IV in the fiifteenth century is of special interest. Plymouth is also historical; Sir Francis Drake started his three-year voyage around the world from here.

FOR FURTHER INFORMATION: Write to: Club Secretary, Churston Golf Club Ltd., Churston, Brixham, South Devonshire, England. Telephone: Churston 2751 or 2218.

Royal North Devon Golf Club

In a superb part of England, right on the shores of Bideford Bay, the Royal North Devon Course offers great golf to the visitor who wishes to try it. In addition, this is a section that has remained relatively free of visitors, and you have that rare combination of good golf, great scenery and no crowds. The soil itself is almost perfect for golf, with the sandhills and high grass forming the main hazards. There is also length—the first 3 holes are all over 400 yards—and variety for everyone's taste—four short holes all different, requiring different approaches and putts. Each step at North Devon is a new experience, all against a beautiful background, with the winds and tides themselves a significant factor in the kind of game you play. Remember these holes: the 4th, with its huge bunker; the 10th, with its rushes; the 15th, with its varying slopes. North Devon is distinctive and well worth a visit.

LOCATION: The course is near Bideford, the closest railway stop. From there, car or bus to the club. Bideford is 9 miles W of Barnstaple, 50 N of Exeter, 105 W of Bristol, and 204 W of London.

OTHER INFORMATION: Open to nonmembers all year, with no limitations. Women golfers have the same rights here as men. No Sunday restrictions. The professional is in daily attendance. There is rarely a crowded time, but the weather is somewhat unpredictable—possibly the best in late spring and August. Practice ground is available.
Number of holes: 18. *Par:* 72. *Length:* 6532 yards.
Green fees: $1.05/round, $1.40/day. *Lessons:* $2/hour. *Caddies:* some available at $1.40/round. *Golfing equipment and caddie carts:* clubs about $0.50/day, carts $0.25/day.

OTHER SPORTS FACILITIES: All water sports: sailing, water skiing, swimming, skin diving, fishing; also tennis.

ACCOMMODATIONS: No living space in the club house, but bar and restaurant are available; meals at any time.
In Bideford: The following hotels offer similar quarters, most rooms without private bath; singles from $3.50, doubles from $6, with breakfast;

full pension from $35/week. They are the *Duart* (Tel. 524, the cheapest, with central heating), *New Inn* (Tel. 83, no central heating), and *Royal* (Tel. 5, no central heating).

In Barnstaple: The *Imperial* (Tel. 3232) and *Royal and Fortescue* (Tel. 2289). Some rooms with private baths, no central heating; singles from $4.20, doubles from $7.50, with breakfast; full pension at the *Imperial* from $48/week.

In Ilfracombe (17 miles): the *Mount* (Tel. 308) and *Imperial* (Tel. 536). Some rooms with private baths; singles from $4, doubles from $8.50; breakfast included; full pension from $42/week. 10% service charge. Both closed during the winter months.

TOURIST ATTRACTIONS: Bideford is an historic town and full of literary references. Charles Kingsley (in *Westward Ho!*), Rudyward Kipling, and Hilaire Belloc all wrote of North Devon. It is an excellent place for walking or driving tours, full of old villages, interesting historic buildings, local products (like pottery). Ilfracombe, to the north, is a well-situated resort backed by lovely forests and valleys. If possible, drive up and down the shoreline following the secondary roads that hug the sea.

FOR FURTHER INFORMATION: Write to: Club Secretary, Royal North Devon Golf Club, Westward Ho, Devon, England. Telephone: Northam 17.

St. Enodoc Golf Club

This is a natural seaside links, and the chief hazards are formed by huge sandhills—both the beauty and the terror of the course. The turf is naturally springy, not at all tiring, and it gives the impression of a much longer course than 6000 yards. St. Enodoc begins with a blast—three holes that average 450 yards and suggest a 7000-yard links. Then the course settles down into careful, precise golf, especially on the blind 6th, where your second shot must climb a mountain and find its way toward the green. The 7th is much the same, except that you already have height. It is not so tough that the holiday player will be discouraged, but it is not easy enough to permit laziness. Combine this course, if you can, with several others in Cornwall and Devonshire for a golfing holiday in stark, spectacular surroundings—far, indeed, from the madding crowd.

LOCATION: The course is 7 miles from Wadebridge, just off the north coast of the Cornwall peninsula, 5 miles S of Padstow; it is accessible by car. Wadebridge is 14 miles N of Newquay, 65 W of Exeter, 40 N of Plymouth, 250 W of London.

OTHER INFORMATION: The course is open to nonmembers, with no restrictions or limitations, all year, and the professional is in daily attendance. During the winter months the course is closed on certain days because of unusually bad weather, especially in January and February. Best weather can be expected in spring and late autumn. The course is rarely crowded. Practice ground is available.

Number of holes: 18. *Par:* 72 (S.S.S.). *Length:* 6056 yards.
Green fees: $1.40 during high season (Easter-Sept. 30), $0.84/round or day the rest of the year; weekly and monthly play at reduction. *Lessons:* by arrangement with the professional. *Caddies:* a few available by arrangement with the professional. *Golfing equipment and caddie carts:* for rent by arrangement.

OTHER SPORTS FACILITIES: All water sports slightly to the north: sandy beaches, safe swimming, water skiing, surfing, fishing; tennis; walking tours.

ACCOMMODATIONS: No living space in the club house, but bar and restaurant are available.
In Newquay (14 miles): the *Headland* (Tel. 2211). Most rooms with private baths, singles from $6.50 (with breakfast), doubles from $12.50; full pension from $55/week; 10% service charge. No central heating; closed during winter months. The *St. Rumons* (Tel. 2978). Some rooms with private baths; singles from $6 (with breakfast), doubles from $12; full pension from $36/week; 10% service charge. Central heating, closed during winter months, all comforts. The *Atlantic* (Tel. 2244), *Bristol* (Tel. 2257), and *Edgcumbe* (Tel. 2061). Most rooms with private baths; singles (with breakfast) from $5, doubles from $8; full pension from $40/week; add 10% service charge. No central heating. *Atlantic* closed during winter months.
In Padstow: the *Dinas* (Tel. 26). Singles from $2.80, doubles from $5.25; full pension from $33/week. No central heating, no private baths. The *Metropole* (Tel. 139). Singles from $4.50, doubles (with breakfast) from $8.40; full pension from $40/week; 10% service charge. A few rooms with private baths; no central heating.

TOURIST ATTRACTIONS: See this section for the *Carlyon Bay Golf Club*, p. 42, and for the *Trevose Golf and Country Club*, p. 47.

FOR FURTHER INFORMATION: Write to: Club Secretary, St. Enodoc Golf Club, Rock, Wadebridge, Cornwall, England. Telephone: Trebetherick 3216.

Trevose Golf and Country Club

Set far out on the Cornwall peninsula, the Trevose Golf and Country Club provides a totally different kind of vacation and golfing experience. It is suitable for the golfer coming alone or with his family, since living quarters are provided in bungalows and flats right on the course grounds. The club is situated on a beautiful stretch of the north coast of Cornwall, with sandy beaches surrounding it. In addition to the regular links, there is a 9-hole course for the beginner, the wife or the children. Trevose is frequently used for championship contests in the southwest of England. It tests the expert golfer trying for par but is also kind to the average player who wants to test his game. The turf is springy and untiring to walk on and dries rapidly after rain. The 18 holes are set in open surroundings with only one blind shot. This adds up to a challenging but very fair links—a true golfing holiday.

LOCATION: Trevose lies in a section of England yet to the discovered by most tourists. It can be reached by air from London or by car from neighboring cities and towns. Padstow is the train stop near Trevose, which is 80 miles W of Exeter, 40 W of Plymouth, 10 N of Newquay, and 4 E of Padstow itself. The eastern boundary of the course is Constantine Bay.

OTHER INFORMATION: The course is open all year to nonmembers, with only three or four ball matches restricted. During the busy season (April to October), beginners are restricted to the 9-hole course. A professional is in daily attendance. The weather is best during May and June but is reasonable all year except in January and February. Limited practice ground is available.

Number of holes: 18 (short: 9). *Par:* 69 (S.S.S., 71; Bogey, 74, short: 29). *Length:* 6516 yards (short: 1357 yards).

Green fees: weekdays $.85-$2.10 (depending on season, with summer and Easter Holiday more expensive); $3.50-$7 week; $9-$14 month. 9-hole course half above prices. *Lessons:* $1.40/½ hour. *Caddies:* rarely available. *Golfing equipment and caddie carts:* limited equipment for rent; carts $0.20/round.

OTHER SPORTS FACILITIES: At the club: tennis and a sports room. In the area: swimming in a pool, surfing, and fishing. Sailing and water-skiing at Padstow. Open sea and surf bathing, and a coast line for walking tours.

ACCOMMODATIONS: The club provides a wide range of excellent lodgings. In addition to these, a bar and restaurant are available, with full catering. The local accommodations (part of the country club) are:

Bungalows with living room, kitchen, 3 bedrooms and all modern conveniences; from $3.50/day in winter to $12.60/day during the height of the summer season.

Chalets with living room, kitchen, 3 bedrooms and all modern conveniences at about the same prices.

Flats (apartments), all self-contained, with a double bedroom and all modern conveniences, plus sitting room with a fine view; from $3.50/day to $9/day, depending on season.

Dormitory suites, with single or double bedroom, kitchenette, bathroom; from $1.50/day to $6-$7/day, depending on size and season.

Extra cots, linen, television sets, etc., can be supplied at nominal cost.

In the district, there are many hotels and guest houses, including the *Treglos Hotel,* about 300 yards from the club.

TOURIST ATTRACTIONS: Cornwall presents a fine background for the novelty seeker, including outdoors, scenery, sandy beaches, dramatic seas. Padstow and Newquay are well developed resort towns. Tours to Lands End at the tip of Cornwall.

FOR FURTHER INFORMATION: Write to: Club Secretary, Trevose Golf and Country Club, Constantine Bay, Padstow, Cornwall, England. Telephone: St. Merryn 208.

Prince's Golf Club (at Sandwich)

Prince's is a seaside links laid out so that it provides the toughest test for the very able player without spoiling the enjoyment of the less experienced golfer. The entire course has been reconstructed to suit modern golf theories, and there is little doubt that the new course will be as famous as its pre-war predecessor. As it was constructed, Prince's favors the long driver; but in addition to the championship course of 18 holes (the Blue), there is a 9-hole course (the Red). Both courses can be adjusted, shortened or lengthened, to fit the quality of the player and to meet weather conditions. In the construction of the links, every possible use was made of the natural terrain, with the result that few bunkers were introduced. A ridge that runs through a good part of the course—called the Himalayas—is one natural obstacle to test the player's skill (and also his nerves).

LOCATION: The course is located less than 3 miles from Sandwich and is best reached by car. Buses and trains run regularly to Sandwich, which is in the heart of the Kent coastal resort area. Margate is 9 miles N, Deal 6 S, Ramsgate 7 N, Dover 12 S, Canterbury 12 W. London is 55 miles (less than 2 hours) W.

OTHER INFORMATION: The course is open to nonmembers, who should have a letter of introduction from their home club. The professional and his assistant are always on hand. The season is from May to October, with the course most crowded from June through August. The weather is always chancy. Two practice grounds are available.
Number of holes: 18 (championship Blue), 9 (Red). *Par:* Blue 74, Red 36. *Length:* Blue 7145 yards (championship; 6681, medal), Red 3494 (championship; 3277, medal).
Green fees: weekdays $2.80, weekends and holidays $4.20/day. *Lessons:* $1.75/½ hour, $2.80/hour, $3.50/round with the professional; $1.05/½ hour, $1.75/hour, $2.10/round with the assistant professional. *Caddies:* $2.80/round. *Golfing equipment and caddie carts:* clubs in limited quantity, rented by arrangement with the professional; carts by arrangement.

OTHER SPORTS FACILITIES: The seaside provides angling, swimming and yachting, as well as tennis nearby; plentiful sandy beaches.

ACCOMMODATIONS: Lodgings are available in the club dormy house, 1 mile from the course. Obtain further information from the Estate Agent, Sandwich Bay, Kent. Restaurant and bar in the club house.
In Sandwich Bay: the *Guildford* (Tel. 2345). Singles with private baths from $6, doubles from $12; full pension from $65/week. Central heating, all comforts. The *Bell* (Tel. 2360). Singles with baths from $4.50, doubles

from $7.50; full pension from $45/week. No central heating. The *Guildford* is set on the edge of the Straits of Dover, standing amidst three golf courses.

In Deal: the *Queen's* (Tel. 702). Singles with baths from $4.50, doubles from $8.50; full pension from $55/week. Central heating, all comforts.

In Canterbury: the *Abbots Barton* (Tel. 63770), the *Slatters* (Tel. 63271), and the *Chaucer* (Tel. 64427). All offer rooms, many with private baths, from $4 for singles, from $8 for doubles; full pension from $45/week, with small variations among the three. No central heat at the *Chaucer*. *Slatters* offers most comforts.

In Margate: the *Grosvenor Court* (Tel. Thanet 22442). Singles from $4.20, doubles from $8; pension from $35/week. Central heating and most comforts; many rooms with private baths.

In Dover: the *White Cliffs* (Tel. 633). Singles from $5.50; full pension from $55/week. Central heating, most comforts, many rooms with private bath. Breakfast comes with all rooms, and for all add 10% service charge or more.

TOURIST ATTRACTIONS: Sandwich itself, one of the ancient Cinque Ports, is of great interest, as are Canterbury (Cathedral), Dover (Castle and Harbor), Deal and Walmer. Churches, museums, large shopping centers and picturesque views offer something for every taste. Several lovely gardens, castles and houses open to the public.

FOR FURTHER INFORMATION: Write to: Club Secretary, Prince's Sandwich, Kent, England. Telephone: 2000.

Royal St. George's Golf Club

The visitor to Royal St. George's will find a championship course with a long history of great matches behind it, and many more to come. Walter Hagen won the Open here, R. T. Jones led an American team to victory in the first Walker Cup match played in England, and Jack Nicklaus received the Royal St. George's Champion Grand Challenge Cup here. The course is an open seaside links, with the wind often a factor. It is so varied and interesting that it favors neither the long nor the short driver; it does, however, favor accuracy. Playing Royal St. George's will be not only a golfing experience but also an aesthetic pleasure—great fairways, exacting holes, towering bunkers and sunlight dancing over dunes and the water of the Bay.

LOCATION: Accessible by train or car, Royal St. George's is 1½ miles from Sandwich, 5 from Deal. Canterbury is 12 miles W, Dover 10 S, London 75 miles W. Ramsgate and Margate are within 10 miles.

OTHER INFORMATION: The course is open all year to nonmembers who are introduced by a member or who have a letter of introduction from the secretary of a recognized golf club. The professional is in daily attendance. The height of the season is the summer, when the weather is usually best. Practice ground is available.

Number of holes: 18. *Par:* 70 (S.S.S., 74). *Length:* 6748 yards (championship), 6484 yards (medal).

Green fees: weekdays $2.80/round, $4.90/day. *Lessons:* by arrangement with the professional. *Caddies:* usually available at $2.80/round. *Golfing equipment and caddie carts:* available, by arrangement with the professional.

OTHER SPORTS FACILITIES: All types of water sports—swimming, sailing and fishing. Horseback riding, yachting and tennis. Excellent sandy beaches.

ACCOMMODATIONS: No living space in the club house, but dining room and bar are available. The immediate region has several excellent hotels in Deal, Margate, Sandwich, Sandwich Bay, Canterbury. See listing for *Prince's Golf Club* at Sandwich, pp. 48-49.

TOURIST ATTRACTIONS: For a listing of attractions, see *Prince's Golf Club* at Sandwich, p. 49.

FOR FURTHER INFORMATION: Write to: Club Secretary, Royal St. George's Golf Club, Sandwich, England. Telephone: Sandwich 3090.

Formby Golf Club

Regarded as one of the leading golf clubs in England, Formby is situated close to the shore on the West Lancashire coast between Liverpool and Southport. Thus the visitor to Formby can enjoy the scenic beauty of the area by day and the facilities of a large city by night. Formby is a natural links, surrounded by stately pine woods, great sand dunes and first-rate turf. As entrances to a number of the greens are narrow and tight, approach shots have to be accurate. Accuracy, in fact, is of primary importance on this course, but there is plenty for everyone, the long and the short driver. Further, in playing many of the holes, visitors experience a feeling of peacefulness and quiet, for the terrain often appears to isolate certain holes from the rest of the links.

The Formby Ladies Course is more open and is situated within the perimeter of the men's course.

The Formby Course has been the scene of many important amateur championship events; in 1967, it will have the honor of staging the Amateur Championship.

LOCATION: Coming from London, the Southport train from Euston Station will leave the visitor at Freshfield Station, two minutes' walk from the course. From Liverpool (15 miles S) and Southport (7 miles N), trains run every 20 minutes. Buses stop at Formby Village, where taxis are available. It is only 20 minutes by car from Liverpool and from Southport. Liverpool is 197 miles NW of London.

OTHER INFORMATION: The course is open all year to nonmembers, who should carry a letter from their parent club or be introduced by a member. Formby is very busy, so prior request to use the course is advisable. Otherwise, arrival on a competition day or during the visit of a society may result in disappointment. The professional or his assistant is on duty every day, with the busy season beginning in April and continuing until early October. Best weather from May until late August, although early fall can also be pleasant. Practice ground is available.

Number of holes: 18. *Par:* Yellow (standard), 73; Red (short), 71. *Length:* 6862 yards (Yellow), 6224 yards (Red).

Green fees: weekdays $2.80/round or day, weekends and holidays $4.20/round or day (half price with member). *Lessons:* $1.40/½ hour, $2.80/hour; the professional charges $2.80/round in a singles match, $4.20/round in a foursome. *Caddies:* $2.80/round; $2.10 for boys. *Golfing equipment and caddie carts:* the professional maintains a well-stocked shop but normally does not rent clubs; carts $0.28/round.

OTHER SPORTS FACILITIES: The entire Lancashire coast area is a sportsman's holiday. The coast offers the entire range of water sports: yachting, sailing, swimming, boating—in and around the Southport area. Also tennis and horseback riding. For the spectator, there is English football, with the championship-caliber Liverpool Football Club. Horseracing at Chester and Haydock Park, coursing at Altcar and the famous Grant National at Aintree fill out the program. In addition, the visitor will find the entire region full of golf clubs.

ACCOMMODATIONS: The Dormy House attached to the club has seven single rooms and one twin-bedded room; charges are $5/night for bed and breakfast. Reservations should be made far in advance. Bar and restaurant in the immediate area in Formby Village. The coast is a resort area, so good accommodations are plentiful.

In Southport: The following hotels offer private baths, central heating and comfortable lodgings; singles (with breakfast) from $5.50, doubles from $10; 10% service charge. *Prince of Wales* (Tel. 4131), *Palace* (Tel. 67021), *Clifton* (Tel. 3131). Full pension also available, from $45/week at *Clifton* to $75/week at *Prince of Wales*.

Ainsdale, Blundellsands, and Hightown in the immediate area provide meals and accommodations on a small scale.

In Liverpool: The *Adelphi* (Ranelagh Place, Tel. Royal 7200). A luxury hotel with all modern conveniences; singles (with breakfast) from $8.50, doubles from $16; 10% service charge. No pension. The *Stork, Exchange* and *Lord Nelson*. Smaller but comfortable.

TOURIST ATTRACTIONS: Both Liverpool and Southport are noted shopping centers. As a great port, Liverpool has connections with every shipping center in the world. Lord Street, Southport, has an international reputation for its shops. Liverpool, of course, offers a wide range of cultural activities including the Walker Art Gallery, the Anglican Cathedral and a tour of the docks. For other kinds of entertainment, there are dancing, night clubs and restaurants in all prices ranges.

FOR FURTHER INFORMATION: Write to: Club Secretary, Formby Golf Club, Formby, Nr. Liverpool, England. Telephone: Formby 2164.

Royal Birkdale Golf Club

Royal Birkdale is a big course in every possible way, and it requires a major brand of golf. But before the average golfer is frightened away, let me say that he can regulate his tees considerably at nearly every hole. Also, Birkdale is perhaps the finest seaside links in England—all the more reason to give it a try. If you do, you will remember it. This is a course with length, narrow fairways and treacherous hazards in the form of sand-hills and roughs filled with scrub. The first hole is enough to discourage you in itself, but don't be discouraged. It is 520 yards and possibly the most difficult hole on the course. There is satisfaction here; get through that and you know what Birkdale has to offer at its best and worst. As on all good courses, it is your second shot that will determine your game. Time and again, an indifferent drive can be corrected by accurate, tight play. Birkdale has variety as well as balance. Play it and match yourself against the world's best—all for $1.05 per round.

LOCATION: The course is at the lower end of Southport, accessible by car or train. The train lets you out at Hillside Station, about ¼ mile from the club house. Southport is 18 miles N of Liverpool, 40 S of Blackpool, 210 W of London.

OTHER INFORMATION: The nonmember is welcome without limitations. The club is open all year, with the professional in daily attendance. The busy season begins in late spring and continues through early autumn, with the best weather to be expected from May through August. Practice ground is available.
Number of holes: 18. *Par:* 74. *Length:* 6844 yards (can be shortened considerably), 5889 yards for women's course.
Green fees: weekdays $1.05/round, $1.40/day, weekends and holidays $2.80/day. *Lessons:* by arrangement with the professional. *Caddies:* by arrangement with the professional. *Golfing equipment and caddie carts:* by arrangement.

OTHER SPORTS FACILITIES: For details, see this section for the *Formby Golf Club,* p. 51.

ACCOMMODATIONS: No living space in the club house, but bar and restaurant are available; meals should be requested in advance.
For details on accommodations in this area—and they are extensive—see this section under the *Formby Golf Club,* p. 51, and the *Southport and*

Ainsdale Golf Club, p. 55. You will find several hotels listed for Southport, Liverpool. For additional hotels in Lytham and Blackpool, see this section for the *Royal Lytham and St. Annes Golf Club*, pp. 53-54.

TOURIST ATTRACTIONS: For Southport, Liverpool, Blackpool, see this section for the following clubs: *Formby*, pp. 51-52; *Southport and Ainsdale*, p. 55; *Royal Lytham and St. Annes*, p. 54.

FOR FURTHER INFORMATION: Write to: Club Secretary, Royal Birkdale Golf Club, Southport, Lancashire, England. Telephone: Southport 68857.

The Royal Lytham and St. Annes Golf Club

The Royal Lytham and St. Annes has the reputation of being one of England's most demanding courses. And it is also one of the finest. For the visiting player there is the opportunity to try out a course that presents problems even for the professionals. Here have been great victories by Bobby Jones, Lawson Little, Bobby Locke and many others. The course is a balance of varying elements—mounds, hollows, sandpits, trees, bushes—all worked out to provide golf at its most strategic and interesting. The soil itself seems made for golf, since most of it is sea-blown sand. Royal Lytham favors the accurate, careful golfer who has a little bit of every kind of magic in his repertory.

LOCATION: The club is accessible by bus, train or car from Preston or Blackpool. Blackpool, the nearest large city, is 4 miles N, Preston, 8 E. Manchester and Liverpool are 45 miles S. There is plane service from London to Blackpool.

OTHER INFORMATION: The course is open all year to nonmembers, who must show letters of introduction from their local clubs. A professional is in daily attendance. The most crowded time is April through October, when the best weather can also be expected. Practice ground is available.
Number of holes: 18. *Par:* 74. *Length:* 6836 yards (championship tees), 6635 yards (medal tees).
Green fees: weekdays $2.10/round, $2.80/day (without introduction by member); weekends and holidays $2.80/round, $4.20/day (without member); $14/week (without member). Half price with member. *Lessons:* $2.80/45 minutes. *Caddies:* limited number available @ $2.10/round. *Golfing equipment and caddie carts:* available by arrangement.

OTHER SPORTS FACILITIES: Tennis, horseback riding, squash, as well as most water sports, including sailing, swimming, sand yachting.

ACCOMMODATIONS: The living space in the club is limited to a dormy house with ten single bedrooms for men only. Arrangements should be made with the club secretary, and reservations should be made far in advance. The club house itself has a large dining room, club room, billiards room with two tables, two bars and ladies' room. Cocktail parties and dinner parties of up to 90 can be handled.

In Lytham St. Annes: *Clifton Arms* (Tel. Lytham 6245). Singles from $6, doubles from $12; including bath and breakfast: *Grand* (Tel. St. Annes 22155) and *St. Annes* (Tel. St. Annes 22111). Singles from $4, doubles from $8; some rooms with private baths.

In Blackpool: The *Imperial* (North Promenade, Tel. 23971), *Savoy* (North Shore, Tel. 52561), *Clifton* (Talbot Square, Tel. 21481), and *Queen's Hydro* (South Promenade, Tel. 42015). All have rooms with private baths; singles from $4.50, doubles from $9-10; 10% tax in most cases. Central heating, garage.

TOURIST ATTRACTIONS: Nearby Blackpool is England's largest pleasure resort, with a full range of entertainment and amusements for the visitor—miles of sandy beaches, with a long promenade, steamer excursions, theaters, ballrooms, an amusement park, a casino and an aquarium.

FOR FURTHER INFORMATION: Write to: Club Secretary, Royal Lytham and St. Annes Golf Club, St. Annes-on-the Sea, Lancashire, England. Telephone: St. Annes 24207.

The Southport and Ainsdale Golf Club

The "S and A," as golfers in the Lancashire area call the Southport and Ainsdale Golf Club, is set in an area known for its fine courses. In Southport alone there are four first-class links. About halfway between Blackpool and Liverpool on the coast, the "S and A" is a championship links with a long pedigree. For many years it served as the site of the Ryder Cup Professional International Matches between Great Britain and the United States, and all the top players have golfed here at one time or another. Many players have worked on their game at this course, which is known as a tough training ground for both the unexpert and the expert. The chief element of the terrain is towering sand hills, which call upon the golfer either to hit between the ridges or to carry over with long sailing shots. Thus, the golfer will always be faced with the problem of whether to be precise or to go for power. For the less expert golfer, "S and A" offers the chance to play a course that one day he may come close to mastering.

LOCATION: The course can be reached conveniently by bus, car or train. The club house is less than ¼ mile from the Ainsdale station on the railway from Liverpool and as near the bus service. Ainsdale and Southport (3 miles apart) are 15 to 18 miles N of Liverpool, 210 W of London.

OTHER INFORMATION: The course is open to nonmembers all year, with a professional in daily attendance. The summer is the most crowded time and also has the best weather. Practice ground is available.

Number of holes: 18. *Par:* 71. *Length:* 6428 yards (for tournaments add another 300 yards).
Green fees: weekdays $2.10/round or day, weekends and holidays $4.20; weekly and monthly tickets at considerable reduction. *Lessons:* by arrangement with the professional. *Caddies:* available, but prices vary according to age and experience. *Golfing equipment and caddie carts:* available by arrangement with the professional.

OTHER SPORTS FACILITIES: Southport is a famous seaside resort full of fine beaches, gardens and parks. There are swimming, boating, fishing, water skiing and yachting; tennis and horseback riding in the general area.

ACCOMMODATIONS: No living space in the club house.
In Southport: *Prince of Wales* (Tel. 4131). Singles with private baths from $5 (with breakfast); doubles $10 plus tax. *Clifton* (Tel. 3131) and *Royal* (Tel. 4101). Singles (with breakfast) from $3.50; doubles $7.50 plus tax.
In Liverpool: The *Adelphi* (Ranelagh Place, Tel. Royal 7200). Very comfortable quarters; singles with baths from $6; doubles from $12; breakfast included; central heating, experienced staff, all amenities. The *Exchange* (Tithebarn St., Tel. Central 5678). Prices same as above. The *Shaftesbury* (Mount Pleasant, Tel. Royal 4421) and the *Stork* (Queen Square, Royal 1231). Comfortable accommodations at prices 10 to 20% below those listed above.

TOURIST ATTRACTIONS: Southport is a famous shopping spot, especially Lord Street. As a popular resort town, it offers a varied program of entertainment. Liverpool, 15 miles away, is a major city with every kind of tourist attraction; recommendations are the docks, St. George's Hall, the Walker Art Gallery, the Anglican cathedral.

FOR FURTHER INFORMATION: Write to: Club Secretary, The Southport and Ainsdale Golf Club, Ainsdale, Southport, Lancashire, England. Telephone: Southport 78000.

Edgbaston Golf Club

Like so many English courses, Edgbaston is only a short distance from a large city but is itself secluded and peaceful. Thus the golfer can enjoy his game in the day and spend his evening in Birmingham, a city of more than one million people. The course is set in Edgbaston Park, with its grassland, woodland, marsh and lake. The links itself is laid out in three loops —the first 9 holes, the next 6 and the final 3—with the 1st, 10th and 16th tees on a line with the club house. As a result, the player who wishes to call it a day at these points can readily do so, or if he wishes he can use any of these as alternative starting points. The course features several long holes, the longest 500 yards (the 17th), and several very short ones, the shortest 140 yards (the 14th), so it has something for every type of golfer.

LOCATION: Two miles from the center of Birmingham, Edgbaston can be reached by car (there is parking) or by the No. 1 bus, which passes the entrance. Birmingham is 113 miles NW of London on A5.

OTHER INFORMATION: The course is open to nonmembers all year, without limitations, but visitors have to be properly clad to enter the club house. The professional or his assistant is always on duty. The most crowded season is summer, when the best weather can be expected.
Small practice area is available.
Number of holes: 18. *Par:* 69 (Bogey, 72). *Length:* 6146 yards.
Green fees: weekdays $2.10, Saturdays and Sundays $3.50/day. *Lessons:* $1.40/½ hour. *Caddies:* not available. *Golfing equipment and caddie carts:* clubs not for rent; carts at nominal price.

OTHER SPORTS FACILITIES: As England's second city, Birmingham offers nearly all facilities: horseback riding, tennis, swimming pools. There are also several other golf courses in the area around the city.

ACCOMMODATIONS: No living space in the club house, but the club does considerable catering for members and visitors—food and drink.
In Birmingham: The *Albany* (Smallbrook, Tel. Midland 8171), *Grand* (Colmore Row, Tel. Central 7301), and *Queen's* (Stephenson Place, Tel. Midland 4433). All very comfortable to luxury hotels; singles (with baths and breakfast), from $7 to $8, doubles from $14. Central heating, experienced staffs, all amenities. No pension available.
The *Arden* (New Street, Tel. Midland 1029) and the *Imperial* (Temple Street, Tel. Midland 6751). Good accommodations, a few rooms with private baths; about half the above prices.
In Edgbaston: the *Norfolk* (259 Hagley Road, Tel. Edgbaston 0870) and the *Grosvenor House* (51 Hagley Road, Edgbaston 4124). Singles from $5.00, doubles from $9, some rooms with private baths; breakfast included. Both very near the course.

TOURIST ATTRACTIONS: Birmingham provides a good deal of interest for the visitor; it has a famous art gallery and the Bull Ring, as well as good shopping on New Street, the Theatre Royal and the Birmingham Symphony Orchestra. Stratford-on-Avon is only 20 miles away. See this section under *Sutton Coldfield Golf Club,* p. 59.

FOR FURTHER INFORMATION: Write to: Club Secretary, Edgbaston Golf Club Ltd., 82, Hagley Road, Edgbaston, Birmingham 16, England. Telephone: Edgbaston 1158.

Notts Golf Club

Notts is an excellent inland course, clearly of championship caliber and by no means an easy test for even the experienced professional. It has been the site of several championship competitions, including the Masters Tournament. Besides providing good golf, it is situated in a lovely part of the English countryside, set in a valley backed by a ridge that isolates it from urban life. Notts clearly favors the powerful hitter; at nearly 7000 yards, it is one of the longest of inland courses. Nevertheless, it has only one hole over 500 yards, with most in the 400 range and three good short holes. Notts begins and ends with several long and tough holes, so if you begin poorly, you have an opportunity to improve your score on the way home. All in all, this is excellent golf, with holes you will remember, like the blind 6th, the narrow 10th and the trickily doglegged 16th.

LOCATION: The course is 10 miles from Nottingham, about 20 minutes by car. There is regular train service to Nottingham, which is 31 miles N of Leicester, 50 NE of Birmingham, 123 N of London, 80 SE of Manchester.

OTHER INFORMATION: The course is open all year to nonmembers, but they should have a letter of introduction from a recognized golf club. The professional is in daily attendance. Weekends are often crowded, although not more so in any particular season. The weather in this area is unpredictable. Practice ground is available.
Number of holes: 18. *Par:* 74 (S.S.S.). *Length:* 6931 yards.
Green fees: weekdays $1.40, weekends $2.80/day. *Lessons:* $2.80/hour. *Caddies:* $1.75/18 holes when available (reserve in advance). *Golfing equipment and caddie carts:* for rent by arrangement with the professional.

OTHER SPORTS FACILITIES: In Nottingham and Derby: tennis, indoor swimming, horseback riding. About an hour's drive to the east, on the Lincolnshire coast, there are numerous seaside resorts, such as Skegness, with sandy beaches, fine swimming.

ACCOMMODATIONS: No living space in the club house, but bar and restaurant are available.
For hotels in Nottingham, Mansfield (14 miles), and Sheffield (25 miles), see this section for the *Sherwood Forest Golf Club Ltd.,* p. 58.

TOURIST ATTRACTIONS: For Sherwood Forest, Nottingham, and Derby, see this section for the *Sherwood Forest Golf Club Ltd.,* p. 58.

FOR FURTHER INFORMATION: Write to: Club Secretary, Notts Golf Club, Hillinwell, Kirkby-in-Ashfield, Nottinghamshire, England. Telephone: Kirkby-in-Ashfield 3225.

Sherwood Forest Golf Club Ltd.

Sherwood Forest is familiar to everyone as the home of the legendary Robin Hood and his followers. It is a peaceful and lovely woodland, full of fine trees and many opportunities for excursions. It provides an attractive background for the club of the same name. The Sherwood Forest Golf

Club is set amidst pine trees, which form one of the chief obstacles to the long hitter. Nevertheless, the course is for the long driver if he remembers also to be precise. In many of the approaches there are unforeseen problems, and here too precision will help the golfer over. This is a course of good length, well planned and of medium-to-difficult standard.

LOCATION: The course is accessible by car from the Mansfield Station, two miles away. Mansfield is 14 miles N of Nottingham—20 minutes by car—25 miles SE of Sheffield, 45 S of Leeds, 48 N of Birmingham, 160 N of London.

OTHER INFORMATION: The course is open all year to nonmembers, who should bring proof of membership in a recognized golf club. The professional is in regular attendance. No single season is crowded, although weekends are usually more crowded than other times. The weather is variable and unpredictable. Practice ground is available.
Numbers of holes: 18. *Par:* 74 (S.S.S.). *Length:* 6691 yards.
Green fees: weekdays $1.40/day, weekends $2.80/day. *Lessons:* $1.40/½ hour, $2.80/hour. *Caddies:* a few available by advance request. *Golfing equipment and caddie carts:* available by arrangement with the professional.

OTHER SPORTS FACILITIES: None in the immediate area, but Nottingham, Sheffield and Derby will provide tennis, indoor swimming and horseback riding.

ACCOMMODATIONS: No living space in the club house, but bar and restaurant are available.
In Mansfield: the *Midland* (Tel. 195) and the *Swan* (Tel. 5). Small hotels, no private baths, comfortable. Singles from $4, doubles from $7; the *Midland* about a third cheaper.
In Nottingham: the *Victoria* (Tel. 48221). The most luxurious and expensive, with all comforts; singles from $8.50, doubles from $13; breakfast included; 10% service charge. The *George* (Tel. 45641), the *Flying Horse* (Tel. 52831), and the *County* (Tel. 46321). Singles from $5, doubles from $7.50; breakfast included. All have rooms with private bath, but no central heating. 10% service charge.
In Sheffield: the *Grand* (Tel. 21001) and the *Royal Victoria* (Tel. 78822). All comforts, private baths, heating, experienced staffs; singles from $9, doubles from $15; 10% service charge; breakfast included. No pension.

TOURIST ATTRACTIONS: The chief attraction is Sherwood Forest; tours of the forest and of the great parks, or Dukeries. Welbeck, home of the Duke of Portland, is the best known of the parks. Nottingham, home of the annual Goose Fair, is famous for lace and as a university city. Also of interest is St. Mary, a fifteenth-century church. In Derby, the porcelain museum, the Derby Racecourse Park, and the art gallery are worth a visit.

FOR FURTHER INFORMATION: Write to: Club Secretary, Sherwood Forest Golf Club, Eakring Road, Mansfield, Notts., England. Telephone: 327.

Sutton Coldfield Golf Club

The scene of many major national professional tournaments, Sutton Coldfield Golf Club is situated in a beautiful residential area only 7 miles from Birmingham. This section of Warwickshire is full of open spaces, and the large city of Birmingham offers the visitor varied entertainment in the evening. The Sutton Coldfield Course is a long driver's paradise, with many holes well over 400 yards. But power isn't the complete answer; very often precision is. Several holes have narrow approaches, and many shots are tricky, with ditches, trees and slopes as the enemy of the blaster. It is a course for all types of players, featuring a fairly easy start, but it has many holes that will try the skills of the most practiced player.

LOCATION: Seven miles N of Birmingham, Sutton Coldfield is within car range of many large cities, including Liverpool, Manchester, Sheffield, Leicester. The course is accessible by bus and train, and the station (Streetly) is only a two-minute walk to the club house. A car from Birmingham will take 15 minutes. Birmingham is 113 miles NW of London on a main artery.

OTHER INFORMATION: The course is open all year to nonmembers, who should have proof of membership in another golf club. The professional is in permanent attendance. Most crowded time is May through September, when the best weather can also be expected. Practice ground is available.

Number of holes: 18. *Par:* 72. *Length:* 6390 yards.
Green fees: weekdays, $2.10, after 4 P.M. $1.40; $5.60 week; $11.20 month. Half price with member. *Lessons:* $1.40/½ hour. *Caddies:* usually unavailable, but on weekends young boys will pull trolleys for $1.05/round. *Golfing equipment and caddie carts:* clubs normally not for rent; carts at nominal cost.

OTHER SPORTS FACILITIES: None in immediate area; in Birmingham, the full range of sports facilities.

ACCOMMODATIONS: No living space in the club house, but several bars and a dining room are available.
Birmingham offers several excellent accommodations. For details, see section for *Edgbaston Golf Club,* p. 56.

TOURIST ATTRACTIONS: As England's second city, Birmingham offers activities for every taste and pocketbook. For the wife of the golfer, there is excellent shopping on New Street; for the visitor who wishes cultural activities, there is the Art Gallery, chiefly known for its collection of pre-Raphaelite works, and not far from there are some windows by Edward Burne-Jones; there are numerous parks, including one with a garden laid out especially for botany students. Only 40 minutes' drive from Birmingham is Stratford-on-Avon, Shakespeare's birthplace.

FOR FURTHER INFORMATION: Write to: Club Secretary, Streetly, Sutton Coldfield Golf Club, Warwickshire, England. Telephone: Streetly 2014 or Walsall 23993.

Ilkley Golf Club

The golf club is situated in a spectacular part of England renowned for its rocks, crags, moors and ravines. What makes the scenery even more attractive is the fact that heather covers everything. The area is historically of great interest and has now become a popular resort region. The golf course has tried to take advantage of these natural surroundings; the first 7 holes follow the curve of the River Wharfe. The course will be of interest to both the medium and the short driver, with special appeal for the precise hitter who can overcome some of the natural hazards.

LOCATION: The course is accessible by car (or taxi) from Ilkley, 1 mile away. Ilkley is 18 miles NW of Leeds, 16 N of Bradford, 21 N of Halifax, 60 N of Manchester, 206 N of London.

OTHER INFORMATION: The course is open for the entire twelve months of the year to nonmembers, unlimited. The professional is in daily attendance, and the busiest time for him and the links is summer. The

Shell's Wonderful World of Golf

Colorful gardens and well-trimmed greens add to the pleasure of golf in England.

weather, as in most of England, is unpredictable. Practice ground is available.

Number of holes: 18. *Par:* 69. *Length:* 6300 yards.
Green fees: weekdays $2.10/day, weekends $4.20/day. *Lessons:* $1.40/½ hour. *Caddies:* available on weekends at $1.05/round. *Golfing equipment and caddie carts:* no clubs for rent; carts $.35/day.

OTHER SPORTS FACILITIES: In the immediate area: horseback riding, tennis, rugby matches and soccer matches for the spectator, as well as an open-air pool.

ACCOMMODATIONS: No living space in the club house, but restaurant and bar are available.

In Ilkley: the *Craiglands* (Tel. 2181). A very comfortable hotel; private baths, central heating, garage; singles from $6, doubles from $12, breakfast included. Full pension from $70 week.

In Leeds: The *Metropole* (King Street, Tel. 20841) and the *Queen's* (City Square, Tel. 31323). Luxury accommodations, with all comforts; at the *Queen's* all rooms have private baths; singles from $8.50, doubles from $16 to $22, with breakfast; 10% service charge. *Great Northern* (Wellington Street, Tel. 30431), *Mount* (Clarendon Road, Tel. 26787), and *Griffin* (Boar Lane, Tel. 36131). ¼ to ½ the above prices.

TOURIST ATTRACTIONS: The chief attraction around Ilkley is the heather-covered moorland. Some of the most spectacular sights are Almescliffe Crag, Cow-and-Calf Rocks, Pancake Rock, Hebers Ghyll, White Wells. At nearby Skipton the fine castle dating from the end of the eleventh century can be visited. Harrogate, 15 miles to the northwest, is a popular spa lying high above the moors. It is renowned as both a health resort and a town noted for its flower gardens, concerts and dramatic presentations.

FOR FURTHER INFORMATION: Write to: Club Secretary, Ilkley Golf Club, Ilkley, Yorkshire, England. Telephone: Ilkley 3505.

Moortown Golf Club Ltd.

Like the Sand Moor Course, only a short distance away, Moortown provides excellent golf in a fine setting that includes typical Yorkshire woods, heather, streams—and the ever-present moors. With the proximity to Leeds, the visitor has a rich country setting by day and the facilities of a lively city by night. Moortown begins with a rush—three par 5s from the start, all legitimate 5s indeed; then the second 9 almost repeats the pattern. But this is a fair test of golf—solid visible greens, broad fairways, good bunkers. The most famous hole is the 176-yard 8th (which follows the 176-yard 7th), called the "Gibraltar"; the green is set atop a large rock formation. But this is only one of several excellent holes, such as the tough 16th on the way home, the 9th leading to the moors on the way out. In 1962 the English

Amateur Championship was played here, an indication of how highly rated Moortown is.

LOCATION: Moortown is 5 miles N of Leeds on the road to Harrogate, accessible by both car and bus (on a regular schedule). There is always regular train service to Leeds, then by car or taxi to the course. Leeds is 190 miles N of London, 40 NE of Manchester, 33 N of Sheffield, 77 N of Birmingham.

OTHER INFORMATION: The course is open all year, weather permitting, with no special restrictions for nonmembers. The most crowded time is spring through autumn, and the professional is in daily attendance. The weather is unpredictable, but your best hope is in late summer. Practice ground is available.

Number of holes: 18. *Par* 73 (S.S.S.). *Length:* 6604 yards.

Green fees: weekdays $1.05/round, $1.40/day; weekends and holidays $2.80/day. *Lessons:* $2.50/hour. *Caddies:* a few available by advance arrangement. *Golfing equipment and caddie carts:* available by arrangement.

OTHER SPORTS FACILITIES: None in the immediate area. In Leeds: tennis, indoor swimming, horseback riding. Some sandy beaches on the inlet to the east.

ACCOMMODATIONS: No living space in the club house, but bar and restaurant are available.

For hotels in Leeds, see this section under the *Sand Moor Golf Club,* p. 63.

TOURIST ATTRACTIONS: For Leeds, see *Sand Moor Golf Club,* p. 63, and for surrounding countryside, see *Ilkley Golf Club,* p. 61.

FOR FURTHER INFORMATION: Write to: Club Secretary, Moortown Golf Club Ltd., Harrogate Road, Leeds 17, England. Telephone: Leeds 68-6521.

Sand Moor Golf Club

Once the site of a barren moor, the Sand Moor Golf Club is now one of the most modern and well-situated courses in England. It is a particularly attractive course, for the setting has not suffered with the construction of modern conveniences. As its name indicates, Sand Moor is laid out over sand and sandstone. Many holes have views of the lake, and in the distance you can see innumerable trees and patches of shrubs, gorse and heather. In this respect the course provides a complete contrast to the city. The sandy subsoil is excellent for playing, and Sand Moor has been the site of several professional tournaments. But that should not frighten away the amateur; while the course possesses many long holes (7 at 450 yards or more), the accurate amateur should also find it rewarding. There is plenty of variety as well as many testing holes. Possibly its greatest attraction is its diversification—each hole is individualized. And don't let the formidable first of 462 yards throw you!

LOCATION: The course is 5 miles N of Leeds, on its outskirts, and accessible by bus or car from Leeds. Leeds is 190 miles N of London, 40 NE of Manchester, 33 N of Sheffield, 77 N of Birmingham.

OTHER INFORMATION: The course is open to nonmembers all year round, and the professional is in daily attendance. The most crowded season is from May through September, when the best weather can also be expected. Practice ground is available.

Number of holes: 18. *Par:* 73 (S.S.S.). *Length:* 6521 yards.

Green fees: weekdays $1.40/round, $2.20/day; weekends and holidays $2.10/round, $2.80/day. *Lessons:* $2.80/hour. *Caddies:* $1.75/round. *Golfing equipment and caddie carts:* no clubs for rent, carts $.35/round.

OTHER SPORTS FACILITIES: There are no special facilities in the immediate area, except other golf courses, but nearby Leeds is a completely modern city with tennis, horseback riding, indoor swimming.

ACCOMMODATIONS: No living space in the club house, but bar and restaurant are available. The club house is one of the most modern in England, with a card room, billiards room, showers, and full catering.

In Leeds: The *Queen's Hotel* (City Square, Tel. 31323). Luxury accommodations; private baths, central heating, experienced staffs, garage; singles from $10, doubles from $21, plus service, breakfast included.

The *Metropole* (King Street, Tel. 20841). Similar facilities at slightly lower prices; singles from $8.40, doubles from $16.

Also available at lower price, *Great Northern* (Wellington Street, Tel. 30431) and *Mount* (Clarendon Road, Tel. 26787). Some rooms with private baths; lower prices.

TOURIST ATTRACTIONS: Leeds is a large industrial city, a center for the clothing industry in this section of England. The visitor can expect excellent shopping, and if he is interested in commerce, he can visit any of the great factories. To the north of Leeds (25 miles) is the famous spa of Harrogate; its waters are famous throughout Europe. In addition, this resort area offers beautiful flower gardens and many drama and music festivals. The entire area is full of interesting buildings and monuments; see Skipton and Ripon. Manchester, to the south, is the heart of industrial England, but it is also a cathedral city with a fine museum, lovely buildings.

FOR FURTHER INFORMATION: Write to: Club Secretary, Sand Moor Golf Club, Leeds, Yorkshire, England. Telephone: Leeds 685180.

Crowborough Beacon Golf Club

Set in the beautiful Sussex countryside, the Crowborough Beacon Golf Course is known as the course with a view as well as the site of good golf. With the entire 18 holes standing 700 feet above sea level, one can look out from the club house and several of the holes over the entire Sussex plain, as far as forty miles away. One can see the Downs, behind Eastbourne, and the Birling Gap to the west, and as far as Brighton and Worthing. The course varies with each hole and features the natural terrain of an English heath, rich in attractive hollows and sweeping uplands, with trees, heather and gorse providing the perfect setting for golf. Crowborough Beacon is not an exhausting course, but it will test your repertory. Bobby Locke is the authority for this. The 6th hole is perhaps its most famous, called "The Speaker," after a former Speaker of the House of Commons. In front of the tee is a ravine, although the hole itself is a short one of 180 yards. Coming home are several holes affording such delightful scenery that even the most avid of players will stop to look.

LOCATION: The club house is less than 2 miles from Crowborough Station, which is one hour S of London by train and 1½ hours by car. Taxis are available at Crowborough Station for the run to the course. London is 40 miles N, Tunbridge Wells 7 N, Brighton 22 S, Eastbourne 27 S.

OTHER INFORMATION: The course is open all year to nonmembers upon payment of the green fee. The professional is always on hand. The most crowded season is from April 1 to September 30, with the worst weather during February and March. Practice ground is available.
  Number of holes: 18. *Par:* 70 (Bogey, 71). *Length:* 6241 yards.
  Green fees: weekdays $1.50/round, $2.10/day; weekends $2.10/round, $2.80/day. Half price with member. After 4:30 P.M. $.85. *Lessons:* $1.05/½ hour, $1.75/hour. *Caddies:* $2.10/round. *Golfing equipment and caddie carts:* available by arrangement with the professional.

OTHER SPORTS FACILITIES: The area is full of golf courses as well as tennis courts and riding stables. A short distance away there is hunting, fishing and shooting. For the climber, there are many fine rock formations.

ACCOMMODATIONS: No living space in the club house, but bar and restaurant are available.
  In Crowborough: the *Crest* (Tel. 394) and the *Links* (Tel. 3213). Rooms with private baths, central heating (at the *Crest*), and general comforts; singles from $3.50, doubles (at *Crest* only) from $9, with breakfast. Full pension at both, from $35/week at *Links* to $50/week at *Crest*. 10% service charge.
  For further lodgings in the area, check the section on Accommodations for *The Royal Ashdown Forest Golf Club*, p. 68; there are recommendations for Tunbridge Wells, Brighton, Eastbourne and Grinstead—all within a short drive of Crowborough.

TOURIST ATTRACTIONS: The scenery around Crowborough will provide the visitor with plenty of diversion whether he walks or drives. Ashdown Forest continues the lovely Sussex countryside. Tunbridge Wells, 7 miles, is a famous and fashionable spa, where in the eighteenth century English royalty came for the waters. Brighton and Eastbourne in the south offer the whole range of facilities one might look for, from swimming and boating to cultural activities for every taste.

FOR FURTHER INFORMATION: Write to: Club Secretary, Crowborough Beacon Golf Club Ltd., Crowborough, Sussex, England. Telephone: Crowborough 511.

Dyke Golf Club, Ltd.

The Dyke is a fine course with wide fairways and plenty of variety, all set in handsome, sloping countryside near Brighton, one of England's most popular seaside resorts. For the holiday golfer the course is just about an ideal length—under 6200 yards—while for the more experienced player there are four short holes, two in each nine, good, solid par 3s. All four are excellent testing shots, a good standard for one's short game; if you come anywhere near the par 3, you can congratulate yourself. The rest of the course will give you whatever you want of golf—clever bunkering, good approaches, plenty of sandy hazards, as well as gorse and trees. And behind it all, there is a fine panorama of sea, rolling downs and wooded land.

LOCATION: The course is accessible by car or bus from the nearest towns, Brighton (5½ miles) and Hove (3½ miles). The bus drops you right in front of the club house. By rail the nearest station is Brighton—from there by car or bus. Brighton is 35 miles S of London.

OTHER INFORMATION: The course is open all year to nonmembers, with no restrictions except that they carry proof of membership in a recognized club anywhere. The professional is in daily attendance. Summer is the most crowded time, with the best weather to be expected then. The weather, however, is unpredictable. Practice ground is available.
Number of holes: 18. Par: 72. Length: 6271 yards (can be lengthened to 6665 yards).
Green fees: weekdays $1.05/round; Saturdays, Sunday afternoons, holidays $1.40/round; Sunday mornings $2.80/round. Reduction after 5 o'clock and during winter. Lessons: $2/hour. Caddies: available through arrangement. Golfing equipment and caddie carts. Available through arrangement.

OTHER SPORTS FACILITIES: The club is near the water, with Brighton only a few minutes away, where there are all types of water sports, including swimming from excellent beaches, boating, water skiing, and tennis, horseback riding, fishing and even hunting and climbing. There are also several golf courses in the vicinity.

ACCOMMODATIONS: No living space in the club house, but bar and restaurant are available. Meals should be ordered in advance.
Accommodations in the general area are numerous and good. For Tunbridge Wells, Brighton, Eastbourne and East Grinstead, see this section for the Royal Ashdown Forest Golf Club, p. 68.
For Worthing, see the Ham Manor Golf Club, p. 67.
In Hove: the Dudley (Lansdown Place, Tel. Hove 36266). A very comfortable hotel with private baths, central heating; singles from $7 to 10,

doubles from $12.50, breakfast included; full pension $70-90/week; 10% service charge. The *Sackville* (Kingsway, Tel. Hove 36292). Most rooms with private baths, central heating, garage, all comforts; singles $6.50-8.50, doubles from $11.50, breakfast included; full pension $65-80/week; 10% service charge.

TOURIST ATTRACTIONS: Brighton and Hove together provide all types of facilities for the visitor, from beaches to music halls and museums and for the children, a good aquarium. For the entire area, see this section under the *Royal Ashdown Forest,* pp. 68-69; *Crowborough Beacon,* p. 64, and *Ham Manor Golf Club,* p. 63.

FOR FURTHER INFORMATION: Write to: Club Secretary, Dyke Golf Club, Dyke Road, Brighton 5, Sussex, England. Telephone: Hove 58713.

Ham Manor Golf Club

Only two miles from the sea, Ham Manor Golf Club is located in the midst of the popular south coast resorts of England, within a short distance of Brighton, Worthing and Littlehampton. The course is divided into two loops of 9 holes each, which provide a variety of golf for every kind of player. Not a championship links, Ham Manor nevertheless might prove pleasing to the medium player who wishes to try his power as well as his putting ability. There are several holes over 500 yards and several at 200 or under. The terrain is a naturally undulating one, with a high expectation of sunshine and lovely breezes from the nearby Channel. One of the many advantages of the course is that several holes can be played according to the strength of the player; the rather long 1st, for example, can be played by the long driver to the right, while the short driver can accomplish much the same by driving straight. With precision on his successive shots, neither player had the advantage of the other.

LOCATION: Ham Manor is one mile from Angmering, on the main line from London (1½ hours by train). Taxis are available at the station for the short run to the club. By car, route A24 via Horsham. London is 60 miles N, Brighton 18 E, Chichester 17 W, Worthing 7 S, Arundel 6 W, Littlehampton 5 S.

OTHER INFORMATION: The course is open to nonmembers all year except under particularly bad weather conditions. The professional or his assistant is available during normal daytime hours. The most crowded season is summer, with the best weather to be expected in June through September. Practice ground is available.

*Number of holes:*18. *Par:* 70 (S.S.S.). *Length:* 6274 yards.

Green fees: weekdays, $1.75/round, $2.50/day (without member); $1.05/round, $1.75/day (with member); weekends, $2.75/round, $4/day (without member); $1.40/round, $2.80/day (with member). *Lessons:* $1.75/½ hour and $2.10/hour with the professional; $1.40/½ hour and $1.75/ hour with the assistant. *Caddies:* available on weekends; men $2.10/round, boys $1.40/round. *Golfing equipment and caddie carts:* clubs $.50/round, carts $.28/round.

OTHER SPORTS FACILITIES: Ham Manor, in Angmering, is within a few miles of many southside resorts. All water sports, as well as tennis, bowls, horseback riding, and river and sea fishing.

ACCOMMODATIONS: No living space available in the club house, but there are bars and lunch and tea facilities. Many first-class restaurants in the immediate area.
   In Angmering: *Palm Court* (Tel. Rustington 3323) and *South Strand* (Tel. Rustington 5086). With and without private baths; singles from $2.80, doubles from $6.50.
   In Worthing: The *Beach* (Tel. 4000) and the *Warnes* (Tel. 2222). Luxury hotels offer all the amenities; singles $5, doubles $10; 10% service charge. *Berkeley, Burlington,* and *Eardley.* Singles from $3.50, doubles from $7.50; 10% service charge.
   In Littlehampton: the *Beach.*
   In Arundel: the *Bridge* and the *Norfolk Arms.*

TOURIST ATTRACTIONS: In addition to many spectator sports—first-class cricket at Hove, racing at Goodwood and Frontwell Park and polo at Cowdray Park-Midhurst—there is excellent shopping in Worthing and Brighton. The Chichester Theatre Festival, only 17 miles from Ham Manor, is also well known. For the devotee of sites and ruins, Worthing offers the first, and Arundel the second.

FOR FURTHER INFORMATION: Write to: Club Secretary, Ham Manor Golf Club, Ham Manor, Angmering, Sussex, England. Telephone: Rustington 3288.

The Royal Ashdown Forest Golf Club

For the visitor to London who wants to relax in a beautiful natural setting, the Royal Ashdown Forest Golf Club will provide peace and quiet— plus excellent golf. Set in the heart of Sussex and in the Ashdown Forest, the club offers perhaps the most natural of English golf courses, without a single artificial hazard, and yet a course developed to suit modern golf architectural standards. Grassy ravines, streams, gorges, fine trees (except when they block a view of the hole), sunken riding tracks—all these make the course a challenge as well as a delight. The 6th is the well-known "Island Hole," a hole to rank with the championship holes at Troon and elsewhere; it is flanked on three sides by streams or ditches. Royal Ashdown favors the precise golfer, although there are plenty of holes and approaches for the short and long driver who isn't too sure where his shots are going.

LOCATION: The course is very close to the Forest Row Station, but the best way to arrive is by car from East Grinstead (4 miles N) or from London (30 miles N). Forest Row is also within short driving distance of the south coast resort cities, like Brighton (22 miles), Eastbourne (22 miles). Tunbridge Wells, the well-known spa and resort, is 12 miles E.

OTHER INFORMATION: The course is open all year; any nonmember who is not introduced by a member should apply to the club secretary and indicate when he would like to play; this can be done by mail. A professional is in daily attendance. The most crowded time is weekends when the weather is good—in the summer months. The weather, however, is unpredictable. Practice ground is available.

Number of holes: 18 (also a 9-hole course). *Par:* 72 (S.S.S., 71). *Length:* 6475 yards (yellow tees), 6210 yards (white tees).

Green fees: weekdays, $2.10; weekends and holidays, $3.50/day. *Lessons:* $2.80/½ hour. *Caddies:* available on weekends and school holidays, $1.75 to $2.80/round. *Golfing equipment and caddie carts:* clubs $.70 to $1.40/round, trolleys $.28/round.

OTHER SPORTS FACILITIES: For the active sportsman there is hunting, shooting, fishing, riding—on quiet ponies or on hacks and hunters. Lingfield Race Course is only seven miles away. There are five or more golf courses, as well as tennis courts in the area.

ACCOMMODATIONS: No living space in the club house, but catering and bar are available.

Near the club: *Ashdown Forest Hotel* (Tel. 2010) and the *Roebuck* (Tel. 2244). Both small, some rooms with private bath; singles from $4, doubles (at *Roebuck* only) from $9; full pension at both from $30 to $60/week.

In Tunbridge Wells: The *Calverly* (Tel. 26455), *Spa* (Tel. 20331), and *Wellington* (Tel. 20286). Private baths, central heating, comfortable; singles from $5, doubles from $9.50, including breakfast; 10% service charge; full pension $45 to $50/week.

In Brighton: The *Grand* (Tel. 26301), the *Metropole* (Tel. 775432), *Old Ship* (Tel. 29001), *Royal Albion* (Tel. 29202), and *Royal Crescent* (Tel. 66311). Accommodations from very comfortable to luxurious (*Metropole*); singles from $6, doubles from $8.50, including breakfast; pension from $55/week; 10% service charge.

In Eastbourne: The *Cavendish, Grand, Burlington, Cumberland.* About the above prices.

In East Grinstead: the *Gravetye Manor, Ye Olde Felbridge.* About the above prices.

TOURIST ATTRACTIONS: Ashdown Forest is a famous scenic spot, and Tunbridge Wells is full of handsome parks and recreation grounds. Crowborough, in the vicinity, is noted for its landscape. Lewes, also nearby, has an attractive museum, the fifteenth-century house of Anne of Cleves (the fourth wife of Henry VIII), the sixteenth-century Bull House and St. Michael's Church, with its Norman tower. London, Brighton and Eastbourne, of course, offer the whole range of entertainment.

FOR FURTHER INFORMATION: Write to: Club Secretary, The Royal Ashdown Forest Golf Club, Forest Row, Sussex, England. Telephone: Forest Row 2018.

BRITISH ISLES—WALES

Royal Porthcawl Golf Club

Wales itself is well worth a visit, and the Royal Porthcawl adds to its natural attractions. This is a beautifully situated links on the south Welsh shore with a view of the sea from every tee. Porthcawl is of championship caliber, a tough course by any standard, and the scene of many tournaments, including the Masters' and Amateur Internationals. But the tees can be lengthened or shortened, and if you lack power, you may still find most of the holes playable. Length, in fact, is not of primary importance from any tee; your second shot will determine how close you come to a respectable game. This is a well-planned course, where accuracy and care determine the game more than power. Each hole has its unique quality, created by well-placed bunkers, interesting contours, the natural heather and gorse and stiff Atlantic breezes that blow in from the Bristol Channel. There is also good overall balance, with holes in every category, although most are in the 350-yard and up range. Of particular interest are the 13th and 18th holes; the entire second 9, in fact, will provide spectacular golf. Forget about your handicap and try Porthcawl.

LOCATION: The course is a short ride by bus or car from Porthcawl Station. There is regular train service to the station. Porthcawl is 26 miles W of Cardiff, on the south Glamorganshire coast, 20 miles SE of Swansea, 186 E of London. It is within driving distance of Bristol and Gloucester—about 2 hours from each.

OTHER INFORMATION: The course is open all year and gets surprisingly little rain for Wales. The visitor needs either an introduction from a member or a letter of introduction from the secretary of his own club. With this even Sunday play is permitted unless members turn up in force. The summer is the most crowded time, with the best weather in spring and summer. Practice ground is available.
Number of holes: 18. *Par:* 74: *Length:* 6658 yards (can be shortened).
Green fees: weekdays, $1.05; weekends, $2.10/day. *Lessons:* by arrangement with the professional, about $2.80/hour. *Caddies:* some available at $2/18 holes. *Golfing equipment and caddie carts:* clubs $1.40/round, carts $.35/day.

OTHER SPORTS FACILITIES: This is a popular seaside resort area, with all types of water sports—swimming from four excellent beaches, boating, fishing—and tennis and bowling.

ACCOMMODATIONS: No living space in the club house, but bar and restaurant are available.
There are excellent accommodations throughout the south Welsh coast. In Porthcawl: The *Esplanade* (Tel. 2201). Rooms with private baths, singles from $4, doubles from $8.50, including breakfast; full pension from $42/week; 10% service charge. No central heating. The *Seabank* (Tel. 2261). Prices about 10% above those for the *Esplanade*. Private baths and central heating.

In Cardiff: The *Angel* (Westgate Street, Tel. 32633). Singles from $5.50 to $10.50, doubles $10.50 and up, including breakfast; no pension. Private baths, central heating, all comforts. The *Park* (Park Place, Tel. 23471). Singles from $5.50 to $9, doubles from $11.50, including breakfast. No pension. Private baths, no central heating. The *Royal* (St. Mary Street, Tel. 23321). Singles from $5.50, doubles from $12, including breakfast. No pension. Private baths, no central heating.

In Swansea: The *Dragon* (Tel. 51074). Singles from $9, doubles from $15.50, including breakfast. This is a luxury hotel with a private bath for each room, central heating, all comforts. The *Dolphin* (Tel. 50011). Singles from $8 to $10, doubles from $14, including breakfast. No pension. Private baths, central heating, all comforts.

TOURIST ATTRACTIONS: Porthcawl is just outside the industrial heart of Wales and has been for many years a popular resort town, rich in entertainment for adults and children. For the youngsters, there is an amusement center, as well as several fine beaches for all. Cardiff offers the Turner House Art Gallery (oil paintings and porcelain), a lovely cathedral, Cardiff Castle. In the Swansea area the visitor is advised to take walking or car tours on the Gower Peninsula.

FOR FURTHER INFORMATION: Write to: Club Secretary, Royal Porthcawl Golf Club, Porthcawl, South Wales. Telephone: Porthcawl 62.

BRITISH ISLES—SCOTLAND

If you come to Scotland, you must golf; and if you golf, you must come to Scotland. Here is the home of the game, beginning with the Old Course at *St. Andrews* and continuing through an illustrious list—*Carnoustie, Royal Dornoch, Troon, Dunbar, Turnberry, Gullane, North Berwick,* and so on.

The number and variety are great, and no matter where you decide to stay in Scotland, there is a course, probably several, within an hour's drive, usually much closer.

You can golf on some of the most famous links in the world for $1 or so in green fees. St. Andrews itself charges $1.40 for the Old Course, $.70 for the New, a little more on weekends. You can take lessons with some of the finest professionals for about $2.50 an hour, often less. And you can have a knowledgeable caddie for 18 holes for around $2.50, sometimes a little more, usually less. This is, indeed, a golfer's paradise.

For your convenience I have grouped 26 of the major courses in the four areas usually most popular with visitors: Edinburgh, Glasgow, Perth-Dundee and the Highlands (Aberdeen-Inverness). For those who want something very different, I have included one other course, *Machrihanish*, which is laid out in a spectacular part of Western Scotland. The water that faces you as you play this interesting course is the Atlantic Ocean, with Scotland behind you and Northern Ireland on the other side.

In the Edinburgh area *Luffness* might be best for the visitor, to be followed by the Number 1 Course at *Gullane* (try Number 2 afterwards), then *Barnton* in Edinburgh itself. If you feel ready, *Dunbar, North Berwick* and *Lundin* await your efforts—but they are tough.

Only an hour's drive southwest of Glasgow is a complex of courses that are among the finest in the world. Try to combine *Troon, Prestwick* and the *Turnberry Hotel* courses (first the Arran, then the Ailsa), all within a few miles of each other. For another tour, west of Glasgow, perhaps try *Gourock, Pollok* and *Cowal*. And if you are south of the city, you have *Lanark*, an excellent test of your game.

In the Perth-Dundee area there are riches to compare with those outside Glasgow. If you are near Perth, you must play *St. Andrews*—there are four courses, all graded according to your game: Jubilee, Eden, New, Old (listed in order of increasing difficulty). A few miles southwest of Perth, *Gleneagles* will provide an exciting holiday in itself. From Dundee you are within easy reach of *Carnoustie, Montrose, Blairgowrie* and *Pitlochry*—each more pleasant and playable than the other.

In the Highlands great golf combines with spectacular scenery. If you are near Aberdeen, the *Royal Aberdeen, Murcar* and *Cruden Bay* are all close together and of equal toughness. Around Inverness, start with *Boat-of-Garten*, move on to *Nairn* and finish up with *Royal Dornoch* and *Golspie*.

Barnton Golf Club
(Royal Burgess Golfing Society of Edinburgh)

Barnton has the advantage of being only four miles from the center of Edinburgh, yet it makes the visitor feel that he has left the city far behind. Barnton is a parkland course of full championship standard. It is, in fact, one of the many championship courses in the Midlothian region, and the visitor may wish to go from one to the other, playing where all the world-famous golfers played their championship matches. Barnton offers the full variety of testing shots of a championship course, and the visitor will find his entire repertory challenged. It is long, at 6600 yards, and yet precision is also a necessity; sheer power will not lead to success here.

LOCATION: Four miles from the center of Edinburgh, Barnton is best reached by car (or taxi). Local buses also run in the general area. Edinburgh is on the main road (A1 or A7) from London, which lies 373 miles S.

OTHER INFORMATION: The course is open to nonmembers, unlimited, who are introduced by a member or who can show a letter of introduction from their own club secretary. The course is open all year, and a member of the professional staff is always on hand. The most crowded season is June through August, when the best weather can also be expected. Practice ground is available.
Number of holes: 18. *Par:* 72. *Length:* 6604 yards.
Green fees: $2.10/round, $3.50/day. *Lessons:* by private arrangement with the professional. *Caddies:* $2.80/round. *Golfing equipment and caddie carts:* clubs and carts for rent at a nominal cost.

OTHER SPORTS FACILITIES: As probably the most popular tourist city in Scotland, Edinburgh offers nearly every kind of sports facility: boating, tennis, riding, English football, rugby football. Winter sports are also within a reasonable distance.

ACCOMMODATIONS: No living space in the club house, but bar and restaurant are available.
Edinburgh offers virtually every kind of accommodation. See that section for the *Gullane Golf Club,* pp. 76-77 for a detailed listing.

TOURIST ATTRACTIONS: Edinburgh offers a wide range of shopping facilities, cultural activities, restaurants and other forms of entertainment. Some of the high points of this diverse and interesting city are Princes Street, famed for its shops, clubs and hotels; The Castle, which overlooks the entire city; the Old Town, in particular High Street; the National Gallery. In addition, Edinburgh is noted for its theater festivals, and has recently come to the fore as a center of exciting artistic activities.

FOR FURTHER INFORMATION: Write to: Club Secretary, Royal Burgess Golfing Society of Edinburgh, Barnton, Edinburgh 4, Scotland. Telephone: Davidsons Mains 2075.

Dunbar Golf Club

The Dunbar Golf Club is situated on historic ground—here Oliver Cromwell camped for six weeks prior to his victory over the Scots in 1650. It is also picturesquely set on a tip of land with a view north of the Firth of Forth. It is a course with a wide variety of holes; the turf has a spring that cuts fatigue, and there is no difficult climbing. It begins with three holes that are inland and then proceeds to become the seaside links that it really is; there is even a strong sea wind. Precision, power and agility will all help the visitor who tries the course. Yet it is not discouraging. It is quite suitable for a short stay, since it is challenging without being exhausting. Dunbar has a good reputation and has been the scene of many championship matches. It should prove an impressive experience.

LOCATION: The course is ½ miles from the railway station of Dunbar, from which a regular bus service drops the visitor within a two-minute walk of the entrance gate. The town is just off the main coast road (A1) between Edinburgh and Newcastle that runs down to London. Dunbar is 30 miles E of Edinburgh, 30 miles N of Berwick, 75 miles E of Glasgow.

OTHER INFORMATION: The course is open to nonmembers all year, weather permitting. This region has the reputation of being one of the sunniest and driest in Great Britain. The most crowded time is the summer months. No professional. Practice ground is available.
Number of holes: 18. *Par:* 71. *Length:* 6444 yards.
Green fees: weekdays, $1.05/day; weekends, $1.75/day. *Lessons:* no professional on hand. *Caddies:* seldom available. *Golfing equipment and caddie carts:* by arrangement.

OTHER SPORTS FACILITIES: All water sports: swimming, boating, fishing. Also tennis and riding as well as several other golf courses up and down the coast.

ACCOMMODATIONS: No living space in the club house, but several bars and restaurants are available nearby, including one at the club that seats 60.
In Dunbar: The following hotels offer approximately the same type of accommodations at about the same prices, from $4 for a single to $8 for a double (with breakfast). *Bellevue* (Tel. 2322, closed during winter), *Craig-en-Gelt* (Tel. 2287), *Lothian* (Tel. 3205), *Roxburghe* (Tel. 2155, closed during winter), *St. George* (Tel. 2213). No private baths or central heating; pension from $35/week.
For the visitor who wishes a wider range of hotels, Edinburgh is the place. For details, see section on Accommodations for the *Gullane Golf Club*, pp. 76-77.

TOURIST ATTRACTIONS: Edinburgh, 30 miles away, is, of course, a major attraction. But the immediate region is interesting for its historical sites and picturesque beauty. Cromwell, Queen Mary (of Scots) and Sir Walter Scott haunt this area, and the interested visitor can spend much of his free time roaming among interesting relics. North Berwick, a few miles up the coast, is a fashionable resort, with excellent beaches and fine shopping.

FOR FURTHER INFORMATION: Write to: Club Secretary, Dunbar Golf Club, Dunbar, East Lothian, Scotland. Telephone: Cockburnspath 225.

Gullane Golf Club

The three courses at Gullane are part of a sports complex in this section of Scotland that makes it a veritable golfer's paradise. The golfer need go no farther than Gullane itself to find a course to his liking. All three of the Gullane courses differ from each other; all three will prove rewarding, although the shorter third course is possibly more suitable for women, young people and relative beginners. The number 1 course has had nothing but praise from the finest amateurs and professionals alike—all this with a lovely view of the Firth of Forth as one climbs the hill. Both the first and second courses call for a variety of shots, with the demanding number 1 definitely favoring the long hitter (11 holes near or over 400 yards). For the less powerful player who can control the ball, course number 2 may be more suitable, and there is no loss of scenic beauty. Whichever you play, your game should get a lift from a course that has seen some of the finest golf in the world.

LOCATION: The courses are in Gullane, accessible by car or bus. Gullane is 5 miles W of North Berwick, 19 E of Edinburgh, 63 E of Glasgow, 376 N of London.

OTHER INFORMATION: The courses are open to nonmembers, without limitations, all year. The professional and his assistants are always in attendance. The most crowded months are April, May and June, with the best weather to be expected in May and October. Very low rainfall. No child under fifteen years of age admitted to the club house. Practice ground is available.

Number of holes: 18 holes for Course No. 1, 2 and 3. *Par:* No. 1, 72; No. 2, 70; No. 3, 70. *Length:* No. 1, 6461 yards; No. 2, 5991 yards; No. 3, 4968 yards.

Green fees: No. 1: weekdays $1.05/round, $1.40/day; weekends $3.50/day; $9 week; $11.20 two weeks. *No. 2:* weedays $.70/round, $1.05/day; weekends, $1.05/round, $1.40/day; $4.20 week; $7 two weeks. *No. 3:* weekday, $.42/round, $.70/day; weekends, $.70/round, $1.05/day; $2.80 week; $4 two weeks. *Lessons:* $2.80/hour. *Caddies:* a few available at $2.10/round. *Golfing equipment and caddie carts:* clubs $1.40/round, carts $.25/round.

OTHER SPORTS FACILITIES: Gullane is a seaside links, so the visitor will find yachting, swimming, boating, as well as tennis, riding, boat trips, sandy beaches. The area is also full of championship caliber golf courses.

ACCOMMODATIONS: No living space in the club house, but bar and restaurant are available.

The general area abounds in comfortable accommodations. For a listing, see this section for *Luffness Golf Course,* p. 78.

In Edinburgh: Luxury hotels include the *Caledonian* (Princes Street),

North British (Princes Street), and *George* (George Street). Comfortable hotels include the *Carlton* (North Bridge), *Darlings Regent* (Waterloo Place) *Grosvenor* (Grosvenor Street), *Old Waverley* (Princes Street), *Roxburghe* (Charlotte Street), *Royal* (Princes Street), *Royal British* (Princes Street), and *Scotia* (5 Great King Street). Singles for luxurious accommodations start at $8.50, doubles at $15. Singles for comfortable accommodations start at $5, doubles at $9. Pension, where available, begins at $35/week.

This is a very popular tourist area, and the visitor should reserve rooms as far in advance as possible, especially during the height of the summer season.

TOURIST ATTRACTIONS: The local Gullane area in East Lothian is noted for its fine views and scenic beauty. The nearby village of Dirleton is especially recommended. North Berwick, 5 miles away, provides a popular and fashionable resort. Excursions to islands in the Firth of Forth as well as to local villages are well organized; or the visitor may tour alone. Good shopping here and in nearby Edinburgh. The latter provides lively entertainment (music and drama festival), a good museum and several sites of interest.

FOR FURTHER INFORMATION: Write to: Club Secretary, Gullane Golf Club, Gullane, East Lothian, Scotland. Telephone: Gullane 2255.

Luffness New Golf Club

The Luffness New Golf Club is tucked away on a lovely promonotory overlooking the Firth of Forth, accessible to Edinburgh, North Berwick and Dunbar, as the visitor may wish. The course is a typical seaside links, with magnificent views of the coast from several tees. It is suitable for the average golfer and for the visitor who will play it only a few times. Short drivers are not unduly punished, although it does have many long holes (like the 530-yard 4th) that favor the power hitter. But there is balance, and the steady player with no particular fireworks in his game will find it to his liking.

LOCATION: The course, in Aberlady, is accessible by car and by bus (regular service) from Edinburgh and North Berwick. These buses pass right by the club. Edinburgh is 17 miles W, North Berwick 11 NE., Dunbar 17 E, Haddington 5 S. Aberlady is just off the main road (A1) from London to Edinburgh.

OTHER INFORMATION: The course is open all year except during interruptions for snow or very heavy frost. Nonmembers are always welcome, but they should have a letter of introduction from their local club secretary. There is no professional in attendance. The busiest time is on weekends, during the summer, with the best weather from June through September. Practice ground is available.

Number of holes: 18. *Par:* 69. *Length:* 6100 yards.
Green fees: weekdays, $1.40/round, $2.45/day; weekends, $2.80/round,
$4.20/day. *Lessons:* not available. *Caddies:* $2.10/round. *Golfing equipment and caddie carts:* no clubs for rent, carts $.35/round.

OTHER SPORTS FACILITIES: The general area, and particularly North
Berwick, is a well-known holiday center, especially as a seaside resort.
Aberlady itself has a wide sandy beach. Besides numerous golf courses
in the region, the visitor will find swimming (in a heated swimming pool
if he wishes), boat trips to various islands in the Firth of Forth, tennis,
bowls, riding and a number of holiday attractions, both cultural and light.

ACCOMMODATIONS: No living space in the club house, but bar and
catering facilities are available.
Most visitors will probably prefer to stay in Edinburgh. If so, see section
on Accommodations for *Gullane Golf Club,* pp. 76-77.
In Gullane (3 miles): The *Greywalls* (Tel. 2144). Rooms with private
baths; singles from $7 with breakfast; no doubles; pension from $70/week.
Closed during the winter months. Booked heavily in advance.
In North Berwick: The *Marine* (Tel. 2406). Rooms with private baths;
singles from $5.50, doubles from $9.50; breakfast included; 10% service
charge. Closed during the winter months. Booked in advance. The *Wester-
dunes* (Tel. 2366). Private baths; singles from $5, doubles from $9.25.
Closed during the winter months. Also heavily booked in advance. *Blen-
heim Arms, Dalrymple Arms, Royal, Yarrow Dene.* No private baths;
singles from $3.50, doubles from $7.

TOURIST ATTRACTIONS: This section is one of the most attractive
for the visitor. Edinburgh has the cultural and entertainment attractions of
a major city, with a music and drama festival in the last two weeks of
August and the first week of September. It is also a good shopping center
and contains many interesting sites: Holyrood Palace, the two Forth Bridges,
the National Gallery (an admirable collection), the Old Town, Edinburgh
Castle and many others.

FOR FURTHER INFORMATION: Write to: Club Secretary, Luffness
New Golf Club, 63 Castle Street, Edinburgh 2, Scotland. Telephone: CAL
8228.

Lundin Golf Club

Lundin is situated in the veritable heart of great golf, in the section of
Fife that includes St. Andrews Royal and Ancient Golf Club. Although not
excessively long by Scottish standards, Lundin is so well planned that it
appears to have an additional 500 yards or more. Even so, the long driver
will find plenty to satisfy him—seven holes well over 400 yards and one
over 550—while the less powerful player will be delighted with the variety
and balance of the holes—three short ones, the rest spread out well for

everyone's range. With its natural hazards and sandhills—this is virtually a seaside links—the course requires constant care, especially the not too modestly titled 14th, named "Perfection." Lundin is made for the adaptable player who can suit his game to the course—its particular hazards, approaches and winds. The chief caution at Lundin is precision, that is, good golf.

LOCATION: The course is ½ mile from the small town of Largo, with the nearest railway station at Lundin Links (which runs close to the 17th green of the course). Lundin Links is 30 miles N of Edinburgh, 12 S of St. Andrews. The course is most easily accessible by car.

OTHER INFORMATION: The course is open all year with the professional in daily attendance. Nonmembers are most welcome, but on Sundays the course is limited to members and temporary members holding a weekly ticket or longer. If you plan to play on Sunday, buy a weekly ticket for $4.20; with this weekly ticket you can introduce up to three guests who may play at $1.40/day. The most crowded time is July to August, with the best weather in April through June. Practice ground is available.
    Number of holes: 18. Par: 72 (Bogey, 76). Length: 6265 yards.
    Green fees: weekdays and weekends, $1.40/day; $4.20 week; $6.30 two weeks; 8.40 month (about one third reduction for women). Lessons: by arrangement with the professional. Caddies: none available. Golfing equipment and caddie carts: clubs not for rent; carts at nominal cost.

OTHER SPORTS FACILITIES: This is a good sports area: plenty of golf, tennis, bowling, fishing in the sea, swimming (good beaches nearby) and walking tours.

ACCOMMODATIONS: No living space in the club house, but bar and restaurant are available.
    For hotels in Edinburgh, see this section for the Gullane Golf Club, pp. 76-77.
    For hotels in Dundee and St. Andrews, see this section for St. Andrews: The Royal and Ancient Golf Club, p. 107.
    In Kirkcaldy (9 miles): The following hotels offer comfortable quarters with a very few rooms with private bath; singles from $3.50, doubles from $7; breakfast included. Abbotshall (Tel. 2803, pension from $35/week), Anthony's (Tel. 3892, pension from $55/week), Ollerton (Tel. 4286, central heating) and Station (Tel. 2093, central heating).

TOURIST ATTRACTIONS: Lundin Links and Largo are the birthplace of Alexander Selkirk, the prototype of Robinson Crusoe in Defoe's novel. The immediate area is full of small historical sites such as this. For further details, see this section for St. Andrews, pp. 107-108. Edinburgh is within an hour's drive from Lundin Links. In addition, the entire region is well known for its summer resorts.

FOR FURTHER INFORMATION: Write to: Club Secretary, Lundin Golf Club, Lundin Links, Fife, Scotland. Telephone: Lundin Links 202.

The North Berwick Golf Club
(West Links)

Like so many other Scottish seaside links, North Berwick will prove pleasant to the eye and professionally satisfying. The course looks out on the famous Firth, and on a sunny day the player can see several beautiful islets in a striking blue water setting. North Berwick has proven popular not only with members of English society but also with persons interested solely in good playing. Several of its holes have become famous, including the 1st ("Point Garry"), the 14th ("Perfection"), and the 15th ("Redan"); the last two have been copied in many American courses. The course favors the accurate player who can find his way between several obstacles and is not afraid of blinds. For example, the par three 4th may seem relatively easy at 180 yards on a straight shot. But hazards exist, for the green lies at the end of a narrow pass with rocky ground on the left and bunkers at the green itself. Clearly, the accurate player who can "thread a needle," rather than the blaster, will find his game here. But for all golfers North Berwick should prove a pleasant experience.

LOCATION: The course is a few minutes' walk from the North Berwick railroad station. The trip from Edinburgh (23 miles W) takes about 45 minutes by train (leaving every hour). By car it is less. Bus from Edinburgh to North Berwick takes about 80 minutes. Glasgow is 70 miles W.

OTHER INFORMATION: The course is open to nonmembers all year round with no limitations except payment of the green fees. The professional is available from May to September; the most crowded season is July through August, and best weather is to be expected from April to October. Practice ground is available.
Number of holes: 18. *Par:* 70 (Bogey, 75). *Length:* 6323 yards (Ladies' tees: 5843 yards).
Green fees: weekdays (April-October), $1.05/round, $1.75/day; weekends and holidays (March-October), $1.40/round, $2.10/day; weekly (April-October), $6.30; monthly (in session), $11.20. For other months, cost is about half that listed above. *Lessons:* $1.05/½ hour, $2.10/hour. Course of six ½-hour lessons, $5.60; twelve 1-hour lessons, $22.40. *Caddies:* $2.10/round. *Golfing equipment and caddie carts:* clubs $1.40/round, carts $.28/round.

OTHER SPORTS FACILITIES: As a popular seaside resort, the area provides swimming in a heated pool, water skiing, beach swimming, yachting, fishing, crazy golf, putting, tennis; other golf courses in the area (Muirfield, 8 miles; Gullane, 8 miles).

ACCOMMODATIONS: No living in the club house, but dining room and bar are available.
For details on hotels in North Berwick, see section on accommodations

for *Luffness New Golf Club,* p. 78. For hotels in Edinburgh, see this section for the *Gullane Golf Club,* pp. 76-77.

TOURIST ATTRACTIONS: The coast provides charming walking and car tours. Also recommended are the ruins of Tantallon Castle, 3 miles from North Berwick, Dirleton Castle and many rocky islets of startling beauty. Edinburgh is nearby; see details in this section for the *Barnton Golf Club,* p. 74.

FOR FURTHER INFORMATION: Write to: Club Secretary, The North Berwick Golf Club, New Club House, Beach Road, North Berwick, Scotland. Telephone: North Berwick 2135.

Cowal Golf Club

Cowal is a solid links whose seeming simplicity is very deceptive. Its varied design and the testing quality of its holes may not be apparent the first time around. The deceptive quality is increased by the relative easiness of the first 9; then comes a reversal with the second 9, which has only one hole under 330 yards, all par 4s and 5s except for the 14th, and that is by no means easy. Another part of the difficulty comes with the greens; their slopes make good putting here a necessity. A difficult course with a lovely background of trees, water, and hills, Cowal should cap your tour of Scottish courses.

LOCATION: The course is 1 mile from Dunoon Pier, which can be reached by train and ferry, or by car. Dunoon is just across the bay from Greenock, about 25 miles W of Glasgow.

OTHER INFORMATION: The course is open all year with no restrictions on nonmembers temporarily in the area. The professional is available at all times. July and August usually prove to be the busiest months, with the best weather generally in May and September. Practice ground is available.
Number of holes: 18. *Par:* 70. *Length:* 6204 yards.
Green fees: $1.05/day; $4.20 week; $6.30 two weeks. *Lessons:* by arrangement with the professional. *Caddies:* none available. *Golfing equipment and caddie carts:* both for rent by arrangement with the professional.

OTHER SPORTS FACILITIES: This is a well-known holiday resort area: water sports of all kinds, other golf courses within a short distance, tennis, bowling, fishing, boating, walking tours.

ACCOMMODATIONS: No living space in the club house, but bar and restaurant are available; meals through arrangement with the catering staff.
In Dunoon: The following are comfortable hotels with no private baths; singles from 3.50, doubles from $7, with breakfast; full pension from

$30/week; no central heating. *Ardnaheim* (Tel. 349), *Argyll* (Tel. 59), *Dhailling* Lodge (Tel. 293), and *Selborne* (Tel. 761). For Greenock and Gourock, see this section for the *Gourock Golf Club*, pp. 82-83. For Glasgow, see this section for the *Pollok Golf Club*, pp. 84-85.

TOURIST ATTRACTIONS: Dunoon is well placed for all kinds of tours—to the Trossachs, the seven Lochs, Inveraray Castle. It offers lovely scenery and all the entertainment facilities of a popular resort—dancing, movie houses, etc. It is lively and colorful. For further details, see this section for the *Gourock Golf Club*, p. 83.

FOR FURTHER INFORMATION: Write to: Club Secretary, Cowal Golf Club, Dunoon (Cowal), Scotland.

Gourock Golf Club

A seaside links, like many in Scotland, Gourock lies on high ground overlooking the Firth of Clyde. This is a particularly beautiful part of the Firth, for here it breaks into several small bodies of water, and the combination of land and water is spectacular. Most of the holes are in the middle-distance range, 250 to 400 yards. Precision is perhaps the key to this course, for even the short holes, like the 3rd, the 5th and the 13th, are full of dangers to the indifferent power man. Possibly the only easy shot is the first, a par four 303-yarder, but after that the visitor will find his game well tested. The course and its views should prove a most pleasant experience.

LOCATION: Gourock is well located, only 26 miles W of Glasgow, 20 NW of Paisley, 3 W of Greenock, 44 N of Ayr, and 69 W of Edinburgh. Gourock is a railway terminal, and therefore is accessible by trains as well as by bus. By car, take route A8 from Glasgow.

OTHER INFORMATION: The course is open to nonmembers with no restrictions for the entire year. The professional is in full-time attendance. The most crowded time is May and June, with the best weather to be expected in May and August. No practice ground is available.
Number of holes: 18. *Par:* 69. *Length:* 5678 yards.
Green fees: weekdays, $1.05/round, $1.40/day; weekends and holidays, $2.10/day; $6.30 week; $11.20 month. Slightly less for women. *Lessons:* by arrangement with the professional. *Caddies:* not available. *Golfing equipment and caddie carts:* available through arrangement with the professional.

OTHER SPORTS FACILITIES: As a coastal town, Gourock offers the full range of water sports, including some of the finest yachting to be found in Scotland, as well as tennis and riding.

ACCOMMODATIONS: No living space in the club house, but bar and restaurant are available.

In Gourock: The following hotels have comfortable quarters, some rooms with private baths: *Bay* (Tel. 31244), *Cloch* (Tel. 32038), and *Queen's* (Tel. 31424). Singles from $4, doubles from $8; with breakfast; 10% service charge; pension from $37/week. Central heating, garage.

In Greenock (3 miles): The *Tontine* (Tel. 23316). Rooms with private baths; singles from $5.25, doubles from $10. Pension from $52/week. Central heating.

For the visitor who prefers to sleep over in Glasgow, see the section on Accommodations for the *Pollok Golf Club,* pp. 84-85.

TOURIST ATTRACTIONS: Gourock is within easy reach of the Burns country, Glasgow, Loch Lomond, the Trossachs, and the West Coast. The scenery is incomparably beautiful for the walker or for the driver. Paisley, the home of the famous print of that name, is 20 miles to the SE. The determined golfer will also find many other courses of repute in the immediate area.

FOR FURTHER INFORMATION: Write to: Club Secretary, Gourock Golf Club, Gourock, Renfrewshire, Scotland. Telephone: Gourock 31001.

Lanark Golf Club

Although not a seaside links, the Lanark Golf Course has a beauty of its own, situated as it is on a former wild moor. It has indeed the reputation of being a splendid course with a splendid atmosphere. Much of the former wasteland has become the rough, and the grass holds the ball up well. The terrain itself is full of dips and hollows. The course, with its wide variety of shots, mostly favoring the longer hitter, is not an easy one. However, there are three somewhat shorter holes and enough attractions to keep every kind of player busy and satisfied.

LOCATION: The Lanark Golf Course is less than a mile from the Lanark Railway Station and Bus Stand and can also be reached by car (just off A74). Lanark is 25 miles SE of Glasgow, 32 SW of Edinburgh.

OTHER INFORMATION: The course is open all year but there is no Saturday or Sunday play for visitors; also no professional on hand. Most crowded period is spring, through early July, with the best weather to be expected in June and July. Practice ground is available.

Number of holes: 18 (also a 9-hole course). *Par:* 71. *Length:* 6403 yards. *Green fees:* $.85/round, $1.40/day. *Lessons:* none available. *Caddies:* none available. *Golfing equipment and caddie carts:* no clubs for rent; carts $.25/round.

OTHER SPORTS FACILITIES: In the area, riding; horse racing in July and September; full sports facilities in Glasgow and Edinburgh.

ACCOMMODATIONS: No living space in the club house, but a bar and lunch counter are available.

In Lanark: *Cartland Bridge* (Tel. 776), *Clydesdale* (Tel. 565), and *Caledonian* (Tel. 84). Singles from $3, doubles from $6; with breakfast; pension at *Clydesdale* from $40/week; No central heating, no private baths. For Glasgow see this section for the *Pollok Golf Club*, pp. 84-85; for Edinburgh see this section for the *Gullane Golf Club*, pp. 76-77.

TOURIST ATTRACTIONS: Very near are Lanark Loch, the Falls of Clyde, and Cartland Crags—all worth seeing. For details on Glasgow, see this section for the *Pollok Golf Club*, p. 85. For details on Edinburgh, see this section for the *Barnton Golf Club*, p. 74.

FOR FURTHER INFORMATION: Write to: Town Clerk, Royal Burgh of Lanark, Lanark, Scotland; or Club Secretary, Lanark Golf Club, The Moo, Lanark, Scotland.

Pollok Golf Club

The Pollok Golf Club has two main advantages: it possesses a fine golf course and it is within commuting distance of Glasgow, in fact only six miles from the center of the city. The course itself is in very pleasant surroundings, well wooded, with fine turf that makes the ball lie high. The terrain is flat and therefore not unduly exhausting. But this is not an easy course—is there an easy one in Scotland?—for the approaches are well bunkered. The word here is precision, not power; a steady game will get you through without too much embarrassment.

LOCATION: The course is accessible by bus or car from the center of Glasgow, 6 miles away. Glasgow is itself on the main road from London, 394 miles S, and from Edinburgh, 45 miles E.

OTHER INFORMATION: Nonmembers are welcome at any time during the season from March through October, but they should have a letter of introduction from their local secretary. There is no professional in attendance. The most crowded time is in June and August, when the best weather can be expected. Practice ground is available.
Number of holes: 18. *Par:* 70. *Length:* 6200 yards.
Green fees: $2.10/day. *Lessons:* not available. *Caddies:* available at varying prices through arrangement, from $1.75/round. *Golfing equipment and caddie carts:* clubs not for rent, carts $.35/round.

OTHER SPORTS FACILITIES: In the immediate area: cricket, riding and indoor ice-skating.

ACCOMMODATIONS: No living space in the club house, but bar and catering facilities are available.
Near the golf course: *Sherbrooke* (Tel. IBR 0674) and *Collingwood* (POL 2623). No private baths; singles from $3, doubles from $6.50; with breakfast; 10% service charge. Most visitors will prefer to stay in Glasgow,

which provides everything from luxury hotels to guest and boarding houses. In the luxury class: *Central* (Gordon Street, Tel. Central 9680). All comforts; singles from $10, doubles from $16; with breakfast; 10% tax. *North British* (George Square, Tel. Douglas 6711), *Royal Stuart* (Jamaica Street, Tel. City 4262) and *St. Enoch* (St. Enoch Square, Tel. Central 7033). All with private baths; singles from $7, doubles from $14; 10% tax; with breakfast; central heating, garages; open all year. At ¼ to ½ less cost: the *Duncan's, Kenilworth, Queen's Park, Green's, Dorchester.* Most with no private baths or central heating.

TOURIST ATTRACTIONS: Glasgow is a fine tourist city with good shopping and many forms of cultural activity and other entertainment. Particularly recommended are the Cathedral, Art Gallery and Museum, the University, Kelvingrove Park, Pollok House, the Zoological Park (5½ miles). Outside of Glasgow the visitor will find a wealth of attractions: Bothwell Castle, Loch Lomond (19 miles), Dumbarton Castle, as well as magnificent countryside and desolate moors.

FOR FURTHER INFORMATION: Write to: Club Secretary, Pollok Golf Club, 122 Wellington Street, Glasgow C2, Scotland.

Prestwick Golf Club

The Prestwick Club is a seaside links situated on the famous Firth of Clyde, whose waters terminate in Glasgow, 33 miles away. The soil of Prestwick is a naturally sandy one and permits year-round golf. Most of the holes are in the middle-distance range, with only two under 200 yards and two over 500 yards (and those barely so). There is, consequently, something here for every type of golfer, with precision, rather than power, probably the most important factor. There is also the beauty of the surroundings for the player who takes his eye off the green to look around.

LOCATION: The course is right at the Prestwick railroad station, 4 miles N of Ayr and about an hour by train from Glasgow (35 miles N). By car, the course is 40 minutes from Glasgow. Prestwick is 78 miles SW of Edinburgh, by way of Glasgow, and the site of an international airport with flights from virtually everywhere.

OTHER INFORMATION: The course is open to nonmembers, unlimited, but if they wish to use the club house, they need a letter of introduction from their local club secretary or from a member of the club. The season lasts the entire year, with the professional in residence. Busy time is May, June, and July, with spring and autumn promising the best weather. Practice ground is available.

Number of holes: 18. *Par:* 72. *Length:* 6571 yards.

Green fees: weekdays, $2.80/round; weekends and holidays, $5.60/round. *Lessons:* $1.40/½ hour, $2.80/hour. *Caddies:* $2.80/round. *Golfing equipment and caddie carts:* clubs $2.80/round, carts $.35/round.

OTHER SPORTS FACILITIES: Water sports of all types at Ayr and other coastal towns: sailing, boating, swimming from sandy beaches, angling; also tennis and many other golf courses in the area.

ACCOMMODATIONS: No living space in the club house; dining room available for male members only; the club has a bar.

In Prestwick: *Queen's* (Tel. 77115) and *Links* (Tel. 77792). Some rooms with private baths; singles from $5, doubles from $9.50; with breakfast; full pension from $50/week; 10% service charge. Central heating, garage, most comforts.

In Ayr: The *Station* (Tel. 63268). The most expensive and most comfortable; many rooms with private baths; singles from $6, doubles from $11.50; with breakfast; pension from $56/week; 10% service charge. Central heating, garage, all comforts. The *Sundrum Castle* (Tel. Joppa 253), *County* (Tel. 63368), and *Savoy Park* (Tel. 66112). Some rooms with private baths; prices about 25% less than those listed above. No central heating.

In Troon: The *Marine* (Tel. 980). All comforts, most rooms with private baths; singles from $7, doubles from $14; with breakfast; full pension from $65/week; 10% service charge. Central heating, garage. The *Sun Court* (Tel. 1066) and *Craiglea* (Tel. 83). Much less cost (and less comfort to some extent); some rooms with private baths; central heating at *Sun Court;* singles from $4.20, doubles from $8.50; full pension from $36/week.

TOURIST ATTRACTIONS: Good shopping for Scottish goods—materials and sweaters—in nearby Ayr. Tours, walking excursions, driving to nearby towns—all of these are recommended. Ayr is the heart of the Robert Burns country and is also of historic interest. In Turnberry (11 miles), Culzean Castle is worth a visit. And, of course, Glasgow.

FOR FURTHER INFORMATION: Write to: Club Secretary, Prestwick Golf Club, Prestwick, Ayrshire, Scotland. Telephone: Prestwick 77404.

Troon Golf Club

Troon is in the very center of great Scottish golf—and that means the best golf in the world. It is a beautifully situated seaside links, the site of numerous championship matches and renowned as a fine test of golf. What competitions have been seen at Troon! What competitors! James Braid, Walter Hagen, Bobby Locke, the Open Championship, the Amateur Championship. The course is balanced; the fairways are not narrow, but the stiff breezes blowing off the Firth of Clyde can force your ball over into bunkers you never dreamed existed. The 6th, a tremendously long 580 yards, is followed two holes later by the "Postage Stamp" 8th, a delicate 122-yarder that can break your game and your will. It is the shortest of championship holes and one of the toughest. The long holes require not only power also but precision, and the short holes demand accurate putting, although possibly not as much accuracy as on other courses where the slopes present more dangers. The player who can hit his tee-shots straight against a strong cross wind will have the advantage. Each hole will present a unique challenge—and all this against a lovely setting by the sea.

Troon also has a less challenging course, the Troon Portland, which lies inland from the championship links. It is an excellent course, at 6113 yards, and lends itself readily to holiday play. It is by no means easy; some claim it is the more difficult of the two. There is also a Children's Course, where young people can practice and improve their game.

LOCATION: Troon is just off the main road (A77) from Glasgow to Kilmarnock-Ayr. It is accessible by car or train (about one hour from Glasgow). Troon is 30 miles SW of Glasgow, 8 N of Ayr, 6 N of Prestwick, 9 SW of Kilmarnock, 72 SW of Edinburgh, 398 NW of London.

OTHER INFORMATION: The course is open all year, weather permitting. Nonmembers can play without restriction, but they should have a letter of introduction from the secretary of their own golf club or an introduction from a Troon member. The professional is in daily attendance. The most crowded time is from late spring through fall, with the weather always unpredictable. Practice ground is available.

Number of holes: 18. *Par:* 72 (S.S.S.). *Length:* 6533 yards (6113 yards for Portland Course).

Green fees: $2.10/day for championship course, $1.40/day for Portland. *Lessons:* $2.80/hour. *Caddies:* $2.25/18 holes. *Golfing equipment and caddie carts:* for rent by arrangement with the professional.

OTHER SPORTS FACILITIES: All water sports: swimming from excellent sandy beaches, boating, water-skiing, fishing.

ACCOMMODATIONS: No living space in the club house, but bar and restaurant are available.

Numerous hotels of all types can be found in this area, or the visitor may live in Glasgow. For hotels in Troon, Ayr and Prestwick, see this section for the *Prestwick Golf Club*, p. 86. For Glasgow, see this section for the *Pollok Golf Club*, pp. 84-85.

TOURIST ATTRACTIONS: See this section for the *Prestwick Golf Club*, p. 86, and the *Pollok Golf Club*, p. 85.

FOR FURTHER INFORMATION: Write to: Club Secretary, Troon Golf Club, Troon, Ayrshire, Scotland. Telephone: Troon 170.

The Turnberry Hotel Golf Courses

AILSA COURSE

Ailsa is a championship links whose undulating dunes border on the seashore just south of the Firth of Clyde. In fact, the first 9 holes of the Ailsa follow the shore, past a lighthouse on the point, and then the second 9 starts back where Ailsa Craig juts out of the sea. The course itself is one of the finest in Scotland, the scene of the Walker Cup Match in 1963 and of several other championship matches. It can be adapted to the long or short hitter, depending on which tee he uses, the closer white ones or the farthest ones, where he can match himself against the strong boys. Most of the holes are in the 350 to 450 yard range, although there are some short ones for the precisionist and some even longer ones for the player who uses muscle.

ARRAN COURSE

The Arran Course may be of greater interest to the visitor because it is less trying and less demanding. It will provide a day or more of excellent golf without appearing so fierce as the Ailsa Course. It is pleasant without being a pushover. The Arran is rather a private type of course because the Scottish gorse growing in great tufts between the holes gives a sense of seclusion. Then, too, there is some fine scenery; the sea is at eye level, and you have the illusion of playing almost into the waves. Like the Ailsa, the Arran features mostly middle-distance holes, but there is something for everyone here. One course in the morning, the other in the afternoon, and you have experienced the best of Scottish golf.

LOCATION: The courses are accessible by car from nearby cities and lie 5 miles from the railway station of Girvan, to the south. Ayr is 20 miles N and is itself very close to Prestwick Airport. Turnberry is 50 miles S of Glasgow, 90 SW of Edinburgh, 34 N of Stranraer.

Shell's Wonderful World of Golf

Turnberry Hotel's Ailsa Course, south of the Firth of Clyde. The first nine holes run close to the shore.

OTHER INFORMATION: The courses are open to nonmembers all year, and a professional is available every day. The most crowded time is during the summer, and the weather is generally unpredictable, although the Gulf Stream provides mild weather year-round.

Number of holes: Ailsa, 18; Arran, 18. *Par:* Ailsa, 73; Arran, 76. *Length:* Ailsa, 6770 yards (can be lengthened); Arran, 6653 yards.

Green fees: for nonresidents of the hotel: weekdays, $2.50; weekends and holidays, $3.85; for residents of the hotel: weekdays, $1.05; weekends and holidays, $1.40; $5.60 week, $8.40 two weeks. Half price November 1 to March 31. *Lessons:* $1.75/½ hour from the professional, $1.05/½ hour from the assistants. *Caddies:* $6.30/day. *Golfing equipment and caddie carts:* clubs $2.80/round or $3.50/day, carts $.35/round.

OTHER SPORTS FACILITIES: The sports lover will find more than enough facilities here. The Girvan River is rich in salmon and sea-trout; on the grounds of the hotel there are two hard tennis courts, an 18-hole putting course, and another of 12 holes for pitch and putt. On cold or wet days there is an indoor swimming pool and swimming in the sea in good weather. Table tennis, snooker, dancing (with dancing lessons) complete the sports calendar.

ACCOMMODATIONS: No living space in the club house but bar and restaurant are available in the Turnberry Hotel.

The *Turnberry Hotel* (Tel. Turnberry 202). Has the two courses on its grounds; a luxury hotel; single room and bath (and breakfast) from $7.50 to $8.50; double with bath from $15 to $17.50; 10% service charge. Special weekend rates; also pension rates. Sitting rooms and apartments also available. The hotel offers all the comforts one expects from luxury accommodations.

For Ayr, see section on accommodations for the *Prestwick Golf Club,* p. 86. For Glasgow, see the section for the *Pollok Golf Club,* pp. 84-85.

TOURIST ATTRACTIONS: The hotel and its surroundings offer a peaceful and secluded type of rest, if desired, with magnificent views of the Firth, charming woods, attractive gardens. For the sightseer, this is Robert Burns country, and memories of the famous Scots poet are everywhere. Many of these remembrances are in the vicinity of Ayr, 20 miles away. Nearby is Girvan, a popular seaside resort. Also, dancing, orchestras, good food in the area.

FOR FURTHER INFORMATION: Write to: Manager, Turnberry Hotel, Turnberry, Ayrshire, Scotland. Telephone: Turnberry 202.

Boat-of-Garten Golf and Tennis Club

Boat-of-Garten is set amidst an unrivaled combination of mountains, crags, huge rock formations, lakes and rivers—the very essence of the Scottish Highlands. As with so many other Scottish courses, the visitor can enjoy

British Travel Association

The unique scenery of the Scottish highlands seen at the Boat-of-Garten course.

good golf here against an impressive background, in its way more sensational than the seaside links. The course itself is not a long one, at 5604 yards, and is therefore most suitable for the occasional player or the brief visitor. It favors neither the long or short hitter but has features for both. The terrain is of an undulating nature, the typical Highland terrain. This should prove a popular course for the visitor passing through the Highlands who wants some good golf to remember for his visit without a setback to his game to ruin his vacation.

LOCATION: The course in Boat-of-Garten is 5 to 6 miles from the nearest train station, Aviemore. From the station the course is accessible by car. Aviemore is 31 miles SE of Inverness, 15 SW of Grantown-on-Spey, 33 S of Nairn, 127 N of Edinburgh and 139 N of Glasgow. London is 500 miles S.

OTHER INFORMATION: The course is open from April to mid-October, with nonmembers welcome without restrictions. A professional is always in attendance. The best weather can be expected in May and June, while August is usually the most crowded time. No practice ground is available.
Number of holes: 18. *Par:* 70. *Length:* 5604 yards.
Green fees: weekdays, $.84; weekends, $2.10/day; $4.20/week, $5.60/ two weeks; $7 month. *Lessons:* $1/½ hour. *Caddies:* available by arrangement with the professional. *Golfing equipment and caddie carts:* both available at nominal cost by arrangement with the professional.

OTHER SPORTS FACILITIES: This is an excellent sports area, with tennis, horseback riding, pony trekking, walking excursions, and fishing as regular activities. High mountains in the region, the Cairngorms, are suitable for skiing in winter and early spring.

ACCOMMODATIONS: No living in the club house.
In Aviemore: The *Cairngorm* (Tel. 233) and *Lynwilg* (Tel. 207). Comfortable accommodations with no private baths; singles from $4.20, doubles $8; with breakfast; full pension from $42/week; 10% service charge. Garage facilities.
In Grantown-on-Spey (15 miles away): The *Grant Arms* (The Square, Tel. 26), *Craiglynne* (Tel. 97), and the *Palace* (High Street, Tel. 7). About the same facilities; some rooms with private baths; singles from $4.50, doubles from $8; with breakfast; 10% service charge. Central heating except at *Palace; Grant Arms* closed during winter months.
In Nairn: The *Golf View* (Tel. 2301) and *Lovat Lodge* (Tel. 3298). Some rooms with private baths; singles from $3.50, doubles from $7.50; full pension from $35/week. Central heating at *Golf View;* 10% service charge there.
In Inverness: The *Caledonian* (Tel. 34322) and *Station* (Tel. 31926). Some rooms with private baths; singles from $5, doubles from $10; full pension at *Station* from $60/week. Central heating, garage; 10% service charge.

TOURIST ATTRACTIONS: This is an excellent part of Scotland for excursions. The Cairngorm Mountains are particularly attractive and popular with visitors. The region is full of historic interest, with parks and lakes to suit everybody's tastes. For those who like larger cities, Inverness and Nairn offer a wider range of activities, including excellent shopping for tweeds.

FOR FURTHER INFORMATION: Write to: Club Secretary, Boat-of-Garten Golf and Tennis Club, Hillcrest, Boat-of-Garten, Inverness-shire, Scotland. Telephone: 605.

Cruden Bay Golf and Country Club

The Cruden Bay Golf Course is a championship links set along the sea, like so many other Scottish courses. It takes advantage of the natural terrain and offers lovely views not only of the course itself but also along the water. The average player should not be frightened off by the "championship" label; Cruden Bay is not exceptionally long—6345 yards—and it offers a full variety of shots, something for every type of player. Several holes are generally considered among the finest in the British Isles: the long tough par five 1st, the short par three 4th, the deceptive 8th, the very long 13th (545 yards), and the 18th—nearly everybody's great 18th. It is ideal for the visitor who might want to get the feel of a major course without feeling the frustration of doing very badly. Cruden Bay will repay a steady game.

LOCATION: Cruden Bay is most accessible by car or train. Aberdeen is 20 miles S, Edinburgh 148 S, Peterhead 9 N. The course is within walking distance of the Cruden Bay railroad station.

OTHER INFORMATION: The course is open to nonmembers, unlimited, the entire year. A professional is available by arrangement; request his services ahead of time. The most crowded season is the height of the summer—July and August—and this is generally the time of best weather. Practice ground is available.
Number of holes: 18. Par: 70. Length: 6345 yards.
Green fees: weekdays $.85/round, $1.40/day: weekends $2.10/day; $6/week, ($5.60 for women); $11.20/two weeks ($8.40 for women). Lessons: by arrangement with the professional. Caddies: from $.70/round. Golfing equipment and caddie carts: no clubs for rent; carts $.28/day.

OTHER SPORTS FACILITIES: Close to the sea, the general area provides swimming, boating, and fishing; also tennis and horseback riding.

ACCOMMODATIONS: No living space available in the club house, but the excellently equipped club does have a restaurant, a cocktail bar, a lounge bar, and a wide variety of facilities for the visitor.
In Cruden Bay: The Kilmarnock Arms (Tel. 213) and Red House (Tel.

216). Comfortable rooms but without private baths or central heating; singles from $3.75, doubles from $7 (at *Red House* only).

In Aberdeen: *Station* (Guild Street, Tel. 27214), *Caledonian* (10/14 Union Terrace, Tel. 29233), *Douglas* (Market Street, Tel. 22255), *Imperial* (Stirling Street, Tel. 29101) and *Gloucester* (Union Street, Tel. 29095). Singles from $5, doubles from $9; pension from $50/week (at *Imperial* only); with breakfast; central heating; private baths.

TOURIST ATTRACTIONS: The immediate area offers lovely scenery for walks and car tours. The beaches and promontories are particularly recommended. For more extensive activities, Aberdeen offers natural beauty plus the facilities of a bustling city. Of special interest for the visitor are the City Cross, the Town House, St. Nicholas Church, the Art Gallery and Museum; also a tour of Old Aberdeen. The entire Harbor area is well worth a visit.

FOR FURTHER INFORMATION: Write to: Club Secretary, Cruden Bay Golf and Country Club, "Emdin" Cruden Bay, Aberdeenshire, Scotland.

Golspie Golf Course

Golspie, the site of the golf course, is located in a spectacular part of Scotland, far up in the Highlands on the main road from Inverness to Wick and Thurso. The view from the course includes the vast expanse of the North Sea to the east and the lovely Dornoch Firth and Ross-shire to the south. To the north lies a range of hills that seem to close off Golspie from the outside. The course is a typical seaside links, and although this is not a long course, there is not much run on the ball. Both long and short drivers will find that they will have an even chance. While there are four short holes, at par 3, most holes are in the longer range, par four 400-yarders. This, then, is not an easy links, but it is certainly a bracing experience in a magnificent setting.

LOCATION: The course is most easily accessible by car, although Golspie itself can be reached by train. Golspie is 80 miles N of Inverness on the main road (A9), 11 N of Dornoch, 17 S of Helmsdale, 228 N of Edinburgh, 238 N of Glasgow, 601 N of London.

OTHER INFORMATION: The course is open to nonmembers, unlimited, during its season, from May through mid-September. A professional is in daily attendance during the season. The best weather can be expected in July and August, which is also the most crowded time. Practice ground is available.

Number of holes: 18. *Par:* 68. *Length:* 5840 yards.

Green fees: weekdays and weekends $.70/day; $2.45/week; $4.20/two weeks; $7/month. *Lessons:* $1.40/hour. *Caddies:* available through arrangements with the professional. *Golfing equipment and caddie carts:* no clubs for rent; carts (limited number) $.35/day.

OTHER SPORTS FACILITIES: Golspie is situated amidst seaside resorts that are still not overcrowded. Thus, there is an abundance of loch fishing, sea swimming and boating. Tennis, bowls, walking excursions and bird-watching are some of the other activities.

ACCOMMODATIONS: No living space in the club house, but several bars and restaurants in the village of Golspie.

In Golspie: *Sutherland Arms* (Old Bank Road, Tel. Golspie 216). Singles from $3.50, doubles from $7; with breakfast; weekly rates relatively less; full pension from $35/week. Central heating, some rooms with private baths. *Ben Bhraggie* (East End, Tel. Golspie 242). Singles from $3.50, doubles from $5.60; with breakfast; full pension $33/week. Reduced rates for children. No private baths or central heating.

In Dornoch: The *Royal Golf Castle* (Castle Street, Tel. 283), the *Dornoch* (Tel. 351) and the *Burghfield House* (Tel. 212). All have rooms with private baths; singles from $4.50, doubles from $7.50; full pension from $45/week. No central heating.

TOURIST ATTRACTIONS: The County of Sutherland, where Golspie is situated, is famous for its ancient monuments, its varieties of rare birds, its many types of rocks and minerals. Also of interest are Dunrobin Castle and Museum, the fine sandy Bays with their fishing, boating, and excursions. In nearby Dornoch the town and cathedral (thirteenth century, restored) attract many visitors.

FOR FURTHER INFORMATION: Write to: Sutherland Tourist Association, Sutherland, Scotland or: Club Secretary, Golspie Golf Club, Golspie, Sutherland, Scotland. Telephone: Golspie 328.

The Murcar Golf Club

Situated along the coastal strip of land north of Aberdeen, the Murcar Golf Club is one of three lying close together. The Murcar Course is laid out so that there is a view of the bay from virtually every hole, which is made even more dramatic by the terraced effect of the sandhill ridges. The course is laid out amid rolling sand dunes, which are crossed by winding streams. The terracing of the dunes is further stressed by the leveling of certain other portions; the result is a series of possible traps for the wild swinger. The course favors the straight hitter, as one can see during the Northern Open Championship, which is often held at Murcar. But the less-than-expert player should not be frightened away. The course is not quite a championship one but is considered a top holiday links, full of uncertainties, delightful twists and turns and natural hazards. It will reward the steady player, and if it proves too much, there is a second course of 9 holes, which also provides a sound test of the player's game.

LOCATION: The Murcar Course is 5 miles from Aberdeen, which is easily reached by train or air. Once in Aberdeen, the visitor can take a bus or car to the course. Aberdeen is 87 miles N of Perth and 157 N of Edinburgh on the main road (A9-A92).

OTHER INFORMATION: The course is open all year to nonmembers, with a professional available at most times. If the visitor comes as a guest of a member (and pays reduced green fees), he must play with the member. The most crowded time is during May and June, with the best weather in June through August. The Secretary says that there is also excellent golfing during late September and October. Small practice ground is available.

Number of holes: 18 (also 9-hole course). *Par:* 69 (S.S.S., 70). *Length:* 6309 yards.

Green fees: weekdays $1.05/round, $1.75/day; weekends and holidays $1.40/round, $2.45/day; $5.90/week, $9/two weeks (for short course, about ½ of above costs). *Lessons:* $1.05/½ hour, $2.10/hour. *Caddies:* not available. *Golfing equipment and caddie carts:* no clubs for rent; some carts.

OTHER SPORTS FACILITIES: As a seaside links, Murcar provides nearly all sports facilities: swimming, boating, as well as tennis, riding and several other golf courses.

ACCOMMODATIONS: No living space in the club house, but a lounge bar and a restaurant are available.

The surrounding area and Aberdeen offer ample accommodations. For hotels in Aberdeen, see this section for the *Cruden Bay Golf and Country Club,* pp. 92-93.

TOURIST ATTRACTIONS: Aberdeen is an excellent shopping center with many tourist attractions. For details, see this section for the *Cruden Bay Golf and Country Club,* p. 93. The area is well known for agriculture, fishing, and granite.

FOR FURTHER INFORMATION: Write to: Club Secretary, Murcar Golf Club, Aberdeen, Scotland. Telephone: 29421.

Nairn Golf Club

One of the most popular of golf courses, in a country filled with popular links, the Nairn Course is situated along the southern shore of the Moray Firth in northern Scotland. Nairn has been renovated in order to bring it up to date, and many of the changes were made by the legendary James Braid. Lying on a small neck of land with the sea in view at all times, Nairn is divided into two loops of 9 holes each. Its carefully cropped seaside turf is intermixed with springy heathland, providing every type of golfer with every type of temptation. As a championship course, Nairn must be played carefully; it contains something for everyone, with several long holes (5 over 450 yards) and three very short ones (true par 3s). Incidentally, this section of Scotland is noted for its low rainfall, making Nairn a good holiday bet. Some of the championship matches here have been the Professional Championship (3 times) and the Scottish Amateur Championship (in 1954 and after), and most of the finest players have tried its full length. It should prove a very satisfying experience—once the visitor can make a choice among the many fine Scottish courses. (There is also a short 9-hole course, the "Newton," at 1864 yards, suitable for women and young people.)

LOCATION: The course, on the outskirts of Nairn, is accessible by car (main route, A96) through the beautiful Highland countryside. There is train service to Nairn from Aberdeen and Inverness, as well as good bus service. Inverness is 15 miles SW, Aberdeen 90 SE, Edinburgh 160 S, Glasgow 171 S.

OTHER INFORMATION: Visitors are welcome, unlimited, all year. The professional is in residence throughout the year. The most crowded time is June through August, and these are also the months of best weather. Practice ground is available.
Number of holes: 18. *Par:* 71. *Length:* 6342 yards.
Green fees: $1.05/round, $1.75/day, $5.60/week, $8.40/two weeks, $11.20/month. *Lessons:* $1.40/½ hour. *Caddies:* available through arrangement with the professional at $2.10 to $2.80/round. *Golfing equipment and caddie carts:* clubs $.70 to $1.40/round, according to type required; carts $.28/round.

OTHER SPORTS FACILITIES: As a seaside links, Nairn offers an area full of excellent swimming, fishing (in sea, river or loch), boating, tennis and bowls, For the walker, the surrounding countryside contains mile after mile of somber moorland and natural heathland.

ACCOMMODATIONS: No living space in the club house, but bar and restaurant are available. The area contains many good hotels.
In Nairn: The *Golf View* (Tel. 2301) and the *Newton* (Tel. 3144). Rooms with private baths; singles from $5, doubles from $10; with breakfast; pension from $55/week; 10% service charge. Central heating. *Golf View* closed during winter. The *Royal* (Tel. 3367), *Windsor* (Tel. 3108), *Highland* (Tel. 3141), *Lovat Lodge* (Tel. 3298). No private baths or central heating, about 1/3 less cost than above. For Inverness, see section on Accommodations for *Boat-of-Garten Golf and Tennis Club*, p. 91.

TOURIST ATTRACTIONS: The country around Nairn is particularly fine for touring. Cawdor Castle provided Shakespeare with the scene for Duncan's murder; Kilravock Castle and Dalcross Castle are within a few miles. A car ride on the coast of Moray Firth will more than repay the time spent. In Inverness, 15 miles away, you will find a bustling and attractive city. As the capital of the Highlands, it is the center of Highland activity—in dress, custom and spirit. Expect very good shopping here; there is a tweed mill in Inverness.

FOR FURTHER INFORMATION: About the club, write to: Club Secretary, Nairn Golf Club, Nairn, Nairnshire, Scotland. Telephone: 3208. About the area, write to: Scottish Tourist Board, 2 Academy Street, Inverness, Scotland.

Royal Aberdeen Golf Club

The Royal Aberdeen Golf Club is an excellent seaside links, of championship caliber, and the regular site of the Scottish Amateur Championship. The terrain is the typical sand and rolling dunes of a Scottish coastal course, even more beautiful because of the views of the bay and harbor. With 9 holes of 400 yards or more, the course at first sight appears to favor the strong hitter. But accuracy is always necessary on these dune courses, where hazards can suddenly loom up and slap your ball back. Of particular interest is the 527-yard 2nd, which includes a huge sandpit, and the short 17th, which is possibly fiercer. Royal Aberdeen will prove a good test of your game, but even if your play is weak, the course, its long tradition and beautiful views will make a trip here worthwhile.

LOCATION: The course is accessible by bus or car from the Aberdeen railroad station, 2 miles away. Aberdeen is 87 miles N of Perth and 157 N of Edinburgh on the main road (A9-A92). Dundee is 65 miles S, Inverness 107 NW.

OTHER INFORMATION: The course is open all year for nonmembers, who should bring a letter of introduction from a recognized local club. The professional is on hand every day. The most crowded time is during the summer months, when the best weather can be expected. No practice ground is available.
Number of holes: 18 (also a short course of 9 holes). Par: 70. Length: 6451 yards.
Green fees: $1.40/round ($.50/round on short course). Lessons: by arrangement. Caddies: schoolboys available on Saturdays at $.70/round. Golfing equipment and caddie carts: both available by arrangement with the professional.

OTHER SPORTS FACILITIES: All types of water sports: swimming, boating, fishing; also several golf courses in the area. In the winter there is skiing.

ACCOMMODATIONS: No living space available in the club house; no meals are served in the club house. Accommodations in Aberdeen are generally good; for details, see the Accommodations section under the Cruden Bay Golf and Country Club, pp. 92-93.

OTHER TOURIST ATTRACTIONS: Aberdeen is the chief city of North Scotland, with a population of almost 200,000. It is full of historical sites and churches, like the Episcopal Cathedral of St. Andrew, well worth seeing. Fifty miles to the west is Balmoral Castle, the Scottish seat of the English Queen (or King). Visiting by arrangement is permitted when the court is not in residence.

FOR FURTHER INFORMATION: Write to: Club Secretary, Royal Aberdeen Golf Club, Aberdeen, Scotland. Telephone: 28755.

Royal Dornoch Golf Club

In the heart of great golfing country, the Royal Dornoch is justly considered one of the finest. This is a seaside links of championship caliber, a tough course by any standard. Part of its glory is its naturalness—the characteristic seaside turf, the sandhills, the generous greens. Dornoch has length—10 holes at 400 yards or over—but power will not be enough. This is a carefully planned course; precision is the key, especially on the deceptively tricky short 2nd and 10th. There are no easy holes. And still the high as well as the low handicapper will find Dornoch rewarding. The setting is lovely, with many tees looking out on the Dornoch Firth and beyond to the curving Moray Coast. Add to that a good climate, and you have golf at its best, with a relief 9-hole course to practice on.

LOCATION: The course is adjacent to Dornoch and accessible by car. Dornoch is just off the main road (A9) that runs from Inverness to Thurso. It is 65 miles N of Inverness, 12 S of Golspie. Edinburgh is 220 miles S.

OTHER INFORMATION: The course is open from May to the end of October, and visitors are most welcome at any time. August is the most crowded time, with the best weather during June, August and September. A professional is in daily attendance. There may be some restrictions on Sunday play if members turn out in great numbers. Practice ground is available.
   Number of holes: 18 (also a 9-hole course). Par: 71. Length: 6404 yards.
   Green fees: $1.05/day, $4.20/week. Lessons: $2.10/hour. Caddies: available in limited quantity; best to reserve them ahead of time. Golfing equipment and caddie carts: clubs not for rent, carts about $.35/round.

OTHER SPORTS FACILITIES: Tennis, swimming (good beaches), shooting, and fishing.

ACCOMMODATIONS: No living space in the club house, but bar and restaurant are available; meals should be ordered in advance.
   There are numerous hotels in the area. For Dornoch and Golspie, see this section for the Golspie Golf Club, p. 94. For Inverness and Nairn see Boat-of-Garten Golf and Tennis Club, p. 91.
   In Tain (25 miles): The Royal (Tel. 13). No private baths, singles from $3.50, doubles from $7; with breakfast, garage; full pension from $35/week.
   In Brora (19 miles): Links (Tel. 225), Royal Marine (Tel. 252), and

Sutherland Arms (Tel. 209). No private bath; singles (with breakfast) from $3.25, doubles from $5.50; full pension, $35 to $40/week.

TOURIST ATTRACTIONS: See this section for the *Golspie Golf Club,* p. 94.

FOR FURTHER INFORMATION: Write to: Club Secretary, Royal Dornoch Golf Club, Dornoch, Sutherland, Scotland.

Blairgowrie Golf Club

Many experts consider Blairgowrie to be Scotland's best inland course. Its natural beauty cannot be disputed, and its balance will become apparent the first time around. For those who like to play in lovely surroundings, Blairgowrie offers fairways lined by pines and birches, holes that are hidden from one another in rustic tranquillity, a course where each approach creates its own natural beauties. As for the golf itself, the present course was designed by James Braid, whose touch is apparent everywhere. The delicate precision required for both the long and the short shots is clearly part of his planning. While there is plenty for the slugger—11 holes at or well over 400 yards—there are several par 3s that should delight every type of player. The 15th, in particular, is a very fine 127-yarder that requires finesse at every point and is followed by the booming 16th, almost 500 yards, a change of pace that will challenge your short and long game. The 16th, incidentally, is the most famous of Blairgowrie's 18; your drive must clear a stream and your second follow a fairway sharply to the left with precision and length in every move. If you plan to play in the British Isles, work up to Blairgowrie. While it is not the most difficult of Scots courses, it is a test for excellent play. There is also a 9-hole course.

LOCATION: The course can be reached by bus or car from Perth (16 miles S) and Dundee (16 miles SE). There is also a railway station at Blairgowrie, which is 62 miles N of Edinburgh.

OTHER INFORMATION: The course is open all year to nonmembers with no limitations. Blairgowrie, however, may be crowded, and it is always a good idea to reserve the course in advance. The professional is always in attendance. The most crowded season occurs during the summer. The weather is unpredictable. Practice ground is available.

Number of holes: 18. *Par:* 73 (S.S.S.). *Length:* 6490 yards.

Green fees: weekdays $1.40; weekends $2.10/day; 9-hole course, $.50/ day. *Lessons:* $3/hour. *Caddies:* $1.75/18 holes. *Golfing equipment and caddie carts:* clubs for rent by arrangement with the professional; carts $.30/ round.

OTHER SPORTS FACILITIES: None in the immediate area. To the northwest, around Pitlochry, the visitor will find water sports on the nearby Lake Tummel.

ACCOMMODATIONS: No living space in the club house, but bar and restaurant are available. Order meals in advance whenever possible. For Perth (16 miles), see this section for the *Pitlochry Golf Club*, p. 105. Particularly recommended is the *Station.* For accommodations in Dundee (16 miles), see this section for *St. Andrews: The Royal and Ancient Golf Club*, p. 107.

In Blairgowrie: *Queen's* (Tel. 17), *Royal* (Tel. 26), *Kinloch House* (Tel. Essendy 237), *Drumore House* (Tel. Blacklunans 218). Singles from $3.50, doubles from $7; with breakfast; full pension from $35/week. No central heating; garage; no private baths.

TOURIST ATTRACTIONS: While the city of Blairgowrie is not particularly attractive in itself, it is very well located as a base of operation for tours, excursions, visits to castles in the area. Some of this territory contains the finest of Scottish scenery—lonely moors, a backdrop of mountains, the famous lochs. Nearby Perth and Dundee provide lively entertainment and good shopping.

FOR FURTHER INFORMATION: Write to: Club Secretary, Blairgowrie Golf Club, Rosemount, Perthshire, Scotland. Telephone: Blairgowrie 622.

Carnoustie Golf Club

Carnoustie has been a famous course for many years, the site of several championship matches, including the British Open of 1953, which Ben Hogan won. But if the unsure player feels awed and not up to the course, it should be added that Carnoustie has something for every kind of golfer, for the great and for the humble. The championship course is very long from the tees, with all kinds of varied hazards: ditches, heather and trees as well as plenty of out-of-bound areas for the long hitter. Then again, there are relatively few bunkers, although those that do exist are cleverly paced for the audacious swinger, so the prudent player can make his way from tee to green without too much trouble. Carnoustie is a seaside course, beautifully situated, so that the avid player as well as the golfer who occasionally looks up to view his surroundings will be pleased.

LOCATION: The Carnoustie Course is 5 minutes' walk from the main railway station of Carnoustie, and this line is on the main Edinburgh to Aberdeen coast route. It can also be reached by bus or car (A92). The town of Carnoustie is 11 miles E of Dundee, 7 miles S of the Royal Burgh of Arbroath and midway between Aberdeen and Edinburgh—about 105 miles from each.

OTHER INFORMATION: The courses are open to nonmembers with no limitation on their use. A visitor needs no introduction and may play at any time upon payment of the green fee. The courses are open all year, and a professional can be made available if specifically requested. Most crowded

time is May through July, with the best weather in June. Practice ground is available.
Number of holes: Medal (Championship) Course, 18; Burnside Course, 18. *Par:* Medal, 74; Burnside, 70. *Length:* Medal, 7160 yards; Burnside, 6740 yards.
Green fees: Medal Course: $1.05/round, $1.50/day. Burnside Course: $.70/round, $1.05/day. *Lessons:* $2.80/hour. *Caddies:* $2.80/round (request in advance.) *Golfing equipment and caddie carts:* clubs $2.94/round, carts $.25/round.

OTHER SPORTS FACILITIES: Carnoustie is a popular seaside resort: swimming and diving, yachting, boating and fishing; also bowling and tennis.

ACCOMMODATIONS: No living space in the club house, but restaurants and bars nearby.
In Carnoustie: The *Bruce* (Tel. 2364). Rooms with private baths; central heating; singles from $6.50, doubles from $12.50; full pension from $55/week.
In Arbroath: The *Seaforth* (Tel. 2232). Some rooms with private baths; singles from $4.20, doubles from $8.40; full pension from $47/week. No central heating.
In Dundee: The *Royal* (Tel. 24074) and the *Queen's* (Tel. 22515). Some rooms with private bath; singles from $5, doubles from $9.20; full pension at *Royal* from $55/week. No central heating at *Royal.* 10% service charge at *Queen's.*

TOURIST ATTRACTIONS: The coast area is attractive for the walker or driver who wishes to explore the villages and towns around the Firth of Tay. Arbroath, the ruins of an abbey where Robert Bruce drew up the "Scottish Declaration of Independence," is of considerable historic interest. Within an hour of Carnoustie there are some very fine glens. Dundee and Arbroath both provide good shopping, as does Carnoustie itself.

FOR FURTHER INFORMATION: Write to: Club Secretary, Carnoustie Golf Course Committee of Management, Carnoustie, Scotland. Telephone: 3335/6.

The Gleneagles Hotel Golf Courses

A visit to the Gleneagles Hotel Golf Courses can be a complete vacation in itself. Here the visitor will find a luxury hotel, three golf courses, including a renowned championship links, superbly tailored greens, scenery full of gorse and heather and lovely environs for after the game or for the player's wife. The two major courses, the King's and the Queen's, were laid out by James Braid and have been the scene of numerous international championships. The King's Course is the more severe, being considerably longer, a test of the long driver and the consistent, precise player. Of particular interest here are the 3rd hole (called the "Silver Tassie"), where the second shot has to carry a high ridge, and the 5th and 7th, where embarrassment awaits the loose hitter. There are no poor holes, and to play the course, regardless of your score, should provide excitement and satisfaction enough. The Queen's Course is more picturesque, shorter by some 600 yards, but not an easy one. The 2nd, 5th and 7th here will also make the ablest player stop to reconsider his game. Playing this course will prove a different kind of stimulation, for the scenery with its fir trees is a delight. There is, in addition, the "Wee Course," suitable for the family, although it too needs good judgment. Many of the holes there are deceptively difficult, like the long 7th (called the "Muckle Bookit"), which would be a test for a professional.

LOCATION: The course can be reached by train to Gleneagles Station or by car. There is a sleeping-car train from Euston Station, London. Gleneagles is 16 miles S of Perth, 21 N of Stirling, 48 N of Glasgow, 45 NW of Edinburgh. It is 440 miles N of London. The international airport at Prestwick, Ayrshire, is 70 miles SW.

OTHER INFORMATION: All three courses are open all year with the nonmember invited to play with no limitations. The resident professional is always in attendance. The most popular season is April through June, and the best weather can be expected in the early summer, although it is unpredictable. Practice ground is available.

Number of holes: 18 (King's Course); 18 (Queen's Course); 9 (Wee Course). *Par:* King's, 69; Queen's 68; Wee, 33. *Length:* King's, 6644 yards; Queen's, 6055 yards; Wee, 2625 yards.

Green fees: For hotel guests: $2.10/day, $8.40/week, $11.20/two weeks, $14/month. For nonresident guests: weekdays $4, weekends and holidays $5.60/day. Special rates when the hotel is closed during the winter months: $1.75/day. *Lessons:* $2.10/½ hour; a round with the professional, $5.60. *Caddies:* $3/round plus tip. *Golfing equipment and caddie carts:* clubs $2.80/round, carts $.35/round, shoes not available.

OTHER SPORTS FACILITIES: Besides its closeness to other golf courses (St. Andrews, for example, is 1½ hours away), Gleneagles offers the facilities of the hotel, which includes excellent fishing in loch and river, tennis courts, miniature golf, putting and bowling greens, croquet lawns, an indoor squash court, a swimming pool, billiards, a motion picture house and nightly dances (black tie on Saturday). Outdoor playground for children.

ACCOMMODATIONS: The club house provides very limited dormy house quarters: one single room, one double-bedded, one twin-bedded; $5/person/night. Reservations for these limited facilities should be made to the hotel or to the golf course secretary. The dormy house has a bar and catering facilities. For nonresidents the hotel has extensive bar and restaurant facilities.

The most immediate and luxurious accommodations are offered by the *Gleneagles Hotel* (Tel. Auchterarder 2231) adjacent to the Courses. It is open from Easter until the end of October, singles from $9 to $17, doubles from $18; with breakfast; full pension from $17/day, with slight variations because of season. Suites also available for one or two persons. All comforts; private baths, central heating, garage, experienced staff. Accommodations also for maids and other servants.

In Perth (16 miles away): The *Station* (Tel. 24141). Rooms with private baths; from $10 for single, $17 for double; with breakfast; pension from $58/week. Suites also available. Prices slightly higher during midsummer—add 10 to 20%.

TOURIST ATTRACTIONS: Gleneagles provides a good central location for excursions in every direction: explorations of the Ochils and Grampians (mountains), of the local lochs, castles, mansions, moors, cathedrals. Perth, Glasgow, Edinburgh are all within reach, the heart of Scott country. The Firth of Forth is only a short drive to the south, the Firth of Tay to the northeast.

FOR FURTHER INFORMATION: Write to: Gleneagles Hotel or to Golf Course Secretary, Dormy House, Gleneagles Hotel, Auchterarder, Perthshire, Scotland.

Montrose Golf Club

Montrose has two 18-hole links—the Medal Course, of championship caliber, and the Broomfield, shorter and somewhat less demanding. The Medal Course is a seaside links, just inland from the sand dunes so characteristic of Scottish courses. Montrose is challenging, suitable for the long driver and yet requiring the precision of a sand course. For the slugger there are 7 holes of good length; for the shorter, possibly more careful player, the 3rd, 12th and 16th will be especially appealing. The Medal is to be taken very seriously; its only "easiness" or softness comes from the beauty of the scenery of the Aberdeenshire coast. For the player still unsure of his game, the Broomfield Course will provide a good workout and preparation for the Medal.

LOCATION: Montrose is on the main East Coast Road (A92) from Edinburgh, as well as a stop on the Edinburgh-Aberdeen train; also trains from Glasgow. From Montrose, the course is a short drive. Aberdeen is 38 miles N, Dundee 29 S, Edinburgh 75 S (depending on route).

OTHER INFORMATION: The courses are open all year. The visitor is most welcome and can get on a course at almost any time. There is no resident professional, and there is no crowded season. This is a section of Scotland still relatively free of visitors, although Montrose itself is popular. Practice ground is available.

Number of holes: 18. *Par:* 70. *Length:* 6365 yards.

Green fees: $.85/round, $1.40/day, $5/week, $15/season. *Lessons:* no professional. *Caddies:* not available. *Golfing equipment and caddie carts:* clubs not for rent; carts at nominal cost.

OTHER SPORTS FACILITIES: Tennis, putting, pitch-and-putt, bowling, indoor swimming; excellent beaches and boating during the warm weather.

ACCOMMODATIONS: No living space in the club house, but there is a bar.

In Montrose: The *Central* (Tel. 52) and the *Park* (Tel. 482). Some rooms with private baths; singles (with breakfast) from $4.20, doubles $8.40 and up. No central heating. The *Star* (Tel. 25). Central heating; no private baths; prices about 25% lower.

For hotels in Arbroath and Dundee, see this section for the *Carnoustie Golf Club,* p. 101. For hotels in Aberdeen, see this section for the *Cruden Bay Golf and Country Club,* pp. 92-93.

TOURIST ATTRACTIONS: Montrose is a good holiday spot for the sportsman and also for the visitor who wants other forms of entertainment. During June there is the Montrose Festival of Music, Art and Drama—various productions and exhibitions; also the Angus Pottery and Craft Shop (for local hand-made pottery), dancing, movie houses, coach tours of surrounding areas. Aberdeen is only a short drive to the north. For details of Aberdeen, see this section for the *Cruden Bay Golf and Country Club,* p. 93.

FOR FURTHER INFORMATION: Write to: Town Clerk, Town Clerk's Office, Montrose, Scotland, telephone Montrose 522; or: Montrose Tourist Association, Town Buildings, Montrose, Scotland. Telephone: Montrose 367.

Pitlochry Golf Club

I know of no other short course in the British Isles that offers the challenge and beauty of Pitlochry. At only 5712 yards and with the longest hole at 430 yards, it is clearly the careful golfer's paradise, although he should play the short holes before he begins dreaming. The glory of Pitlochry is its short holes—the 7th, 11th, and 16th—all par 3s with varying approaches and lovely backgrounds. Such is the balance of Pitlochry that only 2 holes are over 400 yards, and yet the player is barely aware of the shortness of length. For scenic beauty this course can hardly be surpassed. The first 3 holes are all climbing—although not exhausting—and then you are high enough to peer out over the surrounding countryside: snow-capped mountains, pine trees and greens underfoot that are glossy and rich. All in all, this a perfect course for the visiting player; it is demanding enough to give him a taste of Scottish golf and yet not discouraging.

LOCATION: The course is accessible by car and rail from nearby cities. Pitlochry (the town) is 27 miles N of Perth, 50 NW of Dundee, 73 N of Edinburgh, 446 N of London.

OTHER INFORMATION: The course is open all year to nonmembers, with no restrictions except during tournaments; it is a good idea to give advance notice to the secretary and reserve the course. The professional is in daily attendance. The most crowded time is from April through October. The weather is always unpredictable. Practice ground is available. *Number of holes:* 18. *Par:* 70 (S.S.S., 69). *Length:* 5712 yards (5295 yards for women).

Green fees: weekdays $.70, weekends $1.05/day (reduction in winter and after 5 P.M.). *Lessons:* $2.25/hour. *Caddies:* $1/18 holes. *Golfing equipment and caddie carts:* clubs and carts about $.35/day each.

OTHER SPORTS FACILITIES: To the northeast there are several lakes for swimming, fishing, boating—all within short driving distance. Pitlochry itself is a popular summer resort, providing mountains in the background (for climbing), woods (good for walking tours) and the lakes (Tummel, in particular).

ACCOMMODATIONS: No living space in the club house, but bar and restaurant are available.

In Pitlochry: The *Pitlochry Hydro* (Tel. 480). Rooms with private baths, singles (with breakfast) from $5.60, doubles from $11.20; full pension, $55/week. No central heating, closed during winter months. *Atholl Palace* (Tel. 66). Rooms with private baths; singles (with breakfast) from $5.25, doubles from $10.50; full pension $45/week. 10% service charge. No central heating, closed during winter months. *Scotland's* (Tel. 185). Rooms with private baths; singles $4.20 to $5, doubles $8.40; no pension. No central heating.

In Perth: The *Station* (Tel. 24141). Rooms with private baths; singles (with breakfast) $5 to $12, doubles from $10; full pension from $57/week. 10% service charge. Central heating, garage, all comforts. *Isle of Skye* (Tel. 22962), *Queen's* (Tel. 25471), *Royal George* (Tel. 24455). Singles from $4, doubles from $7, full pension from $35/week, some rooms with private baths.

TOURIST ATTRACTIONS: Pitlochry has the usual entertainment facilities of a popular resort. The surrounding countryside has much to recommend it, particularly for walkers; the Pass of Killiecrankie is only one of many picturesque spots. Nearby Perth is a bustling city full of historical sites, fine old churches, and memories of Sir Walter Scott.

FOR FURTHER INFORMATION: Write to: Club Secretary, Pitlochry Golf Club, Pitlochry, Perthshire, Scotland. Telephone: Pitlochry 114.

St. Andrews: The Royal and Ancient Golf Club
(Old Course, New Course, Eden Course, Jubilee Course)

The visitor to St. Andrews can play golf, unrestricted, on the most famous course in the world. And if the Old Course is full, he can play on one of the other three courses, almost equally renowned. For here is the

St. Andrews, world's most famous golf course. The area known as the Old Course, with its spacious greens, begins at the Royal and Ancient Golf Club House.

virtual home of international golf, the premier golf club in the world and the ruling authority on the game. The setting itself is extraordinary—a peninsula on the Fife Coast, projecting into the North Sea, on one side the Firth of Tay, on the other the Firth of Forth, with the St. Andrews Bay at the elbow, Dundee at the northern tip, Edinburgh to the south. In the summer St. Andrews is a crowded, fashionable seaside resort, the home of golfers from everywhere in the world; and all year round it is the home of Scotland's oldest university and a historic town in its own right.

The Old Course remains the favorite of most golfers, the truest test of their game. It starts at the Royal and Ancient Golf Club House, has the biggest greens in the world (the largest being an acre in size) and suits either the long or short driver. Bobby Jones has called it the "finest course in the world."

The New Course, not to be overshadowed, is a first-class links, providing a real test of skill. It starts at the shelter beyond the Ladies' Putting Green.

The Eden Course will prove popular with visitors who are still unsure of their games. It is an ideal holiday course, not too difficult, yet far from easy. It begins on the dunes, at the end of the path leading past the Ladies' Putting Green.

The Jubilee Course is the ideal beginner's course and is nearest to the sea. It is reached by a gate on the right in Guardbridge Road.

The player who may be awed by the tradition and surroundings may well want to start with the Jubilee or Eden Course, work his way up to the New Course and then try out the Old Course. On Sundays, holidays and other crowded days, the members of the club have priority on the Old Course, and during the summer months a ballot is operated by the starter—first come, first served. Thus, if the Old Course is filled, the other three are available until there is an opening.

LOCATION: The courses almost touch on the railway station of St. Andrews. The town of St. Andrews can be reached by bus, train or car. Dundee is 12 miles N, Aberdeen 78 N, Glasgow 76 SW, Edinburgh 49 S, Perth 31 W. London is 422 miles S.

OTHER INFORMATION: All courses are open to nonmembers, but the Old Course is usually closed to nonmembers on Sundays; during the summer months there is a restriction on the number allowed to play through a ballot, with ballot cards available from the starter. A professional is on hand at all times, at McAndrew's Golf School. The course season is from May until October, with the busy season from July until the end of September. Weather is best from May until September. Practice ground is available.

Number of holes: Old Course: 18; New Course: 18; Eden Course: 18; Jubilee Course: 18. *Par:* Old Course: 73; New Course: 73; Eden Course: 70; Jubilee Course: 72. *Length:* Old Course: 6572 yards; New Course: 6516 yards; Eden Course: 6250 yards; Jubilee Course: 6355 yards.

Green fees: Old Course: $1.40/weekdays, $2.10/Saturdays, closed/Sundays; New Course: $.70/weekdays, $1.05/Saturdays, $1.05/Sundays; Eden Course: $.70/weekdays, $1.05/Saturdays, $1.05/Sundays; Jubilee Course: $.45/weekdays, $.45/Saturdays, $1.05/Sundays. *Lessons:* $1.75/½ hour. *Caddies:* $3.50/round. *Golfing equipment and caddie carts:* clubs $1.40/round, carts for rent at small fee.

OTHER SPORTS FACILITIES: Excellent lawn tennis courts, first-class bowling greens and all the facilities of a popular seaside resort: safe swimming, boating, water skiing.

ACCOMMODATIONS: No living space in any of the club houses, but bars and restaurants are within easy reach of the courses.

In St. Andrews: *Rusack's* (Tel. 21), *Rufflets* (Tel. 249), *Scores* (Tel. 82). Some rooms with private baths; singles from $5, doubles from $9; with breakfast; pension from $45/week. Central heating at *Rusack's* and *Rufflets,* also closed during winter months. *Imperial* (Tel. 387), *Kinburn* (Tel. 620), and *Station and Windsor* (Tel. 385). No private baths; less expensive.

In Dundee: The *Queen's* (Tel. 22515) and *Royal* (Tel. 24074). Accommodations at about the same prices as above; a few rooms with private baths.

For the visitor who wishes to return to Edinburgh at night, see the section on Accommodations for the *Gullane Golf Club,* pp. 76-77.

TOURIST ATTRACTIONS: St. Andrews, as a famous university town, has many buildings of great historical interest—the university buildings, Blackfriars Chapel, Holy Trinity, the famous Cathedral, the largest in Scotland, and the Church of St. Rule. The city is also excellent as a center for touring and is within easy reach of Royal Deeside, Balmoral, the Trossachs (the rocky, rugged countryside) and Loch Lomond. St. Andrews and Dundee are also excellent shopping centers.

FOR FURTHER INFORMATION: Write to: Information Center, Town Hall, St. Andrews, Scotland. Telephone: St. Andrews 768.

Machrihanish Golf Club

The backdrop for this course is spectacular; a bay of the Atlantic Ocean, in fact, forms one of the hazards for the first hole. There is also a good-sized river along the run of the course, plenty of other natural hazards, doglegs galore and a spanking wind that can turn your game around. Without the wind this is a slugger's course, with 14 rather long holes but only 2 outsized ones. With the wind you need good judgment and plenty of luck. But it's worth facing the elements to play Machrihanish. It has a springy turf and a variety of holes that will delight every type of player. Forget about score and try to come to terms with the many challenging holes. To list only a few: the 1st, the tricky 8th, where your shot might land in a huge crater, and the long 12th, which also features two considerable sand bunkers. If these sound tough—and they are—the course rewards both in its natural beauty and the fine testing quality of the golf it demands.

LOCATION: Machrihanish (the town and the course) is in the extreme west of Scotland on a peninsula called Kintyre, 140 miles SW of Glasgow, 5 miles from Campbeltown. There is daily air and boat service from Glasgow and buses that take 5 hours. By car, figure about 4 hours.

OTHER INFORMATION: Nonmembers may play with no restrictions; Machrihanish is open all year, weather permitting. The professional is in daily attendance. This section is rarely crowded, even in summer. The weather is unpredictable, especially the winds. Practice ground is available.
Number of holes: 18. *Par:* 70 (S.S.S.). *Length:* 6186 yards.
Green fees: weekdays $.70, Sundays and holidays $1.05 (reduction after 5 P.M.). *Lessons:* by arrangement with the professional. *Caddies:* $1/18 holes. *Golfing equipment and caddie carts:* clubs not for rent; carts $.35/ round.

OTHER SPORTS FACILITIES: Swimming off the sandy beach, walking tours through the surrounding countryside—caves, mountains, bays, inlets, castles, old villages.

ACCOMMODATIONS: No living space in the club house, but bar and restaurant are available. There are ample lodgings in Machrihanish and Campbeltown, comfortable but not luxurious. Do not expect private bath.
In Machrihanish: The *Ugadale Arms* (Tel. 206). Singles from $5.60, doubles from $11.20; breakfast included; full pension from $54/week. A few rooms with private bath; closed during winter months; no central heating. The *Warren* (Tel. 219). Singles from $4.20, doubles from $8.40;

with breakfast; full pension from $42/week. No central heating; closed during winter months.
In Campbeltown: *Ardshiel* (Tel. 2133), *Argyll Arms* (central heating, Tel. 2409), *Royal* (Tel. 2107), *White Hart* (central heating, Tel. 2440). Singles from $3.50, doubles from $6.50; with breakfast; full pension $30 to $35/week; open all year.

TOURIST ATTRACTIONS: For the visitor who wants a quiet and restful time, this is the perfect spot. It is unhurried and uncrowded. Campbeltown and Machrihanish are both small, and their chief attraction (besides the golf course) is their setting. For the walker, this is fine country indeed. And if you drive, the ride from Glasgow should be most rewarding.

FOR FURTHER INFORMATION: Write to: Club Secretary, Machrihanish Golf Club, Machrihanish, Argyllshire, Scotland. Telephone: Campbeltown 2645.

IRELAND and NORTHERN IRELAND

Like her sister courses in England and Scotland, those in Ireland offer first-rate golf played against lovely scenery. And, also like England and Scotland, Ireland is small enough so that you can move around and try courses in several sections, with a drive of only an hour or two between one place and another.

Wherever you go, Irish hospitality and generosity await you in abundance. As an added attraction, the costs are low, possibly the lowest in this part of

Europe, and the services are of a high standard. Under these conditions, golf becomes a double pleasure.

Since most visitors head for Dublin, I have given a cluster of six courses around this popular city, all within 30 minutes of its center. If your game is unsure, or if at first you feel unsure about Irish golf, *Elm Park* and *Milltown* are made to order—good, solid courses that are perfect for holiday play. *Castle* is not far behind. Then, once you feel strong and confident, try *Royal Dublin, Louth* and, finally, *Portmarnock*. The last is one of the greatest courses in Europe, with length, great short holes, superb greens and a majesty that only a few championship links acquire.

As you move around Ireland, you will find courses listed for nearly every part: in the center, the south, the west, in the general Shannon Airport area (*Limerick,* 17 miles; *Lahinch,* 30 miles; *Galway,* 59 miles; *Ballybunion,* 66 miles). But no matter what your other plans, you should try to play at *Sligo,* a most satisfying links in every respect, not the least of which is its spectacular location. If you play only *Sligo* and *Portmarnock,* your Irish stay will have been a success. Also, if possible, *Cork* and *Killarney* should not be missed. Since they are not too far from each other, you can play them on successive days.

The Belfast area offers two great links, *Royal Portrush* and *Royal County Down,* as fine in their way as *Sligo* and *Portmarnock* in the south. These are tough courses, with somewhat easier Number 2 courses for a starter.

North or south, you will find great and entertaining golf in Ireland.

Castle Golf Club Ltd.

The Castle Golf Club (at Rathfarnham) is set in a section 4 miles south of Dublin known as the "gateway" to the Dublin Mountains. The setting for the links, therefore, is a vast panorama of attractive and formidable hills. The course is suitable for both long and short drivers, with several holes almost 500 yards long and many under 200 yards. The artificial hazards are all sand bunkers, while there are numerous water hazards in the form of streams and ditches. Castle is not an excessively difficult course and makes a good beginning for the visitor who plans to play around Dublin. Begin here and work up to Royal Dublin and Portmarnock.

LOCATION: The Castle Golf Club is only a short distance from Dublin and can be reached by bus (No. 47A or No. 61) or car.

OTHER INFORMATION: The course is open to nonmembers, but the visitor should carry proof of membership in his local golf club. The weather permitting, Castle is playable all year, and the professional is in daily attendance. Most crowded season is April through September, when you can also expect the best weather. Practice ground is available.
Number of holes: 18. *Par:* 70. *Length:* 6005 yards.
Green fees: weekdays, $2/day; weekends, $2.80/day; $5.60/weekly; $11.20/monthly. (Reduction if you play with a member.) *Lessons:* $1.40/

hour. *Caddies:* $.75/round. *Golfing equipment and caddie carts:* no clubs for rent; carts $.50.

OTHER SPORTS FACILITIES: Plenty of golf in the immediate area; for the walker, the Dublin Mountains, which lie behind Rathfarnham, are particularly recommended.

ACCOMMODATIONS: No living space in the club house, but restaurant and bar are available.

Dublin is a fine city for good hotels for all tastes and pocketbooks. For details, see this section for the *Elm Park Golf and Sports Club,* p. 114, and *Royal Dublin Golf Club,* p. 117, particularly the first.

TOURIST ATTRACTIONS: There is good camping throughout the immediate region, and in Dublin itself the visitor will find the whole range of attractions from sports to cultural activities of all kinds.

FOR FURTHER INFORMATION: Write to: Club Secretary, Castle Golf Club Ltd., Rathfarnham, Dublin 14, Ireland. Telephone: 905835.

County Louth Golf Club

Louth is a first-rate seaside links of championship caliber. And tough! This is a natural course, with gigantic sandhills, roughs that are really rough and several long holes that call for power and then some. It is not only length that makes Louth so fierce—at 6600 yards, it is not excessively long. But it is the spread, combined with fiendishly placed hazards and narrow approaches, that creates the difficulty. The 7th, for example, at 406 yards makes the good player stumble, not with sheer length but with its unusual approach shot, as does the 11th (at 389 yards) with its approach through two sandhills. The 13th is renowned as an overwhelmingly difficult shot, with an approach from high up that gives a spectacular view of the Mourne Mountains, to a narrow green with a sharp drop on three sides. Louth also has 4 short holes, all good ones and all facing in different directions so that the wind is never the same for two of them. If overall length bothers you, you can shorten your tees considerably and play the course for its other difficulties. Don't, however, come to Louth cold.

LOCATION: The course is in Baltray, near Drogheda, 30 miles N of Dublin, on the main road to Belfast (76 miles N). Drogheda is the closest railroad station; then take bus or car to the course.

OTHER INFORMATION: The course is open all year to nonmembers with no limitations. The professional is in daily attendance. The most crowded time is summer, when the best weather is to be expected. If you don't mind a little rain, the weather never really becomes too bad. Practice ground is available.

Number of holes: 18. *Par:* 72. *Length:* 6606 yards.

Green fees: weekdays, $.70; weekends, $1.40/day. *Lessons:* $2.50/hour. *Caddies:* a few available at $1.50/18 holes. *Golfing equipment and caddie carts:* by arrangement with the professional.

OTHER SPORTS FACILITIES: Baltray has an excellent 3-mile stretch of beach with safe swimming, boating, etc. At Drogheda there is fishing for trout and salmon, hunting, tennis. For the walker, the coastal area is lovely.

ACCOMMODATIONS: The club house has 18 rooms at $2.80 per person for bed and breakfast. Bar and restaurant are available.

For visitors who wish to stay over in Dublin, see this section for the *Elm Park Golf and Sports Club,* p. 114.

In Drogheda: The *Stameen House* (Tel. 8958). Singles from $5, doubles from $10 in high season; breakfast included; full pension $58 to $106/week. Many rooms with private baths; central heating; reductions during off season; 25% reduction for children. *White Horse* (Tel. 8152). Singles from $4, doubles from $7.50; with breakfast; no pension. No private baths; central heating; 25% reduction for children.

OTHER TOURIST ATTRACTIONS: Dublin, of course, offers the attractions of a major city, and it is only 45 minutes away. Drogheda has its own charms; many imposing buildings recall its glorious past; also, it is a good starting point for explorations of the Boyne Valley and of Meath and Louth Counties.

FOR FURTHER INFORMATION: Write to: Club Secretary, County Louth Golf Club, Baltray, Drogheda, Ireland. Telephone: Termonfeckin 2.

Elm Park Golf and Sports Club

Pleasant in appearance and of medium difficulty, Elm Park Golf Club will prove a good test of the visitor's game. Even though it is somewhat on the short side compared with many championship links, Elm Park has enough holes of testing difficulty to give everyone from the average player to the professional a good workout. The main feature of the course is the feeling it gives of the open countryside, although it lies within a built-up area. If you play a careful, precise game, you may do surprisingly well here.

LOCATION: Only 3 miles from the center of Dublin, Elm Park can be reached by car or bus from Dublin. The city bus service (No. 9) passes the club, with the terminus outside the entrance.

OTHER INFORMATION: The course is open to visitors but not when club competitions are being held, usually on Wednesdays, Thursdays and over weekends (not every week or every weekend). Visitors are always welcome and need meet no requirement beyond paying the green fees. Golf is played all year, and the professional is available throughout the year. Most crowded season is April to August, also the time of best weather. Practice ground is available.

Number of holes: 18. *Par:* 69. *Length:* 6022 yards.
Green fees: weekdays, $2.50; Sundays and holidays, $3/day; $6/week;
$9/two weeks. *Lessons:* $2/½ hour. *Caddies:* $.75/round and up. *Golfing
equipment and caddie carts:* clubs $1, carts nominal.

OTHER SPORTS FACILITIES: Tennis, bowling, swimming nearby in
the sea, and horseracing.

ACCOMMODATIONS: No living space in the club house, but dining
room and bar are available.
In Dublin: The visitor will find every type of lodging, with even the fol-
lowing luxury hotels charging reasonable prices. *Gresham* (O'Connell Street,
Tel. 46881), *Intercontinental* (Ballsbridge, Tel. 67511), *Jury's* (College
Green, Tel. 79811), *Royal Hibernian* (48 Dawson Street, Tel. 72991),
Russell (St. Stephen's Green, Tel. 54151), *Shelbourne* (St. Stephen's Green,
Tel. 66471). Singles $7 to $9, doubles $10 to $18; with breakfast. Private
baths, central heating, experienced staffs, all meals available, licensed for
wines and liquors. Expect a slight rise in price during special events; holi-
day rates at Christmas. *Anchor* (Parnell Square, Tel. 40305), *Central*
(Exchequer Square, Tel. 78341), *Clarence* (6/8 Wellington Quay, Tel.
76178), *Dolphin* (Essex Street, Tel. 72886), *Standard* (Harcourt Square,
Tel. 52324), and *Wynn's* (35/39 Lower Abbey Street, Tel. 45131). All
comforts can be expected. Prices about the same as above.

TOURIST ATTRACTIONS: Dublin is 3 miles from the course, and there
the visitor will find the resources of a major capital.

FOR FURTHER INFORMATION: Write to: Secretary of the Elm Park
Golf and Sports Club, Nutley Lane, Dublin 4, Ireland. Telephone: 693438,
693361.

Milltown Golf Club

A flat course with many trees, Milltown favors neither the long nor
the short driver. While there are several holes over 400 yards and several
at about 200 yards or under, the majority are in the 300- to 400-yard class.
For a fairly long links, there is good overall balance, so the average golfer
should feel at home here. So that he isn't lulled into complacency, however,
he should be warned that the holes are of good testing quality and many
fairways are narrow with tricky doglegs awaiting the careless, or presumptu-
ous, driver. The course, incidentally, is kept in very good condition. Since
this is one of the less difficult courses in an area noted for golf, it might be
a good idea to begin here or at Elm Park.

LOCATION: Milltown is 3 miles from the center of Dublin and is accessible by car or bus (Nos. 14 and 61 pass the door).

OTHER INFORMATION: The course is open to nonmembers, who should bring a letter from their local secretary stating that they are members of a recognized golf club. Golf is played all year, and the professional and his assistant are on hand except when playing tournaments. July, sometimes June, is the most crowded time and the period of best weather. Practice ground is available.

Number of holes: 18. *Par:* 72. *Length:* 6145 yards.

Green fees: weekdays, $2.25; weekends and holidays, $3.50/day. *Lessons:* $2.80/hour. *Caddies:* $.50/round plus tip. *Golfing equipment and caddie carts:* no clubs for rent; carts $.35/round.

OTHER SPORTS FACILITIES: The visitor will find all facilities in Dublin.

ACCOMMODATIONS: No living space in the club house, but restaurant and bar are available.

Dublin will provide lodgings for every pocketbook and taste. The Nos. 14 and 61 buses to the Milltown Course pass Dublin hotels in the Harcourt Street and Stephen's Green area. Such hotels are the *Russell, Shelbourne, Ivanhoe* and *Standard.* Also highly recommended is the *Gresham* on O'Connell Street. For details see this section for the *Elm Park Golf and Sports Club,* p. 114.

TOURIST ATTRACTIONS: None in the immediate area, but Dublin is only a short distance away.

FOR FURTHER INFORMATION: Write to: Club Secretary, Milltown Golf Club, Milltown, Dublin 14, Ireland. Telephone: Dublin 976090.

Portmarnock Golf Club

The Portmarnock Golf Course is located in a popular seaside resort area, and the course itself is considered one of the finest not only in Ireland but in all the world. With its tremendous length, Portmarnock offers a challenge to every kind of golfer, from the average player through the top professional. Arnold Palmer, for example, has called the 15th hole the best short hole in the world, and Henry Cotton has called the 14th, with no qualifications, the best hole in the world.

The course is a genuine seaside links lying on a narrow strip of land surrounded on three sides by the sea. Lacking high ground, Portmarnock is open to the wind on all sides. There are no holes where mounds have been raised to create an artificial contour, no holes where the obvious hollow has been used for a green. There are three very long holes—well over 500 yards—and three short ones. The rest are 400 yards and up—a paradise for the long driver. No blind driving here—everything is open and natural.

Portmarnock has been and continues to be the site of many championship matches, such as the Canadian Cup and the Dunlop Masters.

LOCATION: Portmarnock is only 8 or 9 miles N of Dublin and can be reached easily by train, bus or car. It is 5 miles from Howth and 2 S of Malahide. It is 4 miles E of Dublin Airport.

OTHER INFORMATION: The course is open to nonmembers, unlimited, but they should have a letter of introduction from their own club secretary or should make prior arrangements with the secretary of Portmarnock. Ladies are permitted to play only Monday through Friday, inclusive. Large tour parties cannot be accepted at weekends unless by special arrangement. Golf is played all year round, and the professional, Harry Bradshaw, is on hand except when he is playing in tournaments. Then the assistant professional is available. Most crowded seasons are winter, autumn and spring rather than summer, but weekends at any time are popular. Fair weather can be expected most of the year, this section being considered the driest part of Ireland. Practice ground is available.

Number of holes: 18 (two loops of 9). *Par:* 72 (S.S.S., 73). *Length:* 7093 yards.

Green fees: weekdays, $2.80/day; weekends and holidays, $4.25/day. *Lessons:* $2.80/hour. *Caddies:* $.75/round and $1.50/round. *Golfing equipment and caddie carts:* clubs $1.50/round, carts $.35/round.

OTHER SPORTS FACILITIES: Shooting, fishing, yachting and riding facilities are available in the district. Portmarnock has a fine sandy beach that allows safe swimming at all times.

ACCOMMODATIONS: No living space in the club house, but restaurant and bar are available. The dining room can seat 100 persons.

In immediate area: The *Marine, Sutton, Country Club, Portmarnock, Old Shieling, Raheny.* All are within 3 miles of the club. Particularly recommended is the *Country Club* (Tel. 350611). Singles (with breakfast) $4.50 to $6; doubles $9 to $12; full pension from $55/week. 10% service charge. Slightly higher during summer season. Central heating, private baths, licensed to sell wines and whisky.

In Dublin: The *Gresham, Shelbourne, Russell, Royal Hibernian, Jury's.* For details see this section for the *Elm Park Golf and Sports Club,* p. 114.

TOURIST ATTRACTIONS: Portmarnock, while well-provided with its own resort facilities, is also close to Dublin, which provides sports, museums, historic sites. Just south of Portmarnock, Howth has many points of interest, as does Malahide, slightly north: historic sites, the castle, ruins of a medieval church.

FOR FURTHER INFORMATION: Write to: Club Secretary, Portmarnock Golf Club, Co. Dublin, Ireland. Telephone: 323082, 323050.

Royal Dublin Golf Club (Dollymount)

The Royal Dublin Golf Club has an old and honorable past. It is presently considered one of the most honored in Ireland and is justly famous for the high quality of its greens. It is chiefly a course for the fairly skilled golfer, for the ball lies very close and demands accurate hitting. No single hole is easy, but at all times the player is assured of lies from which he can play the required shot. In fact, the close lies are the leading feature of Dollymount; approach play on the outward half is difficult when the wind is following. You will find plenty of balance here, with length a distinct factor; also, several holes feature small hills and drains to test your ingenuity and patience.

LOCATION: About 3 miles from the center of Dublin, within city boundaries, the Royal Dublin can be reached by car or taxi. (Taxis in Ireland, incidentally, are very reasonable.)

OTHER INFORMATION: The course is open to nonmembers with some competition days closed to visitors. Because of the nature of the turf, Dollymount is playable all year. The professional, the well-known Christy O'Connor, is always available. Crowded in summer. Practice ground is available.

Number of holes: 18. *Par:* 73. *Length:* 6657 yards (can be lengthened). *Green fees:* weekdays, $2; weekends, $4. *Lessons:* $4.50/hour. *Caddies:* $1.50/round. *Golfing equipment and caddie carts:* clubs $1.50/round, carts $.35.

OTHER SPORTS FACILITIES: In and around Dublin: horse and dog racing, bowling, tennis, Gaelic football, swimming, boating, basketball, rollerskating.

ACCOMMODATIONS: No living space in the club house, but full restaurant and bar facilities. One pleasant feature for the golfer is a snack bar open to the locker room and available to the golfer prior to and immediately after play without the need to change.

Dublin itself provides first-class accommodations, the *Gresham, Shelbourne, Hibernian, Russell,* and many others. For details, see this section for the *Elm Park Golf and Sports Club,* p. 114.

The Royal Dublin Golf Club has arrangements with all the first-class hotels in Dublin regarding the sale of green-fee tickets to visitors who reside at the hotels. This amounts to a golf reservation that can be made at the hotel.

TOURIST ATTRACTIONS: Dublin provides the whole range of tourist attractions, from plays in the famous Abbey Theater to fine museums and historical sites; excellent shopping at reasonable prices—tweeds, linens, knitted goods, glassware.

FOR FURTHER INFORMATION: Write to: Club Secretary, Royal Dublin Golf Club, Dollymount, Dublin 3, Ireland. Telephone: 336346.

Athlone Golf Club

The Athlone Golf Course is a typical Irish course in that it combines good golf with beautiful surroundings. The course is located beside Lough Ree, Ireland's second largest lake, right off the main road between Athlone and Roscommon. While Athlone is not particularly long at 5846 yards, it will prove a test for the visitor's skill. The fairways are narrow and nearly always call for accuracy rather than power. One of the special features of the course is that its many plateau greens require extremely accurate approach shots. All greens are watered. This is a good course for the average golfer who wants to play without the pressures of a full championship links and yet wants a solid game.

LOCATION: The course is 3 miles from Athlone on the road to Roscommon; it is served by train and bus as well as by car. Athlone is 78 miles W of Dublin on the main road from Dublin to Galway. It is 56 miles from Galway, 84 NE of Shannon Airport, 134 N of Cork.

OTHER INFORMATION: The course is open all year to nonmembers with no limitation except proof that they belong to a golf club. The professional is always on hand. The weather is good from March through October, best in June, July and August; most crowded months are May, June and September.
Number of holes: 18. *Par:* 70. *Length:* 5846 yards.
Green fees: $1.05/day, $4.20/week, $5.60/month. *Lessons:* $1.40/hour. *Caddies:* $.70/round. *Golfing equipment and caddie carts:* through arrangement with the professional.

OTHER SPORTS FACILITIES: The course is next to the *Hodson Bay Hotel,* which has hardcourt tennis courts; there are all types of water sports on the nearby lake: swimming, yachting, boating, fishing and water skiing. Fishing in season for pike and perch, trout in surrounding bays and rivers; hunting in season.

ACCOMMODATIONS: No living space in the club house, but bar and restaurant in the hotel 50 yards from the club house.
The *Hodson Bay Hotel.* Next to the course; comfortable lodgings, with fresh food from an extensive farm attached to the hotel; singles from $4, doubles $8; with breakfast; no private baths.
In Athlone: The *Prince of Wales* (Church Street, Tel. 2626). Singles from $4.20, doubles from $8.40; with breakfast; full pension from $50/week. 10% service charge. Some rooms with private baths; central heating throughout, baby-sitting. Prices 10 to 20% higher during summer season. *Shamrock Lodge* (Tel. 2601). About the same price range as above; same services except no baby-sitting. *Mont Vista* (Tel. 2065) and the *Royal*

(Mardyke Street, Tel. 2924). A few rooms with private baths. Slightly lower prices.

TOURIST ATTRACTIONS: Besides all the sports facilities, the visitor may take boating trips on the lake and make excursions to many villages famous in English and Irish literature. Athlone is close to the former center of Christian civilization, and many of the villages are of great historic interest. It also provides good shopping, motion picture houses, several places of amusement, various rowing and sailing events.

FOR FURTHER INFORMATION: Write to: Tourist Information Bureau, Church St., Athlone, Co. Westmeath, Ireland. Telephone: 2073.

Mullingar Golf Course

The Mullingar Golf Course has the reputation of being one of the best inland courses in Ireland and without question one of the most picturesque. Situated 3 miles from the town, it is set on the shores of Lough Ennell, a lovely body of water, and is laid out on a beautiful wooded piece of land. The course was designed by James Braid, who needs no introduction to golfers. So well thought of is Mullingar that it has attracted the Irish Professional Championship on three occasions as well as amateur players of the highest standing. Not excessively long, the course, with its good greens, tight fairways and varied approaches, will nevertheless provide a challenge for every type of game.

LOCATION: The golf course is 3 miles from Mullingar, which is 52 miles NW of Dublin on the main road from Dublin to Sligo. It is 109 miles from Shannon Airport and is accessible by car, bus or train, with regular daily line service.

OTHER INFORMATION: The course is open all year to nonmembers with no restrictions. A professional is in attendance from March 1 to October 31. The season goes on throughout the year, weather permitting. Practice ground is available.

Number of holes: 18. *Par:* 71 (S.S.S., 70). *Length:* 6264 yards.

Green fees: weekdays, $1.40; weekends, $2.10 (half price for women); weekly tickets at reduction. *Lessons:* $1 to $1.75/session. *Caddies:* available on weekends at $.70/round plus tip. *Golfing equipment and caddie carts:* clubs available by arrangement with professional at reasonable cost; carts $.28/round.

OTHER SPORTS FACILITIES: The lakes in the area provide fine fishing (trout, perch, pike) and boating facilities; also good hunting, shooting, tennis and swimming.

ACCOMMODATIONS: No living space in the club house, but bar and dining facilities are available.

In Mullingar: *Greville Arms* (Tel. 563). Single from $5, double at $10; with breakfast. 10% service charge. Slightly higher during the summer season. Central heating; some private baths. *Lake Country* (14 Pearse Street, Tel. 230). Single $3.50, double $7; breakfast included; full pension from $40/week. 10% service charge. Slightly higher during the summer season. Some private baths. *Broder's* (Green's Bridge, Tel. 439). About same as *Lake Country*; full pension from $35/week.

TOURIST ATTRACTIONS: Besides being rich in fine scenery (particularly around Lough Ennell), Mullingar is an excellent shopping center for linens and other Irish products. At Newbrook, one mile away, there is a fine race course, and there is a greyhound track in the town. Local sites include a cathedral of some interest.

FOR FURTHER INFORMATION: Write to: Club Secretary, Mullingar Golf Club, Belvedere, Mullingar, Co. Westmeath, Ireland. Telephone: Mullingar 8366.

Kilkenny Golf Club

Set in the pleasant Irish countryside, the Kilkenny Golf Course offers the visitor some relaxing golf along with a lovely holiday in a relatively uncrowded spot. Not that the course is easy—far from it. But it will prove a solid challenge for the visiting player, favoring neither the long nor the short hitter. There are several strong holes requiring precision and sound strokes. Most holes are in the middle range of 350 yards, with the fairways and greens of good texture. There are, however, a semirough and a rough that are a good test of one's game. All in all, a good course for the golfer who has not yet set his sights too high or the player who is still feeling his sea (or air) legs.

LOCATION: The course is at Newtown, about 1 mile N of Kilkenny; it is accessible by bus, train or car. Kilkenny is 75 miles SW of Dublin, 92 NE of Cork, 88 E of Shannon Airport, 52 NW of Rosslare Harbour.

OTHER INFORMATION: The course is open all year to nonmembers, who should bring proof of membership in a recognized golf club and have a handicap. The professional is available every day, all day. The weather is best from April through September, and the course is never really crowded. Practice ground is available.
Number of holes: 18. *Par:* 71. *Length:* 6085 yards.
Green fees: $1.05/day, $2.80/week, $4.20/two weeks, $5.60/month. *Lessons:* $1.05/½ hour. *Caddies:* $1.05/round. *Golfing equipment and caddie carts:* both available through arrangement with the professional.

OTHER SPORTS FACILITIES: For golfers, there are additional 9-hole courses at Callan and Castlecomer. Other facilities include those for tennis, hunting, fishing (for brown trout and salmon), walking excursions and mountain climbing.

ACCOMMODATIONS: No living space in the club house, but bar and food facilities are available.
In Kilkenny (3 minutes from the course by car): *Imperial* (Rose Inn Street, Tel. 54). Single from $3.50, double from $7; breakfast included; full pension from $40/week. No central heating. Prices 10% higher during summer season and Beer Festival. *Club House* (Patrick Street, Tel. 4) and the *Rose Hill House* (College Road, Tel. 207). Similar lodging at about the same prices as above; with central heating. 10% service charge. *Rose Hill House* has baby-sitting facilities.

TOURIST ATTRACTIONS: Kilkenny is well situated as a base for tours of the fine river and mountain country. The city itself is ancient, going back to 1200, and the streets retain their medieval flavor. Of particular interest are St. Canice's Cathedral, Kilkenny Castle (overlooking the Nore, famous for its excellent art gallery), the Black Abbey, and several other landmarks. For the walker, there are several charming walking tours of the city and its environs. For the beer drinker and celebrant, the annual Beer Festival from May 30 to June 6 features drinking, folk dancing, boxing, a circus, greyhound racing, football, golf competitions, variety shows and all kinds of other attractions. For reservations at this time, write to: Accommodations Bureau, Kilkenny Beer Festival Committee, City Hall, Kilkenny, Ireland.

FOR FURTHER INFORMATION: Write to: Club Secretary, Kilkenny Golf Club, Glendine, Kilkenny, Ireland.

County Sligo Golf Club

Sligo is a superb links, a combination of everything that makes golf pleasurable and satisfying. The course is of championship caliber, the scenery spectacular—a view of sea, mountains, ocean and the roofs of the town itself—and the layout is natural, as if nature intended this to be a golf course and nothing else. Not surprisingly, Sligo is popular, and many of Ireland's most famous golfing events are held there. Curiously enough, length is not a great factor; all the par 5s are in the 400-yard range, the longest being the 491-yard 12th. The real toughness lies in the balance of obstacles (natural and otherwise), the approaches to the green, the narrowness of some fairways, the deceptive largeness of others, the strong wind. The 17th, possibly the best hole at Sligo, is a good example of what the course demands: a dogleg to the left, to the base of a hill; if you hit too far left, a ravine, if too hard to the right, an extremely difficult second shot to a now distant green. And the 17th, also the 12th, the 14th and several others are similar; this is a true test of your golf, on a matchless course.

LOCATION: The course is at Rosses Point, 5 miles W of Sligo and is accessible by car or bus (regular service). Sligo is the nearest railroad station, 134 miles NW of Dublin and about the same distance N of Shannon Airport.

OTHER INFORMATION: The course is open all year, weather permitting, with no limitations for nonmembers. The professional is always on hand. The most crowded time is the summer, when Sligo fills even without visitors, and the best weather can be expected then. It is a good idea to reserve the course ahead of time, especially on weekends. Practice ground is available.

Number of holes: 18. *Par:* 72 (S.S.S.). *Length:* 6372 yards.

Green fees: weekdays, $1.40; weekends, $3.50 for entire weekend or $1.40/day. *Lessons:* $2/hour. *Caddies:* $1.75/18 holes. *Golfing equipment and caddie carts:* clubs occasionally available for rent by arrangement; carts $.25/round.

OTHER SPORTS FACILITIES: This is a fine seaside resort, with all water sports: safe swimming from sandy beaches, diving, boating, water skiing, fishing; also tennis, shooting, riding.

ACCOMMODATIONS: No living space in the club house, but bar and restaurant are available.

In Sligo: A wide variety of lodgings, pensions, boarding houses. *Great Southern* (Lord Edward Street, Tel. 2101). Most luxurious. Singles from $6, doubles $8.40 to $17.50 during summer season; with breakfast. Private bath, central heating, all comforts. Other seasons about 25% cheaper; one-third reduction for each child. *Grand* (Teeling Street, Tel. 2591). Less luxurious. Singles $4 to $8, doubles $5 to $10, during high season; full pension $50 to $100/week. Most rooms with private baths; reductions for children; reductions during off season; central heating. *Imperial* (John F. Kennedy Parade, Tel. 2677). Singles from $4.50, doubles from $7.50 to $15, during high season; with breakfast; full pension $45 to $90/week. Many rooms with private baths; reductions for children; reductions during off season; central heating. Add 10% service charge to all of the above hotels.

TOURIST ATTRACTIONS: The entire County Sligo area is fine for touring by car or on foot. The coastal areas are full of popular resorts, and the villages are picturesque. If possible, take a boat trip on Lough (Lake) Gill just east of the city of Sligo. Strandhill and Rosses Point provide not only sporting facilities but also good dancing and other light entertainment. The drive from Sligo to Bundoran along the coast is outstanding for scenic beauty and historical interest. At Drumcliff is the grave of William Butler Yeats, the great Irish poet and possibly the greatest poet of the twentieth century. Not far is Lissadell, well worth a visit.

FOR FURTHER INFORMATION: Write to: Club Secretary, County Sligo Golf Club, Rosses Point, Co. Sligo, Ireland. Telephone: Rosses Point 20.

Ballybunion Golf Club

The Ballybunion Golf Course is set against the beautiful background of northwest County Kerry, where the River Shannon meets the sea. The coastline with its caves, cliffs, coves and beaches provides a fine setting for this championship course. One of the leading links in Ireland, Ballybunion is situated in the sandhills south of the town itself and favors long and straight driving, with 11 holes of 400 yards or more. In one sense, it is unique because of its varying features; it is a challenge for the golfer who wishes to try out his entire repertory. Of particular interest—and possible difficulty—are the sand ridges that run across the course, especially the so-called "Sahara" at the 13th. This is tough, satisfying golf.

LOCATION: From Shannon Airport, bus or car to Ballybunion, 66 miles W. Or from Limerick to Ballybunion, bus or car, 50 miles W. There is also train service.

OTHER INFORMATION: The course is open to nonmembers, unlimited, for the entire year, and there is always a professional on hand. July and August are the most crowded times, and the weather never seems to be very bad. The course is playable all year because of the sandy soil of the region. A practice ground is available.
Number of holes: 18. *Par:* 71 (S.S.S., 75). *Length:* 6417 yards.
Green fees: $1.25/day, less in the evening; weekly and monthly tickets at considerable savings. *Lessons:* $1/½ hour. *Caddies:* $.75/round. *Golfing equipment and caddie carts:* limited clubs at $.75/round, carts $.75/day.

OTHER SPORTS FACILITIES: Deep-sea angling as well as rod and line fishing, greyhound racing, Gaelic football and swimming along a fine stretch of beach; add to these boating, and shooting (duck, snipe, mallard, teal, grouse, and woodcock).

ACCOMMODATIONS: The club provides no living space, but does have bar and restaurant facilities.
Within 5-10 minute walking distance of the Links, the following hotels and guest houses are available, some rooms with private baths: *Castle* (Tel. 4). Single from $4, double from $8; with breakfast; full pension from $45/week. 10% service charge. Prices slightly higher during summer and racing season. *Central* (Tel. 5). About 10% cheaper than above; similar lodgings. *Marine* (Tel. 17). Prices as above; no private baths. *West End* (Tel. 13), *Greenmount* (Tel. 21), *Mountain View* (Tel. 10). Prices slightly below those listed for the *Castle*. Full pension if desired; no private baths.

TOURIST ATTRACTIONS: Besides the beautiful sandy beaches and scenic walks, there is a public dance hall as well as frequent motion-picture and concert performances. Highly recommended are tours of the famous ring of Kerry, Killarney and Dingle Peninsula. Good shopping in town and in Listowel, 10 miles away, and the nearby regions are full of castles and sites of historic interest.

FOR FURTHER INFORMATION: Write to: Club Secretary, Ballybunion Golf Club, Ballybunion, Co. Kerry, Ireland. Telephone: Club House Ballybunion 20.

Cork Golf Club (Little Island)

The Cork Golf Club, situated in a beautiful area, is a championship course that will test any visitor's game. Cork, Cobh, and the other cities along the southern Eire coast have become very popular as resort areas. The course takes advantage of the scenery, and as the player goes from hole to hole, he has glimpses of the sea estuary. Little Island is about evenly divided between short and long holes, with the latter perhaps having the advantage. The course opens with a tough 372-yard par 4, played to an immensely large green, over a thousand square yards on two levels, with a variety of puzzling ridges. From here on, the player is faced by one natural obstacle after another—a quarry, furze, gorse and tangled undergrowth —but all blended into a mixture of the lovely and the dangerous. Precision is the key here, and the visitor will enjoy his game—if he remembers not to lose his temper.

LOCATION: The club is ¼ mile from the bus and train stop at Little Island. But since there might be long waits between service, a car is the best way to reach the course. Cork City is 6 miles away; Cobh 8, Middleton 8, Limerick 60 N, Macroom 32 W.

OTHER INFORMATION: The course is open all year to nonmembers provided the visitor is a member of a recognized golf club and does not interfere with regularly scheduled competition. The professional is in daily attendance. Although the course is usually not crowded at any single time, September and May are popular. The best weather is in the summer. Practice ground is available.
Number of holes: 18. *Par:* 71 (S.S.S., 69). *Length:* 6071 yards (medal tees), 6246 yards (championship tees).
Green fees: $1.40/day ($1.05 with a member); after 5 P.M. $.70; half for women. *Lessons:* $1.40/hour. *Caddies:* available in three classes: at $1.05, $.85, $.60. *Golfing equipment and caddie carts:* clubs $.70, carts $.28/round.

OTHER SPORTS FACILITIES: This is a popular resort area, with full water sports: fishing, swimming, sailing, yachting, yacht racing; also tennis.

ACCOMMODATIONS: No living space in the club house, but bar and catering facilities are provided.
In Cork: *Metropole* (MacCurtain Street, Tel. 23271). A luxury hotel; singles $5, doubles $10; with breakfast; no pension. 10% service charge; central heating. *Imperial* (South Mall, Tel. 23304). A luxury hotel; single $5, double $10; with breakfast. 10% service charge. Central heating. *Intercontinental* (Lancaster Quay, Tel. 26651). Add 10% to 15% to above prices. Summer rates slightly higher.
In Cobh: *Commodore* (Westbourne Place, Tel. 811277). Single $4, double $7; with breakfast; no pension. 10% service charge. Summer rates slightly higher.

In the immediate area of the Golf Course, there are the following hotels, from $3.50 up for bed and breakfast, some with private baths: *Ashbourne, Tullagreine, Silversprings.*

TOURIST ATTRACTIONS: Cork City and Cobh provide excellent shopping for Waterford glass, tweeds, other fabrics, especially Irish linen, and footwear. For the walker, a tour of Cork and its environs will prove rewarding, starting at St. Patrick Street. Twelve miles from the club is the Blarney Castle and famous Blarney Stone; Cobh has a lovely harbor, a cathedral and other sites worth a visit.

FOR FURTHER INFORMATION: Write to: Club Secretary, Cork Golf Club, Little Island, Co. Cork, Ireland. Telephone: Cork 821037.

Douglas Golf Club

The Douglas Golf Club lies near historic Cork City, only a short distance from Blarney and Cobh, a large port where trans-Atlantic ocean liners call. Although the course is flat, making it easy for those pulling caddie carts, it is situated on a high hill overlooking Cork City and Cork Harbor, providing a fine view of these areas. Douglas favors the long hitter, although the variety of its holes and approaches leaves much for the short driver. It is a well-rounded course and almost perfect for the visitor who plays an average game and is still looking for his golf legs. From here he can well move on to some of the tougher championship courses scattered around the country.

LOCATION: The club is 3 miles from Cork City, 2 from Cork Airport, 16 from Cobh. Shannon Airport is 82 miles N and Dublin is 164 NE. There is a regular bus service (every 20 minutes) from Cork City to within a mile of the entrance of the club; better is a taxi service from Cork City to the club—cost about $1.70. No train service.

OTHER INFORMATION: The course is open to nonmembers with the only limitation being that a visitor must play with a member on Sunday. The season lasts all year, with a professional on hand every day and even during the evenings in summertime. The most crowded time is the fall, with the summer relatively quiet. Practice ground is available.
Number of holes: 18. *Par:* 70. *Length:* 6270 yards.
Green fees: weekdays, $1.50; Saturdays the same; Sundays only with a member. *Lessons:* $3/hour. *Caddies:* normally available at $1.50/round but should be reserved a day or two ahead. *Golfing equipment and caddie carts:* clubs available by arrangement with the professional; carts $.35.

OTHER SPORTS FACILITIES: The course is within 5 to 10 miles of beaches for swimming and boating. The Royal Munster Yacht Club is 11 miles away, and there are many famous hunting grounds within easy reach of Cork City; there is also tennis and fishing (at Cobh).

View of Ireland's Killarney Golf Club, where you play close to the lake shore.

ACCOMMODATIONS: No living space in the club house, but restaurant and bar are available. Meals should be arranged in advance with the catering staff.

For hotels, see this section for the *Cork Golf Club* (Little Island), pp. 124-125.

TOURIST ATTRACTIONS: See this section for the *Cork Golf Club* (Little Island), p. 125.

FOR FURTHER INFORMATION: Write to: Club Secretary, Douglas Golf Club, Douglas, Co. Cork, Ireland.

Killarney Golf and Fishing Club

Justly considered one of the finest golf courses in Ireland, Killarney has as its background some of the most beautiful lakes and mountains in Europe. The course is undulating, though not hilly, and each of its holes presents completely different features, thereby making it suitable for the average as well as the superior golfer. Depending on his game, the visitor can use either the regular or the championship tees. In either case, there is plenty of length—half of the holes at or over 400 yards. Many holes are played along the lake—all natural and open golf—but as counterbalance there are the holes played near a hidden stream, or the short 6th and 18th, which seem to merge with the lake itself. Killarney is held in such high regard that it has been chosen as the site of several championship matches, such as the Irish Open Amateur Championship, the Walker Cup trials and the Home Internationals.

LOCATION: Killarney can be reached by car or train from all ports of entry. From Cork it is 56 miles W, from Shannon Airport 84 S, from Dublin 191 SW, from the town of Killarney 3 miles.

OTHER INFORMATION: The course is open to nonmembers, who may play at any time, the year round. The regular season is from May to October, with the professional available by arrangement. August and September are the busiest times, with decent weather to be expected during the entire regular season. Practice ground is available.
Number of holes: 18. *Par:* 72. *Length:* 6353 yards (medal play), 6741 yards (championship play).
Green fees: $2/day (less if you are introduced). *Lessons:* $2.25/hour. *Caddies:* $1.25/round. *Golfing equipment and caddie carts:* full set of clubs $1.25 (half set $.75); carts $.50.

OTHER SPORTS FACILITIES: This section is a mecca for the sportsminded. The Killarney area offers sea fishing (mackeral, bass, plaice, cod) for the pro and the amateur, shooting (wild duck, pheasant, pigeon), riding (at very nominal fees), tennis, climbing; in addition, there are sandy beaches for picnics, swimming and holiday outings. In the third week in July, Killarney celebrates a three-day holiday meeting for racing.

ACCOMMODATIONS: No living space in the club house, but restaurant and bar are available.
   In immediate area, virtually every kind of lodging, from luxury hotels to guest houses. In Killarney town (3 miles from the course): *Europe* (Tel. 300) and *Southern* (Tel. 262). Luxury hotels: singles $5 to $8.50, doubles $9.50 to $17; with breakfast. 10% service charge. Prices slightly higher during summer season. Private baths, central heating, baby-sitting, all meals by arrangement. *Cahernane* (Tel. 95). 28 rooms, 8 with private baths; singles from $4, doubles from $7; with breakfast; full pension from $35/ week. 10% service charge. Central heating. *Casterosse* (Tel. 144). 40 rooms with private baths; prices 10% to 20% higher than above. Central heating. *International* (Tel. 16). 120 rooms, 45 with private baths; same prices as *Casterosse.* No pension; central heating.
   There are numerous Grade B and C hotels, from $2.50/day, without private bath.
   For a brochure on accommodations, write for the Killarney Tourist Directory, Co. Kerry, Ireland.

TOURIST ATTRACTIONS: There are tours by car or on horseback of the famous lakes of Killarney; interesting ruins, castles, old villages. Also shopping for souvenirs, traditional Irish goods and other items at very reasonable prices.

FOR FURTHER INFORMATION: Write to: Club Secretary, Killarney Golf and Fishing Club, Killarney, Co. Kerry, Ireland.

Galway Golf Club

A visit to the Galway Golf Club can be a full vacation experience. In addition to the course, Galway County offers fine scenery and nearly every variety of tourist attraction. The course is of championship caliber and of inland texture. It is ideally suited to long drivers from the back tees, while short drivers will find it more attractive from the forward tees. The course strikes a good balance between 3-par short holes (200 yards and under) and 5-par long holes (over 450 yards), with most in the middle range of 350 to 450 yards. Many of the holes overlook beautiful Galway Bay and the popular seaside resort of Salthill.

LOCATION: The course is in Salthill, a suburb of Galway (1½ miles away), accessible by bus, train and car; the most convenient way is by car. Galway is 135 miles W of Dublin, 130 N of Cork, 59 N of Shannon Airport (75 minutes by coach), 56 W of Athlone.

OTHER INFORMATION: The course is open all year to nonmembers, who need only show membership in any golf club. The club professional and his assistant are in daily attendance. While the course remains playable all year, the best time is from the end of April to the end of October, with best weather to be expected in spring, summer and autumn. July and August are the most crowded times. Practice ground is available and has an illuminated driving range.

Number of holes: 18. *Par:* 70 (S.S.S., 71). *Length:* 6595 yards.

Green fees: weekdays, $1.40; weekends (June 1-Sept. 30), $2.10; $5.60/week; $8.40/two weeks; $11.20/month. *Lessons:* $1.40/hour. *Caddies:* not always available; should be requested in advance. *Golfing equipment and caddie carts:* clubs and bag $.85/round, carts $.25/round.

OTHER SPORTS FACILITIES: Since the course is in the heart of a coastal resort town, the visitor will find nearly every sports facility: tennis, sea swimming (a swimming pool for children), deep-sea fishing, angling in nearby lakes and river, even shark fishing, shooting (wild geese and duck), riding; and for the less active there is dancing.

ACCOMMODATIONS: No living space in the club house, but bars and light meals are available. Nearby Salthill has several restaurants.

In Salthill the following hotels offer comfortable accommodations, some with private bath (reserve far in advance): *Banba* (Tel. 2438). Single (with breakfast) at $3.50-$7, for a double; full pension, from $40/week. Prices about 20% higher during summer season. No central heating. *Eglinton* (Tel. 2025), *Rio* (Tel. 2439), and *Warwick* (Tel. 4325). Similar facilities at somewhat lower prices—about 10% less. Central heating at *Warwick* and *Eglinton*.

In Galway: The *Great Southern* (Tel. 4041). A luxury hotel with all the comforts, including private baths; singles $5 to $6.50, doubles $10 to $12.60, with breakfast. 10% service charge. No pension. Central heating; baby-sitting available.

TOURIST ATTRACTIONS: This section of western Ireland, called Connemara, is one of the most popular tourist regions, most famed for its scenic grandeur. For those who like to walk, the area offers a wealth of interesting excursions. For those who wish to climb, there are both rocks and hills. There are also bus and boat excursions, including one to the Aran Islands (2½ hours by steamer), famous for their magnificent ruggedness and lovely products (knitted wear). Galway offers several attractions: Church of St. Nicholas, the Spanish Arch, the Corrib Salmon, the Claddagh (an ancient fishing village), with Coole Park, Oughterard, Ballintubber Abbey, and Cong not too far away; also good shopping for Aran Island sweaters, Irish linen.

FOR FURTHER INFORMATION: Write to: Tourist Board, Eglinton Street, Galway, Co. Galway, Ireland or to: Club Secretary, Galway Golf Club, Salthill, Galway, Ireland. Telephone: Galway 2422.

Lahinch Golf Course

Lahinch Golf Course lies in a beautiful spot behind the sandy beach bordering on Liscannor Bay. On the edge of the Atlantic, the links is subject to sea winds, which may do strange things with your game; but nevertheless it favors the average player. Lahinch provides a natural course and is well known as the site of many championship matches, such as the South of Ireland Open Amateur Championship. The coastal scenery on both sides of the town makes the course an ideal site to visit as well as to play golf. It especially suits the visiting player who wants a course that challenges without discouraging him. Particularly exciting are the par-5 fifth and the par-3 6th. The latter involves a shot to an invisible green that lies between two large hills that must be carried.

LOCATION: Lahinch is 30 miles NW of Shannon Airport, by bus or car, 40 NW of Limerick, 160 W of Dublin. The nearest town is Ennistymon.

OTHER INFORMATION: The course is open to nonmembers all year, with visitors very welcome indeed. The professional is in daily attendance. There is no especially crowded time, and the weather generally holds good except for some strong winds. Practice ground is available.

Number of holes: 18 for championship course; 9 for new course. *Par:* 71 for championship course; 72 (twice around) for 9-hole course. *Length:* 6434 yards for championship course.

Green fees: weekdays, $1.50/day; weekends and holidays $2/day; $9/

week. Reduction for women. *Lessons:* $1.50/hour. *Caddies:* $1.25 to $1.50/round. *Golfing equipment and caddie carts:* clubs $.75, carts $.50.

OTHER SPORTS FACILITIES: Fishing for trout and salmon, shooting (rough), swimming west of Liscannor, tennis and boating. Particularly recommended are tours of the cliffs west of Liscannor, which rise 700 feet above the Atlantic.

ACCOMMODATIONS: No living space in the club, but restaurant and bar facilities are available to visitors.

In Lahinch: *Aberdeen Arms* (Tel. 20). Singles $4 to $6, doubles $8 to $10; with breakfast; full pension from $40/week. 10% service charge. Slightly higher during season. No private baths; baby-sitting.

In Lisdoonvarna: *Hydro* (Tel. 27). Singles from $3, doubles from $6; with breakfast. Other facilities as above.

In Ennistymon: *Falls* (Tel. 4). Singles from $3, doubles from $6; breakfast included. Other facilities as above.

In Ennis: *Old Ground* (Tel. 126). Prices as at *Hydro* in Lisdoonvarna. Private bathroom, central heating, baby-sitting.

TOURIST ATTRACTIONS: In nearby Ennistymon (2½ miles from Lahinch), there is swimming as well as movies and places of historic interest. Ten miles from Lahinch is Ireland's most famous spa, Lisdoonvarna, famous as a health resort and as a place where a holiday atmosphere prevails.

FOR FURTHER INFORMATION: Write to: Club Secretary, Lahinch Golf Club, Lahinch, Co. Clare, Ireland. Telephone: Lahinch 3.

Limerick Golf Club

The Limerick Golf Course is an excellent starter for the visitor who wishes to work his way up to the championship courses in Ireland (Royal Dublin, Killarney, Portmarnock) or for the player who intends to go on a golfing tour. It is also suitable for the average golfer or the golfer unsure of what to expect in a new country under different conditions. The course provides straightforward golf and is comparatively easy and flat. With good greens, not too narrow fairways and natural obstacles, Limerick is a good bet for a relaxing day or two. Furthermore, the course is only 17 miles from Shannon Airport and in Limerick City, the heart of a section known for its good accommodations.

LOCATION: Two miles from the center of Limerick City, the course is accessible by either bus or car. Limerick City is 123 miles SW of Dublin, 17 SE of Shannon Airport, and 24 NW of Tipperary. Galway is 64 miles N.

OTHER INFORMATION: The course is open, unlimited, all year to nonmembers. A professional is always on hand, with the most crowded months May and June. The best weather can be expected in May and August. Practice ground is available.

Number of holes: 18. *Par:* 71 (S.S.S., 69). *Length:* 6187 yards. *Green fees:* $1.10/day. *Lessons:* $1.50/½ hour. *Caddies:* $1.10/round; arrangements should be made ahead. *Golfing equipment and caddie carts:* full set of clubs for $1.25, carts $.25.

OTHER SPORTS FACILITIES: Tennis, fine hunting, trout fishing, a race course, riding, boating, water skiing, sailing; also greyhound racing on Monday, Friday and Saturday from February to November.

ACCOMMODATIONS: No living space in the club house, but restaurant and bar are available.

In Limerick, a city of good hotels, there are numerous accommodations, with prices generally below those in Dublin, Cork, Galway, or Belfast: *Intercontinental* (Ennis Road, Tel. 47266). A luxury hotel; singles $6 to $9, doubles $10 to $14.50; with breakfast; no pension. 10% service charge. Slightly higher during summer; central heating, private baths in every room, baby-sitting. *Ardhu House* (Ennis Road, Tel. 45811), *Royal George* (109/111 O'Connell Street, Tel. 44566), *Cruise's* (5/7 O'Connell Street, Tel. 44977), *Hanratty's* (Glentworth Street, Tel. 45627). Excellent hotels with private baths, central heating, baby-sitting facilities, at 10% to 20% less than for *Intercontinental*. *Glentworth* (Glentworth Street, Tel. 45031), *National* (Baker Place, Tel. 44672), *Shannon Arms* (93 Henry Street, Tel. 46855), *Cecil* (Cecil Street, Tel. 44094). Singles from $4, doubles from $7.50; with breakfast. No private baths.

In addition there is a "bed bureau," an organization that will find you lodgings. Apply either by mail or in person.

TOURIST ATTRACTIONS: One of the oldest cities in the British Isles, Limerick had its charter 12 years before London. It is steeped in tradition, with churches, monuments, old buildings. In addition, the visitor may be interested in purchasing Limerick lace and cured hams and bacon. The club will arrange a "Hooley" for parties of 15 or 20, an evening of social entertainment in which a good time is guaranteed.

FOR FURTHER INFORMATION: Write to: Club Secretary, Limerick Golf Club, Ballyclough, Co. Limerick, Ireland. Telephone: 44083.

Balmoral Golf Club Ltd.

Along with Belvoir Park and Royal County Down, Balmoral forms part of a trio of excellent courses ringing Belfast—a quartet, if the somewhat more distant Royal Portrush is counted. They give the visitor a choice of parkland courses and seaside links, each the best of its type. Balmoral is parkland, with luxurious greens that have a particularly high reputation among British golfers. While Balmoral is not particularly long at 6100 yards, several holes give the power hitter plenty of opportunity. This is a well-balanced course and, like Belvoir, a pleasant holiday experience for the average as well as the seasoned player.

LOCATION: The course is accessible by car or bus from Belfast, two miles away. It is just off the main route from Dublin to Belfast. Dublin is 106 miles S.

OTHER INFORMATION: The course is open and playable all year, and nonmembers are most welcome; the sole requirement is that the visitor show proof of membership in a recognized golf club. The professional is in daily attendance. Most crowded time is April through June— very busy—and it is a good idea to reserve the green. Best weather is April through October. Practice ground is available.

Number of holes: 18. *Par:* 69. *Length:* 6100 yards.

Green fees: weekdays, $1.40; weekends and holidays, $2.80/day; $7/ week. Half price for women. *Lessons:* $1.75/½ hour. *Caddies:* available on weekends only at $1.40/round. *Golfing equipment and caddie carts:* limited number of clubs for rent at $.70/set; carts $.28/round.

OTHER SPORTS FACILITIES: All the water sports: swimming, diving, fine beaches, boating, fishing; also tennis, bowling, riding. This is a fine area for the active sportsman.

ACCOMMODATIONS: No living space in the club house, but excellent restaurant and bar are available every day.

For hotels in Belfast, see this section for the *Royal Portrush Golf Club,* p. 135.

TOURIST ATTRACTIONS: For details, see this section for *Belvoir Park Golf Club,* p. 133.

FOR FURTHER INFORMATION: Write to: Club Secretary, Balmoral Golf Club, Belfast, Northern Ireland. Telephone: 668514 Belfast.

Belvoir Park Golf Club

While Belvoir cannot compete in terms of toughness and championship caliber with Portrush and Down, it is nevertheless a fine parkland course in its own right. Furthermore, it is advantageously situated very close to Belfast, so you can combine good golf with a pleasant city stay. Belvoir has its own type of scenic beauty; trees surround the course, and from the front of the club house one has a sweeping view of the mountains and the nestled city of Belfast, lying as though in an amphitheater. Lacking special eccentricities, Belvoir requires solid, careful golf. Its length is not so great that the short driver is penalized, and its fairways are not so narrow or its approaches so testing that the power hitter will suffer. There is good over-all balance with 5 par 3s, 5 par 5s, which except for the 15th are not excessively long. The 4s are in the legitimate range of 350 to 400 yards. All in all, this is a very pleasant holiday course—demanding enough to challenge your game but not so demanding that it ruins your stay.

LOCATION: The course is 3 miles from Belfast and accessible by bus (regular city service) or car. Belfast is 106 miles N of Dublin.

OTHER INFORMATION: The course is open to nonmembers all year with no limitations. The professional is in daily attendance. The most crowded time is during the spring and summer, when the best weather can be expected (usually spring and late summer or early autumn). Practice ground is available.
Number of holes: 18. *Par:* 72 (S.S.S.). *Length:* 6328 yards.
Green fees: weekdays, $.85; weekends and holidays, $1.75/day. *Lessons:* $2.80/hour. *Caddies:* $1.75 and up/18 holes. *Golfing equipment and caddie carts:* by arrangement with the professional.

OTHER SPORTS FACILITIES: Belfast is close to the water, so the visitor will find all types of water sports: good sandy beaches, boating, fishing, swimming and diving; also tennis, bowling, riding.

ACCOMMODATIONS: No living space in the club house, but bar and restaurant are available.
For hotels in Belfast, see this section for the *Royal Portrush Golf Club,* p. 135.

TOURIST ATTRACTIONS: As the capital of Northern Ireland, Belfast is a lively city with good shopping, pleasant parks and numerous public buildings worth seeing (including the Municipal Museum and Art Gallery). The environs of Belfast are especially lovely, for the blight of cities has not yet ruined the countryside. The coast route from Belfast, either north or south, is particularly recommended. All through this area, including Newcastle in the south and Bangor in the north, are popular holiday resorts, with a great variety of entertainment: beaches by day and good dining and dancing at night.

FOR FURTHER INFORMATION: Write to: Club Secretary, Belvoir Park Golf Club, Newtownbreda, Belfast 8, Northern Ireland. Telephone: Belfast 6411591.

Royal County Down Golf Club

Although not so well known to visitors as Royal Portrush, County Down compares favorably with that great links. This, too, is seaside golf of championship caliber, with great length, great scenic beauty and great natural hazards. The view of hills and sea alone would make the visit worthwhile, but this added to the game makes an unbeatable combination. A course of famous holes, like the sharply doglegged 5th and the much-copied 13th, Down also has balance. Its almost 7000 yards require plenty of strength, but the testing quality of most of the holes is still precision. The par 5s (5 of them) are balanced by 4 interesting par 3s, each of which may appear easy and then prove heartbreaking. Another attractive feature is a Number 2 course for the holiday player who finds the championship links too tough. Try Number 2, but be sure to play Royal Down's best before you leave.

LOCATION: The course is accessible by car from Newcastle, which is the closest railway station. Newcastle is 31 miles S of Belfast, 75 miles N of Dublin.

OTHER INFORMATION: The course is open all year, weather permitting, with visitors allowed to play unrestricted except during the tournament season. Women must be accompanied by a man to enter the club house and may not enter at all on Saturdays. The professional is in daily attendance. Most crowded time is weekends during spring and summer, with the best weather usually in spring and fall.
    Number of holes: 18. *Par:* 72 (S.S.S., 72). *Length:* 6952 yards.
    Green fees: weekdays, $1.05; weekends, $1.75/day (reduced fee after 5 P.M. and for No. 2 course). *Lessons:* by arrangement with the professional, about $2.80/hour. *Caddies:* $1.75/18 holes. *Golfing equipment and caddie carts:* by arrangement with the professional.

OTHER SPORTS FACILITIES: The visitor will find all types of water sports: swimming from sandy beaches, diving, fishing, water skiing, boating, yachting; also tennis, bowling.

ACCOMMODATIONS: No living space in the club house, but bar and restaurant are available. Order meals in the morning, however. Hotels in Belfast are excellent, and if you wish to stay there, see this section for the *Royal Portrush Golf Club,* p. 135.
    In Newcastle: the *Arkeen* (Tel. 3173). Small but comfortable, singles $3.50 to $4.50, doubles from $7.25; with breakfast; full pension from $28/week. No private baths, but one public bath for each two rooms; no central heating. *The Slieve Donard* (Tel. 3291). Singles from $6.50, doubles from $12.50; with breakfast; full pension from $28/week. A few rooms with private baths; no central heating.

TOURIST ATTRACTIONS: For Belfast and the general area, see this section for the *Belvoir Park Golf Club,* p. 133.

FOR FURTHER INFORMATION: Write to: Club Secretary, Royal County Down Golf Club, Newcastle, County Down, Northern Ireland. Telephone: Newcastle 2209.

The Royal Portrush Golf Club

This famous golf course is a seaside links, situated close to a popular resort, Portrush, which is washed on three sides by the Atlantic. Royal

Portrush has been the site of many championship matches and has, through the years, become especially popular for ladies' golf. The course is laid out in a remarkable stretch of natural golfing country, including dunes that often take on two or three distinct levels. The championship links looks out on the sea from all but a few of its holes through a tangle of hills. This very long course, with 13 holes at or over 400 yards, tests the first-class golfer who counts on precision without discouraging the medium handicap player. But precision is really the key; the fairways are tight, the greens are full of deceptive slopes, the roughs are potential nightmares.

The Valley Course, somewhat shorter and less difficult (fewer bunkers, for example), is more sheltered and has become quite popular with golfers who wish to work up to championship caliber.

LOCATION: The course is 1 mile from the railway station of Portrush, 6 miles N of Coleraine, 38 miles NE of Londonderry, 61 N of Belfast. Portrush is accessible by bus or train and by car or taxi to the course.

OTHER INFORMATION: The course is open, unlimited, to visitors, all year. The professional is always on hand. The most crowded time is July and August, with the best weather expected in spring and early fall. Practice ground is available.

Number of holes: Dunluce (championship) Course, 18; Valley Course, 18; Short Course, 9. *Par:* Dunluce, 73; Valley, 68. *Length:* Dunluce, 6809 yards (up to 6842 yards); Valley, 6207 yards (up to 6641 yards); (For women, Dunluce, 6094 yards; Valley, 5894 yards).

Green fees: Dunluce: weekdays, $1.40; weekends and holidays, $2.80/day, $6.30/week, $10.50/two weeks. Valley: about half the above fees (also evening rates $.56 for weekdays, $.70 for weekends and holidays after 4:30 P.M.). *Lessons:* $2.10/½ hour. *Caddies:* $1.75/round. *Golfing equipment and caddie carts:* clubs $.70/round, carts $.28/round.

OTHER SPORTS FACILITIES: This is a holiday-conscious area, with facilities for every kind of recreation and hobby: tennis, bowling, yachting, boating, swimming, diving, fishing; also plenty of good golf courses.

ACCOMMODATIONS: No living space in the club house, but bar and restaurant are available nearby.

Belfast offers all kinds of lodgings, from luxury hotels to boarding houses and apartments. The following hotels all offer excellent accommodations, private bath, central heating, experienced staffs; include breakfast in the price and add 10% service charge: *Grand Central* (18 Royal Avenue, Tel. 21001). Singles from $7, doubles from $14; no pension. *International* (Donegall Square South, Tel. 20661). Singles from $4.50, doubles from $8.50; no pension. *Midland* (Whitla Street, Tel. 745251). Singles from $8, doubles from $15.50; no pension. *Royal Avenue* (23 Royal Avenue, Tel. 26611). Singles from $6.50, doubles from $11.50; no pension.

TOURIST ATTRACTIONS: Although Belfast (61 miles) is excellent for shopping and rich in historical sites, the visitor who heads north toward Portrush will find more than enough to interest him: from Dunluce and

Dunseverisk Castles to the Giant's Causeway (many-sided columns caused by lava formations), to lovely promontories and inlets. Scenically and culturally, the area is rich in rewards: theater companies and concert tours join with dance halls, movies and an amusement park to cater to every taste.

FOR FURTHER INFORMATION: Write to: Club Secretary, Royal Portrush Golf Club, Co. Antrim, Ireland. Telephone: Portrush 2311.

FRANCE

Wherever you choose to tour or vacation in France, you will find first-rate golf courses. And in the most popular places, like Paris and its elegant suburbs, there are fully nine courses of varying degrees of difficulty. Five of these are for the average golfer, the others for the more experienced player who is ready for championship golf.

On the Riviera (the Côte d'Azur) three courses of average difficulty in spectacular surroundings await you. The links overlooking Monte Carlo is possibly the most beautiful in all France, perhaps in all Europe.

If you are in the north, try the famous cathedral city of Reims, which is also excellent for touring World War I battle sites. In the south-central part, near the Spanish border, there is the rewarding city of Toulouse. Marseilles offers a course with a rich background in an area noted for its historical interest. The Lyons course, just west of the Alps, is of championship caliber, and in addition you are in one of the most famous restaurant areas of France.

If you want a seaside vacation on the Normandy coast, the two courses in Deauville and Le Havre will give you immediate access to fine beaches and fine golf. (Start with Le Havre; Deauville is more difficult.) The same holds true for Biarritz—a famous resort, a good links and superb beaches and swimming.

For those who like vacations in a region with a sports background, Megève and Le Mans are a must—Megève with its fine skiing, Le Mans with its well-known car racing.

Near big cities, in sports areas, at seaside resorts, north, south, east, west and center—France has courses in virtually every geographical location to accommodate the visitor.

Let me suggest a little tour of the nine Paris courses, which ring the city within a radius of 25 miles, most within 10 to 12 miles. Start with one of the following: *Ozoir, Racing-Club, Fourqueux, St. Cloud, Morfontaine;* then move on to either *Saint-Nom-la-Breteche, Saint-Germain-en-Laye* or *Marly;* and finish your tour with *Chantilly,* which I consider the most difficult of the Parisian courses. After this, you'll be ready for any French links.

Golf de Chantilly

The Golf Club is a short distance north of Paris, near the famous forest, ponds and streams of Chantilly. The town is small and old, dating back to the Renaissance, and is well known throughout Europe for its racing course and magnificent Château, which houses the Condé Museum featuring paintings from most schools and periods. Like so many other French courses, this one combines a superb location with good golf. The course is possibly one of the best in Europe and the biggest test for long drivers in France. Its length, nearly 6800 yards, places it in the championship class with similar courses in Scotland and England. Tough and challenging, it demands accurate play as well as careful, precise putting. Possibly some practice on less challenging European courses should precede your play here. But don't miss it.

French Government Tourist Office

The Golf de Chantilly, just 25 miles north of Paris, is a particularly challenging course.

LOCATION: 25 miles N of Paris. The course is easily accessible by train from Gare du Nord (northern railroad station in Paris) or by car (route N 16).

OTHER INFORMATION: The course is open to nonmembers for the entire year, with a professional always on hand. Most crowded months are May and June, with weather best from May to October. Practice ground is available.

Number of holes: A, 18; B, 9. *Par:* A, 71; B, 35. *Length:* A, 6750 yards; B, 2900 yards.

Green fees: weekdays, $3; Saturdays, $7; Sundays and holidays, $9. *Lessons:* $6/hour. *Caddies:* $3/18 holes. *Golfing equipment and caddie carts:* only caddie carts for rent at $1/day.

OTHER SPORTS FACILITIES: Riding.

ACCOMMODATIONS: No living space in the club house, but restaurant and bar are available.

In Gouvieux (3 miles from Chantilly): *Château de la Tour* (Tel. Chantilly 7.39). A good, comfortable, quiet hotel situated in a park, lovely view, open all year. Rooms from $5.50 for a single to $9.50 for the best double with private bath; central heating; taxes and services not included.

In Toutevoie (4 miles from Chantilly): *Pavillon St-Hubert* (Tel. Chantilly 7.04). A good comfortable, quiet hotel with a pleasant view, open all year. Room from $5 for a single to $11 for the best double with private bath and shower; central heating; full pension from $8/day; services and taxes not included.

In Chantilly: *Angleterre* (4 Place O.-Vallon, Tel. Chantilly 0.59). A plain, comfortable hotel, open all year. Rooms from $3 for a single to $6 for the best double with bath and shower for general use; central heating; full pension from $6.50/day; services and taxes included.

TOURIST ATTRACTIONS: This area is noted for its many streams and small lakes and its magnificent Renaissance castle. It also has a famous race-track. Nearby Senlis has an old quarter dating back to the Renaissance, full of narrow streets and ancient houses; and its Cathedral a good example of Gothic architecture, is well worth a visit. The Château Royal has the only hunting museum in Europe.

FOR FURTHER INFORMATION: Write to: Secretary of Golf de Chantilly, Vineuil (Oise), Chantilly, France. Telephone: Chantilly 443 and 1358.

Golf Club de Fourqueux

The Golf Club de Fourqueux, on the western outskirts of Paris in the elegant resort area of Saint-Germain-en-Laye, is situated near the foundation of a twelfth-century castle built by Louis the Fat to protect the Seine valley. Close by and still intact is the room where Louis XIV, the "Sun King," was born. A more luxurious background for golf can hardly be found. The course itself is hilly, of medium difficulty and requires accurate driving and putting. It is made for long as well as short drivers, although the length of some of the holes favors the power hitter. The fairways and greens are always beautifully kept, as one would expect in such surroundings.

LOCATION: The course is about 10 miles west of Paris and 1½ miles from St-Germain-en-Laye; it is accessible by car.

OTHER INFORMATION: The course is open to nonmembers for the entire year, with two professionals always on hand. Practice ground is available.

Number of holes: 18. *Par:* 74. *Length:* 6000 yards.

Green fees: weekdays, $3; weekends, $5/day. *Lessons:* $3.50/half hour. *Caddies:* $3.50/18 holes. *Golfing equipment and caddie carts:* only caddie carts for rent at $1/day.

OTHER SPORTS FACILITIES: Tennis.

ACCOMMODATIONS: No living space in the club house, but restaurant and bar are available. For accommodations, see this section under *Golf de Saint-Nom-La-Bretèche,* pp. 144-145.

TOURIST ATTRACTIONS: See this section under *Golf de Saint-Nom-La-Bretèche*, p. 145, and of course there is Paris, only 10 miles away.

FOR FURTHER INFORMATION: Write to: Secretary of the Golf Club de Fourqueux, 8, rue de Saint-Nom, Fourqueux (S. & O.), France. Telephone: 963.41.47.

Marly-Country-Club

In the heart of the famous Saint-Germain-en-Laye resort area in the outskirts of Paris, the Marly Country Club golf course is interesting but difficult. It favors the short hitter and calls for accurate driving. The approaches to the fairways are good and well defended, with all hazards clearly marked. The relative shortness of the course should not fool you into thinking it is too easy; there are plenty of testing shots even for the expert. And if your game is not up to standard, there is always Saint-Germain itself—relaxing and luxurious.

LOCATION: In Port-Marly, about 12 miles W of Paris. Easily accessible by car and bus (take bus No. 258 from Pont de Neuilly in Paris). Saint-Germain-en-Laye is 2 miles north of Port-Marly.

OTHER INFORMATION: The course is open to nonmembers for the entire year, with a professional always on hand. Most crowded time is Saturdays and Sundays, with best weather from June to September. Practice ground is available.
Number of holes: 18. *Par:* 65. *Length:* 5580 yards.
Green fees: weekdays, $3.50; Saturdays, Sundays, holidays, $7.50/day.
Lessons: $3/half hour; $5/an hour. *Caddies:* $2/9 holes; $3/18 holes.
Golfing equipment and caddie carts: clubs $3/day, carts $.50/day.

OTHER SPORTS FACILITIES: None.

ACCOMMODATIONS: No living space in the club house, but restaurant and bar available. For accommodations see this section under *Golf de Saint-Nom-la-Bretèche*, pp. 144-145.

TOURIST ATTRACTIONS: See this section under *Golf de Saint-Nom-la-Bretèche*, p. 145.

FOR FURTHER INFORMATION: Write to: Secretary, Marly-Country-Club, Port-Marly (Seine-et-Oise), France. Telephone: 963.0312.

Golf Club de Morfontaine

The Golf Club de Morfontaine is in the western part of the Forest of Ermenonville, a wild and haunting forest landscaped by the Marquis René

Louis de Girardin, an apostle and close friend of Jean Jacques Rousseau. A disciple of Romanticism, the Marquis filled the area with false ruins, long winding roads and melancholy paths, all designed to stir the heart and the imagination. It is indeed a strange background for a golf course. The course itself is charming and pleasant, with pines, birches and heather everywhere in sight. Although it is a lengthy course—nearly 6500 yards— and appears to favor the long driver, it should not discourage the short one. There are enough testing approaches and tough tee shots to make a difference. It has good fairways and greens and is of average difficulty.

LOCATION: The course is about 25 miles N of Paris, 7 miles S of Senlis, and 9 miles E of Chantilly. Best way to get there is by car by way of La Porte de la Villette, Le Bourget and Pontarmé (N17).

OTHER INFORMATION: The course is open to nonmembers on weekdays only; the most crowded months are April, May, June, October, November, with the weather best from May through September. Practice ground is available.
Number of holes: 18. *Par:* 72. *Length:* 6425 yards.
Green fees: weekday, $5.50; weekend, $13/day. *Lessons:* $7/hour. *Caddies:* $3.50/18 holes. *Golfing equipment and caddie carts:* none for rent.

OTHER SPORTS FACILITIES: None.

ACCOMMODATIONS: No living space in the club house, but restaurant and bar are available.
In Senlis: *Grand Cerf* (rue République, Tel. 1.11). A good, comfortable hotel, open all year. Rooms from $4 for a single to $7.50 for the best double, with central heating and private bath; taxes and services not included.
In Chantilly: See accommodations under *Golf de Chantilly,* pp. 139-140.

TOURIST ATTRACTIONS: See this section under *Golf de Chantilly,* p. 140.

FOR FURTHER INFORMATION: Write to: Director, Golf de Mortefontaine, par Mortefontaine (Oise), France. Telephone: Mortefontaine 5.

Golf Club D'Ozoir-la-Ferrière

Here is a pleasant flat course between the Bois Notre-Dame and the Forest of Armainvilliers; it is one of the best on the eastern outskirts of Paris. It is made for long as well as short drivers, with a slight edge to the long driver. There should be no great difficulties here for the average golfer, although the variety of the fairways, bunkering and greens should prove challenging. There is also a somewhat shorter course for women— about 500 yards less. This is, in all, a course that will not discourage you and one that, at the same time, will give you a good feel of a European links.

LOCATION: About 20 miles east of Paris. Best way to get there is by car (N4).

OTHER INFORMATION: The course is open all year, but nonmembers may play only on weekdays. A professional is always on hand. The most crowded months are May, June, September. Practice ground is available. *Number of holes:* 18. *Par:* 71. *Length:* 6160 yards. *Green fees:* weekdays, $5; weekends, $11/day. *Lessons:* $5/half hour. *Caddies:* $3.50/18 holes. *Golfing equipment and caddie carts:* only carts for rent at $2/day.

OTHER SPORTS FACILITIES: None.

ACCOMMODATIONS: No living space in the club house. It is best to live in Paris and drive out to use the course. The club has a restaurant and bar.

TOURIST ATTRACTIONS: Paris is the chief attraction.

FOR FURTHER INFORMATION: Write to: Manager of the Golf Club D'Ozoir, Château des Agneaux, Ozoir-la-Ferrière (Seine-et-Marne). Telephone: 79 Ozoir.

Golf du Racing-Club de France à La Boulie (Versailles)

One of the best and most attractive clubs in France, the Golf du Racing-Club de France favors the long hitter (longest hole about 530 yards and many others near 500 yards) but should by no means discourage the short driver. Many of the holes are just over 200 yards, including the very short 2nd, 6th and 15th. The approaches to the fairways are good, and all hazards are clearly marked. The course should present no difficulties to the seasoned golfer. The less expert player can golf from the front tees, a difference on many holes of 50 to 75 yards. The club has the added advantage of being just outside of Versailles, so you can combine good golf with a visit to the palace—a fabulous, magnificent creation of French royalty at the height of its pomp and glory, with the famous gardens and the small pavilions.

LOCATIONS: The course is about 13 miles W of Paris. It is easily accessible by car (take auto-route West) and train (station stop: Versailles-Chantiers).

OTHER INFORMATION: The course is open to nonmembers for the entire year, with five professionals always on hand. The most crowded months are June, July, September; the weather best from June to September. Practice ground is available. *Number of holes:* 18. *Par:* 72 (S.S.S., 74). *Length:* 6426 yards. *Green fees:* weekdays, $5; weekends, $11/day. *Lessons:* $4.50/half hour.

Caddies: $3/18 holes. *Golfing equipment and caddie carts:* clubs $3.50/ day, carts $.50/day.

OTHER SPORTS FACILITIES: Tennis.

ACCOMMODATIONS: No living space in the club house, but restaurant and bar are available. See accommodations under *Golf de Saint-Nom-la-Bretèche,* pp. 144-145.

TOURIST ATTRACTIONS: See this section under *Golf de Saint-Nom-la-Bretèche,* p. 145.

FOR FURTHER INFORMATION: Write to: Secretary of Golf du Racing-Club de France, La Boulie (près Versailles), France. Telephone: 950.59.41.

Golf de Saint-Nom-la-Bretèche

On the outskirts of the famous forest and château country southwest of Paris, the Golf Club of Saint-Nom-la-Bretèche has two championship courses, the Red and the Blue. Both are a must for long hitters, but they may create difficulties for the short driver. Not only the length but also the narrow fairways, sharp doglegs and natural barriers will prove challenging. These are both medium-to-difficult courses, and you might find it better to tune up on less demanding French links first. In 1963 Jack Nicklaus established the record for the Red Course with a 6-under-par 66.

LOCATION: The course is in Saint-Nom-la-Bretèche, 19 miles W of Paris, 5 miles SW of St-Germain-en-Laye, 8 miles NW of Versailles. It is accessible by car (use the West Highway).

OTHER INFORMATION: The course is open to nonmembers, with four professionals always on hand. Most crowded months are May, June, September and October; the weather is best May-October. Practice ground is available with 50 balls for $.50.
Number of holes: Red, 18; Blue, 18. *Par:* Red, 72; Blue, 73. *Length:* Red, 6713 yards; Blue, 6684 yards.
Green fees: weekdays, $5; Saturdays, Sundays, holidays, $10. *Lessons:* $4/half hour. *Caddies:* $4/18 holes; $2.50/9 holes. *Golfing equipment and caddie carts:* clubs $7/day, carts $1/day.

OTHER SPORTS FACILITIES: Tennis.

ACCOMMODATIONS: No living space in the club house, but restaurant and bar available.
In Saint-Germain-en-Laye (about 4 miles from the golf course): *Pavillon Henri IV* (21 rue Thiers, Tel. 963.20.66). One of the best and loveliest hotels of its kind in the Paris area, open from March through November.

Rooms from $15 for a single to $40 for the best double, with private bath, central heating; full pension from $25/day; taxes and services not included. *Pavillon d'Estrées* (1 rue Arcades, Tel. 963.20.83). A good, comfortable hotel, open all year. Rooms from $8 for a single to $20 for the best double, with private bath, central heating; full pension from $14/day; taxes and services included.

In Versailles (about 7 miles from the golf course): *Trianon Palace* (1 blvd. Reine, Tel. 950.34.12). A first-class hotel in a lovely park, quiet and secluded, open all year. Rooms from $11 for a single to $21 for the best double with private bath; central heating; services and taxes not included. *Royal* (3 rue Pétigny, Tel. 950.03.51). A good, comfortable hotel, open all year. Rooms from $5.50 for a single to $12.50 for the best double with private bath; central heating, continental breakfast; services and taxes included. *St-Louis* (28 rue St-Louis, Tel. 950.23.55). A simple, comfortable hotel, open all year. Rooms from $3.50 for a single to $7.50 for best double, with private shower; central heating; services and taxes included.

TOURIST ATTRACTIONS: The area is famous for its attractions. Saint-Germain-en-Laye is an elegant country resort noted for its forest, château, terrace and the centuries-old lime trees. There is also a fine English garden. Versailles is a veritable grand tour of French history from the sixteenth to the twentieth century. Don't miss the château, the formal gardens, trianons and the night festivals from July to September on the first Sunday of each month. And, of course, 15 miles away there is Paris.

FOR FURTHER INFORMATION: Write to: Director, Golf Club de Saint-Nom-la-Bretèche, Seine-et-Oise, France. Telephone: 923.50.80.

Golf de Saint-Cloud

Set in a lovely forest in the Buzenval Park and surrounded by chestnut and oak trees, the Golf Club de Saint-Cloud is one of the best in the outskirts of Paris. The golfer has two courses to choose from, both challenging, but because of their well-defined fairways they present no great difficulties to the long accurate driver. Although all hazards can be clearly seen, one of the major difficulties of the course is its slopes, which seem to defy accurate judgment. The Saint-Cloud area is one of the loveliest outskirts of Paris, with woods, small lakes and pleasant open fields.

LOCATION: The course is in Garches, 9 miles W of Paris and 2 miles from Saint-Cloud. It is accessible by car.

OTHER INFORMATION: The course is open to nonmembers, limited, for the entire year, with a professional always on hand. Most crowded season is June through September with best weather in the summer. Practice ground is available.

Number of holes: Green, 18; Yellow, 18; *Par:* Green, 72; Yellow, 68.
Length: Green, 6592 yards; Yellow, 5477 yards.

French Government Tourist Office

The pleasant scenery of the Golf de Saint-Cloud, which includes some tricky slopes.

Green fees: weekdays, $7; weekends, $16/day. *Lessons:* $4/half hour. *Caddies:* $4/18 holes. *Golfing equipment and caddie carts:* clubs $3.50/day, carts $.50/day.

OTHER SPORTS FACILITIES: Tennis. Paris, of course, offers every type of sports facility.

ACCOMMODATIONS: No living space in the club house, but restaurant and bar available. Nearest accommodations are in Paris.

TOURIST ATTRACTIONS: The attractions of Paris need no description. For a short and excellent guide, however, see the English editions of *Michelin Green Guide to Paris.*

FOR FURTHER INFORMATION: Write to: Secretary of Golf de Saint-Cloud, Garches (Seine-et-Oise), France. Telephone: 970.22.83.

Golf de Saint-Germain-en-Laye

In one of the most elegant resorts in the outskirts of Paris, near the famous Château and forest of Saint-Germain-en-Laye, this course should please both the long driver (the longest hole is about 550 yards) and the short driver (many holes are under 200 yards). All hazards are clearly defined, and the rules of St. Andrews are strictly enforced. This is not an easy course, as you will see from the several par-5 holes, the well-guarded greens and the testing quality of many of the holes. But if you are in the Paris area and want to play at a course that has an international reputation, then the Golf de Saint-Germain-en-Laye is a must.

LOCATION: The course is about 14 miles W of Paris, 8 miles N of Versailles, and 2 from Saint-Germain-en-Laye. It is easily accessible by car (take auto-route West from Port Maillot) or train (from Gare St. Lazare).

OTHER INFORMATION: The course is open all year, but to nonmembers on weekdays only, with a professional on hand every day except Monday. May, June and October are the most crowded months; the weather is best from May to October. Practice ground is available.
Number of holes: 18. *Par:* 72 (S.S.S., 73). *Length:* 6305 yards.
Green fees: weekdays, $5; Saturdays, Sundays, holidays, $11. *Lessons:* $3.50/half hour. *Caddies:* $3.50/18 holes. *Golfing equipment and caddie carts:* clubs $3/day.

OTHER SPORTS FACILITIES: Tennis.

ACCOMMODATIONS: No living space in the club house, but restaurant and bar available. See accommodations under *Golf de Saint-Nom-la-Bretèche*, pp. 144-145.

TOURIST ATTRACTIONS: See this section under *Golf de Saint-Nom-la-Bretèche*, p. 145.

FOR FURTHER INFORMATION: Write to: Secretariat du Golf de Saint-Germain-en-Laye, (Seine-et-Oise) France. Telephone: 963-0590 and 963-0591.

Golf Club d'Hossegor

The Hossegor Golf Club is on the southwest coast of France in the small, pleasant resort town of Hossegor, just north of Biarritz. The area is noted for its villas, beaches and a famous salt-water lake surrounded by pine forests. Hossegor is of average difficulty, flat and made for long as well as short drivers, although its length is considerable for a European course. It is of medium difficulty and not discouraging to the visitor. If you want to combine a seaside vacation with good golf, then this is your course.

LOCATION: The course is in Hossegor, about 15 miles N of Biarritz, 112 miles SW of Bordeaux, 462 miles W of Marseille, 458 miles SW of Paris. It is accessible by car.

OTHER INFORMATION: The course is open to nonmembers, unlimited, for the entire year, with a professional on hand April through October. The most most crowded months are July, August, September; the weather is best from May to October. Practice ground is available. *Number of holes:* 18. *Par:* 72. *Length:* 6348 yards. *Green fees:* weekdays, $5. *Lessons:* $4/half hour. *Caddies:* $2.50/18 holes. *Golfing equipment and caddie carts:* clubs $2.50/day, carts $.50/day.

OTHER SPORTS FACILITIES: Water skiing, tennis, riding, fishing.

ACCOMMODATIONS: No living space in the club house, but restaurant and bar are available.
In Hossegor: *Mercédès* (Hossegor, Tel. 12.23). A very good, comfortable, modern hotel, open June through September. Rooms from $5 for best single to $11 for best double; private baths, central heating; full pension from $10/day; taxes and services included. *Parc* (av. Touring-Club, Tel. 0.14). A very good, comfortable hotel, open April to September. Rooms from $4 for best single to $12 for best double; private baths, central heating; full pension from $11/day; taxes and services included.

TOURIST ATTRACTIONS: Especially recommended are walks along the beach, excursions to neighboring seaside villages and, of course, all the attractions of Biarritz (gambling) casino, nightclubs, museums, vast beaches and salt-water springs. For the visitor who wishes to travel, the proximity to Spain is a particular recommendation; there are regular excursions to San Sebastian, for example.

FOR FURTHER INFORMATION: Write to: Secretary, Golf Club d'Hossegor, Hossegor (Landes), France. Telephone 0.59.

Golf Club de Wimereux

In the heart of the great resort areas of northwest France, the Wimereux Golf Course is set against a background of the sea, picturesque and cool. While the course is a paradise for the longer driver (with many holes over 500 yards), it should not discourage the short driver, who will find several holes to his liking (the shortest being 160 yards). The course, therefore, is of medium difficulty, presenting only a few clearly marked hazards. It is an interesting course and gains from its location in a favorable area; it is accessible to the sea and to England as well as to the French heartland.

LOCATION: About 155 miles N of Paris, Wimereux is on the northwest coast of France, on the sea, easily accessible by bus, train or car (Route N1). It is 200 miles S of Calais and only 4 miles N of Boulogne-sur-Mer; the trip across the Channel from Folkestone, England, takes 1½ hours.

OTHER INFORMATION: The course is open to nonmembers, unlimited, for the entire year, with a professional always on hand. Most crowded season is July and August, with the best weather in June and September. Practice ground is available. *Number of holes:* 18. *Par:* 74. *Length:* 7000 yards. *Green fees:* weekdays, $5/day. *Lessons:* $3/half hour. *Caddies:* $3/18 holes. *Golfing equipment and caddie carts:* clubs $3/day, carts $.50/day.

OTHER SPORTS FACILITIES: Swimming, tennis and yachting.

ACCOMMODATIONS: No living space in the club house, but restaurant and bar are available.
In Wimereux: *The Belle-Vue* (2 quai de Vimille, Tel. 32.42.03). A good, comfortable hotel, open Easter to end of September. Rooms from $3 for a single to $7 for the best double with private bath; central heating; full pension from $5.50/day; taxes and services included. *Centre* (78 rue Carnot, Tel. 32.41.08). Plain but comfortable hotel, open Feb. 15 to Nov. 15. Rooms from $2.50 for a single to $3.50 for a double; central heating, bathroom for general use on each floor; full pension $5 to $6/day; taxes and services included.

TOURIST ATTRACTIONS: This area is rich in varied entertainment: dancing, bowling, gambling casino, tennis, concerts, walking tours along the sea and to historic sites, weekly or monthly festivities.

FOR FURTHER INFORMATION: Write to: Secretary of the Golf Club de Wimereux, Route d'Ambleteuse, Wimereux (Pas-de-Calais), France. Telephone: 32.43.20 Wimereux.

Cannes Country Club

On the outskirts of Cannes, a town once described by Napoleon as a "paradise," and set against a background of small villages perched on strong hills, the Cannes Country Club is one of the most attractive in France. The area is a perfect blend of air, sea, sky and earth, with soft nights and clear sunny days. The course is fairly lengthy and suitable for long as well as short drivers. The roughs are mostly heather or woods, and the hazards are, for the most part, water holes clearly marked. You can always expect the fairways and greens to be well kept. This is a good, playable links of medium difficulty. If you want to combine fine golf with life in one of the most sophisticated and vital cities in the world, then this is the course for you.

LOCATION: The course is in Mougins, about 6 miles N of Cannes, 11 miles NW of Antibes, 22 miles W of Nice, 105 miles E of Marseille, 268 miles S of Lyon, 200 miles S of Grenoble, 570 miles SE of Paris, 292 miles S of Geneva.

OTHER INFORMATION: The course is open to nonmembers, unlimited, for the entire year, with 3 professionals always on hand. The weather is best from February to October; most crowded season from January 15 to March 15. Practice ground is available. *Number of holes:* 18. *Par:* 70. *Length:* 6000 yards. *Green fees:* weekdays, $4.50; weekends, $6/day. *Lessons:* $5/hour. *Caddies:* $2.50/18 holes. *Golfing equipment and caddie carts:* clubs $3/day, carts $.50/day.

OTHER SPORTS FACILITIES: Swimming, tennis, fishing, sailing, riding, water skiing.

ACCOMMODATIONS: No living space in the club house, but restaurant and bar are available.
In Cannes: *Majestic* (12 blvd. Croisette, Tel. 39.17.92). A luxury hotel of international standing, open all year. Rooms from $13 for a single to $32 for best double with private bath; central heating; full pension from $22/day; taxes and services not included. *Grand* (45 blvd. Croisette, Tel. 38.13.00). A modern first-class hotel, open all year. Rooms from $15 for the best single to $30 for best double with private bath; central heating; taxes and service included. *Canberra* (Rond-Point Duboys-d'Angers, Tel. 38.20.70). A very good, modern, comfortable hotel, open all year. Rooms from $8.50 for best single to $21 for best double with private bath; central heating; taxes and services included.

TOURIST ATTRACTIONS: Napoleon was right in calling Cannes a "paradise," for there is just about everything here to make your stay a memorable one: beaches, fashionable shops, first-class restaurants, museums, a gambling casino, nightclubs, a film festival, historical landmarks and a procession of kings, princes, statesmen, scientists, artists and movie stars from all over the world.

FOR FURTHER INFORMATION: Write to: Secretary, Cannes Country Club, Mougins (A.M.), France. Telephone: Mougins 90.00.04.

Golf Cannes-Antibes-Biot

A few miles from the Mediterranean, at the foot of the famous Maritime Alps, the Golf Club of Biot is one of the most picturesque and colorful in all France. It's a perfect course for the short driver since many of the holes are less than 200 yards. No great obstacles here, but the course does call for careful and accurate play. The wild swinger will find himself incurring many penalties. Biot itself, built on terraces on the side of a hill, is an old village that seems never to have moved into the modern world. But its golf course is modern and highly enjoyable—all against a spectacular scenic background.

LOCATION: The course is about 4 miles N of Antibes, 12 miles SW of Nice, 13 miles NE of Cannes, 31 miles SW of Monte-Carlo, 112 miles E of Marseille, 581 miles SE of Paris. It is accessible by car.

OTHER INFORMATION: The course is open to nonmembers for the entire year, with 3 professionals always on hand. The most crowded season is from July 20 to September 20; the weather is good throughout the year. Practice ground is available. *Number of holes:* 18. *Par:* 70. *Length:* 6014 yards. *Green fees:* $5.50/day (summer), $4.50/day (winter, fall, spring). *Lessons:* $3.50/half hour; $6/hour. *Caddies:* $3/18 holes. *Golfing equipment and caddie carts:* clubs $2.50/day, carts $.50/day.

OTHER SPORTS FACILITIES: Tennis, riding, swimming, water skiing, boating.

ACCOMMODATIONS: No space in the club, but hotels of every category in nearby towns. Restaurant and bar at the club.
In Biot: *Mas des Orangers* (Biot, Tel. 34.90.33). A good, comfortable hotel with a pleasant view, open all year except November. $4 for a single to $8.50 for best double with private bath; central heating; full pension from $7.50/day; taxes and services included.
In Antibes: *Royal* (blvd. General-Leclerc, Tel. 34.03.09). Good and very comfortable hotel with a pleasant view, open from December 21 to October 19. Rooms from $5 for single to $11 for best double with private bath or shower; central heating; full pension from $8.50/day; taxes and services included.
In Nice: *Atlantic* (12 blvd. Victor-Hugo, Tel. 88.40.15). A first-class hotel, open all year. $7 for single to $18 for the best double with private bath/shower; central heating; full pension from $14/day; taxes and services included. *Napoléon* (6 rue Grimaldi, Tel. 80.10.07). A first-class modern hotel, open all year. $6.50 for a single to $13 for best double with private bath or shower; central heating; taxes and services included.
In Cannes: *Fouquet's* (2 Rond-Point Duboys-d'Angers, Tel. 39.15.81). A very good and very comfortable modern hotel with a pleasant view and a garden, open all year. Rooms from $9 for a single to $20 for the best double, with private bath and shower; central heating; taxes and services included; continental breakfast. *Corona* (55 rue Antibes, Tel. 39.69.85). A good, comfortable modern hotel, open all year. Rooms from $7.50 for best single to $8.50 for best double with private bath and shower; central heating; taxes and services included.

TOURIST ATTRACTIONS: The area has about everything a visitor would want: golf tournaments, yachting races, flower festivals and the famous Cannes movie festival. Biot itself is an important ceramic center. It also has the famous Fernand Léger Museum, devoted solely to his works.

FOR FURTHER INFORMATION: Write to: Secretary, Golf Cannes-Antibes-Biot, Biot (Alpes-Maritimes), France. Telephone: 34.50.27.

Monte-Carlo Golf Club

This is possibly the most breathtaking course in Europe. No visitor should miss it! The first 9 holes offer a panoramic view of the Maritime Alps and the coastline around Nice, and the second 9, a sweeping view of the Mediterranean from Cap Ferrat to the coast of Italy. The course itself is short and interesting but by no means easy; the mountain air makes it especially tiring. At times, it gives the impression of being much longer. Most holes favor the short, accurate driver. The approaches to the fairways are good, and all hazards are clearly defined.

LOCATION: The course is in Mont Agel on the outskirts of La Turbie, 4 miles NW of Monte-Carlo, 9 miles W of Menton, 8 miles NE of Beaulieu, 26 miles NE of Nice, 48 miles NE of Cannes, 588 miles SE of Paris, 32 miles W of San Remo, Italy. The only way to get there is by car.

OTHER INFORMATION: The course is open to nonmembers, unlimited, for the entire year, with two professionals always on hand. Most crowded season is from June to September, with best weather from April to October. Practice ground is available.
Number of holes: 18. *Par:* 68. *Length:* 4986 yards.
Green fees: weekdays, $5; weekends, $7/day. *Lessons:* $3.50/half hour.

Shell's Wonderful World of Golf
The French Riviera is the perfect setting for relaxed golf. Here, the Monte Carlo course high above the Mediterranean.

Caddies: $3/18 holes. *Golfing equipment and caddie carts:* $3 for set of best clubs. Course is not suited for caddie carts.

OTHER SPORTS FACILITIES: Water skiing, deep-sea fishing, tennis, swimming, pigeon-shooting.

ACCOMMODATIONS: No living space in the club house, but restaurant and bar are available.

In Monte-Carlo: *Paris* (Place Casino, Tel. 30.80.80. One of the great luxury hotels of Europe, open all year. Rooms from $16 for single to $45 for the best double with bath and shower; central heating; taxes and services not included. *Balmoral* (12 av. Costa, Tel. 30.62.37). A very good, comfortable hotel with a pleasant view. Open all year. Rooms from $5 for single to $13 for the best double with bath and shower; central heating; full pension from $10/day; taxes and services included. *Helder et Rôtisserie Chapon Fin* (2 av. Madone, Tel. 30.63.07). A good, comfortable hotel, open all year. Rooms from $3.50 for a single to $9 for best double with bath and shower; central heating; full pension from $8/day; taxes and services not included.

In Menton: *Napoléon* (29 quai Laurenti, Tel. 35.89.50). A very good, comfortable modern hotel with a pleasant view, open all year. Rooms from $8 for single to $13 for best double with bath or shower; central heating; full pension from $11/day; taxes and services not included. *Viking* (2 av. Général-de-Gaulle, Tel. 35.80.44). A very good, comfortable modern hotel, open all year except November. Rooms from $7 for single to $14 for best double with bath or shower; central heating; full pension from $11/day; taxes and services not included; continental breakfast.

TOURIST ATTRACTIONS: Monte-Carlo offers just about everything a tourist would want, from the famous casino, with gambling and a nightclub, to fashionable shops, numerous festivals, the palace, the famous Oceanographical Museum and boat trips along the Riviera. In Menton, don't miss the International Festival of Chamber Music in August and the Jean Cocteau Museum in the Town Hall.

FOR FURTHER INFORMATION: Write to: Director, Monte-Carlo Golf Club, Mont Agel, France. Telephone: 82.14.01.

Golf Club du Mans

Here is a course that should present no unforeseen difficulties for the average golfer. It is mostly flat with medium-sized fairways and greens and only slightly favors the long driver on a few holes. It is an excellent course for a tuneup, especially for a small game. Le Mans itself, known to sports-car racing fans throughout the world, is also a charming medieval town with many old cobblestoned streets, a famous cathedral and Roman walls that recall an age long since past. The combination of the ancient background, the "Grand Prix," and the golf course adds up to a pleasant, varied holiday.

LOCATION: The course is about 7 miles from Le Mans, 140 miles SW of Paris, 80 miles SW of Chartres, 90 miles NE of Nantes, 53 miles N of Tours. It is accessible by car.

OTHER INFORMATION: The course is open to nonmembers, unlimited, for the entire year (closed in August), with a professional on hand every Friday. Most crowded month is June, with best season May to July. Practice ground is available.
Number of holes: 9. *Par:* 74 (for twice around). *Length:* 5758 yards. *Green fees:* weekdays, $3; weekends, $5/day. *Lessons:* $3/hour. *Caddies:* none available. *Golfing equipment and caddie carts:* clubs $3/day, carts $.50/day.

OTHER SPORTS FACILITIES: Riding, clay-pigeon shooting.

ACCOMMODATIONS: No living space in the club house, but restaurant and bar are available.
In Le Mans: *Paris* (16 av. Général Leclerc, Tel. 28.15.28). A very good, comfortable modern hotel, open all year. Rooms from $9 for a single to $16 for the best double with private bath or shower; central heating; full pension from $9/day; taxes and services included. *Moderne* (14 rue Bourg-Belé, Tel. 28.16.50). A good, comfortable hotel, open all year. Rooms from $4 for a single to $10 for the best double with private bath; central heating; taxes and services not included. *Central* (5 blvd. R. Levasseur, Tel. 28.08.93). A good, comfortable hotel, open all year. Rooms from $3 for a single to $11 for best double with private bath and shower; central heating; taxes and services not included.

TOURIST ATTRACTIONS: The great event here is the 24-hour Grand Prix of Le Mans, one of the most famous sportscar races in the world. The town also has a magnificent cathedral, St. Julien, a charming old section and an automobile museum. Le Mans, moreover, is on the edge of the famous châteaux country of the Loire region.

FOR FURTHER INFORMATION: Write to: Secretary, Automobile-Club de l'Ouest, 13, blvd. René Levasseur, Le Mans, France. Telephone: 28.54.57.

Golf Club de Lyon

Here is a tough, challenging course in the heart of the gastronomic center of France. It is flat, favors the long accurate driver and has narrow fairways but large greens. This is by no means an easy course; with several par-5 holes and much length, it compares favorably with the best Scottish championship links. You may need some practice first. If you want to combine good golf with good food, don't miss this course. And if you are a gourmet, you've got a very special delight waiting for you, for about 17 miles south of Lyons in Vienne is the Pyramide, probably the best restaurant in France, if not the whole world.

LOCATION: The course is in Villette D'Anthon, about 15 miles S of Lyon, 196 miles N of Marseille, 263 miles NW of Nice, 52 miles NW of Grenoble, 308 miles SE of Paris. It is accessible by car.

OTHER INFORMATION: The course is open to nonmembers, unlimited, for the entire year, with a professional always on hand except in August. Most crowded seasons are spring and autumn, with the weather best in June, July and August. Practice ground is available.
Number of holes: 18. *Par:* 72. *Length:* 6686 yards.
Green fees: weekdays, $4.50; weekends, $11/day. *Lessons:* $3/half hour.
Caddies: $2/18 holes. *Golfing equipment and caddie carts:* none available.

OTHER SPORTS FACILITIES: Tennis, riding, swimming.

ACCOMMODATIONS: No living space in the club house, but restaurant and bar are available.
Royal (20 Place Bellecour, Tel. 37.57.31). A modern, first-class hotel, open all year. Rooms from $8 for best single to $25 for best double with private bath; central heating; full pension from $14/day; continental breakfast; taxes and services included. *Bordeaux et Parc* (24 cours Verdun, Tel. 37.58.74). A very good, comfortable hotel, open all year. Rooms from $5 for best single to $14 for best double with private bath; central heating; continental breakfast; taxes and services included. *Bristol* (28 cours Verdun, Tel. 37.56.55). A very good, comfortable hotel, open all year. Rooms from $5 for best single to $15 for best double with private bath; central heating; continental breakfast; taxes and services included.

TOURIST ATTRACTIONS: Lyon's attractions include a cathedral, some old churches, a fine art museum, the Guimet Museum with its collection of Oriental art, some beautiful gardens and, of course, many of the very best restaurants in France (don't leave Lyon without eating at Mère Guy, 35 quai J.-J. Rousseau).

FOR FURTHER INFORMATION: Write to: Secretary, Golf Club de Lyon, Villette D'Anthon, Isère, France. Telephone: 49.75.82.

Golf Club Marseille-Aix Les Milles

In the heart of Provence, on the outskirts of Aix-en-Provence and within easy commuting distance of Marseille, the club lies in a section of France, famous for its history and tradition. Phoenicians, Greeks and Romans settled here, and in 49 B.C. Julius Caesar conquered the area and made it a province of Rome. Against such a rich and varied background, golf possibly gains in pleasure and certainly takes on an added interest, particularly when it is played on an excellent course. The course itself is for the long, accurate driver and has well-defined fairways and greens. Nevertheless, short hitters have enough testing holes to make the course an enjoyable experience. Neither too difficult nor too easy, the Golf Club Marseille should prove the happy medium for the visitor.

LOCATION: The course is about 6 miles S of Aix-en-Provence, 12 miles N of Marseille, 189 miles S of Lyon, 108 miles W of Nice, 45 miles SE of Avignon, 482 miles S of Paris. It is accessible by car.

OTHER INFORMATION: The course is open to nonmembers, who live more than 30 miles from Marseille. It is open all year, with a professional always on hand. The weather is best from April to November. Practice ground is available.
Number of holes: 18. *Par:* 73. *Length:* 6267 yards.
Green fees: weekdays, $4.50; weekends, $5.50/day. *Lessons:* $4.50/half hour. *Caddies:* $3.50/18 holes. *Golfing equipment and caddie carts:* clubs $3/day, carts $.50/day.

OTHER SPORTS FACILITIES: Tennis, riding, swimming.

ACCOMMODATIONS: No living space in the club house, but restaurant and bar are available.
In Marseille: *Splendide* (31 blvd. Athènes. Tel. 20.81.50). A first-class hotel, open all year. Rooms from $4.50 for single to $16 for the best double with private bath or shower; central heating; full pension from $11/day; taxes and services included. *Royal St-Georges* (10 rue Cap-Dessemond, Tel. 33.56.92). A good, modern, comfortable hotel, open all year. Rooms from $8 for single to $10 for best double with private bath and shower; central heating; continental breakfast; taxes and services included.
In Aix-en-Provence: *Thermes Sextius* (55 cours Sextius, Tel. 1.18). A very good, comfortable hotel, open all year. Rooms from $4 for single to $13 for best double with private bath and shower; central heating; full pension from $10/day; taxes and services included. *Moderne* (34 av. Victor Hugo, Tel. 5.16). A simple, comfortable hotel, open all year. Rooms from $3.50 for single to $7 for best double with private bath and shower; central heating; taxes and services included.

TOURIST ATTRACTIONS: The second city of France and one of the oldest, Marseille, offers some of the best and liveliest tourist attractions. It has many museums, old, old churches, parks, gardens, tours and boat trips along the Riviera coast. Don't miss the old port, the world-famous bouillabaisse (marvelous fish stew) and the celebrated Canebière, the most famous street in Marseille, a gay, bustling, noisy Broadway with luxury shops, cafés and hotels.
Aix-en-Provence is the old capital of Provence; it is famous for its university, museums, cathedrals, elegant mansions, graceful square and charming eighteenth-century fountains. Above all, don't miss the studio of Paul Cézanne, where the painter lived most of his life, and the International Festival of Music in July.

FOR FURTHER INFORMATION: Write to: Secretary, Golf Club Marseille-Aix Les Milles, 10 rue de Coq 9, Marseille, France. Telephone: 62.17.93.

Golf Club du Mont-d'Arbois

There is a new championship course just outside Megève, one of the most magnificent winter sports resorts in the world. Since the course is at a height of nearly 3000 feet, the air is fresh and cool even on the hottest day; and the surrounding mountains and forests give one the feeling of grandeur and beauty. Mont-d'Arbois favors the medium-strength hitter, although the nature of the mountain course will not penalize the accurate, steady player. This links was designed for variety, and it should appeal to every type of golfer. And if it proves too challenging, there are always the great views!

LOCATION: The course is in Mont-d'Arbois, about 3 miles from Megève, 47 miles SE of Geneva, 64 miles E of Aix-les-Bains, 41 miles E of Annecy, 78 miles NE of Grenoble, 280 miles N of Nice, 136 miles E of Lyon, 359 miles SE of Paris. It is accessible by car.

OTHER INFORMATION: The course is open to nonmembers, unlimited, for the entire season (June 25-September 10), with a professional available from July 1 to September 10. Most crowded month is August, with weather best in July. Practice ground is available.
Number of holes: 18. *Par:* 70 (anticipated). *Length:* 5873 yards (anticipated length).
Green fees: $3.50/day. *Lessons:* $4/half hour. *Caddies:* $2.50/18 holes. *Golfing equipment and caddie carts:* only carts available at $1/day.

OTHER SPORTS FACILITIES: Tennis, ice-skating, riding, fishing, summer skiing, mountain-climbing, swimming.

ACCOMMODATIONS: No living space in the club house, but restaurant and bar are available.
In Megève: *Hermitage* (Megève, Tel. 0.86). A very good, comfortable hotel, open all year except May and November. Rooms from $4.50 for best single to $15 for best double with private bath; central heating; full pension from $11/day; services and taxes of 24% not included. *Mont Blanc et Réserve* (Megève, Tel. 0.04). A very good, modern hotel, open all year. Rooms from $5.50 for best single to $15 for best double with private bath; central heating, full pension from $11/day; taxes and services of 25% not included.

TOURIST ATTRACTIONS: For the visitor, trips into the French Alps and breathtaking panoramic views can be mixed with excursions into nearby cities, like Geneva and Megève. There is, in addition, very fine shopping in Megève.

FOR FURTHER INFORMATION: Write to: Secretary, Club du Mont-d'Arbois, Megève (Haute-Savoie), France. Telephone: Megève 503.

New-Golf Deauville

Situated on a hill dominating a wide and beautiful landscape, the New-Golf Deauville is one of the most impressive on the Continent, both for its scenery and for its layout. From almost every hole a golfer can see the English Channel as well as the ruins of a magnificent old castle built by Louis XIV for Mlle. de Montpensier. The course has rich, thick grass and favors the long driver, although it is by no means discouraging for the short driver. The diversity of the design, particularly the bunkering, makes this a challenging course, especially if you play the White and Blue courses, a total of 6700 yards.

LOCATION: The course is in Deauville, about 120 miles from Paris on the northwest coast of France. Easily accessible by car, train or plane. It is 25 miles NE of Caen, 45 S of Le Havre, 40 E of Bayeux, 100 E of Cherbourg, 60 W of Rouen.

OTHER INFORMATION: The course is closed to nonmembers, but there is no difficulty in becoming a member. Just sign the entrance book and pay your green fees. The season lasts from March 16 to September 30, when there are from one to four professionals on hand. The weather is best from June to September, with the most crowded season from July 15 to August 15.
Number of holes: Red, 9; White, 9; Blue, 9. Par: Red, 35 (S.S.S., 35); White, 36 (S.S.S., 36); Blue, 36 (S.S.S., 36). Length: Red, 2963 yards; White, 3326 yards; Blue, 3379 yards.
The golfer can combine any two of the three courses for his 18 holes.
Green fees: weekdays, $6; weekends, $13/day. Lessons: $4.50/half hour. Caddies: $1.50/9 holes, $2.50/18 holes. Golfing equipment and caddie carts: clubs $2.50/day, carts $.50/day.

OTHER SPORTS FACILITIES: Riding, polo, yachting, tennis, swimming, clay-pigeon shooting.

ACCOMMODATIONS: No living space in the club house, but restaurant and bar are available.
In Deauville: Golf Hotel (Deauville, Tel. 882901). An impressive luxury hotel in the Normandy countryside facing the sea and the valley, open from April 14 to April 21 and from June 2 to September 6. Rooms from $9 for a single to $27 for the best double with private bath; central heating; taxes and services of 25% not included. Normandy (rue J. Mermoz, Tel. 882921). One of the great luxury hotels of France, open all year. Rooms from $17 for a single to $25 for the best double with private bath; central heating; continental breakfast; taxes and services of 25% not included. Marie-Anne (142 av. République, Tel. 882742). A good, comfortable hotel, open all year. Rooms from $4 for a single to $11 for the best double with private bath; central heating; taxes and services included. Paradis (av.

Courses, Tel. 882016). A simple, comfortable hotel, with a good view, open Easter to the end of September. Rooms from $4 for a single to $6 for the best double with private shower and bath; full pension from $7/day; taxes and services not included.

TOURIST ATTRACTIONS: This luxurious worldly resort probably has more than you can handle; there are regattas, tennis and polo matches, presentations of the latest Paris collections, elegant dining and dancing, and a splendid beach with colorful booths. There is also an international horse fair and, of course, the Normandy beach where our troops landed on June 6, 1944. The season ends the fourth Sunday in August with the famous Grand Prix of Deauville.

FOR FURTHER INFORMATION: Write to: Secretary of the New-Golf Club, Deauville, Calvados, France. Telephone: 882901.

Golf Club du Havre

One of the modern and important ports of France, Le Havre dates back to Roman times, and some old ruins, especially that of a theater, are still very much in evidence. For the leisurely traveler a stopover here after an ocean voyage might be a good idea. Only a short distance away is the golf course. The course itself is flat, not at all tiring and made for the long as well as the short driver. It has good fairways and well-defended greens and should give the average golfer an enjoyable time. At 6000 yards there is enough distance to demand power, but its variety will stimulate every type of player.

LOCATION: In Octeville-sur-Mer, about 6 miles from Le Havre, 136 miles NW of Paris, 151 miles E of Cherbourg, 50 miles N of Deauville, 62 miles W of Rouen. It is accessible by car.

OTHER INFORMATION: The course is open to nonmembers (but golfer should be a member of a club back home) for entire year, with a professional always on hand. The best time to play is on weekdays, with good weather from May through August. Practice ground is available.
Number of holes: 18. *Par:* 73. *Length:* 6030 yards.
Green fees: weekdays, $4.50; weekends and holidays, $5/day. *Lessons:* $3/half hour. *Caddies:* not available at present. *Golfing equipment and caddie carts:* clubs and carts for rent at $2.50/day.

OTHER SPORTS FACILITIES: Tennis, swimming and riding in nearby Le Havre.

ACCOMMODATIONS: No living space in the club house, but restaurant and bar are available.
In Le Havre: *Grand Hôtel Bordeaux* (Place Gambetta, Tel. 428073). A good, comfortable hotel, open all year. Rooms from $5 for a single to $11

for best double with private bath and shower; central heating; continental breakfast; taxes and services included. *Printania* (13 cours République, Tel. 423306). A good, comfortable hotel, open all year. Rooms from $3.50 for single to $6 for best double with private bath and shower; central heating; full pension from $7/day; taxes and services included. *Gambetta* (20 rue J-Macé, Tel. 422594). A simple, good hotel, open all year. Rooms from $3 for single to $6.50 for best double with private bath and shower; central heating; taxes and services included.

TOURIST ATTRACTIONS: Chief attractions are visits to ocean liners, promenades with magnificent views of the Channel, and the port itself, one of the largest and busiest in the world. The surrounding areas provide lovely views of the Seine estuary.

FOR FURTHER INFORMATION: Write to: General Secretary, Golf Club du Havre, Octeville-sur-Mer (Seine Maritime), France. Telephone: 202007.

Golf de Reims

The Golf Club of Reims is in the famous champagne country of fertile plains, wooded hills and rich vineyards. If you are also a World War I buff, you will know this as "invasion country" and recall such names as Sedan, Verdun, Valmy, Montmirail and Champaubert. The course, on the outskirts of Reims, is flat, in pleasant surroundings and of average difficulty because of its relative shortness. It favors the less powerful driver and requires careful, accurate play. It is a good tuneup course if you plan to go on to some of the championship links around Paris or Lyon; or played by itself, it should prove more than satisfactory.

LOCATION: The course is in Gueux, about 5 miles from Reims, 95 miles NE of Paris, 110 miles SE of Amiens, 130 miles S of Brussels, 128 miles NW of Nancy, 84 miles N of Troyes. It is easily accessible by car.

OTHER INFORMATION: The course is open to nonmembers, unlimited, for the entire year, with a professional always on hand. Most crowded months are May and June, with weather best from May to late September. Practice ground is available.
Number of holes: 9. *Par:* 68 (for twice around). *Length:* 5919 yards.
Green fees: weekdays, $3.50; weekends and holidays, $4.50/day. *Lessons:* $2.50/half hour. *Caddies:* evenings and on weekends at $1.50/9 holes. *Golfing equipment and caddie carts:* none for rent, but available from the professional on hand.

OTHER SPORTS FACILITIES: Tennis and riding.

ACCOMMODATIONS: No living space in the club house, but restaurant and bar are available.

In Reims: *Lion d'Or* (58 place Drouet-d'Erlon, Tel. 47.54.28). A very good, comfortable hotel, open all year. Rooms from $8 for a single to $15 for best double with private bath and shower; central heating; continental breakfast; taxes and services included. *Bristol* (76 place Drouet-d'Erlon, Tel. 47.35.08). A good, comfortable hotel, open all year. Rooms from $4.50 for a single to $8 for the best double with private bath; central heating; taxes and services included. *Univers* (41 blvd. Foch, Tel. 47.52.71). A good, comfortable hotel with a pleasant view, open all year. Rooms from $4 for a single to $9 for the best double with private bath and shower; central heating; full pension from $8/day; taxes and services included.

TOURIST ATTRACTIONS: Reims is in the heart of the champagne country, so don't miss a visit to the vineyards and the cellars in deep catacombs and old stone quarries. A must is the great Notre-Dame Cathedral and the war room where the Armistice was signed in 1945. Also of interest is the Museum of Fine Arts (Cranach, Corot and others). Soissons and its environs are recommended as well.

FOR FURTHER INFORMATION: Write to: Secretary, 46, rue de la Justice, Reims, France. Telephone 47.39.06.

Golf Club de Toulouse

For the visitor interested in both tourism and golf, Toulouse will provide an amply rewarding experience. The tourist will be interested because the city was the center of activity for the Romans, then later became the seat of the most magnificent court in Europe and finally was almost destroyed by a Papal Army. For the golfer, the course is only 9 holes, but it is an interesting 9 holes overlooking the city, good for the long as well as the short driver. The course is hilly and calls for careful, accurate play, but the approaches to the greens are good, and the hazards are clearly defined. For the more expert player the course will provide a good tuneup for some of the more demanding European links.

LOCATION: The course is about 4 miles from Toulouse and is accessible by car. Toulouse is 157 miles SE of Bordeaux, 182 miles E of Biarritz, 256 miles W of Marseille, 366 miles W of Nice, 432 miles S of Paris.

OTHER INFORMATION: The course is open to nonmembers, unlimited, for the entire year, with a professional on hand daily except in August and first half of September. Most crowded time is on weekends, with weather best from April through October. Practice ground is available.
Number of holes: 9. *Par:* 72 (for twice around). *Length:* 5418 yards.
Green fees: weekdays, $3; weekends, $5/day. *Lessons:* $3.50/half hour.
Caddies: $1/9 holes. *Golfing equipment and caddie carts:* clubs $3/day, carts $.50/day.

OTHER SPORTS FACILITIES: Swimming, tennis and riding.

ACCOMMODATIONS: No living space in the club house, but restaurant and bar are available.
In Toulouse: *Grand Hôtel et Tivollier* (31 rue Metz, Tel. 22.39.93). The finest hotel in Toulouse, open all year. Rooms from $7 for a single to $17 for best double with private bath; central heating; continental breakfast; taxes and services included. *Caravelle* (62 rue Raymond IV, Tel. 62.70.65). A very comfortable, modern hotel, open all year. Rooms from $10 a single to $15 for the best double with private bath; central heating; taxes and services included. *Victoria* (76 rue Bayard, Tel. 62.28.90). A good, comfortable hotel, open all year: Rooms from $5 a single to $9 for best double with private bath; central heating; taxes and services included.

TOURIST ATTRACTIONS: Toulouse is called "The Red Town" because nearly every building is constructed of red brick (this is, in fact, what gives the city its character and peculiar charm). Toulouse is one of the great cultural and artistic centers of France, especially for the St-Sernin Basilica, the best known Romanesque church in southern France, and for its museums (Augustins' Museum in particular).

FOR FURTHER INFORMATION: Write to: Secretary, 20, rue Ozenne, Toulouse, France. Telephone: 85.11.99.

ITALY

The visitor to Italy will find golf courses in every kind of setting, from the coast of the Italian Riviera, to the beautiful Lake Country of the North, to the mountains above Venice and Milan. If he is in the large cities—Rome, Florence, Milan—there are several courses of varying difficulty to test his game.

Italian courses are particularly pleasant because the holes are laid out for aesthetic as well as sporting reasons. Usually the golfer has a spectacular view of mountains, lakes or coastline whenever he takes a shot. All the courses are accessible—best if you have a car, but within range of bus, train or taxi. And the welcome? You know you can be sure of that. The Italians are delighted to have visitors.

If you are in the North, may I suggest that you try a little combined tour of Swiss courses in the Lake Lugano area with those in the Italian

Lake Country. Possibly start with *Menaggio e Cadenabbia* just south of Como, then move on to *Lanzo* or *Villa d'Este*, and finish with *Varese*. In the Venice area, perhaps start with *Miramonti* or *Cansiglio* and work into *Condulmer* and the *Lido di Venezia*. If you are driving through the Riviera and find some free time, start with the *Ulivi* (at San Remo), which is not too trying, then move on the leisurely *Rapallo* course, working your way south to *Punta Ala,* which will challenge your game. From here you are in a good position to go either north to Florence or south to Rome. Good golf awaits you in either place.

Circolo Golf Olgiata

The Olgiata Golf Club is well situated on the Via Cassia, leading to Florence, but only 12 miles from Rome. The golf course is one element of a complex of sporting facilities all arranged as part of a sporting center and residential area. Golf here will keep the visitor within driving distance of a great city, Rome, yet he will find himself in the peaceful surroundings of the beautiful Campagna Romana.

The recently designed West Course of 18 holes and the East Course of 9 holes wind their way over undulating countryside. Both courses follow the natural lay of the land. The greens are large, with many bunkers protecting them. The lengthy West is not an easy course; it provides problems for both the long and the short driver. For the accurate player there are numerous chances for birdies, but the golfer with only a big game and an imprecise short game will find several opportunities for punishment. This is a course that should challenge the game of any player, while the surrounding countryside helps him forget his bad shots and soothe his nerves.

LOCATION: Twelve miles N of Rome on the via Cassia, leading to Florence, the Olgiata is best reached by car. Florence is 174 miles N.

OTHER INFORMATION: The course is open to nonmembers, but visitors should have proof of membership in a home club. Course is open all year, with the professional always on hand. Mild weather can be expected at all times. Large practice ground is available, and also an indoor practice room.

Number of holes: West Course, 18 holes; East Course, 9 holes. *Par:* West Course, 72; East Course, 34. *Length:* West Course, 6833 yards; East Course, 3092 yards.

Green fees: weekdays, $4; Saturdays, Sundays, and holidays, $8/day. *Lessons:* $3.50/hour. *Caddies:* $2.50/round. *Golfing equipment and caddie carts:* $2.50/day, carts $.70/day.

OTHER SPORTS FACILITIES: There is a swimming pool on the grounds, and within easy reach of the links are tennis courts and a riding center. The background of Olgiata is rich in a sporting tradition, for here thoroughbred horses were raised before the property was converted into a golf course.

ACCOMMODATIONS: No living space in the club house, but restaurant and bar are available. The bar is open to players coming in from the course. The club house was carefully designed so that it gives the golfer every convenience as well as recapturing the atmosphere of the links.

In the immediate area: The *Bela Motel* (about ½ mile from the course). Comfortable rooms, some with baths; $4/single. Central heating.

Rome offers every type of accommodation, from luxurious to more reasonable hotels and pensions. See information on accommodations for *Rome Golf Club*, p. 166.

TOURIST ATTRACTIONS: The locale of the club offers fine walking trips through the rolling countryside, into the adjoining forests or around the various lakes. Nearby Rome is a mecca for visitors, with every type of attraction—culture, sports, night life, as well as excellent shopping.

FOR FURTHER INFORMATION: Write to: Club Secretary, Circolo Golf Olgiata, Via Cassia, Rome, Italy. Telephone: 6990393/5.

Circolo del Golf di Roma
(Rome Golf Club)

The Rome Golf Club is set in a typical section of the Roman countryside on varied and rolling terrain. The course is open and undulating with well-prepared greens and fairways. There are only two par-5 holes (7th and 10th), but the course is varied enough to interest every kind of player. For example, the short 2nd hole (par 3) requires a delicate tee shot to a double green well guarded on all sides; and the middle distance 17th requires a second shot that must carry over three water hazards to a green guarded on the left by the stream and on the right by a large grass bunker. For the power hitter the 8 holes over 400 yards will prove satisfying.

The course is picturesquely set within pines, cypresses, clusters of oaks and evergreen oaks, crossed by a stream that divides into rivulets. On one side are the Alban Hills, with the Roman aqueduct in the foothills, and on the other the old Appian Way, which stretches to the ancient walls of the town.

LOCATION: The Rome Golf Club is 9 miles N of Rome, accessible by car or bus.

OTHER INFORMATION: The course is open to visitors and nonmembers, unlimited, except during tournaments; visitors, however, should bring proof of membership in home club. Professional in daily attendance. Season lasts the entire year, except on Mondays. Bungalow-styled club house with changing and locker rooms, showers. Practice ground is available.

Number of holes: 18. *Par:* 71 (S.S.S., 71). *Length:* 6344 yards (championship tees), 5874 yards (men's normal tees), 5513 yards (women's tees).

Green fees: weekdays, $3.50; Saturdays or Sundays, $5. *Lessons:* $2.50/½

Italian State Tourist Office
Ancient ruins are visible from the Circolo del Golf di Roma.

hour. *Caddies:* $2/round. *Golfing equipment and caddie carts:* clubs $2.50/ round.

SPORTS FACILITIES: The club has an outdoor swimming pool set amidst trees as well as two tennis courts. Rome, of course, offers every type of sports facility for the visitor.

ACCOMMODATIONS: No living space in the club house, but restaurant and bar are available.

Rome offers the visitor accommodations suitable for every pocketbook. Luxury hotels: *Cavalieri Hilton* (via Cadolo 53, Tel. 3151), *Hassler-Villa Medici* (piazza Trinità dei Monti 6, Tel. 672651), *Grand Hotel et de Rome* (via Vittorio Emanuele Orlando 3, Tel. 489011), *Excelsior Palazzo* (via Vittorio Veneto 125, Tel. 489031), *Bernini Bristol* (piazza Barberni 23, Tel. 463051). All have singles with private baths from $10, doubles $18 to $20; pension $20 to $24/day.

Very comfortable hotels (in central Rome) start at $4 to $5 for single, $8 for double: the *Universe, Eliseo, Milano, Rex, Esperia, Reale.*

TOURIST ATTRACTIONS: Rome, one of the great cities of the world, offers every possible tourist attraction. It also provides some of the best shopping in Europe. The immediate area of the golf club has its own attractions—many small villages, the old Appian Way and the Roman Aqueduct. All of these will provide pleasant excursions. The less crowded season for Rome is late April, May, June and early October.

FOR FURTHER INFORMATION: Write to: Club Secretary, Circolo del Golf di Roma, via Appia Nuova (Acquasanta), Rome, Italy. Telephone: 783.407 or 786.129.

Golf Club Bologna

The Bologna Golf Club combines the attractions of the lovely Emilia countryside with proximity to a major city. The course has been remodeled from a 9-holer to its present full 18 holes set against the spectacular Italian landscape. It favors the long hitter, although, as on most Italian courses, steadiness and precision are helpful. There are several testing holes that should keep the visiting player on the alert without spoiling his holiday.

LOCATION: 10 miles from Bologna, the golf club is accessible by car. Bologna is 65 miles N of Florence, 130 miles SE of Milan, 250 miles N of Rome, and within short distances by car, train or bus of Ferrara, Modena, Reggio, Parma, Mantua and Pistoia.

OTHER INFORMATION: The club is open all year with nonmembers most welcome with no limitations. A professional is in attendance. The best weather is in the spring and autumn, and the worst is in the winter, when it becomes quite cold. Practice ground is available.
Number of holes: 18. *Par:* 72. *Length:* 6484 yards.
Green fees: weekdays, $3.50/day; weekends and holidays, $5/day. *Lessons:* $4/hour. *Caddies:* $2.50/10 holes (weekdays). *Golfing equipment and caddie carts:* clubs $2 and up/day, carts $.50/day.

OTHER SPORTS FACILITIES: In the immediate area the visitor will not find any sports facilities, but in Bologna he can find tennis and riding. There is stream fishing and some hunting as well. For the skiing enthusiast, Bologna is backed by mountains.

ACCOMMODATIONS: No living space in the club house, but restaurant and bar are available.
In Bologna: *Jolly* (piazza 20 Settembre 2, Tel. 264405). A luxury hotel with private baths, central heating, experienced staff; singles from $7, best double $13.50; service included; pension from $20/day. *Grand Hotel Majestic Baglioni* (via dell'Indipendenza 8, Tel. 274771). Luxury hotel with private baths, central heating, experienced staff; single from $6, best double $17; service included; pension $16 to $18/day. *Nettuno* (via Galliera 67, Tel. 260964) and the *Roma* (via Massimo d'Azeglio 9, Tel. 231330). Singles from $3, best double $8; private baths; central heating; pension at *Roma* $7.50 to $8.50/day.

TOURIST ATTRACTIONS: Full of towers and campaniles, the home of good restaurants, famous for its university, known for local products like shoes and silks, Bologna has much to offer the visitor. Things to see: Basilica of S. Petronio, Palazzo Comunale, Piazza di Porta Ravegnana, the Picture

Gallery (Pinacoteca) and the Civic Museum. And of course the surrounding countryside will provide joy for every visitor.

FOR FURTHER INFORMATION: Write to: Club Secretary, Golf Club Bologna, Chiesa Nuova di Monte San Pietro (Bologna), Italy. Telephone: 715.154.

Ugolino Golf Club

The Ugolino Golf Course is set in the hills of the Chianti district only 6½ miles from Florence. It is a varied links, with perfect greens and spectacular views from several holes. The first 9 holes, surrounded by cypresses and pines, follow a hilly layout, which provides a panorama of the Tuscan landscape. The next 9 holes have an almost level layout and will prove somewhat more challenging. Except for the 9th (504 yards) and 17th (522 yards), the course favors the medium driver with a diversity of shots in his repertory. Ugolino has been the scene of several tournaments and is a pleasant test both for experts and for the Sunday player.

LOCATION: 6½ miles S of Florence, Ugolino can be reached easily by car, either from the city itself, or from the "Firenze-Sud" (Florence-South) terminus of the Autostrada del Sole (Highway of the Sun). Rome is 174 miles S.

Italian State Tourist Office

Looking toward the ninth hole at the Ugolino Golf Course in the hills near Florence.

OTHER INFORMATION: The course is open to nonmembers, who may play at any time throughout the year. Two professionals are in daily attendance. Weather is generally good during the whole year. Especially well-equipped dressing rooms. Practice ground is available (a 9-hole putting green).
Number of holes: 18. *Par:* 69. *Length:* 5891 yards.
Green fees: weekdays, $3.25; Saturday and all holidays, $5; weekly, $14; monthly, $33. *Lessons:* $3/hour. *Caddies:* $2.25/round. *Golfing equipment and caddie carts:* clubs $2.50/round.

OTHER SPORTS FACILITIES: At the club: large open-air swimming pool, a tennis court, and a putting green. In Florence: the full range of sports activities.

ACCOMMODATIONS: No living space in the club house, but restaurant and bar are available.
In Florence: the visitor will find every kind of accommodation to suit his taste, including 1st, 2nd, 3rd and 4th class hotels, with prices from $3/night, according to the type desired. First-class luxury hotels (*Grand, Villa Medici, Excelsior Italie*) run from about $9 to $10 for single with bath to $18 for double. Pension $17 to $20/day. Middle-range hotels (*Londra, Signoria, Kraft*), $5 to $6 for single with bath, $10 to $12 for double. Pension $13 to $14/day. There are also numerous pensions of every kind, from $4/day, according to type desired. Near the golf course, the Secretary recommends the *Hotel Mediterraneo* and *Villa La Massa*. For further information about these, write the Secretary.

TOURIST ATTRACTIONS: Florence provides every possible kind of tourist attraction, including some of the best shopping in Europe. Especially recommended are the Duomo, Piazza della Signoria, the Uffizi Museum, the Palazzo del Bargello and Museum, the Giardini (Gardens) of Bobili, the Palazzo Pitti and Gallery, the Museum of San Marco, numerous churches, trips into the nearby hills, especially to San Miniato al Monte by way of the Viale Michelangelo and an excursion to Fiesole, 10 miles away.

FOR FURTHER INFORMATION: Write to: Club Secretary, Circolo del Golf dell'Ugolino, via Chiantigiana, Grassina (Firenze), Italy. Telephone: 696.003.

Golf Club Lanzo

For the visitor who wishes to explore the beauties of northern Italy, especially in and around the Lake Country (Como, Lecco, Lugano, Maggiore), the Golf Club Lanzo will more than suit all golfing needs. Although only 9 holes and somewhat short by championship standards, the course is a very pleasant one, possibly because the visitor will find himself on a mountain links for the first time. Even though the length of the holes is normal—3 under 155 yards, 5 under 400, 1 over 400—many of the tees are on a "salita" or rising ground and the terrain is somewhat irregular. All in all, it is an interesting course because of the unexpected nature of the ground and the approaches.

LOCATION: The club is in Lanzo Intelvi, tucked between Lake Como and Lake Lugano, accessible by car or bus. Como is 20 miles S, Lugano (in Switzerland) 15 miles W, Campione 6 miles W, Milan 50 miles S. Rome is 440 miles S.

OTHER INFORMATION: The course is open from May to September, with nonmembers always welcome. All visitors, however, should bring a letter of introduction from their local secretary. A professional is always on hand. The best weather can be expected from June through September, inclusive. Practice ground is available.
Number of holes: 9. Par: 69 (for 18 holes). Length: 5598 yards.
Green fees: weekdays, $3.50/day; weekends and holidays $5/day. Lessons: $3.50/hour. Caddies: $1.60/18 holes; $1/9 holes. Golfing equipment and caddie carts: a small number of clubs for rent by arrangement; no carts for rent.

OTHER SPORTS FACILITIES: This is magnificent country for the active sportsman: fishing, hunting, water skiing (on Lake Lugano), lake swimming and bathing, mountain climbing or walking excursions, tennis, riding through the forests.

ACCOMMODATIONS: No living space in the club house, but bar and restaurant are available.
In Lanzo Intelvi: Park Hotel Villa Violet (Tel. 84139). Fine view of the lake and mountains; open for the golf season (May-September); from $4 for a single, $7 for a double; plus service. Central heating, and, if requested, private bath.
In Campione d'Italia (6 miles away): The Grand Hotel Campione d'Italia (Tel. 87031). Faces Lake Lugano; single with bath from $12, doubles from $18; plus service. No restaurant.
In Lugano (15 miles away): The Splendide Royal (March 15–Nov. 15), the Grand Hotel Eden (April 15–Oct. 15), the Europa Grand Hotel au Lac, Excelsior, Arizona, Villa Castagnola. All offer accommodations from very comfortable to luxurious at prices somewhat above those in Campione and Lanzo Intelvi; singles, $4 to $10, $15 to $20 for best double. Pension $10/day. 18% to 20% service charge.

TOURIST ATTRACTIONS: This is one of the most beautiful sections of Italy. Walking or driving tours will bring the visitor to picturesque lake scenes, breathtaking mountains and beautiful forests. Cable cars offer a view of the entire region. Near Campione there is a gambling casino; and Lugano is a world-famous resort. The various villages and sites along Lake Como, as well as an island in the lake, are of great interest. Nearly every site is famous for its resort facilities.

FOR FURTHER INFORMATION: Write to: Club Secretary, Golf Club Lanzo, Lanzo Intelvi (Como), Italy. Telephone: 84169.

Menaggio e Cadenabbia Golf Club

Like so many other Italian courses, Menaggio e Cadenabbia is set amidst lovely countryside, here in the beautiful Val Menaggio of the North. Mountains, lakes and rich growths of trees and other vegetation mark the boundaries of the fairways. Menaggio e Cadenabbia is an interesting and undulating course, with many varied holes. Since it is not long, it favors the short driver and is excellent for family play. But even the expert golfer will find much to his liking and will perhaps use this course as a warmup for longer and more challenging ones in the area. He can hardly find a more lovely setting in which to tune up his game.

LOCATION: Accessible by car from Menaggio (2 miles), Lugano (16 miles W, in Switzerland), Milan (52 miles S), Como (20 miles S). Rome is 445 miles S, Venice 220 miles SE.

OTHER INFORMATION: Visitors may play, unlimited, but they must show proof of membership in a home golf club. The season is from March to November, and the professional is always on hand. The club is normally crowded on weekends but rarely during the week; good weather can nearly always be expected. Practice ground is available.
Number of holes: 18. *Par:* 65. *Length:* 4433 yards.
Green fees: weekdays, $3; Saturday and Sundays, $4; $16/week, $42/month. *Lessons:* $3.50/hour. *Caddies:* $2.75/18 holes; $2.25/12 holes; $1.90/9 holes. *Golfing equipment and caddie carts:* clubs $1.60/day, carts $.50/day.

OTHER SPORTS FACILITIES: Numerous water sports in Menaggio, on Lake Como, including water skiing, boating, swimming. In Como (20 miles) all sports facilities.

ACCOMMODATIONS: No living space in the club house, but restaurant and bar are available. Club house looks out on Lake Como and contains lounge, changing and locker rooms.
In Menaggio: *Grand Hotel Victoria* (via al Lago 7, Tel. 2003). 106 rooms, singles from $4, doubles from $9; pension $8 to $10/day. 18% service charge. Very quiet and secluded, tennis, parking. Season: April–October. *Grand Hotel e Menaggio* (via 4 Novembre 23, Tel. 2019). 72 rooms, singles from $3, doubles from $12; with baths; taxes included; pension $9 to $12/day. Parking. Season: April 15–October. *Hotel Bellevista* (via 4 Novembre 9, Tel. 2136). 35 rooms, singles from $2, doubles from $6.50; with baths; pension $8 to $10/day. 19% service charge; parking. Season: April 15–October. In addition, Como and Milan offer every type of hotel facility. For Como, see accommodations for *Villa d'Este Golf Club,* p. 174. For Milan, see *Barlassina Golf Club,* pp. 175-176.

TOURIST ATTRACTIONS: There are tourist attractions of every kind in Como and Milan. The immediate area offers beautiful walks, rides, boat trips, sightseeing and bars and cafés; there is excellent shopping and good restaurants in lovely locations.

FOR FURTHER INFORMATION: Write to: Club Secretary, Menaggio e Cadenabbia Golf Club, Grandola e Uniti (Como), Italy. Telephone: 2103.

Golf Club Varese

The golf course is 3 miles from the center of Varese, situated in the spectacular Lake Country of northern Italy. Caught between the lake and the mountains, Varese has tree-lined fairways and well-situated greens. One of the longest courses in Italy, it favors the power hitter but does not unduly punish the shorter, accurate player. The Varese Golf Course should delight those golfers who are looking for a links in lovely surroundings for a playing holiday. The area is known for its healthy air and invigorating climate. If you've tuned up your game a little before coming to Varese, this is an ideal course.

LOCATION: The course can be reached from Varese by car (3 miles). Varese is 28 miles W of Como and 38 miles N of Milan. It can be reached by bus or car from either place. There is also a railway station at Varese. Rome is 395 miles S.

OTHER INFORMATION: The course is open to nonmembers, for unlimited playing, but all visitors should bring proof of membership in a home club. The season lasts the entire year, and a professional is in daily attendance. The most crowded seasons are late autumn and winter; spring and early autumn are excellent for golf, less crowded, with very pleasant weather. Practice ground is available.
Number of holes: 18. *Par:* 72. *Length:* 6644 yards.
Green fees: weekdays, $3.50; Saturdays and Sundays, $6.50. *Lessons:* $2.50/½ hour; $4/hour. *Caddies:* 1st class: $2.50/9 holes, $4/18 holes; 2nd class: $1.75/9 holes, $2.50/18 holes. *Golfing equipment and caddie carts:* no clubs or shoes for rent; caddie carts $.50/round.

OTHER SPORTS FACILITIES: None at the club, but the immediate area—Como and the entire Lake region—is rich in water sports, plus fishing and hunting.

ACCOMMODATIONS: No living quarters in the club house, but lounge, changing and locker rooms, restaurant, and bar are available:
In Varese: the *Europa* (via Sacco, Tel. 35535), *Rosa Ticino* (via Vittorio Veneto 16, Tel. 34355), and *Manzoni* (via Magatti 2, Tel. 31238). All medium-priced hotels, singles from $2.50, doubles $4 to $6; private baths available, central heating, parking.
In Camp dei Fiori (6 miles away): *Grand Hotel dei Fiori* (Tel. 22878). Season: June–September. A quiet, restful place, 110 rooms with baths;

singles from $6, doubles from $10; full pension from $11 to $12/day. 18% service charge. Parking, tennis, beautiful view of the lakes. In addition, Como and Milan furnish hotel accommodations for every pocketbook. For Como, see accommodations for *Villa d'Este Golf Club*, p. 174. For Milan, see accommodations for *Barlassina Golf Club*, pp. 175-176.

TOURIST ATTRACTIONS: The superb scenery provides the background for tours, walking trips, steamer excursions around Lake Maggiore, shopping trips in Varese or nearby Como (particularly for shoes). In Varese, the Public Garden is particularly recommended, as are trips to Sacro Monte (10 miles N) for the village and church, and to Campo dei Fiori (14 miles N) for the panoramic view of six lakes.

FOR FURTHER INFORMATION: Write to: Club Secretary, Golf Club Varese, Monastero di Luvinate, Varese, Italy. Telephone: 34333 or 36568.

Villa d'Este Golf Club

Set in one of the most beautiful regions of Italy, the well-known Lake Como area, the Villa d'Este Golf Club takes full advantage of the extraordinary natural terrain. The course is an interesting one, wooded and narrow, with carries from all tees to the fairway. Constructed nearly forty years ago to fit in with its surroundings, the layout calls for precision from the player rather than sheer long driving. Despite its good length—over 6000 yards—it is a course for the player who attempts accuracy rather than the golfer who relies chiefly on brute strength. But regardless of your game, the course and its surroundings will make for a memorable experience.

LOCATION: The course is situated 3 miles from Como, in Montorfano, and is accessible by car or taxi. From Milan, on the superhighway, it is about 35 miles N. Rome is 345 miles S.

OTHER INFORMATION: The course is open to visitors and nonmembers for unlimited play, although tournaments, of course, take precedence. The professional is on hand for the entire season, which lasts from late March to early November. The course may be crowded at all times of the year. Good weather can usually be expected. Practice ground is available. *Number of holes:* 18. *Par:* 70 (S.S.S., 71). *Length:* 6070 yards.
Green fees: For those residing at the Villa d'Este Hotel: $3.25/day, $15/week. For those not residing at the Hotel: $4.25/day, $6.50/Saturdays, Sundays, holidays. *Lessons:* $2.50/½ hour. *Caddies:* 1st category: weekdays, $3.25/round; Saturdays and Sundays, $4.25/round. 2nd category: weekdays, $2/round; Saturdays and Sundays, $2.50/round. *Golfing equipment and caddie carts:* clubs $2.50/round, carts (not motorized) $1/round.

OTHER SPORTS FACILITIES: This is a great sports area as well as a popular health resort. The nearby *Hotel Villa d'Este* (8 miles away), on the shores of Lake Como, offers all kinds of activities for the outdoorsman:

Villa d'Este Golf Club is set in the famous Lake Como area.

swimming, fishing, water skiing. The hotel has a new floating swimming pool, four tennis courts in its large private park, riding facilities. The whole area offers similar facilities.

ACCOMMODATIONS: No living space in the club house, but restaurant and bar are available.

In Cernobbio: *Hotel Villa d'Este.* Single and double rooms facing Lake Como. Rates include service and state tax; singles with baths, $11 to $16; doubles with baths, $16 to $24. Additional bed $4. Breakfast $1.50, lunch $5, dinner $6. Complete pension and half pension also available. All amenities, experienced staff, 20% reduction for children.

In Como: *Barchetta Excelsion* (piazza Cavour 1, Tel. 32931). From $6 for single with bath, $11 for double. *Villa Flori* (strada per Cernobbio, Tel. 57642). Open April–October. $3 for single with bath, $10 for double. *Metropole e Suisse* (piazza Cavour 19, Tel. 22105). $5 and up for single with bath, $12 for double. Pension and half pension $8 and up/day. 19% service charge. All of these can be reached from the golf course by car.

TOURIST ATTRACTIONS: The Lake Como area offers splendid scenery, tours of old and picturesque villages, leisurely living in graceful and quiet surroundings, beautiful old buildings, gardens and mansions. Como is also known for its production of high quality silk. For the determined golfer, the Villa d'Este Course is an excellent jumping-off place for other equally fine courses in the Como region and across the Swiss border.

FOR FURTHER INFORMATION: Write to: Dr. Willy Dembré, Honorary Secretary, Villa d'Este Golf Club, Como, Italy. Telephone: 37471.

Barlassina Country Club

Only 15 miles from Milan, the Barlassina Country Club should appeal to all golfers, whether high or low handicappers. The course, located in the typical landscape of the Lombard plain, is not only of championship caliber but is also entertaining. The fairways and greens are framed by the pines, birches, firs, poplars and oaks that make the Italian landscape distinctive. The relatively inexperienced as well as the expert golfer will find something to his taste here. There are 3 long holes with par 5 and several short ones at 200 yards or under with par 3. On the whole, the lengthy course favors the power golfer, but the variety of the testing shots will make the wild hitter wince. This is an excellent course if you want a break from business or tourism in the Milan area.

LOCATION: The Barlassina Country Club is located on the Milan–Como highway, halfway (15 miles each way) between the two cities. The nearest towns are Barlassina and Lentate on Seveso, less than a mile away. The best way to arrive at the course is by car. Rome is 325 miles S.

OTHER INFORMATION: The Barlassina Country Club is private, but play is unlimited for visitors. During the height of the season, however, it is best to make arrangements ahead for Saturdays and Sundays. Visitor should bring proof of membership in a home golf club. The course is open all year; the most crowded season is in April, May, June, September, October, and November; the best weather is in spring and autumn. The professional is on hand all year, except August, and is available for nonmembers. Practice ground (driving range and putting green) is available.
 Number of holes: 18. *Par:* 71 (S.S.S., 71). *Length:* 6540 yards (championship), 6252 (men), 5644 (women).
 Green fees: weekdays, $4; Saturdays, Sundays, and holidays, $5.50/day. *Lessons:* $3.25/½ hour; $4.10/hour. *Caddies:* 1st class: $4.10/18 holes, tip included. 2nd class: $3.25/18 holes, tip included. *Golfing equipment and caddie carts:* clubs $1.75/round, carts $.80/round.

OTHER SPORTS FACILITIES: None in the immediate area, but all water sports at Lake Como.

ACCOMMODATIONS: Living space in the club house is only for members, but restaurant and bar are available.
 In Como: *Barchetta Excelsior, Villa Flori,* and *Metropole e Suisse.* See p. 174 for details (*Villa d'Este Golf Club*).
 In Milan: *Grand Hotel Continental* (via Manzoni 7, Tel. 807641). Very luxurious, 180 rooms, singles $10, doubles $20; pension from $20/day. 21% service charge. All amenities. *Grand Hotel Duomo* (via San Raffaele 1, Tel. 8833), the *De la Ville* (via Hoepli 6, Tel. 867061), the *Marino alla*

Scale (piazza della Scala, Tel. 867803). All rooms have private baths; central heating; parking, experienced staff; about 20% less than the above. *Principe e Savoia* (piazza della Repubblica 17, Tel. 6230). The *Excelsior Gallia* (piazza Duca d'Aosta 9, 637044). The *Palace* (piazza della Repubblica 20, Tel. 6336). Singles from $7, doubles from $15 to $16; pension from $15/day (not at *Principe e Savoia*). Very luxurious. 21% service charge. All amenities.

In Seveso: *Calypso* (Corso Garibaldi 5, Tel. 53223). 15 rooms; singles from $2.50, doubles from $5.50; some with baths. Central heating.

TOURIST ATTRACTIONS: Tourist attractions of every kind abound— cultural, aesthetic, athletic. Como offers scenic delights: while Milan offers the cultural—opera, museums, churches. See particularly the Duomo, the Brera Palace and Picture Gallery, Da Vinci's *Last Supper*. The district, named Brianza, is well known for the production of furniture, and there is excellent shopping through the area and in Milan.

FOR FURTHER INFORMATION: Write to: Club Secretary, Barlassina Country Club, Birago di Camnago, Milan, Italy. Telephone: 7556 and 70230.

Golf Club Bergamo ("L'Albenza")

Located at Almenno San Bartolomeo, near Bergamo, the Bergamo Golf Club is excellent for the visitor to the Italian Lake Country who wishes a golfing holiday. In addition, many major cities are within easy reach— Milan, Venice, as well as Verona, Padua, Mantua. Here you will find a course of medium difficulty for both long and short drivers with natural doglegs and fairways circled by numerous trees. Although the power hitter will be favored, there is something for everyone. The length of the course —unusually long for a continental links—might lull the strong hitter into carelessness, while the tightness of many of the holes will challenge his short game.

LOCATION: Accessible by car, the links is located 7½ miles from Bergamo, near the superhighway running from Turin (85 miles SW) and Milan (30 miles SW) to the East (Brescia, Verona, Vicenza, Padua, and Venice). Venice is 140 miles E, Rome 373 miles S.

OTHER INFORMATION: The course is open to nonmembers, although the Director has the right to establish the number of players if excessive. It is best to apply ahead of time for a permit to play. All visiting players should bring proof of membership in their home clubs. Two professionals are on hand during the season, which runs from March to November. The height of the season is May to June and September to October, with the best weather during the latter time. Closed Monday. Equipped practice ground is available.

Number of holes: 18. *Par:* 72 (S.S.S., 72). *Length:* 6626 yards. *Green fees:* weekdays, $3.50; Saturdays and Sundays, $5/day; holidays, $6.50/day. *Lessons:* $2/½ hour; $3.50/hour. *Caddies:* $2/hour. *Golfing equipment and caddie carts:* clubs $1.75/day.

OTHER SPORTS FACILITIES: At the club, no other sports facilities exist. In Como and around the Lake area proper, all types of sports activities are available: swimming, boating, fishing, water skiing.

ACCOMMODATIONS: No living space in the club house, but an excellent bar and restaurant are available.

In Bergamo: *Excelsior San Marco* (viale Vittorio Emanuele 11, Tel. 232132). 93 rooms; singles from $6, doubles from $10, service included. Luxurious, view from roof garden, air conditioning. *Grand Hotel Moderno* (viale Roma 106, Tel. 233033). 70 rooms, singles from $3.50, doubles from $9, service included; pension, $9 to $11 inclusive/day. Private baths, central heating. *Touring* (piazza Vittorio Veneto 10, Tel. 242280). 42 rooms; singles from $3, doubles from $7; service included. Breakfast but no restaurant. Private baths, central heating. Recommended restaurants: Manarini (viale Vittorio Emanuele 5), Moro (via Tiraboschi 7).

TOURIST ATTRACTIONS: Bergamo offers many tourist attractions: Piazza Vecchio, the historical center of the town; Capella Colleoni, a beautifully decorated chapel; Rocca, the citadel; the Carrara (painting) Academy. Also, the general area is known for its spun goods.

FOR FURTHER INFORMATION: Write to: Club Secretary, Golf Club Bergamo, Almenno San Bartolomeo, Bergamo, Italy. Telephone: 54.11.33.

Golf Club Punta Ala

Situated on the west coast of Italy, about halfway between Rome and Florence, Punta Ala is set against the extremely blue waters where the Ligurian Sea meets the Tyrrhenian. If you are near the lower Italian Riviera, a golfing trip to Punta Ala is well worth the time. The course is one of the best in Italy and possibly among the best in continental Europe. It has length (over 6700 yards), variety and many holes of testing quality for both the long and short driver. The natural undulations of the ground provide the terrain for the course, and the fairways unroll amidst stately evergreen trees. The course is only ¼ mile from the sea, and gentle breezes cut the heat of the summer. One further advantage is that this part of coastal Italy is still not too crowded. A trip here should prove a rewarding experience for both play and touring.

LOCATION: The nearest large city to Punta Ala is Grosseto (28 miles), on the main highway between Rome (140 miles SE) and Siena-Florence (120 miles NW). There is complete bus and train service to Grosseto from all points in Italy or to Follonica (13 miles N of Punta Ala). Then take either taxi, private car or bus to the course.

OTHER INFORMATION: The course is open to nonmembers the entire year; a professional and his assistant are always on hand. During the height of the season (the summer months) three professionals are available. Because of the mild climate, it is possible to play right through the winter months. Driving range is available.

Number of holes: 18. *Par:* 72. *Length:* 6708 yards.

Green fees: $5/day; $24/week; $72/month. *Lessons:* $4/hour with professional; $3.25/hour with assistant professional. *Caddies:* $2/9 holes, $3.50/18 holes, tip included. *Golfing equipment and caddie carts:* clubs $2.50/day, carts $.50/day.

OTHER SPORTS FACILITIES: All types of water sports: swimming, diving, water skiing, boating, fishing; also tennis, riding, polo and even hunting.

ACCOMMODATIONS: No living space in the club house, but a snack bar is available.

In Punta Ala: *Gallia Palace Hotel* (open June to Sept., Tel. 52022). 95 rooms; single with bath $7.50, doubles to $14; service included; pension $16 to $17/day, all inclusive. Very quiet, restful, facing the sea; air conditioning, parking, experienced staff. *Golf Hotel* (open only during the summer season, Tel. 52026, 7, 8). *Hotel Alleluiah* (Tel. 52050). *Hotel Welt-Ring* (Tel. 52044). Price range for all generally from $6 for single, $12 and up for double. All comforts, experienced staff.

In Grosseto: *Lorena* (via Truste 3, Tel. 25501).

In Follonica: *Minerva* (via Bicocchi 44, Tel. 84010).

TOURIST ATTRACTIONS; During the summer season there are numerous events: polo, horsemanship contests, and evening spectacles; also excursions to Follonica, Riva del Sole and other popular coastal resorts.

FOR FURTHER INFORMATION: Write to: Club Secretary, Punta Ala Golf Club, Punta Ala (Grosseto), Italy. Telephone: 52251.

Rapallo Golf Club

Rapallo has become an internationally known resort area, justly renowned for its mild climate and beautiful scenery. Located on the so-called Italian Riviera, the town makes an attractive background for the golf course, which is small but interesting in its variety. What creates its chief interest is a small canal that crosses several holes and provides a challenge for every type of player. Principally, the course is for the short driver, the golfer who is accurate and precise. But the more powerful driver may find this an excellent place to tune up his game, possibly in preparation for the more demanding courses in the North or around Venice and Rome.

LOCATION: About ½ mile from Rapallo proper, the golf course is accessible by car and by bus. A regular bus line runs from the railway station to the club. Rapallo is connected by boat to Portofino and San Fruttuoso. It is only 18 miles from a major city, Genoa (north), and is near a main highway (N1) leading south along the western coast of Italy.

OTHER INFORMATION: The course is open to nonmembers all year, but visitors should bring proof of membership in their home golf club. The two professionals and one assistant professional are always on hand. Summer is most crowded, but the best season is spring. Weather mild all year round. Practice ground is available.

Number of holes: 9. *Par:* 33. *Length:* 2461 yards.

Green fees: $3.50/day. *Lessons:* $3.50/hour with the two professionals; $2.50/hour with the assistant professional. *Caddies:* 1st class: $1.60/9 holes, $3.50/18 holes. 2nd class: $1.25/9 holes, $2.50/18 holes. *Golfing equipment and caddie carts:* clubs $.85, carts $.50.

OTHER SPORTS FACILITIES: Tennis at the Rapallo Golf Club's tennis courts. In the immediate area: swimming, boating, water skiing, skin diving, fishing.

ACCOMMODATIONS: No living space in the club house, but restaurant and bar are available.

In Rapallo: *Excelsior Palace* (via San Michele 10, Tel. 50841). View of the sea and the city; 112 rooms; single with bath, $10, doubles $17; 21% service charge; pension, $15 to $19/day. *Grand Hotel Bristol* (via Aurelia Orientale 240, Tel. 50216). 70 rooms; singles $8, doubles $14; taxes included; pension $14 to $15/day. Parking, swimming pool on the panoramic terrace. Other excellent hotels include *Grand Hotel, Grand Hotel ed Europa, Moderne et Royal,* and several others of differing prices and types. If the visitor wishes to commute to the course from Genoa (18 miles), he will find every type of accommodation there (*Columbia-Excelsior* and *Savoia-Majestic,* in the luxury class; *Bristol Palace* and *Plaza,* in very comfortable class; *Atlantico* and *Park,* in comfortable class).

TOURIST ATTRACTIONS: This section of the lower Italian Riviera is famous for its shopping as well as its beauty. There are many boutiques in Rapallo, in San Margherita and Portofino, all within a mile or two of each other. The visitor might tour the nearby hills or the fishing villages in the area or the Portofino promontory. A well-known church, Madonna di Montallegro, is worth a visit and can be reached by cablecar, which departs hourly. Many smart bars and clubs are found in the area. Genoa, of course, offers a wide range of tourist attractions—the Port, via Garibaldi, the various palaces.

FOR FURTHER INFORMATION: Write to: Club Secretary, Rapallo Golf and Tennis Club, via Mameli 99, Rapallo (Genova), Italy. Telephone: 50.210.

Golf Club degli Ulivi

Only a short distance from the French border, the Golf Club degli Ulivi at San Remo is beautifully located for golf and for tourism. San Remo is a world-renowned resort with a delightful year-round temperature and gay festivals and it is the principal flower market of Italy. The name of the course is Golf Club of the Olive Trees because of the presence of so many of these lovely trees in and around it. The course is almost perfect for the casual visitor—not too demanding and yet challenging enough to keep up one's game. It is a hilly links suitable for both long and short drivers. Somewhat short at 5316 yards, it is splendidly balanced with enough long holes, short holes, tight approaches and good fairways to keep everyone satisfied.

LOCATION: The golf course is on the outskirts of San Remo, about 3 miles behind the città vecchia, or old part of the city. The course is most accessible by car on the road from San Remo to San Romolo. San Remo is 35 miles E of Nice, 23 E of Monaco, 90 miles SW of Genoa on the superhighway, 420 NW of Rome, 188 SW of Milan.

OTHER INFORMATION: The course is open all year, although the season starts on November 1 and lasts until the end of April. The course is open to nonmembers who can show membership in any regular golf club. Two professionals are available during the season, and four assistants are on hand all year. The most crowded period is from December 15 to the end of February. The weather is generally always good. There is no special practice ground, but the first few holes are used for practice. Putting green is available.

Number of holes: 18. Par: 65. Length: 5316 yards.

Green fees: weekdays, $2.25; Sundays and holidays, $3.50/day; $1.25 for practice. Special fees for 7 consecutive days, for 2 weeks, and for a month. Lessons: $3.50/hour from the professional, $2.50/hour from the assistant. Caddies: 1st class: $2.50/18 holes. 2nd class: $1.50/18 holes. During competition, caddies are reserved for competitors. Golfing equipment and caddie carts: clubs $1.60; no caddie carts because of hilly terrain.

OTHER SPORTS FACILITIES: Well placed in the Italian Riviera and only a few miles from the French Riviera, San Remo offers every type of sports facility: seabathing, swimming (in pools), water skiing, boating, tennis, riding.

ACCOMMODATIONS: No living space in the club house, but an excellent restaurant and smart bar are available. Also other first-rate restaurants in San Remo.

In San Remo (136 hotels and boarding houses): Royal (corso Imperatrice 74, Tel. 84321). Closed Sept. 20–Dec. 20; most luxurious; single with bath from $12, double from $20; 18% service charge. Pension from $18.50/day.

Swimming pool, floral gardens, all comforts. *Savoy* (via Nuvoloni 28, Tel. 84921). Closed Oct.–Dec. 5; a luxury hotel with all comforts at prices about 10% to 15% lower than the *Royal. Miramare* (corso Matuzia 9, Tel. 85486; closed Nov.–Dec. 20); *Astoria West-End* (corso Matuzia 8, Tel. 70791); *Grand Hotel Londra* (corso Matuzia 2, Tel. 70801); *Vittoria e Roma* (corso Cavallotti 30, Tel. 85264). Nearly all have views overlooking the sea. $6 to $8 for a single, $10 to $15 for double; private bath; pension $10 to $15/day.

TOURIST ATTRACTIONS: San Remo needs no introduction to the tourist; its flower gardens, fine shops, lovely beach and other facilities for entertainment speak for themselves. Its proximity to other Italian cities like Genoa, Rapallo and Portofino (as well as its closeness to Nice, Cannes and Monaco) adds to its luster.

FOR FURTHER INFORMATION: Write to: Club Secretary, Golf Club degli Ulivi, San Remo, Prov. Imperia, Italy. Telephone: San Remo 85932.

Golf Club Cansiglio
(Vittorio Veneto)

This small golf course is situated in a lovely section of Italy that has not yet been fully discovered by tourists. It is within two hours' driving distance of Venice and even closer to many picturesque cities of the Northeast; it is only 60 miles from Cortina d'Ampezzo, for example. The course is for both long and short drivers; the fairways are natural, and even the obstacles, such as they are, are not artificial. The English architects who designed the course found that they were able to follow the natural terrain, including the numerous pine trees, and come up with a very playable course. The visitor should find it to his liking.

LOCATION: The golf course is 12 miles from Vittorio Veneto, which can be reached by train or car. Vittorio Veneto is 50 miles N of Venice, 25 N of Treviso, 18 S of Belluno, 225 NE of Milan, 350 NE of Rome.

OTHER INFORMATION: The club is open from April to October; nonmembers are welcome, unlimited. The weather is best during July, August, and September. The club professional is always available during the season. Practice ground is available.
Number of holes: 9. *Par:* 72 (for 2 x 9). *Length:* 5450 yards (2 x 2725). *Green fees:* $1.75/day. *Lessons:* $3.25/hour. *Caddies:* $1.25/9 holes. *Golfing equipment and caddie carts:* no clubs for rent; carts $.70/day.

OTHER SPORTS FACILITIES: This is rugged country, and the outdoorsman will find it a sports paradise: hunting, fishing, plenty of mountain excursions and riding. Nearby is horse racing. For the less active sports enthusiast, there are innumerable walking trips into the lovely northern Italian countryside.

ACCOMMODATIONS: No living space in the club house, but restaurant and bar in a nearby hotel, the *Albergo San Marco* (Tel. 57404). Located only a few yards from the course, this hotel offers modern facilities with all comforts. Newly built and with private bath for each room, it is open from December 20 to February and then from June 15 to September. Singles from $3, doubles from $6; pension $6.50 to $8.50/day.

In Vittorio Veneto: The *Terme* (viale della Vittoria, Tel. 57025) and the *Vittorio Veneto* (via San Gottardo 7, Tel. 55229). Comfortable quarters, private baths, central heating, from $3 for singles, from $5 for doubles. No restaurant in the *Vittorio Veneto.*

TOURIST ATTRACTIONS: The town of Vittorio Veneto is attractive, with lovely Gothic and Renaissance-style houses and a fifteenth-century town hall. The surrounding woods are famous, as is the nearby "Forest of Cansiglio." Belluno, to the north, is known for its lovely architecture, and Conegliano, to the south, is also a picturesque town. Venice is less than 2 hours away by car or train.

FOR FURTHER INFORMATION: Write to: Azienda Soggiorno Turismo, Vittorio Veneto, prov. di Venetia, Italy. Telephone: 57402.

Golf Club Villa Condulmer

The Villa Condulmer Golf Course is small—only 9 holes—but it was specially designed by an English architect so that it provides something of interest for every type of golfer. Each hole has a particular feature, with sand bunkers, grass bunkers, plus the usual other obstacles of trees, streams and roughs. It is of medium difficulty, with a variety of testing shots; it is excellent for the less experienced golfer as well as for the more advanced player. Condulmer contains a watering system, so it remains in excellent shape for the entire season of nine months. The setting of the links is particularly beautiful, between Venice and Treviso, and the course is so laid out that the golfer can enjoy the beauty of the Italian countryside as he plays.

LOCATION: The best way to reach the course, in Mogliano, is by car (N3) either from Venice, 13 miles S, or from Treviso, 12 miles N. The club is also accessible from Padua, Vicenza and Verona.

OTHER INFORMATION: The course is open to nonmembers, but all visitors should bring proof of membership in their local club. Hotel guests can play unlimited. The season is from March 15 to December 15, with best weather in April and May and in September and October. The course is rarely so crowded that newcomers cannot play. A professional is in daily attendance. Practice ground is available without additional charge except for balls.

Number of holes: 9. *Par:* 35. *Length:* 2800 yards.

Green fees: weekdays, $2.50; Saturdays, Sundays, and holidays, $3.15/day; $13.75/week; $48.00/month. *Lessons:* $2.50/hour; practice balls

$.40/basket of 25. *Caddies:* $.65/9 holes, $1.25/18 holes. *Golfing equipment and caddie carts:* golf clubs $.80/day, caddie carts $.50/day.

OTHER SPORTS FACILITIES: The club provides swimming in a filtrated and heated pool on the grounds. In nearby Venice: tennis and riding.

ACCOMMODATIONS: No living space in the club house, but restaurant and bar are available at low cost. At the course: *Hotel Villa Condulmer.* A very comfortable and attractive eighteenth-century building, now modernized, with full modern conveniences; bath, shower, telephone. 32 rooms; $4 to $8/person; pension $9 to $10/day; service included. If the *Villa Condulmer* is full, which is rare, golfers can stay in hotels within a range of 2 or 3 miles. The region is full of new lodgings, restaurants and inns with a wide variety of prices to suit every pocketbook. For these arrangements, write to the *Villa Condulmer.*
For accommodations in Venice, see *Circolo Golf Lido di Venezia,* p. 184.

TOURIST ATTRACTIONS: Nearby cities—Venice, Padua, Treviso, Verona and Mantua—provide everything of interest—cultural, historical, architectural—that any visitor could possibly want. Especially recommended are the Giotto frescoes in Padua, the central part of Verona, as well as the Art Museum and the Ducal Palace and apartments in Mantua.

FOR FURTHER INFORMATION: Write to: Club Secretary, Villa Condulmer, Zerman di Mogliano Veneto, Treviso-Venezia (Venice), Italy. Telephone: 450.001.

Circolo Golf Lido di Venezia
(Alberoni Golf Course)

One could hardly hope for a more beautiful setting than that of the Alberoni Golf Course. It is set on the western limit of the Lido landstrip, resting betwen the lagoon and the Adriatic Sea, only 20 minutes from Venice itself. This is a seaside links—a spectacular one. It is of championship caliber—long for a continental course at 6536 yards. While the several par 5s would seem to favor the long hitter, an analysis of the course indicates overall balance, since it features many long drives as well as testing shots. It provides a good workout for the visitor who has a broad repertory without unduly penalizing the golfer who is strong in a single department. Here is a lot of golf in a setting that is incomparable.

LOCATION: The Alberoni Course can be reached from Venice by car and by boat. A public bus (No. 8) also runs out to the Lido. By boat: to the Lido and then a car to the course. In all, a trip of 20 to 30 minutes from Venice. Milan is 170 miles W, Rome 340 SW.

OTHER INFORMATION: The season lasts from March through Novem-

ber, and the club is open to nonmembers, who should bring proof of membership in their local club. The professional is in daily attendance. The best weather is in July, but the most crowded time is usually in August. Practice ground is available.
  Number of holes: 18. *Par:* 72 (S.S.S., 72). *Length:* 6536 yards (championship), 6242 yards (normal tees).
  Green fees: $6.50/day. *Lessons:* $4/hour. *Caddies:* $2.50/18 holes, $1.50/9 holes. *Golfing equipment and caddie carts:* clubs $2.50/day, carts, $.50/day.

  OTHER SPORTS FACILITIES: Since the course is minutes away from one of the most famous beaches in the world, the visitor can expect first-rate swimming, skiing, boating, etc. In addition, riding, tennis and the sports facilities of a large city.

  ACCOMMODATIONS: No living space in the club house, but bar and restaurant are available.
  The Lido: The *Excelsior Palace Hotel* (Tel. 60201). A luxury hotel; singles from $12, doubles to $22; 23% service charge; pension from $16/day. Air conditioning, lovely view of sea and beach, tennis courts. Season: May 15–Sept. *Grand Hotel des Bains* (season: May–September, Tel. 60381), the *Quattro Fontane* (season: April–September, Tel. 60227), and the *Grand Hotel Lido* (open for summer season, Tel. 60213). Approximately the same accommodations as the above at prices about 10% to 25% lower. Experienced staffs, private baths, all amenities.
  In Venice: The *Gritti Palace Hotel* (campo Santa Maria del Giglio 2467, Tel. 26044), the *Danieli Royal Excelsior* (riva degli Schiavoni 4196, Tel. 26480), the *Grand Hotel* (season, March–November, calle larga 22 Marzo 2321, Tel. 31781). All offer the facilities of great luxury hotels; singles with baths $6 to $12, doubles $17 to $24; full pension from $12/day. 18% service charge. The *Bauer Grunwald, Grand Hotel Europa e Britannia, Cipriani,* and *Grand Hotel Luna* offer excellent accommodations at slightly lower cost. Several small hotels around the golf course provide full pension from $6/day/person.

  TOURIST ATTRACTIONS: Besides the beaches of the Lido, Venice (20 minutes away) offers a range of entertainment, cultural or otherwise, that hardly needs enumeration. The chief attractions are walking trips through the 117 connected islands, the Doges' Palace, the Grand Canal, the Rialto Bridge, the Academy of Fine Arts, San Marco, the Scuola San Rocco.

  FOR FURTHER INFORMATION: Write to: Club Secretary, Golf Club Lido, Venice, Italy. Telephone: 60.815.

Golf Club Miramonti

  The Miramonti Golf Course is located in one of the most famous resort areas in Italy, indeed in all of Europe—Cortina d'Ampezzo. Cortina is the center of numerous cultural and athletic activities suitable for every taste. The golf course is a typically mountain links, that is, one without numerous long holes or many straightaways. At only 2100 yards, it is for the short and accurate driver. It is an interesting course, however, and the long hitter might find it useful to sharpen his short game here. For the less determined golfer, the surroundings of Miramonti are superb, with snow-covered mountains and rich vegetation in the background. A new 18-hole course is to be opened in the near future.

LOCATION: The golf course is on the ground of the Miramonti Majestic Hotel, one mile from Cortina. A bus runs from the course to Cortina, on a regular timetable. Cortina, the capital of the Dolomites, is 250 miles NE of Milan, 100 miles N of Venice, 45 N of Belluno, 70 E of Bolzano, all on direct lines by car or rail. There is also bus service from each major city to Cortina. Rome is 435 miles S.

OTHER INFORMATION: The course is open to nonmembers, unlimited; the season is from July 1 to September 10, with the most crowded time from July 20 to August 20. A professional is always in attendance. Weather is good from July on and very good in the second half of August and in September. Practice ground is available.
Number of holes: 9. *Par:* 31 (S.S.S., 30). *Length:* 2100 yards.
Green fees: $2/half day, $2.50/day, $11.50/week, $20/two weeks, $33/month, $40/season. Special discount for guests of the hotel; $.80 for practice. *Lessons:* $4/hour. *Caddies:* $.70/9 holes, $1.40/18 holes. *Golfing equipment and caddie carts:* clubs $3.25/day; no caddie carts.

OTHER SPORTS FACILITIES: Cortina is of course a sportsman's paradise: tennis, riding, swimming, fishing, ice-curling, ice-skating, climbing, bowling.

ACCOMMODATIONS: Restaurant and bar are always open, and golfers, whether hotel guests or not, are welcome.
Miramonti Majestic Hotel (Tel. 4201). Low season (June 20–July 20): singles from $5 to $10, doubles to $15; pension $9 to $15/day. High season (July 20–August 25): 3 days minimum stay; singles $5 to $10, doubles $10 to $20; pension $10 to $18/day. 18% service charge. Season: December 20 to March 10 for skiing and June 20 to September 10 for other sports.
In Cortina: *Cristallo Palace* (via Menardi 20), *Grand Hotel Savoia* (via Roma 22), *Excelsior Cademai* (at Cademai, ½ mile away). All have lovely views, experienced staffs, private baths, parking, breakfast, and full pension. Very comfortable hotels; prices 10% to 30% below those of the Miramonti.
In addition, there are dozens of less expensive lodgings in the locality, as well as numerous excellent restaurants, including Foghèr.

TOURIST ATTRACTIONS: The region is colorful; the natives dress in their local costumes, hold fêtes and still speak in their old dialect. Cortina has fine shops, mostly for sports and casual wear. During the season there are tennis tournaments, ice hockey matches and other sports events. Night clubs with good international orchestras, several picture galleries, a wide variety of entertainment and artistic events fill out the diverse offerings.

FOR FURTHER INFORMATION: Write to: Secretary, Golf Club Miramonti, Cortina d'Ampezzo, Italy. Telephone: 4201.

LOW COUNTRIES

In an area as small as Belgium and Holland, you can make a tour of all eight courses I have listed without going out of your way. They are among the best in terms of the challenge they offer and their proximity to attractive and interesting cities. They are easily accessible, and you will feel most welcome.

All three Belgian courses are of championship caliber—the more reason to try them. Nearly everyone who visits Belgium passes through Brussels, now also the capital of the Common Market. The *Royal Golf Club de Belgique* will suitably reward your efforts, and on your way up to Brussels you might want to stop at Waterloo to visit the famous battle site. While there, play *Royal Waterloo;* take your pick of two courses according to your game. And if you're going north through Belgium on the way to Holland, stop in Antwerp to sightsee and to play *Royal Antwerp.* The full course is 6600 tough yards, and it's one you'll remember.

In Holland, either *Rosendaelsche,* a leisurely 9-holer in Arnhem, or *Kennemer* in Amsterdam will make a good beginning. Then move on to the tougher *Haagsche* and *Hilversumsche* in Amsterdam, and by all means try *Toxandria,* one of Holland's best. If you're coming up from Belgium, you might add *Toxandria* to your plans, which already include *Belgique, Royal Waterloo* and *Royal Antwerp.* They lie in line between Brussels and Rotterdam.

The Low Countries, like equally small Switzerland, are hospitable, comfortable and relaxing for the visitor. If you don't plan to tour them directly, you might consider adding them as a side trip. Their golf alone will provide a pleasant diversion.

BELGIUM

Royal Golf Club de Belgique

Only a few miles from the center of Brussels, in a lovely country setting, the Royal Golf Club de Belgique has built two courses, one of championship caliber. The average player should not be frightened, however; the 18-hole Green Course is not so difficult that the casual player or visitor will find it impossible. Whatever your game, the course is playable. The terrain is undulating, lined by all types of firs and many other kinds of trees that produce blossoms during the year. The tight fairways are also lined by some of Belgium's famous rhododendron bushes. The course starts with a rush, two very long holes with the green guarded on both sides by heavy bunkers. Once past this and the 514-yard 5th, the visitor should find the first 9 to his liking. Generally there is good balance—numerous long holes (4 near 500 yards or over), several short ones and enough precision work for the steady player.

LOCATION: The club is in the eastern suburbs of Tervuren (also spelled Tervueren), connected to Brussels by an electric train that leaves every 20 minutes from Parc du Cinquantenaire. The club is also accessible by car or taxi; it is 6 miles from the Grand'Place, the center of Brussels.

OTHER INFORMATION: The course is open all year to nonmembers, although on certain Saturdays and Sundays it is open only to visitors playing with a member. All visitors should check first with the secretary's office (Brussels 57.58.01). Four professionals are on hand during the year. The best weather can be expected from April to the end of October, with the most crowded season April to the end of July, and September to the end of October. Practice ground, heated and covered, can accommodate ten players; automatic ball service and special floodlighting for night practice.

Number of holes: 18 (also a 9-hole course). *Par:* 73 (33 for 9 holes). *Length:* 6615 yards for the Green championship course, 2058 yards for the new 9-hole course.

Green fees: weekdays, $2; Saturdays and Sundays, $5/day; entire weekends, $8. *Lessons:* $3.50 to $5/hour. *Caddies:* $2.50/round. *Golfing equipment and caddie carts:* clubs $1/day or round, carts free.

OTHER SPORTS FACILITIES: Riding, tennis, indoor swimming pools, soccer matches, ice skating.

ACCOMMODATIONS: No living space in the club house, but a permanent bar and restaurant are available in the club house; closed on Mondays.

Brussels has a full range of first-class accommodations and restaurants. *Palace* (22 pl. Rogier, Tel. 176200), *Plaza* (118 bd. A.-Max, Tel. 179140), *Métropole* (31 pl. de Brouckère, Tel. 172300), *Westbury* (popular with

American visitors, 6 r. Cardinal-Mercier, Tel. 136480), *Amigo* (1 r. de l'Amigo, Tel. 115910). The last is in the heart of the city. Luxury hotels; private baths with nearly every room, central heating, excellent restaurants, experienced staffs; singles from $8, doubles up to $30; 20% service charge. *Bedford, Marie-José, Astoria, Colonies, Vendôme, Central.* Singles from $4, doubles from $8; many rooms with private baths; central heating.

TOURIST ATTRACTIONS: As headquarters for the Common Market, Brussels is an excellent shopping center for laces, linens, glassware, jewelry, furniture, among other items. The shopping areas are all located uptown between Porte Louise and Porte de Namur and downtown between Gare du Midi and Gare du Nord, with public transportation circulating from one area to the other. Brussels also offers cultural, architectural and historical points of interest: Grand'Place, Musée d'Art ancien, Place Royale, Cathédrale St.-Michel et Ste.-Gudule, Manneken Pis and many others.

FOR FURTHER INFORMATION: Write to: Club Secretary, Royal Golf Club de Belgique, Chateau de Ravenstein, Tervueren, Belgium. Telephone: 57.58.01.

Royal Waterloo Golf Club

The Royal Waterloo Golf Club is 3 miles east of the historic Waterloo battlefield, where in 1815 the Duke of Wellington's armies defeated the forces under Napoleon. Only a few miles further north is Brussels, with all the facilities of a major city. Golf at Waterloo combines proximity to a large city, an historic background and fine golfing on two lovely courses, one for the average player and the other for championship matches. The major course (called the "A.B.") has great length—over 6700 yards—and provides a real challenge for the best of players. This is a course for the long driver who can also control his short game. Luckily, the tees can be shortened by about 500 yards if necessary. The secondary course (called the "C.D.") is by no means easy. At a little over 5000 yards, it does not require great power, but it does combine narrow fairways with some clever bunkering to provide a good game. There's a lot of golf at Waterloo, whichever course you choose to play.

LOCATION: The club is in Ohain, 3 miles E of Waterloo. Waterloo is 15 miles S of Brussels, about 25 to 30 minutes by car. The club is accessible by car or taxi, on the main road from Brussels to Charleroi (N5). Brussels is 175 miles N of Paris, 125 S of Amsterdam.

OTHER INFORMATION: The course is open all year to the nonmember with no limitation except that on weekends members have first call on the green. For weekend play it is best to reserve the course ahead of time. The professional is in daily attendance. The official season is from April 1st through the end 'of October, with the most crowded time from June until September. Weather is always unpredictable. Practice ground is available.

Number of holes: A.B., 18; C.D., 18. *Par:* A.B., 73; C.D., 69. *Length:* A.B., 6714 yards; C.D., 5049 yards.

Green fees: weekdays, $3; weekends, $5/day. *Lessons:* $3.50 to $5/hour. *Caddies:* $3/round. *Golfing equipment and caddie carts:* clubs about $1/day.

OTHER SPORTS FACILITIES: None in the immediate area; in Brussels: tennis, riding, indoor swimming, ice skating.

ACCOMMODATIONS: No living space in the club house; no bar or restaurant available.

Accommodations in Brussels are abundant and lavish or simple, as you wish. See this section for the *Royal Golf Club de Belgique,* pp. 189-190, for details of hotels in Brussels.

In Waterloo: *Wellington* (379 rte Lion, Tel. 542314) and *1815* (369 rte Lion, Tel. 542358). Singles from $2.50, doubles from $3 to $4; a few private baths; pension from $6/day at the *1815.*

TOURIST ATTRACTIONS: Waterloo, of course, provides a tour of the battlefield, a museum and other monuments celebrating the event. For Brussels, see this section for the *Royal Golf Club de Belgique,* p. 190.

FOR FURTHER INFORMATION: Write to: Club Secretary, Royal Waterloo Golf Club, Ohain, Belgium. Telephone: 53.18.50.

Royal Antwerp Golf Club

Only a short distance from Antwerp, the Royal Antwerp Golf Club provides two courses, a long 18-hole course and an interior 9-hole course, with

Typical Belgian caddies.

Shell's Wonderful World of Golf

the advantages of a lovely country setting not too far from city facilities. The rural location is evident in the pine trees and heather that line the course. The tees can be set forward and backward, depending on the power of the player. The back tees provide many long holes in the 400-yard class and up (8 in all). This is not an easy course, but it should not discourage the visitor who can combine length with precision. If possible, you should work up to Royal Antwerp.

LOCATION: The course is accessible by train or car. From the Kapellenbos Station (10 miles from Antwerp) there is a five-minute walk to the club. Antwerp is 25 miles N of Brussels, 60 S of Rotterdam.

OTHER INFORMATION: The course is open all year to nonmembers, who must show proof of membership in a home club. The professional or his assistant is always on hand; request caddies ahead of time from the professional. It is crowded on weekends from Easter through August, with the weather always uncertain in this area. Practice ground is available.
Number of holes: 18 (also a 9-hole course). *Par:* 74 (34 for 9 holes). *Length:* 6600 yards (about 700 yards shorter for women's tees), 2407 yards for 9 holes.
Green fees: weekdays, $2; weekends and holidays, $3/day. *Lessons:* $3/hour. *Caddies:* $2/round. *Golfing equipment and caddie carts:* not for rent.

OTHER SPORTS FACILITIES: Riding and tennis.

ACCOMMODATIONS: No living space in the club house, but there is a dormy house; write secretary of the club for further arrangements there. Bar and restaurant in the club house.
In Antwerp (all first-class hotels): *Century et Rest Ambassadeurs* (De Keyserlei 60, Tel. 331820). A deluxe hotel; prices by arrangement. *Grand Hôtel Londres* (De Keyserlei 58, Tel. 325960). Singles (with bath) from $5, doubles from $10. All comforts. 20% service charge. *Antwerp Docks* (Nooderlaan 100, Tel. 411850). Singles from $3, doubles from $7 to $9; full pension from $6 to $7/day. 20% service charge. All comforts. *Tourist Hôtel et Restaurant* (Pelikaanstraat 22, Tel. 325870). Singles from $3, doubles from $6; most rooms with baths; full pension $7/day. 20% service charge.
A highly recommended restaurant: La Pérouse (open, October to May; reservation necessary).

TOURIST ATTRACTIONS: In Antwerp there is good shopping as well as interesting tours of the town and docks. Recommended: the cathedral, the largest in Belgium; the art museum, with a fine collection of Flemish painting of the seventeenth century; the Museum Plantin-Moretus; for the children, a first-rate zoo.

FOR FURTHER INFORMATION: Write to: Club Secretary, Royal Antwerp Golf Club, Kapellen-Lez-Anvers, Antwerp, Belgium. Telephone: 74.84.56.

NETHERLANDS

Haagsche Golf en Country Club

The Haag Golf and Country Club is in a lovely section of Holland, accessible to all the major cities—Rotterdam, Amsterdam, Utrecht, Haarlem, Leiden—and yet countrified. The course is almost a seaside links, with many holes running adjacent to the North Sea only a short distance away. Haagsche is full of dunes and is suitable for the long driver. In fact, the first six holes (except for the 4th) might lead the visitor to believe he is playing a 7000-yard course. But there are several shorter holes for the less powerful player, and precision is obviously a requisite on any dune links. All in all, Haagsche should prove a happy combination for any visitor eager to try out a variety of shots and willing to take the consequences!

LOCATION: The course, in Wassenaar, is easily accessible by car from The Hague, 6 miles to the south. Amsterdam is 36 miles N, Rotterdam 15 miles S, Antwerp 75 miles S, Brussels 101 miles S, Paris 290 S.

OTHER INFORMATION: The course is open all year to visitors, who should show proof of membership in their home club. The professional or his assistant is always in attendance. Spring and autumn are the most crowded seasons, with the best weather to be expected at that time. Practice ground is available.
Number of holes: 18. *Par:* 73. *Length:* 5951 (from front tees; 5307 yards for women).
Green fees: weekdays, $1.60; weekends and holidays, $3.15/day; entire weekend, $4.30; $8 week, $20 month. *Lessons:* $2/½ hour with the professional, $1.60/½ hour with the assistant professional. *Caddies:* sometimes available through arrangement with the professional. *Golfing equipment and caddie carts:* for rent through arrangement with the professional.

OTHER SPORTS FACILITIES: In the immediate area: tennis courts; to the west of Wassenaar and The Hague, there are fine beaches and seaside facilities, particularly at Scheveningen, a suburb of The Hague. To the north, Katwijk aan Zee and Noordwijk aan Zee offer the same facilities.

ACCOMMODATIONS: No living space in the club house, but a bar and restaurant are available.
In Wassenaar: The *Kasteel Oud Wassenaar* (Park Oud Wassenaar 1, Tel. 9045). Luxurious quarters, all comforts, private baths, central heating, garage; lovely view of the park and the sea; singles start at $4, doubles $8 to $17; full pension $9 to 14. The *De Kievet* (Stoeplaan 27, Tel. 9203). 7

rooms; singles from $4.50, doubles from $8; private baths, central heating, parking, good restaurant.

In the Hague: *Indes et Rôtiss. Copper Kettle* (Lange Voorhout 56, Tel. 184545), *Central* (Lange Poten, Tel. 184930), *Terminus* (Stationsweg 80, Tel. 184300), *Parkhotel et Queen's Garden* (Molenstraat 53, Tel. 184030). The last includes an excellent restaurant. 10% to 20% higher than above.

In Scheveningen: *The Wittebrug* (Badhuisweg 251, Tel. 512361). Luxurious accommodations at prices about 20% to 40% above those listed for Wassenaar.

TOURIST ATTRACTIONS: Besides its proximity to popular seaside resorts and many other major cities, The Hague offers the visitor good shopping and many interesting museums and historical sites. The principal museums are the Mauritshuis, with its exceptional collection, which includes Rembrandt, Vermeer, Steen and Hals, and the Municipal Museum, with its fine collection of French Impressionists and Moderns (Picasso, Braque, Rouault, Dufy, Léger).

FOR FURTHER INFORMATION: Write to: Club Secretary, Haagsche Golf en Country Club, Groot Haesebroekseweg 22, Wassenaar, Netherlands. Telephone: 01751-9607.

Hilversumsche Golf Club

Hilversum, the site of the course, is really a large suburb of Amsterdam, a lovely spot near the Lake of Loosdrecht and the wild forest land of Gooi. Set amidst all these contrasting features—water, woods and villages—is the course. Hilversumsche is by no means the easiest in Holland; it ranks with Toxandria. It compares favorably with Toxandria in length, although its 6650 yards can be shortened by playing front tees. But this is a long driver's course, with the careful player—through trees and heather—also standing a good chance. Work up to Hilversumsche, if you can.

LOCATION: The course is accessible by car from Hilversum, 2 miles away. Hilversum is 20 miles S of Amsterdam, within easy reach of Utrecht (16 miles S), The Hague, Rotterdam and Arnhem.

OTHER INFORMATION: Barring important matches, the course is open to visitors without limitation. All nonmembers, however, should have a letter of introduction from their home club. The professional is in daily attendance. The season usually lasts all year, except when the course is frozen or covered with snow; spring and autumn are the most crowded. Weather is unreliable—like British weather. Practice ground is available.

Number of holes: 18. *Par:* 74. *Length:* 6652 yards (from yellow tees), 6206 yards (from blue tees), 5663 yards (from red tees, for women).

Green fees: weekdays, $2; weekends and holidays, $4/day. *Lessons:* $2/fifty minutes. *Caddies:* $1.50/18 holes, but they must carry two bags or you pay double; reserve in advance. *Golfing equipment and caddie carts:* clubs not for rent, carts $.40/round.

OTHER SPORTS FACILITIES: Tennis, yachting (on Lake Loosdrecht); walking in the Gooi forest; fishing, water skiing.

ACCOMMODATIONS: No living space in the club house, but bar and restaurant are available.

In Hilversum: The *Grand Hôtel Gooiland et Rôtiss. Le Clairon* (Emmastraat 2, Tel. 48441). Singles from $5, doubles from $12; full pension from $10/day. A luxury hotel with all comforts, private baths, central heating, experienced staff. *Hof van Holland* (Kerkbrink 1, Tel. 46141) and *Heidepark* (on route to Baarn, Tel. 49630). Singles from $3, doubles from $7.50; full pension from $6/day. Some rooms with private baths, central heating, most comforts.

In Utrecht: *Smits* (Vredenburg 14, Tel. 26041). Singles from $4, doubles from $7; full pension from $7/day. Private baths, central heating, all comforts.

In Amsterdam: The *Amstel* (Professor Tulpplein 1, Tel. 226060), *Carlton* (Vijzelstraat 8, Tel. 222266), *Victoria et Rest. Stuyvesant* (Damrak 1, Tel. 234255), *Europe* (Nieuwe Doelenstraat 2, Tel. 234836), *American* (Leidsekade 97, Tel. 245322). All offer luxury accommodations with private baths, central heating, experienced staffs; singles from $7, doubles $12 to $18; full pension from $13/day.

TOURIST ATTRACTIONS: The region of the lake and the forest is extremely picturesque and not too crowded; this section seems to recall a Holland of several centuries ago, especially in the small villages that dot the area. Amsterdam is very lively, with good restaurants and plenty of evening entertainment. Also recommended are the various museums, particularly the Rijksmuseum (with its great collection of Rembrandt paintings) and the Stedelijk Museum (for its collection of Van Gogh), a tour of the canals, the flower market and the new market.

FOR FURTHER INFORMATION: Write to: Club Secretary, Hilversumsche Golf Club, Soestdijkerstraatweg 172, Hilversum, Holland. Telephone: 47688.

Kennemer Golf and Country Club

Kennemer is a pleasant dune course within 30 minutes' driving distance of Amsterdam and only a few miles from Haarlem. It combines the seaside advantages of Zandvoort without relinquishing the pleasures of large city life at night. The course favors the long driver on most holes, although there are three of good testing quality for the less powerful hitter. But the slugger seems to have the better of it—9 holes well up in the 400-yard category, the rest above 300. This is a dune course, however, and even when length is a factor, care and precision must count. The chief hazards are sandhills, and no matter what your power, the ball must be played accurately or your score will skyrocket. Without being too difficult, Kennemer provides good golf, a most pleasant setting and excellent vacation facilities.

LOCATION: The course is about ½ mile from Zandvoort. Zandvoort is accessible by car, bus or train. Haarlem is 5 miles E, Amsterdam 18 miles E, The Hague 32 S.

OTHER INFORMATION: The course is open from April through November, with visitors most welcome; all nonmembers, however, should be members of a recognized golf club and have an official handicap. The professional and his assistant are always on hand. The most crowded season is May, June, September, with the best weather from June through September. Weekends are usually crowded, and you might reserve the green in advance. Practice ground is available.
Number of holes: 18. *Par:* 74. *Length:* 6508 yards.
Green fees: weekdays, $2.50; weekends and holidays, $4/day. *Lessons:* $2/¾ hour. *Caddies:* $1.50/18 holes. *Golfing equipment and caddie carts:* clubs $2/day, carts $.30/18 holes.

OTHER SPORTS FACILITIES: All water sports at Zandvoort, a popular resort area; also tennis and riding.

ACCOMMODATIONS: No living space in the club house, but first-class restaurant and a bar are available.
   In Zandvoort: The *Bouwes* (Badhuisplein 7, Tel. 3046). A luxury hotel with all comforts; central heating, private baths, experienced staff, garage facilities; singles from $4.50, doubles from $12; full pension $10 to $11/day. Good view of the sea. *Badhotel* (Bd Paulus Loot 1, Tel. 4841). Very comfortable, private baths, central heating; singles from $9, doubles to $15; full pension from $9 to $12/day. View of the sea.
   In Haarlem: The *Lion d'Or* (Kruisweg 34, Tel. 22180). Some rooms with private bath or shower; central heating in all rooms; singles from $4, doubles to $10; full pension $7 to $9/day.
   In Amsterdam: see this section for the *Hilversumsche Golf Club,* p. 195.

TOURIST ATTRACTIONS: Besides the entertainment facilities of Zandvoort, the visitor might visit Haarlem and the Franz Hals Museum and the "champs de fleurs" (the flower fields). For Amsterdam, see this section for the *Hilversumsche Golf Club,* p. 195.

FOR FURTHER INFORMATION: Write to: Club Secretary, Kennemer Golf and Country Club, Zandvoort, Holland. Telephone: 02507-2836.

Rosendaelsche Golf Club

Rosendaelsche is a good relaxing course within easy driving distance of nearly every major Dutch city; it is on the superhighway from Amsterdam, Utrecht, The Hague and Rotterdam. It is also close to two interesting smaller cities, Arnhem and Apeldorn; thus it combines enjoyable golf in a pleasant setting with nearby city life. Rosendaelsche has no eccentricities; of good length, it favors the medium driver. With average-sized greens and fairways, the high as well as low handicapper will be satisfied. If you find yourself in Holland, this is a good place to begin your European golf tour. Then move on to the tougher 18 holes in Holland, such as Toxandria and The Hague.

LOCATION: The course is most easily reached by car, from Arnhem 2 miles away; take the road to Zutphen. Arnhem is a major stop on the railroad and is also the center of converging major roads. It is 59 miles SE of Amsterdam, 55 E of The Hague and Rotterdam, 37 E of Utrecht.

OTHER INFORMATION: The course is open to nonmembers, without restriction, the entire year; the visitor has only to sign the guest book and pay the green fee. The professional is in daily attendance. Summer is generally the most crowded season, with the weather unpredictable. Practice ground is available.
Number of holes: 9. Par: 71. Length: 6065 yards (twice around).
Green fees: weekdays $2; weekends and holidays, $3.25/day; entire weekend, $5. Lessons: $2/fifty minutes. Caddies: $1.50/18 holes. Golfing equipment and caddie carts: limited number of each available.

OTHER SPORTS FACILITIES: Tennis, swimming, riding.

ACCOMMODATIONS: No living space in the club house, but bar and restaurant are available.
In Arnhem: The Haarhuis (Stationsplein 1, Tel. 27441). Singles from $4, doubles to $18; full pension from $6 to $7/day. All comforts: private baths, central heating, experienced staff. Twente (Stationsplein 44, Tel. 35641) and the Bosch (Apeldoornsestraat 4, Tel. 35150). Singles from $3, doubles from $6; full pension $5 to $6.50/day. Many rooms with private baths, central heating, most comforts.
In Apeldoorn: Keizerskroon (Koningstraat 7, Tel. 17744) and Bloemink (Loolaan 56, Tel. 14141). Singles from $3.50, doubles $8 to $10; full pension from $6/day. Private bath, central heating, comfortable.
For Amsterdam, see this section for the Hilversumsche Golf Club, p. 195.

TOURIST ATTRACTIONS: There is good shopping in Arnhem. Just 20 miles from Arnhem is the Kröller Müller Museum, with a remarkable collection of 200 paintings by Van Gogh. The Museum is set in the Park de Hoge Veluwe, a national park of great scenic beauty. Utrcht and Amsterdam (both within an hour's drive on the superhighway) offer the full range of entertainment for the visitor. Amsterdam is especially interesting.

FOR FURTHER INFORMATION: Write to: Club Secretary, Javastraat 100, Nijmegen, Netherlands. Telephone: 26824.

Noord-Brabantsche Golf Club "Toxandria"

Just inside the Dutch border, near the city of Breda, the Toxandria Golf Club offers the visitor a little bit of everything: good Dutch scenery, proximity to large cities and an interesting course, which was the scene of the Dutch International Open Championship in 1965. This is a part of Holland that is not overcrowded and Breda, 6 miles away, is a city of some historical interest—especially during the wars with Spain—and is immortalized in a painting by Velásquez. The course provides a challenge for the visitor and favors the long driver; from the back tees, it extends for 6500 yards. But all kinds of players will find enough to interest them here. There are no special idiosyncrasies to the course; in fact, variety is the key. Each hole brings its own kind of challenge. Toxandria is excellent for the average player up.

LOCATION: The Toxandria Course is 6 miles from Breda and is most easily reached by car. Breda can be reached by train, bus or car. It is on the main highway from Brussels and Antwerp from the south, and Amsterdam, The Hague and Rotterdam from the north. The Belgian frontier is 8 miles S, Antwerp 34 miles S, Rotterdam 34 miles N, Amsterdam 60 miles N, Brussels 55 miles S.

OTHER INFORMATION: The course is open all year to nonmembers, who must only show proof of membership in any golf club. The professional is always in attendance. The most crowded season is April through October, with the exclusion of August, with the best weather to be expected during this general period. Driving range is available.
Number of holes: 18. Par: 73. Length: 6500 yards (from the back tees).
Green fees: weekdays, 2; weekends, $4/day; entire weekend, $5.50.
Lessons: $2/hour, including practice balls. Caddies: $1.50/18 holes. Golfing equipment and caddie carts: not for rent.

OTHER SPORTS FACILITIES: In the immediate area: swimming (in pool); in Rotterdam and Antwerp: tennis, riding. Beach facilities are within an hour's drive.

ACCOMMODATIONS: No living space in the club house, but a bar and restaurant (no hot meals) are available.
In the environs of Breda: The Mastbosch (Burg. Kerstenlaan 20, Tel. 22344). Some rooms with private baths; singles from $4; doubles $11; with breakfast; pension $8/day. Meals provided if desired. Parking.
In Breda: Cosmopolite (Stationsplein 4, Tel. 30550), Oranje (Stationsplein 7, Tel. 31850), Wapen van Nassau (Prinsenkade 7, Tel. 38350). Comfortable lodgings, some rooms with private baths; from $3 for singles to $8 for doubles; pension (none at Oranje) from $5/day. Central heating, shower.
On the road to Antwerp: The Motel Breda (Rijsbergseweg, Tel. Breda 01600). Facilities similar to those above at about the same prices.
For the visitor who wishes greater luxury, Rotterdam, an hour away, offers traditionally grand hotels, with the Hilton, the Parkhotel, the Atlanta, as well as gourmet restaurants.
Antwerp, one hour to the south, in Belgium, provides luxury accommodations with the Century and Restaurant Ambassadeurs, the Grand Hôtel Londres, and many gourmet restaurants. See this section for the Royal Antwerp Golf Club, p. 192.

TOURIST ATTRACTIONS: Breda and its environs invite some sight-seeing. In Breda recommended sites are the Grote Markt, Grande Église and the Château. In Rotterdam the visitor has the facilities of a large city, with excellent restaurants, shopping, museums and other attractions. A visit and tour of the Port are highly recommended. The Museum Boymans-Van Beuningen has major collections of the northern European schools, as well as many examples of Italian and French painting and a rich collection of old glass, furniture and pottery.

FOR FURTHER INFORMATION: Write to: Club Secretary, P.O. Box 207, Breda, Netherlands. Telephone: 01600-24231.

SCANDINAVIA

Golf in Scandinavia? Possibly the idea never occurred to you. And yet what fine golfing awaits you in Denmark, Norway and Sweden. Even when the courses are small and only 9 holes—and most are huge and 18 holes— you feel a sense of expansiveness, of large tracts of land, enormous lakes, immense skies. Golf in the northern countries has its own kind of beauty, and the courses range from relatively easy to very difficult.

In Denmark you can golf only a short distance from Copenhagen; then move up the coast to Helsingør, a beautiful place with or without sport. If you plan to move on to Sweden, you can take the car ferry at Copenhagen for Malmö and play golf almost as soon as you touch land. Five courses ring Malmö, some only a few miles north or south. Then you might move up the southwest coast of Sweden toward Göteborg, by way of Hälsingborg and Halmstad, with three more courses on your way. In Göteborg four excellent courses close out this part of your trip. Altogether, you have a choice of fourteen courses, including the two in Denmark.

If you explore other parts of the Danish islands, like the picturesque little Fyn (due west of Copenhagen), then two beautifully located courses await you. Play *Odense* first, before *Sct. Knuds;* it is small, befitting the fairytale land of Hans Christian Andersen. On the peninsula of Jutland, try *Ebeltoft* and *Esbjerg* before venturing on to *Randers* and *Silkeborg Bryghus;* they are lovely, but the latter two are tough.

The Oslo Course is the best in Norway; it is a full championship links with a lake as background. All four Norwegian courses will offer a rewarding game in often awe-inspiring surroundings. Golf is a relatively new game here, but the Norwegians have picked wonderful spots: one in the capital, one west, one south, one north. The northern one is remarkable indeed; you can play in the middle of the night under a blazing sun. And then 24 courses in Sweden. Why so many? Sweden has been rapidly developing its golfing facilities and welcomes visitors. There are courses all over this vast country, many of them good-sized and 18 holes. Since most Americans are not familiar with this side of Sweden, I thought I would give you a good taste. Within ten miles of Stockholm there are three courses of varying difficulty. Begin with *Lidingö, Stockholm* or *Drottningholms;* then take a leisurely drive (of about an hour) along several lakes to Uppsala and try the more difficult course there.

If you enter from Denmark, in the southwestern part, Malmö alone can give you a good taste of Swedish links. Start with either *Falsterbo* or *Mölle;* then move on to *Rya,* and finish up with *Ljunghusens* and *Lunds.* The last will be a real test of your game.

If you have time for a good workout, play your way up the coast from Malmö to Göteborg. Both the countryside and the golf are fine. Start with *Båstad,* which lies between Hälsingborg and Halmstad; it is not too tough for the average player. Then try either *Falkenbergs* or *Halmstad,* and you are ready for the somewhat more demanding courses around Göteborg. In that area play *Öijared* and *Göteborgs* before trying *Delsjö* and *Borås.* None of these will spoil your stay in Sweden—it would be difficult to do that— but the latter two are stubborn.

Distances in Sweden, north and south, are huge, and I have included no course north of Söderhamns, about 150 miles from Stockholm. But there are numerous courses extending all the way up. You can obtain the names of these from the Swedish Golf Union in Stockholm. At last count Sweden had about 100 courses ready for visitors.

DENMARK

Copenhagen Golf Club

In the middle of the Royal Deer Park, surrounded by lovely trees and hedges, the Copenhagen Golf Course is the oldest in Scandinavia and one of the best (don't be surprised if you see deer watching you as you get ready for an approach shot). Its length of 6400 yards favors the long driver with three 500-yarders, but there is an overall balance. The fairways should please any golfer, the very playable turf being several hundred years old and absolutely free from weeds. The greens, which have a good putting surface, are undulating, and the slopes around the greens are a bit tricky and require careful, accurate play. Nearly every approach is a challenge. This is an excellent course of some difficulty, but not enough to upset your stay in Copenhagen.

LOCATION: The course is 7 miles north of Copenhagen. Best way to get there is by car or train (get off at Springforbi station). If you phone the club before leaving, a caddie will meet you at the parking lot or train station and carry your bags to the clubhouse.

OTHER INFORMATION: The course is open to nonmembers, unlimited, for the entire year, with a professional always on hand. The most crowded seasons are spring and autumn; the weather is best from May to September. Practice ground is available.
Number of holes: 18. Par: 72. Length: 6328 yards (6427 from back tees).
Green fees: weekdays, $3; weekends, $5/day. Lessons: $2.50/½ hour. Caddies: $2.50 for 18 holes. Golfing equipment and caddie carts: clubs $3/day, carts $1/day.

SPORTS FACILITIES IN AREA: Tennis, riding, fishing, swimming and boating.

ACCOMMODATIONS: No living space in the club house, but restaurant and bar available.
In Copenhagen: D'Angleterre (Kongens Nytorv 34, Tel. Central 95). A luxury hotel of international standing, open all year. Rooms from $9.50 to $13 for best single, $19 to $53 for best double; private baths, central heating; taxes and services not included. Richmond (Vester Farimagsgade 33, Tel. Byen 9701). A first-class hotel of international standing, open all year. Rooms from $10 to $11.25 for best single, $16 to $30 for best double; private baths, central heating, continental breakfast; taxes and services not included. Codan (Sct. Anne Plads 21, Tel. Byen 8485). A very good, com-

203

fortable hotel, open all year. Rooms from $6.50 to $9.50 for best single, $11.50 to $15.50 for best double; private baths, central heating; taxes and services not included. *Astoria* (Vesterbrogade 7B, Central 1419). A very good, comfortable hotel, open all year. Rooms from $7.50 to $8.50 for best single, $10.50 to $15.50 for best double; private baths, central heating; taxes and services not included. *Grand* (Vesterbrogade, Tel. Central 3600). A very good, comfortable hotel, open all year. Rooms from $7 to $11.50 for best single, $10.50 to $17.50 for best double; private baths, central heating; taxes and services not included.

See *Helsingør Golf Club* for further accommodations.

TOURIST ATTRACTIONS: Copenhagen has just about every variety of sights and activities to make it a tourist's paradise: wonderful boat excursions on the harbor canals that go right into the heart of the city, museums (including an excellent art museum), theaters, a circus, night life, dancing, a palace and, of course, for the young in heart, Tivoli Gardens, one of the most delightful amusement parks in Europe.

FOR FURTHER INFORMATION: Write to: Secretary, B. Bjerre Pedersen, Copenhagen Golf Club, Springforbi, Denmark. Telephone: Bellevue 283 & 483.

Helsingør Golf Club

In the northernmost part of the island of Zealand, near Hamlet's castle, the Helsingør Golf Club is set against a beautiful background of sea and woods. The area also has some of the finest bathing beaches in Scandinavia, lovely private homes and many castles, among them Fredensborg, spring and fall residence of the royal family. The course is slightly hilly, the greens are always in good condition, and many of the fairways are narrow and edged by forests. It strongly favors the short driver. The average, even the inexperienced, golfer should have no difficulties here. Helsingør has the added advantage of combining good golf with the delights of Copenhagen, only about 45 minutes by car from the course.

LOCATION: The course is about 2 miles N of Helsingør, 30 miles N of Copenhagen, 107 miles NE of Odense, 212 miles N of Hamburg (Germany), about a half-hour ferry trip from Hälsingborg (Sweden), 45 miles NW of Malmö (Sweden). It is accessible by car.

OTHER INFORMATION: The course is open to nonmembers, unlimited, the entire year; a professional is on hand from May to September. The most crowded months are June and July; the weather is best in June and September. Practice ground is available.

Number of holes: 9 (to be extended to 12). *Par:* 66 (for twice around). *Length:* 5213 yards.

Green fees: weekdays, $2.50; weekends & holidays, $4/day. *Lessons:* $3/45 minutes. *Caddies:* $.75/9 holes. *Golfing equipment and caddie carts:* clubs $2/day, carts $.50/day.

OTHER SPORTS FACILITIES: Swimming, riding, tennis, badminton and yachting.

ACCOMMODATIONS: No living space in the club house, but restaurant is available.

In Helsingør: *Marienlyst* (Helsingør, Tel. [03] 211801). A first-class hotel of international standing, open all year. Rooms from $6.50 to $9.50 for best single, $11 to $19 for best double; private baths, central heating; taxes and services not included. *Prins Hamlet* (Kronborgvej, Tel. [03] 213233). A very good, comfortable hotel; no singles with bath, $10.50 to $11.50 for best double with private bath, central heating; taxes and services not included.

In Copenhagen: *Royal* (Hammerichsgade, Tel. Minerva 7600). A first-class hotel of international standing, open all year. Rooms from $9 to $15 for the best single, $13.50 to $27 for the best double; private baths, central heating; taxes and services not included. *Alexandra* (Hans Christian Andersens Blvd. 8, Tel. Central 2200). A very good, comfortable hotel, open all year. Rooms from $7.50 to $8.75 for best single, $12.50 to $16 for best double; private baths, central heating; taxes and services not included.

See *Copenhagen Golf Club* for further accommodations.

TOURIST ATTRACTIONS: Helsingør, one of the oldest trading towns in Denmark, dates back to the twelfth century. It has some unusual chemist shops and two magnificent Gothic churches, Skt. Olai and Skt. Marie. And be sure to take the excursion boats for a panoramic view of the northwest coast of Denmark.

Elsinore needs no introduction. The important attraction here is Kronborg, Hamlet's castle. Of special interest are the royal apartments, the banquet hall and the chapel. And in nearby Marienlyst Castle, you'll find the Hamlet Museum with the tomb of Hamlet and Ophelia.

FOR FURTHER INFORMATION: Write to: Secretary, Solnavej 1, Søborg, Denmark. Telephone: (01) 692351.

Odense Golf Club

The Odense Golf Course is on the island of Fyn, just outside of Odense, Denmark's third largest city. The course is one of the smallest in Europe and a paradise for short drivers, with well-tailored fairways and greens. Even though short, Odense is laid out to give balance. This is a perfect place for a tune-up before you tackle some of the longer Danish courses. But what makes Odense so charming is that it is about a mile from Hans Christian Andersen's birthplace, in the lovely, quiet countryside he loved and wrote about in his fairy tales. And if you visit the picturesque estates surrounded by moats and parks and walk through the little streets in the neighboring villages, with their half-timbered houses and flower gardens, many of the fairy tales will almost come to life before your eyes.

LOCATION: The course is about a mile from Odense, 87 miles W of Copenhagen, 41 miles NW of Nakskov, 19 miles W of Nyborg, 93 miles S of Aarhus, 90 miles SE of Silkeborg, 88 miles E of Esbjerg. It is accessible by car.

OTHER INFORMATION: The course is open to nonmembers, unlimited, for the entire year. The most crowded months are September and October, with the weather best in June, August and September. Practice ground is available.
Number of holes: 9. *Par:* 58 (for twice around). *Length:* 4000 yards.
Green fees: weekdays, $1; weekends, $1.50/day. *Lessons:* not available. *Caddies:* $1.25/18 holes. *Golfing equipment and caddie carts:* clubs $1.25/day, carts $.50/day.

OTHER SPORTS FACILITIES: Tennis, swimming, badminton.

ACCOMMODATIONS: See this section for *Sct. Knuds Golf Club,* p. 207.

TOURIST ATTRACTIONS: You should see Hans Christian Andersen's birthplace, which contains many of his books, letters, drawings and personal possessions; Skt. Hans Kirke, a fifteenth-century church; the Odense Castle; the Odense Cathedral, dating back to the fourteenth century and probably the best example of Gothic architecture in Denmark; a little Tivoli; a zoo and a race course. Also recommended are excursions to the surrounding villages. For more details see section under *Sct. Knuds Golf Club,* p. 208.

FOR FURTHER INFORMATION: Write to: Secretary, Odense Golf Club, Odense, Denmark. Telephone: 126889.

Sct. Knuds Golf Club

Situated on a very small peninsula on the island of Fyn, this seaside and inland course is one of the most attractive and picturesque in Denmark. From many of the holes there is a good view of the Nyborg Fjord and its small sailing boats. The island itself is full of old castles and stately mansions, farmhouses, lovely neat gardens and fields surrounded by high hedges. This combined seaside and inland course favors the long driver but should not discourage the short one. Some of the holes are in a wood and call for careful, accurate play. Like the roughs on many Danish courses, Sct. Knuds' are difficult to play in the summer. This is a links of medium difficulty but well worth the attempt. If this one proves tough, try the Odense Course, also on the island of Fyn and somewhat easier at 9 holes.

LOCATION: The course is about 2 miles from Nyborg, 21 miles E of Odense, 37 miles N of Nakskov, 70 miles W of Copenhagen, 113 miles SW of Aarhus, 108 miles SW of Silkeborg. It is accessible by car.

OTHER INFORMATION: The course is open to nonmembers, unlimited, for the entire season (May-September); a professional is always on hand. The most crowded month is July; the weather is best from June to mid-September. Practice ground is available.
Number of holes: 18. *Par:* 70. *Length:* 5995 yards.
Green fees: weekdays, $3; Saturdays, $4.50; Sundays, $5.50. *Lessons:* $1.50/half hour. *Caddies:* $1/18 holes. *Golfing equipment and caddie carts:* clubs $2.50/day, carts $.50/day.

OTHER SPORTS FACILITIES: Riding, tennis, swimming.

ACCOMMODATIONS: No living space in the club house, but restaurant and bar are available.
In Nyborg: *Nyborg* (Adelgade 6, Tel. 994). A very good, comfortable hotel, open all year. Rooms from $3 to $3.50 for best single, $6.50 to $10.50 for best double; private baths, central heating; taxes and services not included. *Strand* (Nyborg, Tel. 112). A very good, comfortable hotel, open all year. Rooms from $4.50 to $5 for best single, $7.50 to $8.50 for best double; private baths, central heating; taxes and services not included.
In Odense: *Grand* (Jernbanegade 18, Tel. 117171). A first-class hotel, open all year. Rooms from $5.75 to $8 for best single, $11.50 to $26 for best double; private baths, central heating; taxes and services not included. *Park* (Aalykkegade 2, Tel. 122939). A very good, comfortable hotel, open all year. Rooms from $4 to $5 for best single, $5.75 to $8 for best double; private baths, central heating; taxes and services not included.

Danish National Travel Office
Sct. Knuds Golf Club, on the island of Fyn. View from the club house.

TOURIST ATTRACTIONS: This area is made for visitors. Nyborg was the first capital of Denmark. About 2 miles from the center of town you can see the medieval castle of Holckenhavn, with its battlements and loopholes. It's the oldest royal castle in Scandinavia, dating back to the middle of the twelfth century. The island of Fyn has many old castles open to tourists.

Odense, only 19 miles west of Nyborg, is world famous as the birthplace of Hans Christian Andersen. Don't miss his house and the Andersen Museum.

FOR FURTHER INFORMATION: Write to: Secretary, Sct. Knuds Golf Club, Nyborg, Denmark. Telephone: Nyborg 1212.

Ebeltoft Golf Club

Here is one of the best, and certainly one of the most difficult, courses in Denmark, despite its relatively short length. Carefully planned and laid out by the Danish Committee for Golf, it strongly favors the long, accurate driver and requires careful putting on the greens. Ebeltoft is full of tricky bunkering, sharp doglegs and unexpected hazards. It is really a must for all golfers visiting Scandinavia, particularly the player who desires a challenge and isn't afraid of running up his score. But good golf is not the only thing you find here. This beautiful area is rustic, with open heath-covered hills, ravines and meadows. Life seems to flow in the quiet, easy rhythm of an age long gone. Golf here should indeed be satisfactory.

LOCATION: The course is on the NE coast of Jutland, 30 miles NE of Aarhus, 56 miles E of Silkeborg, 85 miles SE of Aalborg, 122 miles N of Odense, 96 miles NW of Copenhagen. It is accessible by car.

OTHER INFORMATION: The course is open to nonmembers, unlimited, for the entire year, with a professional always on hand. The weather is best from May to September. Practice ground is available.
Number of holes: 18. *Par:* 70. *Length:* 5488 yards.
Green fees: weekdays, $2; weekends, $3/day. *Lessons:* $3/hour. *Caddies:* $1/18 holes. *Golfing equipment and caddie carts:* clubs $1.50/day, carts $.50.

OTHER SPORTS FACILITIES: Tennis, riding, fishing and boating.

ACCOMMODATIONS: No living space in the club house, but restaurant and bar are available.
In Ebeltoft: *Hvide Hus* (Ebeltoft, Tel. 93511). A first-class hotel, open all year. Rooms from $8.50 to $9.50 for best single, $12 to 13 for best double; private baths, central heating; taxes and services not included.
In Aarhus: *Ritz* (Banegaardspalads 12, Tel. 3444). A very good, comfortable hotel, open all year. Rooms from $4 to $5.50 for best single, $7.50 to $8.50 for best double; private baths, central heating; taxes and services not included. See *Silkeborg Bryghus Golf Club,* pp. 211-212, for further accommodations.

TOURIST ATTRACTIONS: Ebeltoft itself is a small provincial town that looks about the same now as it did in the sixteenth century. There are charming, crooked old houses, stone steps, iron handrails and small gardens everywhere. The Town Hall has a good collection of local folklore.

FOR FURTHER INFORMATION: Write to: Manager, Hotel Hvide Hus, Ebeltoft, Denmark. Telephone: (063) 41466.

Esbjerg Golf Club

Near the North Sea and sheltered by the island of Fanö, one of the finest resorts in Scandinavia, the Esbjerg Golf Club Course should prove rewarding to long and short drivers, although most holes do not require special length. But the fairways are surrounded by trees and heather, so the straight, accurate driver has a decided advantage here. The roughs are almost impossible to play in the summer. The area is famous for its beaches, high dunes, hedges and woods that come down to the sea. This is golf at its most pleasant—an interesting course in lovely surroundings.

LOCATION: The course is in Gjesing Skov on the west coast of Jutland, about 3 miles N of Esbjerg, the fifth-largest town in Denmark, 80 miles SW of Silkeborg, 92 miles SW of Aarhus, 88 miles W of Odense, 175 miles W of Copenhagen. It is accessible by car and by bus (route No. 2) from the center of Esbjerg. Buses leave every half-hour.

OTHER INFORMATION: The course is open to nonmembers, unlimited, for the entire year; a professional on hand April, May, June and August but for only one week each month. The most crowded months are April through September; the weather is best in May, June, and August. Practice ground is available.
Number of holes: 9. *Par:* 70 (for twice around). *Length:* 6200 yards (2 x 3100).
Green fees: $2/day. *Lessons:* $2/half hour. *Caddies:* $.75/9 holes. *Golfing equipment and caddie carts:* not available at present.

OTHER SPORTS FACILITIES: Tennis, swimming, soccer, cycling and boating.

ACCOMMODATIONS: No space in the club house, but restaurant and bar are available.
In Esbjerg: *Britannia* (Torvet, Tel. [051] 30111. A first-class hotel, open all year. Rooms $4.25 to $5.75 for best single, $7.25 to $9.50 for best double; private baths, central heating; taxes and services not included. *Palads* (Skolegade 14, Tel. [051] 23000). A very good, comfortable hotel, open all year. Rooms $4 to $5 for best single, $7.50 to $8.50 for best double; private baths, central heating; taxes and services not included.

TOURIST ATTRACTIONS: In Esbjerg, get to see the fish market, a hall about 640 feet long, where you can attend a fish auction every morning except holidays. During the summer take a ferry to the international resort of Fanö for bathing and fishing. It has one of the best sand beaches in northern Europe.

FOR FURTHER INFORMATION: Write to: Secretary, 7 Skovstien, Spangsberg (near Esbjerg), Denmark. Telephone: (051) 21868.

Randers Golf Club

Set in a lovely region of Denmark, Randers is suitable for both long and short drivers and calls for accurate driving and careful putting. It is up and down, so some of the best shots can go awry. Nevertheless, this is a pleasant course, particularly if you are golfing in Denmark for the first time. The club is on the outskirts of Randers, one of the largest cities in Jutland, near the spot where the Gudenaa River flows into the Randers fjord. A medieval town dating back to the twelfth century, with a historic old quarter, Randers is now famous for its salmon and gloves. Nearby, to the north, is the Forest of Rold, the largest forest in Denmark.

LOCATION: The course is in NE Jutland, about 5 miles from Randers, 25 miles N of Aarhus, 48 miles S of Aalborg, 35 miles NE of Silkeborg, 117 miles N of Odense, 90 miles NW of Copenhagen plus a 3-hour ferry from Kalundborg to Aarhus. It is accessible by car.

OTHER INFORMATION: The course is open to nonmembers, unlimited, for the entire season (May-October), with a professional on hand 14 days each month. The most crowded seasons are spring and autumn with the weather best from June to September. Practice ground is available.
Number of holes: 9. Par: 70 (for twice around). Length: 5509 yards (2 x 2754½).
Green fees: weekdays, $2; weekends, $3/day. Lessons: $2/half hour. Caddies: $1/18 holes. Golfing equipment and caddie carts: none available.

OTHER SPORTS FACILITIES: Swimming, tennis, boating and riding.

ACCOMMODATIONS: No living space in the club house, but restaurant and bar are available.
In Randers: Randers (Tel. [064] 23422). A first-class hotel, open all year. Rooms $4.50 to $7 for best single, $9 to $12.50 for best double; private baths, central heating; taxes and services not included. Westend (Vestergade 53, Tel. [064] 25388). A good comfortable hotel, open all year. Rooms $3 to $4 for best single, $6 to $7 for best double; private baths, central heating; taxes and services not included.
In Aarhus: Royal (Store Torv 4, Tel. [061] 20011). A first-class hotel, open all year. Rooms $4.50 to $6.50 for best single, $7.50 to $12.50 for best double; private baths, central heating; taxes and services not included.

See *Ebeltoft Golf Club* and *Silkeborg Bryghus Golf Club* for further accommodations in Aarhus.

TOURIST ATTRACTIONS: Randers is one of the busiest commercial centers in Denmark, famous for salmon, gloves, horses and pretty girls. There are some magnificent stone houses to visit, dating back to the Middle Ages. For those interested in Viking encampments, be sure to see Fyrkat, a small village about 18 miles northwest of Randers.

FOR FURTHER INFORMATION: Write to: Secretary, Randers Golf Club, Randers, Denmark, Telephone: (064) 288699.

Silkeborg Bryghus Golf Club

Surrounded by the hills of the Jutland highlands, this championship course is tucked away in a wood near the Gudenaa, the longest river in Denmark. The surrounding country with its forests, heather-covered hills and strikingly beautiful lakes, all within short distances of each other, is typical of this region of Jutland. The course is tough and made for the long driver (9 holes well over 400 yards). The fairways and greens are cleverly laid out; numerous doglegs and a large creek add to the difficulty. The overall layout is huge—be prepared to do a lot of walking. This is a course you might work up to, but the area is lovely and the views wonderful, even if the course should dwarf your game.

LOCATION: The course is in central Jutland on the outskirts of Resenbro, about 3 miles E of Silkeborg, 22 miles W of Aarhus, 24 miles S of Viborg, 94 miles W of Copenhagen, 87 miles NW of Odense, and 22 miles E of Herning. It is accessible by car.

OTHER INFORMATION: The course is open to nonmembers, unlimited, for the entire season (April-November); a professional is on hand from May through August. The weather is best from June through August. Practice ground is available.
Number of holes: 18. *Par:* 74. *Length:* 7025 yards.
Green fees: weekdays, $3; weekends, $4/day. *Lessons:* $2/half hour. *Caddies:* $1.50/18 holes. *Golfing equipment and caddie carts:* unavailable at present.

OTHER SPORTS FACILITIES: Sailing, riding, tennis.

ACCOMMODATIONS: In Silkeborg: *Dania* (Torvet 5, Tel. [068] 6). A very good, comfortable hotel, open all year. Rooms $4.50 to $5.50 for best single, $8 to $9 for best double; private baths, central heating; taxes and services not included. *Missionshotellet Grand* (Hostruspsgade 39, Tel. [068] 9). A good, comfortable hotel, open all year. No singles with bath; $7.25 to $8 for best double with private bath; central heating; taxes and services not included.

In Aarhus: *Regina* (Søndergade 53, Tel. [061] 35300). A very good, comfortable hotel, open all year. Rooms $3.75 to $5 for best single, $8 to $10.50 for best double; private baths, central heating; taxes and services not included. See this section for *Ebeltoft Golf Club*, p. 208.

In Viborg: *Preislers* (Viborg, Tel. [076] 1087). A very good, comfortable hotel, open all year. Rooms $3.25 to $4.50 for best single, $6 to $7.50 for best double; private baths, central heating; taxes and services not included.

TOURIST ATTRACTIONS: Hans Christian Andersen said that the forests, hills and lakes around Silkeborg reminded him of the beauty of Scotland and the Black Forest. Don't miss the boat ride from Silkeborg to Himmelbjerget on a 90-year-old paddle steamer. The town has one of the best collections of modern art in Denmark.

FOR FURTHER INFORMATION: Write to: Mr. Edouard Jørgensen, Hotel Dania, Silkeborg, Denmark. Telephone: 0681 (6).

NORWAY

Oslo Golf Club

Here is a championship course in the western suburbs of Oslo by Lake Bogstad, one of the most beautiful in Scandinavia. It is the oldest course in Norway, and many of Scandinavia's most important tournaments (the Scandinavian International Amateur Championship and the Scandinavian Professional Championship) are held here. Long as well as short drivers should feel at home at Oslo, but many of the holes are fairly difficult and demand careful, accurate play. Although the length is good and the 18th is a monumental 572 yards, there is overall balance; the 11 par-4 holes are nearly all in the 350-to-400-yard range. The par-3 holes (4) are all in the 150-to-200-yard range. The great charm of the course lies in its picturesque surroundings and in the fact that the very good as well as the average golfer can enjoy a fine game. If you are in Norway, don't miss Oslo and its course.

LOCATION: About 6 miles W of the center of Oslo, 118 miles S of Lillehammer, 346 miles S of Trondheim, 304 miles E of Bergen, 222 miles NE of Kristiansand. It is accessible by car or bus.

OTHER INFORMATION: The course is open to nonmembers (but golfer must be a member of another club) for the entire season (May-October); a professional is always on hand. The most crowded months are May and June; the weather is best in July and August. Practice ground is available.
Number of holes: 18. *Par:* 71. *Length:* 6580 yards (6340 front tees).
Green fees: weekdays, $3; weekends, $5/day. *Lessons:* $3/hour. *Caddies:* $1.50/18 holes. *Golfing equipment and caddie carts:* clubs $2.50/day, carts $.50/day.

OTHER SPORTS FACILITIES: Swimming, fishing, tennis, sailing.

ACCOMMODATIONS: No living space in the club house, but restaurant and bar are available.
In Oslo: *Grand* (Karl Johansgatan 31, Tel. 415820). A luxury hotel of international standing, open all year. Rooms $14 to $15 for best single, $19 to $22 for best double; private baths, central heating; taxes and services not included. *Continental* (Stortingsgatan 24-26, Tel. 417060). A first-class hotel, open all year. Rooms $11.50 to $12.50 for best single, $17 to $18.50 for best double; private baths, central heating; taxes and services included. *Nobel* (Karl Johnsgatan 33, Tel. 337190). A very good, comfortable hotel,

213

Shell's Wonderful World of Golf
Oslo Golf Club, in a beautiful location in the suburbs of Oslo, is the oldest course in Norway.

open all year. Rooms from $9.50 to $10.50 for best single, $14 to $15 for best double; private baths, central heating; taxes and services not included.

TOURIST ATTRACTIONS: Oslo is a good town for tourists. Some of the attractions you should not miss are the Royal Palace, the University of Oslo, the National Art Museum, where one room is devoted to some of the best paintings of Edvard Munch, the National Theater, the Frognerparken with the sculpture park by Norway's great sculptor, Vigeland, the Hall of Viking Boats and the famous Kon Tiki Raft, which took Thor Heyerdahl and his men across the Pacific.

FOR FURTHER INFORMATION: Write to: Secretary, Oslo Golfklubb, Bogstad, Oslo 7, Norway. Telephone: 246027.

Bergen Golf Club

This is a beautiful, cool course on the outskirts of Bergen with a good view of the surrounding hills and mountains. Bergen is the second-largest city in Norway, its former capital and the birthplace of Edvard Grieg. It is also the home of Norway's oldest theater and one of the oldest symphony orchestras in the world, the *Harmonien,* founded in 1765. The course is small and for short drivers, but the fairways are often so narrow that you have to drive carefully to keep your score down. There is also some up-and-down play that may upset your game. On the whole, however, this is a balanced course for the average player.

LOCATION: The club is in Aastvedt, about 8 miles N of Bergen, 318 miles W of Oslo, 170 miles N of Stavanger, 418 miles SW of Trondheim, 331 miles NW of Kristiansand. It is accessible by car.

OTHER INFORMATION: The course is open to nonmembers, unlimited, for the entire season (April-October); a professional is always on hand. The weather is best in May and June.
Number of holes: 9. *Par:* 68 (for twice around). *Length:* 4832 yards.
Green fees: $2.50/day. *Lessons:* $1.75/half hour. *Caddies:* $1.25/18 holes. *Golfing equipment and caddie carts:* clubs about $1.50/day, carts $.50/day.

OTHER SPORTS FACILITIES: Swimming, tennis, archery, fishing.

ACCOMMODATIONS: No living space in the club house, but restaurant is available.
In Bergen: *Bristol* (Torvalmenningen 11, Tel. 32600). A luxury hotel of international standing, open all year. Rooms $8.50 to $9.50 for best single, $14 to $17 for best double; private baths, central heating; taxes and services included. *Norge* (Ole Bulls Plass 4, Tel. 33000). A luxury hotel of international standing, open all year. Rooms $9 to $10 for best single, $12.50 to $15.50 for best double; private baths, central heating; taxes and services

included. *Orion* (Bradbenken 3, Tel. 31610). A first-class hotel, open all year. Rooms $7.50 to $8.50 for best single, $10.50 to $14 for best double; private baths, central heating; taxes and services included. *Neptun* (Walckendorffsgatan 8, Tel. 32015). A very good, comfortable hotel, open all year. Rooms $5.75 to $6.50 for best single, $10 to $12.75 for best double; private baths, central heating; taxes and services included.

TOURIST ATTRACTIONS: Here are some absolutely breathtaking excursions by boat that you should not miss, about nine museums of every variety from old Norwegian farming to merchant life in the Hansa days, Edvard Grieg's home, Troldhaugen, a Gothic Cathedral, a Cistercian abbey built in 1146 in Lysekloster and some stimulating walking tours.

FOR FURTHER INFORMATION: Write to: Secretary, Bergen Golfklubb, P. O. Box 1223, Bergen, Norway. Telephone: 10090.

Stavanger Golf Club

The Stavanger Golf Club is on the southwestern coast of Norway along a beautiful lake near a small peninsula between Östre and Vestre Våg. The town, with its picturesque winding streets and old-world markets, is one of the oldest in Norway, going back to the beginning of the eleventh century. The course, just outside the center of town, is for both long and short drivers but requires straight, accurate drives because many of the fairways are narrow and tree lined. Its location along a lake gives it many incomparably lovely views, all visible from the tees, and its clever layout gives the player a lot of interesting, unusual golf.

LOCATION: The course is about a mile from the center of Stavanger, 275 miles W of Oslo, 165 miles S of Bergen, 182 miles NW of Kristiansand, 310 miles SW of Lillehammer. It is accessible by car.

OTHER INFORMATION: The course is open to nonmembers, unlimited, for the entire season (May-October); a professional is always on hand. Good weather in spring and summer. Practice ground is available.
Number of holes: 18. *Par:* 68. *Length:* 5653 yards.
Green fees: weekdays, $1.50; weekends, $2.50/day. *Lessons:* $2.50/hour. *Caddies:* $1/18 holes. *Golfing equipment and caddie carts:* clubs $1/day, carts $.50/day.

OTHER SPORTS FACILITIES: Trout fishing, sailing, swimming, tennis.

ACCOMMODATIONS: No living space in the club house.
In Stavanger: *Atlantic* (Jernbaneveien 1, Tel. 27520). A luxury hotel of international standing, open all year. Rooms $7.50 to $9 for best single, $14 to $15 for best double; private baths, central heating; taxes and services included. *KNA* (Lagärdsvegen 61, Tel. 29512). A first-class hotel, open all year. Rooms $7 to $8 for best single, $10.50 to $11.50 for best

double; private baths, central heating; taxes and services included. *Victoria* (Skansegatan 1, Tel. 20526). A very good, comfortable hotel, open all year. Rooms $5.75 to $7 for best single, $9.75 to $10.50 for best double; private baths, central heating; taxes and services included.

TOURIST ATTRACTIONS: Worth a visit are a fascinating cathedral dedicated to Saint Swithin and dating back to the twelfth century, a good museum (of archeological remains), ancient caves and, of course, boat excursions to fjords.

FOR FURTHER INFORMATION: Write to: Secretary, Stavanger Golfklubb, Stavanger, Norway. Telephone: 24182.

Trondheim Golf Club

If you are looking for a small, out-of-the-way course, fascinating, bizarre and utterly unique, then the Trondheim Golf Club is what you want. The course is of average difficulty and length, suitable for the relatively inexperienced player. But the narrow fairways should keep everyone on his toes. What makes Trondheim so fascinating, however, is that you can golf from midnight until early morning under a blazing sun. A memorable experience!

LOCATION: The course is about 2 miles outside Trondheim, 343 miles N of Oslo, 540 miles N of Kristiansand and 429 miles NE of Bergen. It is accessible by train and then car.

OTHER INFORMATION: The course is open to nonmembers, unlimited, for the entire season (May-October), with a professional always on hand. The most crowded months are June and August; the weather is best in July and August. Practice ground is available.

Number of holes: 9. *Par:* 69 (for twice around). *Length:* 5815 yards.

Green fees: daily: $1.50. *Lessons:* $1.50/half hour. *Caddies:* $1.50/18 holes. *Golfing equipment and caddie carts:* clubs $1.25/day, carts $.50/day.

OTHER SPORTS FACILITIES: Swimming, tennis, hunting, fishing.

ACCOMMODATIONS: No living space in the club house, but restaurant is available.

In Trondheim: *Prinsen* (Kongensgatan 30, Tel. 30650). A first-class hotel, open all year. Rooms $5.75 to $7 for best single, $9.75 to $15 for best double; private baths, central heating; taxes and services included. *Astoria* (Nordregatan 24, Tel. 29550). A very good, comfortable hotel, open all year. Rooms $5.75 to $6.50 for best single, $9 to $11 for best double; private baths, central heating; taxes and services not included. *Britannia* (Dronningensgaten 5, Tel. 30040). A very good, comfortable hotel, open all year. Rooms $5.75 to $6.25 for best single, $9 to $10.50 for best double; private baths; central heating; taxes and services not included.

TOURIST ATTRACTIONS: Trondheim is one of the oldest cities in Scandinavia, dating back to the year 1000, and architecturally, one of the most beautiful. Be sure to see the Nidaros Cathedral, probably the largest medieval cathedral in Scandinavia, as well as the Museum of Decorative Arts with a good assortment of Viking relics; and take advantage of the excursions to neighboring fjords and islands.

FOR FURTHER INFORMATION: Write to: Secretary, Trondheim Golfklubb, Trondheim, Norway. Telephone: 21060.

SWEDEN

Drottningholms Golf Club

Only a few miles from Stockholm, the Drottningholms Golf Club has one of the newest and best courses in Scandinavia. It is on an island on Lake Mälaren, where the King of Sweden has a summer palace. The small park near the palace has a lovely pavilion in Chinese and rococo style, built in the eighteenth century by King Adolf Frederick for his queen. The course itself is rather flat and more suitable for the long driver. Its considerable length, however, is offset by a well-conceived layout, which favors the accurate player without too much of a long game. Altogether, this is not too difficult a course for the average player.

LOCATION: The course is about 10 miles W of the center of Stockholm, 208 miles NE of Jönköping, 311 miles NE of Göteborg, 366 miles NE of Hälsingborg, 394 miles NE of Malmö. It is accessible by car.

OTHER INFORMATION: The course is open to nonmembers, unlimited, for the entire season (May-October); two professionals are always on hand. The most crowded seasons are May to June 15 and August 15 through October; the weather is best in June, August and September. Practice ground is available, the best in Sweden.
   Number of holes: 18. *Par:* 71. *Length:* 6544 yards (6175 from front tees).
   Green fees: weekdays, $3; weekends, $5/day. *Lessons:* $2/20 minutes; $8/18 holes. *Caddies:* $1.75/18 holes. *Golfing equipment and caddie carts:* clubs and carts $2/day.

OTHER SPORTS FACILITIES: Tennis, swimming, boating, fishing.

ACCOMMODATIONS: No living space in the club house, but restaurant and bar are available. See the section for accommodations under *Lidingö Golf Club*, p. 220 and *Stockholms Golf Club*, p. 221.

TOURIST ATTRACTIONS: Of chief interest here are the Drottningholm Castle and the Drottningholm Theater. For other attractions, see this section under *Stockholms Golf Club*, pp. 221-222.

FOR FURTHER INFORMATION: Write to: Secretary, Drottningholms Golfklubb, Drottningholm, Sweden. Telephone: 7720300.

219

Lidingö Golf Club

The course is surrounded by trees and has well-planned fairways and greens. Long drivers should feel at home here, but many of the holes call for careful, accurate play. In essentials Lidingö doesn't differ too much from Drottningholms and Stockholms, the other two courses in Sweden's capital. The great advantage of golfing here—besides a fine course—is that you are just outside the center of Stockholm (2 miles).

LOCATION: The course is about 2 miles from the center of Stockholm, 220 miles NE of Jönköping, 325 miles NE of Göteborg, 380 miles NE of Hälsingborg, 407 miles NE of Malmö. It is accessible by car.

OTHER INFORMATION: The course is open to nonmembers, unlimited, for the entire season (May-October), with a professional always on hand. The most crowded months are May through August; the weather is best in May, June and September. Practice ground is available.
Number of holes: 18. Par: 72. Length: 6598 yards (6206 from front tees). Green fees: weekdays, $3; weekends, $5/day. Lessons: $4/hour. Caddies: $1.50/18 holes. Golfing equipment and caddie carts: clubs $2.50/day, carts $.50/day.

OTHER SPORTS FACILITIES: Riding, swimming, tennis.

ACCOMMODATIONS: No living space in the club house, but restaurant and bar are available.
In Stockholm: Foresta (Lidingö 5, Tel. [08] 652700). A first-class hotel of international standing, open all year. Rooms $11 to $13 for best single, $16 to $18 for best double; private baths, central heating, taxes and services not included, swimming pool; fully licensed for liquor, wine, beer. Apollonia (Nybrogatan 53, Tel. [08] 631240). A first-class hotel, open all year. Rooms $9 to $11 for best single, $13 to $15 for best double; private baths, central heating, taxes and services included; fully licensed for liquor, wine, beer. Aston (Adolf Mariatorget 3, Tel. [08] 440690). A very good, comfortable hotel, open all year. Rooms $8 to $9 for best single, $11 to $14 for best double; private baths, central heating, taxes and services not included; fully licensed for liquor, wine, beer. Reisen (Skeppsbron 12-14, Tel. [08] 223260). A very good, comfortable hotel, open all year. Rooms from $9 to $10 for best single, $12 to $13 for best double; private baths, central heating, taxes and services included; fully licensed for liquor, wine, beer. See this section for Stockholms Golf Club for further accommodations, p. 221.

TOURIST ATTRACTIONS: See this section under Stockholms Golf Club, pp. 221-222.

FOR FURTHER INFORMATION: Write to: Secretary, Lidingö Golfklubb, Lidingö, Sweden. Telephone: 651911.

Stockholms Golf Club

Here is a fine, undulating course, well-bunkered with some tough, challenging holes. The long driver has a decided advantage here, with many of the holes 400 yards and over, and 2 over 500 yards. But there is balance, so length alone doesn't predominate. The clever bunkering and general layout, characteristic of many Swedish courses, provide good golf whatever the state of your game. The course has the added advantage of being only a few miles from the center of Stockholm.

LOCATION: The course is about 4 miles N of Stockholm, 218 miles NE of Jönköping, 377 miles NE of Hälsingborg, 320 miles NE of Göteborg, 404 miles NE of Malmö. It is accessible by car and bus (get bus at Jarlaplan and get off at Mörby Centrum).

OTHER INFORMATION: The course is open to nonmembers (but golfer must be a member of a golf club), unlimited, for the entire season (April-October 15); a professional is always on hand. The most crowded months are April, May, June, September; the weather is best in June and September. Practice ground is available.
Number of holes: 18. Par: 72. Length: 6355 yards (5970 and 5520 from front tees).
Green fees: weekdays, $3; weekends, $5/day. Lessons: $3.75/hour. Caddies: $2/18 holes. Golfing equipment and caddie carts: clubs carts $.75/day.

OTHER SPORTS FACILITIES: Swimming, tennis, fishing, boating.

ACCOMMODATIONS: No living space in the club house, but restaurant and bar are available.
In Stockholm: Grand (Blasieholmshamnen 8, Tel. [08] 221020). A luxury hotel of international standing, open all year. Rooms from $12 to $17 for best single, $18 to $28 for best double; private baths, central heating, taxes and services included; fully licensed for liquor, wine, beer. Carlton (Kungsgatan 57, Tel. [08] 223400). A first-class hotel, open all year. Rooms from $11 to $14 for best single, $16 to $21 for best double; private baths, central heating, taxes and services included; fully licensed for liquor, wine, beer. Palace (Eriksgatan 115-7, Tel. [08] 241220). A first-class hotel, open all year. Rooms from $9 to $11 for best single, $13 to $18 for best double; private baths, central heating, taxes and services included; fully licensed for liquor, wine, beer. Gillet (Brunkebergstorg 13-15, Tel. [08] 221120). A very good, comfortable hotel, open all year. Rooms from $10 to $11 for best single, $16 to $17 for best double; private baths, central heating, taxes and services included; fully licensed for liquor, wine, beer. See this section for Lidingö Golf Club for further accommodations, p. 220.

TOURIST ATTRACTIONS: Stockholm has just about everything a

tourist could want—museums (particularly the National Museaum), parks, gardens, churches, excursions into the archipelago, wonderful shopping districts (especially for glassware, knitted wear), theaters, opera, a very good amusement park called Skansen and abundant night life.

FOR FURTHER INFORMATION: Write to: Secretary, Stockholms Golfklubb, Kevinge, Danderyd 1, Sweden. Telephone: 550031.

Uppsala Golf Club

On the outskirts of the oldest and most important university town in Sweden, this long, varied course is one of the best and most challenging in Scandinavia. Part of the course is in the open and part of it is cut out of a dense wood. Seven of the tees are high up on hills overlooking Uppsala and the surrounding countryside. The links also has a charming artificial lake and a small river—charming until you hook into them at the 4th, 13th and 17th. It favors the long, accurate driver and has fairways and greens that many pros have praised. This is a course of medium difficulty for the slightly better than average golfer.

LOCATION: The course is about 5 miles from the center of Uppsala, 50 miles N of Stockholm, 250 miles NE of Jönköping, 314 miles NE of Göteborg, 407 miles NE of Hälsingborg, 435 miles NE of Malmö. It is accessible by car.

OTHER INFORMATION: Uppsala is open to nonmembers, unlimited, for the entire season (April 15-November 15); a professional is always on hand. The most crowded months are May, June, September and October; the weather is best from June to September. Practice ground is available. *Number of holes:* 18. *Par:* 72. *Length:* 6706 yards (6413, front tees). *Green fees:* weekdays, $2; weekends, $4/day. *Lessons:* $2.25/25 minutes. *Caddies:* none available. *Golfing equipment and caddie carts:* clubs $2/day, carts $.50/day.

OTHER SPORTS FACILITIES: Tennis, swimming, riding, fishing.

ACCOMMODATIONS: No living space in the club house, but restaurant is available.

In Uppsala: *Rullan* (Dragarbrunnsgatan 32, Tel. [018] 120260). A first-class hotel, open all year. Rooms from $7 to $8 for best single, $12 to $18 for best double; private baths, central heating, full pension from $7/day, taxes and services included; fully licensed for liquor, wine, beer. *Gillet* (Fyristorg 6, Tel. [018] 139260). A good, comfortable hotel, open all year. Rooms from $6 to $7 for best single, $10 to $11 for best double; private baths, central heating, full pension from $7/day, taxes and services included; fully licensed for liquor, wine, beer. *Grand* (Barngårdsgatan 1, Tel. [018] 139380). A good, comfortable hotel, open all year. Rooms from $5 to $6 for best single, $10 to $11 for best double, private baths, central heating, taxes and services included; licensed for wine and beer.

TOURIST ATTRACTIONS: You may be interested in the *Domkyrkan,* the largest cathedral in the country and one of the largest in Scandinavia. Behind the pulpit you can see the Shrine of St. Erik, the patron saint of Sweden. Many famous men are interred in the Cathedral, among them Emmanuel Swedenborg. Uppsala also has Botanical Gardens, some interesting museums and, of course, the University.

FOR FURTHER INFORMATION: Write to: Secretary, Uppsala Golfklubb, Box 76, Uppsala, Sweden. Telephone: (018) 61241.

Eskilstuna Golf Club

Here is a course of good variety for all kinds of golfers, with possibly a nod to the cautious player. It lies a few miles from Eskilstuna, a town named after St. Eskil, a British bishop who lived and preached there in the eleventh century. Most of the holes are well sheltered from wind, and accurate play is a must here if you are to stay anywhere near par. Like the fairways and greens on most other Swedish courses, these are large, giving good approaches to the tees.

LOCATION: The course is about 4 miles from Eskilstuna, 70 miles W of Stockholm, 220 miles NE of Göteborg, 310 miles NE of Malmö. It is accessible by car.

OTHER INFORMATION: The course is open to nonmembers (but golfer must be a member of another club), unlimited, for the entire season (May-October), with a professional always on hand. Practice ground is available.
Number of holes: 18. *Par:* 71. *Length:* 5818 yards.
Green fees: weekdays, $3; weekends, $5/day. *Lessons:* $3/hour. *Caddies:* $1.25/18 holes. *Golfing equipment and caddie carts:* clubs $1.50/day. No carts.

OTHER SPORTS FACILITIES: Swimming and fishing.

ACCOMMODATIONS: No living space in the club house, but snackbar is available.
In Eskilstuna: *Stads* (Hamngatan, Tel. [016] 37225). A very good, comfortable hotel, open all year. Rooms from $8 to $10 for best single, $11 to $16 for best double; private baths, central heating, taxes and services included; fully licensed for liquor, wine, beer. *Smeden* (Drottninggatan 9, Tel. [016] 37690). A good, comfortable hotel, open all year. Rooms from $6 to $7 for best single, $8 to $9 for best double; private baths, central heating; taxes and services included.

TOURIST ATTRACTIONS: The visitor will find an interesting twelfth-century church (Fors Kyrka), a museum devoted to the history of the town and region, good shopping (especially for cutlery), a lovely park (Djurgården).

FOR FURTHER INFORMATION: Write to: Secretary, Eskilstuna Golf-klubb, P. O. Box 238, Eskilstuna, Sweden. Telephone: (016) 42629.

Karlstad Golf Club

Set in central eastern Sweden in the lovely Värmland district, with its rich, fertile plains, pastures, hills, thick forests and traditional red farm-houses, the Karlstad Golf Club is among the best and most challenging in Sweden. About 25 miles north of Karlstad on the shores of Lake Fryken are some of the manor houses associated with Selma Lagerlöf's famous *Gösta Berlings Saga*. The course is hilly but not difficult and is made for long as well as short drivers. Some of the fairways are very narrow and bordered by forests and therefore call for accurate, straight driving if you don't want to lose your sliced or hooked balls. The fairways and greens are well kept and the hazards (and there are plenty of them) usually clearly defined. This is a better-than-average course, almost of championship caliber, and the 605-yard 10th hole should become quite a conversation piece.

LOCATION: The course is 8 miles N of Karlstad, 165 miles N of Göte-borg, 318 miles N of Hälsingbor, 354 miles N of Malmö, 210 miles W of Stockholm. It is accessible by car.

OTHER INFORMATION: The course is open to nonmembers, un-limited, for the entire season (May-October), with a professional always on hand. The most crowded months are May, June, August, with the weather best from June to September.
Number of holes: 18. *Par:* 72. *Length:* 6560 yards.
Green fees: weekdays, $3; weekends, $4/day. *Lessons:* $3/50 minutes.
Caddies: $1.75/18 holes when available. *Golfing equipment and caddie carts:* none for rent.

OTHER SPORTS FACILITIES: Riding, tennis, skiing, skating, curling.

ACCOMMODATIONS: No living space in the club house, but restaurant is available.
In Karlstad: *Grand* (Västra Torggatan 8, Tel. [054] 15240). A very good, comfortable hotel, open all year. Rooms from $7 to $8 for best single, $11 to $14 for best double; private baths, central heating, taxes and services included; fully licensed for liquor, wine, beer. *Savoy* (Torggatan 1a, Tel. [054] 56640). A very good, comfortable hotel, open all year. Rooms from $6.50 to $7.50 for best single, $9 to $14 for best double; private baths, central heating, taxes and services included; fully licensed for liquor, wine, beer. *Stads* (Kungsgatan 22, Tel. [054] 15220). A fiirst-class hotel, open all year. Rooms from $8 to $9 for best single, $11 to $22 for best double; private baths, central heating, taxes and services not included; fully licensed for liquor, wine, beer.

TOURIST ATTRACTIONS: Karlstad offers the Rottneros Garden, an open-air museum, containing some old Värmland houses, excursions into the countryside. Try to see the Fryken Lake, one of the outstanding sights in the area.

FOR FURTHER INFORMATION: Write to: Secretary, Karlstad Golf-klubb, Fack, Kalstad 1, Sweden. Telephone: (054) 33090.

Örebro Golf Club

Northwest of Örebro, one of the oldest and most important cities in central Sweden, dating back to medieval times (the great hero of Swedish independence, Engelbrekt, lived there for a period and in 1434 drove the Danes from Örebro castle), lies the Örebro Golf Course, perhaps the best in central Sweden. It's a beautiful course, at the foot of a small mountain ridge called Kilsbergen, with a small river and a valley in the center. Long as well as short drivers will be at home here, but Örebro does call for accurate driving. The up-and-down nature of the course gives an interesting aspect to many of the holes. Örebro has the feel of something different and is worth playing for the golfer with a balanced game.

LOCATION: The course is 15 miles NW of Örebro, 146 miles W of Stockholm, 175 miles NE of Göteborg, 277 miles NE of Hälsingborg, 302 miles NE of Malmö. It is accessible by car.

OTHER INFORMATION: Örebro is open to nonmembers, unlimited, for the entire season (May-October), with a professional always on hand. The most crowded times are May 15 to July 1 and August 20 to September 30. The weather is best in July and August. Practice ground is available.
Number of holes: 18. *Par:* 72. *Length:* 6284 yards.
Green fees: weekdays, $2; weekends, $3/day. *Lessons:* $2/50 minutes. *Caddies:* not available. *Golfing equipment and caddie carts:* clubs $1.50/day, carts $.50.

OTHER SPORTS FACILITIES: Tennis, riding, swimming.

ACCOMMODATIONS: No living space in the club house, but restaurant is available.
   In Örebro: *Grey Rosen* (S. Grev Rosengatan 2, Tel. [019] 130240). A very good hotel, open all year. Rooms from $5.75 to $7 for best single, $9 to $11 for best double; private baths, central heating; taxes and services included. *Bergsmannen* (Drottninggatan 42, Tel. [019] 130320). A very good, comfortable hotel, open all year. Rooms from $6 to $7 for best single, $10 to $11 for best double; private baths, central heating, taxes and services included; fully licensed for liquor, wine, beer. *Stora* (Drottninggatan 1, Tel. [019] 124360). A very good, comfortable hotel, open all year. Rooms from $8 to $9 for best single, $12 to $15 for best double; private baths, central heating, taxes and services included; fully licensed for liquor, wine, beer.

TOURIST ATTRACTIONS: The chief attractions are a fifteenth-century castle, boat excursions on Lake Hjälmaren, walking tours into the surrounding countryside, and the Wadköping Museum, where you can buy Swedish handicrafts.

FOR FURTHER INFORMATION: Write to: Secretary, Örebro Golf-klubb, Fredsgatan 42, Örebro, Sweden. Telephone (019) 121162.

Falsterbo Golf Club Malmö

Here is a cool, pleasant seaside course on the southwestern tip of Sweden, between the Sound and the Baltic Sea. It favors long drivers even though its overall length is not too great. The course is cleverly planned, with about 100 bunkers and numerous other hazards. This is a good, average links, combining the advantages of pleasant golf with all the attractions of Malmö, the third largest city in Sweden. It is, incidentally, a good starting point for your game in Sweden, particularly if you enter from Copenhagen on the ferry to Malmö, only a few miles away. From here, go on to the championship course at Lund.

LOCATION: The course is in Falsterbo, about 23 miles SW of Malmö, 355 miles SW of Stockholm, 60 miles SE of Copenhagen (take ferry from Helsingør to Hälsingborg and then drive south to Falsterbo). It is accessible by car.

OTHER INFORMATION: The course is open to nonmembers, unlimited, for the entire year, with a professional on hand from March through October. The weather is best in May, August and September; the most crowded months are June and August. Practice ground is available.
Number of holes: 18. *Par:* 73. *Length:* 5742 yards.
Green fees: weekdays, $3; weekends, $4/day. *Lessons:* $2.50/half hour. *Caddies:* available June-August at $2/18 holes. *Golfing equipment and caddie carts:* clubs can be rented from June to August at $2/day and carts at $.50/day.

OTHER SPORTS FACILITIES: Riding and water-skiing.

ACCOMMODATIONS: No living space in the club house, but restaurant is available.
In Falsterbo: *Falsterbohus* (Falsterbo, Tel. [040] 470800). A first-class hotel, open all year. Rooms from $8 to $13 for best single, $13 to $22 for best double; private baths, central heating, full pension from $12/day, taxes and services included; fully licensed for liquor, wine, beer.
In Malmö: *Arkaden* (Balzarsgatan 20, Tel. [040] 70120). A very good, comfortable hotel, open all year. Rooms from $7 to $8 for best single, $10.50 to $11 for best double; private baths, central heating, taxes and services included; fully licensed for liquor, wine, beer. *Kramer* (Stortorget 7, Tel. [040] 70120). A first-class hotel, open all year. Rooms from $8.50

to $9 for best single, $12 to $15 for best double; private baths, central heating, taxes and services included; fully licensed for liquor, wine, beer. See this section for *Lunds Akademiska Golf Club,* p. 228, for accommodations in Malmö.

TOURIST ATTRACTIONS: Falsterbo has a famous beach and the ruins of an old fortress. Malmö is an ideal tourist town, with its many parks, fashionable shops, impressive squares, churches (St. Peter's, dating back to 1319, is the second largest in Sweden), canals and a good museum you shouldn't miss, the Malmöhus.

FOR FURTHER INFORMATION: Write to: Secretary, Falsterbo Golf-klubb, Malmö, Sweden. Telephone (040) 470990.

Ljunghusens Golf Club

This club is on the southwestern tip of Sweden, just north of the narrow sandy promontory between Örsend and the Baltic Sea and near several old fishing (herring) villages dating back to the thirteenth century. Ljunghusens is tough, challenging and made for the long driver (many of the holes are well over 400 yards). It has many waterholes and a hard rough. If you want a good workout, this is your course. One of its advantages is that you can regulate its length by as much as 500 yards by selecting which group of 9 holes you wish to play. Try to work it in with the several other courses around Malmö.

LOCATION: The course is in Ljunghusens, about 20 miles S of Malmö, 350 miles SW of Stockholm, 55 miles SE of Copenhagen (take ferry from Helsingør to Hälsingborg and then drive south to Ljunghusens). It is accessible by car.

OTHER INFORMATION: The course is open to nonmembers, unlimited, for the entire season (April-December) with a professional always on hand. The weather is best in May, August, September; the most crowded months are June and August.
Number of holes: 27, which you can play in 3 different combinations.
Par: 70 and 72. *Length:* 6418, 5942, 6142 yards.
Green fees: weekdays, $4; weekends, $5/day. *Lessons:* $3.50/hour. *Caddies:* none available. *Golfing equipment and caddie carts:* none available.

OTHER SPORTS FACILITIES: Riding, water-skiing, sailing, tennis.

ACCOMMODATIONS: No living space in the club house, but restaurant is available.
See the section on accommodations under *Falsterbo Golf Club, Malmö,* pp. 226-227.

TOURIST ATTRACTIONS: See this section under *Falsterbo Golf Club, Malmö,* p. 227.

FOR FURTHER INFORMATION: Write to: Secretary, Ljunghusens Golfklubb, Stortorget 9, Malmö C, Sweden. Telephone: Malmö 75800.

Lunds Akademiska Golf Club

Here is a championship course well worth the effort. Northeast of Malmö, it lies near Lund, one of the oldest and most charming cities in Sweden, founded in 1035 by Knut the Great of Denmark. But there is a legend that the city was founded by King Canute of England, who named it after London. At 6600 yards the course obviously favors the power hitter, but experience shows that many of the holes are also suitable for the short driver. Lunds provides plenty of variety—what you might expect on a championship course—including hazards that fit into the natural terrain, clever bunkering, stubborn roughs. Don't begin here if you can help it— your game may suffer.

LOCATION: The course is about 3 miles NE of Lund, 9 miles NE of Malmö, 390 miles SW of Stockholm, 30 miles S of Hälsingborg. It is accessible by car.

OTHER INFORMATION: Lunds is open to nonmembers, who must belong to another club, unlimited, for the entire season (March-September). The most crowded months are May, June, September; the weather is best from June through September. Practice ground is available.
Number of holes: 18. *Par:* 74 (S.S.S. 73). *Length:* 6586 yards.
Green fees: weekdays, $3; weekends, $5/day. *Lessons:* $2/half hour. *Caddies:* available on request. *Golfing equipment and caddie carts:* clubs $2.50/day, carts $1/day.

OTHER SPORTS FACILITIES: Tennis and riding.

ACCOMMODATIONS: No living space in the club house, but restaurant is available.
In Lund: *Grand* (Lund, Tel. [0412] 17010). A very good, comfortable hotel, open all year. Rooms from $7 to $8 for best single, $11 to $12 for best double; private baths, central heating, taxes and services included; fully licensed for liquor, wine, beer.
In Malmö: *St. Jörgen* (St. Nygatan 35, Tel. [040] 77300). A very good, comfortable hotel, open all year. Rooms from $8 to $9 for best single, $12 to $14 for best double; private baths, central heating, taxes and services included; fully licensed for liquor, wine, beer. *Savoy* (N. Vallgatan 62, Tel. [040] 70230). A first-class hotel, open all year. Rooms from $9 to $13 for best single, $12 to $17 for best double; private baths, central heating, taxes and services included; fully licensed for liquor, wine, beer.
See this section for *Falsterbo Golf Club, Malmö,* pp. 226-227, for further accommodations in Malmö.

TOURIST ATTRACTIONS: Besides dating back to the very beginning of the Middle Ages, Lund has one of the most famous universities in Scandinavia. The city still preserves its ancient quality and has many parks, gardens, old, somber, dignified houses and a cathedral (Domkyrkan) built in 1080. The crypt under the choir is one of the largest in Europe. The Historical Museum of the University has a fine collection of Medieval and Renaissance art.

FOR FURTHER INFORMATION: Write to: Secretary, Lunds Akademiska Golfklubb, P. O. Box 719, Lund 7, Sweden. Telephone [0412] 99005.

Mölle Golf Club

Near the shore of the Kattegat just north of Hälsingborg and at the foot of the great Kulleberg Cliffs, the Mölle Golf Club is surely one of the best situated in Sweden. Nearby is the famous Krapperup Castle with its magnificent parks and gardens. The course itself, even after considerable lengthening, is primarily for short drivers (5 of the holes are under 200 yards), but there are enough holes to interest the long driver, the longest being about 500 yards. With the recent revisions of the course, there is now good balance, and Mölle should fit the needs of the average golfer. It is a good course to tackle if you are just beginning your European tour.

LOCATION: About a mile outside of Mölle, 22 miles N of Hälsingborg, 45 miles N of Malmö, 400 miles SE of Stockholm, and about 50 miles N of Copenhagen (drive from Copenhagen to Helsingør, take the ferry to Hälsingborg, and then drive directly north to Mölle). It is accessible by bus and car.

OTHER INFORMATION: The course is open to nonmembers, unlimited, for the entire season (middle of April until end of October), but the player must be a member of a golf club; a professional is on hand from June 15 to August 30. The weather is best in the spring and autumn; the most crowded month is July.
Number of holes: 18. Par: 70. Length: 5943 yards.
Green fees: weekdays, $3; weekends and holidays, $4/day. Lessons: $3/40 minutes. Caddies: $1.75/18 holes. Golfing equipment and caddie carts: clubs $1.50/day, carts $.50/day.

OTHER SPORTS FACILITIES: Tennis, fishing, boating.

ACCOMMODATIONS: No living space in the club house, but restaurant and bar are available.
In Mölle: Grand (Mölle, Tel. [042] 47280). A good, comfortable hotel, open April 30 to August 31. Rooms from $5 to $6 for best single, $9 to $10 for best double; central heating, bath and toilet on the floor, taxes and services not included; fully licensed for liquor, wine, beer.
In Hälsingborg: Grand (Stortorget 8, Tel. [042] 20170). A first-class hotel, open all year. Rooms from $8 to $9 for best single, $13 to $14 for

best double; private baths, central heating, taxes and services included; fully licensed for liquor, wine, beer. *Mollberg* (Stortorget 18, Tel. [042] 20270). A very good, comfortable hotel, open all year. Rooms from $7 to $8 for best single, $12 to $15 for best double; private baths, central heating, taxes and services included; fully licensed for liquor, wine, beer.

TOURIST ATTRACTIONS: Mölle offers some magnificent views of the Kattegat, good walks, lovely parks and gardens, prehistoric caves and the sixteenth-century Krapperup Castle, whose owners, the Gyllerstierna family, were immortalized in *Hamlet* (as Guildenstern).

FOR FURTHER INFORMATION: Write to: Secretary, Mölle Golfklubb, P. O. Box 61, Hälsingborg, Sweden. Telephone (042) 47012.

Rya Golf Club

The Rya Golf Club combines the best features of seaside, country and city. It offers the golfer a stunning view of the narrows between Sweden and Denmark, lovely grounds and all the facilities of Hälsingborg and Copenhagen (the course is less than three hours from the center of Copenhagen). Rya favors long hitters but should not put off short drivers. Like so many other Swedish links, this combined seaside and park course is full of variety; a balanced game is the key here. Sandwich Rya in between Falsterbo and Lunds if you can.

LOCATION: 5 miles S of Hälsingborg, 35 miles N of Malmö, 380 miles SW of Stockholm, 40 miles N of Copenhagen (drive up to Helsingør, take the ferry to Hälsingborg and drive 5 miles south). Best way to get there is by car.

OTHER INFORMATION: Rya is open to nonmembers, unlimited, for the entire season (March-December), with a professional always on hand. The most crowded month is July, and the weather is best in September. Practice ground is available.
Number of holes: 18. *Par:* 72. *Length:* 6202 yards.
Green fees: weekdays, $2; weekends, $4/day. *Lessons:* $3/hour. *Caddies:* $1.75/18 holes. *Golfing equipment and caddie carts:* clubs $2.50/day, carts $.50/day.

OTHER SPORTS FACILITIES: Tennis and swimming.

ACCOMMODATIONS: No living space in the club house, but restaurant and bar are available.
See the section for accommodations under *Mölle Golf Club*, pp. 229-230.

TOURIST ATTRACTIONS: The Kärnan, a tower of a medieval castle, offers an impressive view of the city. There are some interesting gardens, a number of old houses going back to the seventeenth century and a modern concert hall. Don't miss the Vikingsberg Art Gallery, where you can see the original portrait of the French philosopher Descartes by Franz Hals. In the summer there are many excursions to the very lovely countryside surrounding Hälsingborg.

FOR FURTHER INFORMATION: Write to: Secretary, Rya Golf Club, Box 150, Hälsingborg, Sweden. Telephone: 91082.

Söderhamns Golf Club

On the northern shore of the Söderhamn Sound, near the Baltic Sea, the Söderhamn Golf Club, with its many roughs, trees and beautiful summer flowers, is one of the most picturesque in Sweden. If you are lucky, you may get to see elk and roe deer as you move from hole to hole. The course itself is considered an interesting one by both high and low handicappers. Each hole has its own character, and the course is full of well-placed and planned hazards, bunkers or hills with trees—all calculated to provide excitement and a challenge. This is an average links, with the chief difficulty in the length.

LOCATION: The course is about 5 miles N of Söderhamn and 150 miles N of Stockholm. It is accessible by car.

OTHER INFORMATION: The course is open to nonmembers, unlimited, for the entire season (May-October); a professional is on hand at least two days a week. The weather is best in June, July, August. Practice ground is available.
Number of holes: 18. Par: 72. Length: 6392 yards.
Green fees: weekdays, $2; weekends, $3/day. Lessons: $1.75/half hour.
Caddies: usually not available. Golfing equipment and caddie carts: clubs $2/day, carts $.50.

OTHER SPORTS FACILITIES: Tennis, soccer, swimming, riding and sailing.

ACCOMMODATIONS: No living space in the club house, but restaurant is available.
In Söderhamn Stads-Central (Söderhamn, Tel. 11410). A good, comfortable hotel, open all year. Rooms from $4 to $5 for best single, $8 to $9 for best double; private baths, central heating; taxes and services not included.

TOURIST ATTRACTIONS: Try the boat excursions through the archipelago to nearby islands, salmon fishing (Ljusne), museums, long sandy beaches, churches and good shopping for local homecrafts. Stenö Havsbad (6 miles) is a large resort area.

FOR FURTHER INFORMATION: Write to: Secretary, Söderhamns

Golfklubb, Oxtorgsgatan 14, Söderhamn, Sweden. Telephone: (0270) 13030.

Åtvidabergs Golf Club

Tucked away between rich fertile meadows and great stretches of forest, on the shores of a beautiful lake and surrunded by magnificent oak groves, the Åtvidabergs Course is one of the most delightful and challenging in all of Sweden. Nearby are vast pine and fir forests abounding in deer, pheasant and moose and about 50 lakes, many of them excellent for fishing. The course favors the power golfer; long driving is necessary at many holes for the scratch player. Nevertheless, except for holes 4 and 17, there should be no driving difficulties for the shorter hitter. The layout of the course gives the visitor a great variety of different tees. In sum, it is an interesting and challenging links of championship caliber.

LOCATION: The course is about 2 miles from Åtvidaberg, 25 miles SE of Linköping, 45 miles S of Norrköping, 145 miles S of Stockholm, 210 miles E of Göteborg and 286 miles NE of Malmö. It is accessible by car.

OTHER INFORMATION: The course is open to nonmembers (but golfer must show membership in his own club) for the entire season (April 15-October 15), with a professional always on hand. Most crowded months are August and September; the weather is best July through September. Practice ground is available.
Number of holes: 18. Par: 71. Length: 6392 yards.
Green fees: weekdays and Saturdays, $2.50, Sundays and holidays, $4.
Lessons: $2.25/25 minutes. Caddies: none available. Golfing equipment and caddie carts: clubs $2/day, carts $.50/day.

OTHER SPORTS FACILITIES: Hunting, fishing, boating, tennis.

ACCOMMODATIONS: No living space in the club house, but restaurant and bar are available.
Near course: Trädgårds (Åtvidaberg, Tel. [0120] 11800). A good, comfortable hotel, open all year. Rooms from $5 to $6 for best single, $7 to $8 for best double; private baths, central heating; taxes and services included.
In Åtvidaberg: Stallet (Åtvidaberg, Tel. [0120] 11940). A very good, comfortable hotel, open all year. Rooms from $6 to $7 for best single, $8 to $9 for best double; private baths, central heating, taxes and services included; fully licensed for liquor, wine, beer.

TOURIST ATTRACTIONS: The general area offers a large oak forest, attractive walking tours, lakes with excellent fishing, bird watching, old manor houses and medieval castles.

FOR FURTHER INFORMATION: Write to: Secretary, Åtvidabergs Golfklubb, Åtvidaberg, Sweden. Telephone (0120) 11800.

Jönköping-Huskvarna Golf Club

Jönköping-Huskvarna is certainly one of the most beautiful courses in Sweden. Lying at the southern tip of Lake Vättern in south central Sweden, the course is surrounded by large forests, moors, hills and lakes. Everything in Jönköping is geared to a healthy outdoor life. The course is hilly, with good opportunities for the long as well as the short driver. With back tees, club tees and front tees, you can come out to the fairway with a modest drive, depending on your own power. The greens are of large size, but well bunkered. This is an exceptionally well-kept course and well liked by visitors, even though it is not too easy.

LOCATION: The course is 2 miles from Jönköping, 105 miles E of Göteborg, 160 miles NE of Hälsingborg, 188 miles NE of Malmö, 220 miles SW of Stockholm. It is accessible by car.

OTHER INFORMATION: The course is open to nonmembers, unlimited, for the entire year; a professional is always on hand. The most crowded months are May and August; the weather is best from May-September. Practice ground is available.
Number of holes: 18. *Par:* 70. *Length:* 6246 yards (5393, from front tees).
Green fees: weekdays, $3; weekends, $4/day. *Lessons:* $2/25 minutes. *Caddies:* $1.50/18 holes. *Golfing equipment and caddie carts:* clubs $2/day, carts $.75/day.

OTHER SPORTS FACILITIES: Swimming, boating, tennis, riding, indoor ice-skating, fishing.

ACCOMMODATIONS: No living space in the club house, but restaurant is available.
In Jönköping: *Portalen* (Storgatan 9, Tel. [036] 118200). A first-class hotel, open all year. Rooms from $7 to $8 for best single, $11 to $12 for best double; private baths, central heating, full pension from $11/day, taxes and services included; fully licensed for liquor, wine, beer. *Stora* (Hotellplan 1, Tel. [036] 119300). A first-class hotel, open all year. Rooms from $9 to $10 for best single, $12 to $13 for best double; private baths, central heating, taxes and services included; fully licensed for liquor, wine, beer. *City* (Brunnsgatan 15, Tel. [036] 119280). A very good, comfortable hotel, open all year. Rooms from $6 to $8 for best single, $9 to $15 for best double; private baths, central heating, full pension from $10/day, taxes and services not included; fully licensed for liquor, wine, beer.

TOURIST ATTRACTIONS: Jönköping has been called the "Geneva of Sweden." The town is a paradise for those who love an active life—with many lakes, walking tours, excursions and just about every form of outdoor activity.

FOR FURTHER INFORMATION: Write to: Secretary, Jönköping-Huskvarna Golfklubb, Box 1266, Jönköping, Sweden. Telephone: (036) 118400.

Kalmar Golf Club

The Kalmar Club is in southeastern Sweden, on a straight line between the mainland and Öland, the second largest island in Sweden. Kalmar is an ancient town, going back to pagan times and, historically, one of the most important in Sweden. The course itself is suitable for every type of player. It is particularly good for the visitor who plays 15 or 20 over par, and yet it is still a challenge for the pro. This used to be a rather easy 9 holes, but during its expansion it was stiffened—in hazards, bunkers and roughs. A pleasant course for the average golfer.

LOCATION: The course is 5 miles N of Kalmar, 208 miles E of Hälsingborg, 219 miles E of Malmö, 245 miles SE of Göteborg, 302 miles S of Stockholm.

OTHER INFORMATION: The course is open to nonmembers, unlimited, for the entire year; a professional is always on hand. The weather is best from June to October. Practice ground is available.
Number of holes: 18. *Par:* 72. *Length:* 6392 yards.
Green fees: daily, $2. *Lessons:* $1.50/half hour. *Caddies:* not available.
Golfing equipment and caddie carts: clubs $2/day, carts $.50.

OTHER SPORTS FACILITIES: Swimming, boating, tennis.

ACCOMMODATIONS: No living space in the club house, but restaurant is available.
In Kalmar: *Stads* (Kalmar, Tel. [0480] 15180). A very good, comfortable hotel, open all year. Rooms from $7 to $9 for best single, $10 to $17 for best double; private baths, central heating; full pension from $9/day, taxes and services included; fully licensed for liquor, wine, beer. *Frimurare* (Kalmar, Tel. [0480] 15230). A good, comfortable hotel, open all year. Rooms from $6 to $7 for best single, $10 to $11 for best double; private baths, central heating, taxes and services included; fully licensed for liquor, wine, beer. *Witt* (Kalmar, Tel. [0480] 15255). A good, comfortable hotel, open all year. Rooms from $6 to $7 for best single, $8 to $9 for best double; private baths, central heating, taxes and services included; fully licensed for liquor, wine, beer.

TOURIST ATTRACTIONS: The most important attraction here is Kalmar Castle, built at the end of the twelfth century by Magnus Erikson. It is one of the most picturesque castles in Sweden. There are also a seventeenth-century cathedral and attractive shops. Just across from Kalmar is the island of Öland, with about 500 windmills and rare Scandinavian plants.

FOR FURTHER INFORMATION: Write to: Secretary, Kalmar Golf-klubb, Hornsgatan 3, Kalmar, Sweden. Telephone: (0480) 13357.

Linköpings Golf Club

In the province of Östergötland, often called "the cradle of Swedish civilization," and within easy touring distance of medieval castles and old manor houses, the Linköpings Golf Club has one of the best and most challenging courses in Sweden. Many of Sweden's most important tournaments—the Swedish Amateur, the Scandinavian Dunlop Professional Tournament and the Scandinavian Penfold Professional Tournament—have been held here. The course favors the long driver, especially many of the par-5 and long par-4 holes, which require great length if they are to be reached on the second shot. In addition, the tree-lined fairways and well-guarded greens demand accuracy. This is a balanced course, with a famous 16th hole, the "Bauer," and one you shouldn't miss if you are touring Sweden, especially if your game is above average.

LOCATION: The course is about 2 miles outside of Linköping, 140 miles SW of Stockholm, 180 miles NE of Göteborg, 205 miles NE of Hälsingborg, 242 miles NE of Malmö. It is accessible by car.

OTHER INFORMATION: The course open to nonmembers (golfer must be a member of a recognized golf club), unlimited, for the entire season (April-October); a professional is always on hand. The most crowded months are May, June and September; the weather is best in June, July and August. Practice ground is available as well as driving range with automatic tees.
Number of holes: 18. Par: 71. Length: 6350 yards.
Green fees: weekdays, $2; weekends, $3/day. Lessons: $2/half hour. Caddies: $1.75/18 holes. Golfing equipment and caddie carts: clubs $2/day, carts $.50/day.

OTHER SPORTS FACILITIES: Tennis, swimming and fishing.

ACCOMMODATIONS: No living space in the club, but restaurant is available.
In Linköping: Frimurare (Larsgatan 14, Tel. [013] 29180). A first-class hotel, open all year. Rooms from $7 to $8 for best single, $11 to $13 for best double; private baths, central heating, taxes and services included; fully licensed for liquor, wine, beer. Rally (Storgatan 72, Tel. [013] 30200). A very good, comfortable hotel, open all year. Rooms from $7 to $8 for best single, $10 to $11 for best double; private baths, central heating, taxes and services included; fully licensed for liquor, wine, beer. Stora (Stora Torget 9, Tel. [013] 29630). A very good, comfortable hotel, open all year. Rooms from $7 to $8 for best single, $9 to $10 for best double;

private baths, central heating, taxes and services included; fully licensed for liquor, wine, beer.

TOURIST ATTRACTIONS: Chief attractions are the Domkyrkan, one of the largest medieval cathedrals in Scandinavia, gardens, parks, a huge fountain by Sweden's greatest sculptor, Carl Milles, and excursions into the lake country.

FOR FURTHER INFORMATION: Write to: Secretary, Linköpings Golfklubb, Kalmarvägen, Linköping, Sweden. Telephone (013) 120646.

Borås Golf Club

The club is on the outskirts of Borås, a charming, pleasant town within touring distance of picturesque lake country. Borås is the leading textile center in Scandinavia and is a must for anyone interested in the colorful, unique Swedish fabrics. The course is for both long and short drivers and requires precision because of the heavy roughs around many holes. It is a varied course, requiring many abrupt changes of pace from a long to short game. This is a course to keep the average and above-average golfer on his toes.

LOCATION: The course is about 3 miles from Borås, 44 miles E of Göteborg, 158 miles N of Hälsingborg, 196 miles N of Malmö, and 277 miles SW of Stockholm. Best way to get there is by car.

OTHER INFORMATION: The course is open to nonmembers (but golfer must be a member of another club), unlimited, for the entire season (April-November), with a professional always on hand. Practice ground is available.
Number of holes: 18. *Par:* 70. *Length:* 5775 yards.
Green fees: daily, $3/day. *Lessons:* $3/hour. *Caddies:* none available. *Golfing equipment and caddie carts:* none available.

OTHER SPORTS FACILITIES: Swimming, ice-skating.

ACCOMMODATIONS: No living space in the club house, but restaurant is available.
In Borås: *Hôtel du Nord* (Yxhammarsgatan 8, Tel. [033] 17165). A good, comfortable hotel, open all year. Rooms from $6 to $7 for best single, $10 to $11 for best double; private baths, central heating, taxes and services not included; fully licensed for liquor, wine, beer. *Stads* (Österlanggatan 12, Tel. [033] 27950). A good, comfortable hotel, open all year. Rooms from $7 to $8 for best single, $10 to $11 for best double; private baths, central heating; fully licensed for liquor, wine, beer.

TOURIST ATTRACTIONS: You will find here a typical Swedish marketplace, parks, a seventeenth-century church, a cultural museum devoted to the area, Turkish baths and cotton and woolen mills. The chief advantage is proximity to fine countryside, and good shopping for fabrics.

FOR FURTHER INFORMATION: Write to: Secretary, Borås Golfklubb, Borås, Sweden. Telephone: 131618.

Delsjö Golf Club

The Delsjö Golf Club is ideal for the golfer who wants to combine big city life with a good, tough course. Göteborg has a variety of entertainment, fashionable shops, good restaurants and exciting night life. The outskirts are well worth touring if you want to see the way the Swedish people work and live. The course itself is good for both long and short drivers, with possibly the narrowest fairways in Europe. Straight, accurate driving is a must here. Delsjö requires an above average game; there are a lot of tricky approaches, some uncooperative roughs, sharp doglegs, many holes not visible from the tees.

LOCATION: The course is 3 miles from Göteborg, 151 miles N of Hälsingborg, 191 miles N of Malmö, 321 miles W of Stockholm. It is accessible by car or taxi (tell driver to go to "Golfbanan 1 Kallebäcksliden").

OTHER INFORMATION: The course is open to nonmembers, unlimited, for the entire year, with a professional on hand from April through October. The weather is best from May to August. Practice ground is available.
Number of holes: 18. Par: 71. Length: 6154 yards.
Green fees: weekdays $2.50; weekends, $3.75/day. Lessons: $2/20 minutes. Caddies: $1.75/18 holes. Golfing equipment and caddie carts: clubs $2.50/day, carts $.50/day.

OTHER SPORTS FACILITIES: Swimming, fishing, boating, tennis.

ACCOMMODATIONS: No living space in the club house, but restaurant is available.
In Göteborg: Park Avenue (Kungsportsavenyn 36-38, Tel. [031] 176520). A luxury hotel of international standing, open all year. Rooms from $11 to $12 for best single, $16 to $19 for best double; private baths, central heating, taxes and services included; fully licensed for liquor, wine, beer. Grand Hôtel Haglund (Södra Hamngatan 49-57, Tel. [031] 171520). A first-class hotel, open all year. Rooms from $10 to $12 for best single, $14 to $19 for best double; private baths, central heating, taxes and services included; fully licensed for liquor, wine, beer. Palace (Södra Hamngatan 2, Tel. [031] 174240). A very good, comfortable hotel, open all year. Rooms from $9 to $10 for best single, $12 to $16 for best double; private baths, central heating, taxes and services included; fully licensed for liquor, wine, beer.

See this section for *Göteborgs Golf Club*, pp. 238-239, for further accommodations.

TOURIST ATTRACTIONS: There are typical Swedish attractions: numerous parks, gardens, theaters, museums (the Maritime Museum shows the development of the Swedish merchant marine from its beginning until the present), concerts and excursions into the surrounding suburbs.

FOR FURTHER INFORMATION: Write to: Secretary, Delsjö Golfklubb, Sweden. Telephone (031) 406959.

Göteborgs Golf Club

The Göteborgs Golf Club in Hovås is in an attractive seaside resort facing the Kattegat, with picturesque walks along the coast and a leisurely old-world way of life. Should you want the excitement of big city life. Göteborg is only a half hour away by car or train. The course is rather short, hilly, with good sandy soil. The nature of the soil fortunately keeps it dry no matter what the weather. While Göteborgs favors a short game, long drivers will have enough holes to keep them interested. The layout is clever, so that there is balance despite the relative lack of length. Good for the average golfer.

LOCATION: The course is in Hovås, about 7 miles S of Göteborg, 144 miles N of Hälsingborg, 184 miles N of Malmö, 317 miles SW of Stockholm. It is accessible by car.

OTHER INFORMATION: The course is open to nonmembers (but golfer must be a member of a recognized club), unlimited, for the entire year, with a professional always on hand. The weather is best in May, June and September; the most crowded months are June, July, August. Practice ground is available.
Number of holes: 18. *Par:* 70. *Length:* 5525 yards.
Green fees: weekdays, $4; weekends, $7/day. *Lessons:* $2/half hour. *Caddies:* $1.75/18 holes. *Golfing equipment and caddie carts:* clubs $1.75/ day, carts $.50/day.

OTHER SPORTS FACILITIES: Swimming, fishing, yachting.

ACCOMMODATIONS: No living space in the club house, but restaurant and bar are available.
In Göteborg: *Eggers* (Drottningtorget 1, Tel. [031] 171570). A very good, comfortable hotel, open all year. Rooms from $9 to $10 for best single, $13 to $14 for best double; private baths, central heating, taxes and services included; fully licensed for liquor, beer, wine. *Göteborg* (Skeppsbroplan 1, Tel. [031] 170965). A very good, comfortable hotel, open all year. Rooms from $7 to $8 for best single, $12 to $13 for best double; private baths, central heating, taxes and services included; fully licensed for

liquor, wine, beer. *Opalen* (Engelbrektsgatan 73, Tel. [031] 810300). A very good, comfortable hotel, open all year. Rooms from $8 to $9 for best single, $12 to 18 for best double; private baths, central heating, taxes and services included; fully licensed for liquor, wine, beer.

TOURIST ATTRACTIONS: You will find delightful gardens, lovely walks along the shore and through thick woods, excursions to the island of Styrsö and, of course, all the attractions in Göteborg. See this section for *Delsjö Golf Club,* p. 238.

FOR FURTHER INFORMATION: Write to: Secretary, Göteborg Golf Club, Box 110, Hovås, Sweden. Telephone: (031) 282444.

Öijared Golf Club

The course is just outside of Floda, at the mouth of the Säveån River and near Floda Castle, built in the early part of the twelfth century. The town is world renowned because before World War II professors from all over the world met there for special seminars in their field. Öijared itself is for long drivers but also calls for careful, accurate play. It is a natural course, where the hazards and bunkering come from the very nature of the terrain. You can see elk and deer from many of the holes. This is the kind of course for which Scandinavia is justly famous.

LOCATION: The course is in Floda, 15 miles SE of Alingsås, 25 miles NE of Göteborg, 176 miles N of Hälsingborg, 216 miles N of Malmö, 296 miles SW of Stockholm. It is accessible by car.

OTHER INFORMATION: The course is open to nonmembers (but golfer must be a member of another club), unlimited, for the entire season (April-October); a professional is always on hand. The weather is best from May through September; the most crowded months are May, June, August and September. Practice ground is available.
Number of holes: 18. *Par:* 72. *Length:* 6312 yards.
Green fees: weekdays, $3; weekends, $5/day. *Lessons:* $1.75/half hour.
Caddies: not available. *Golfing equipment and caddie carts:* clubs $3/day.

OTHER SPORTS FACILITIES: Tennis, riding, fishing.

ACCOMMODATIONS: No living space in club house, but restaurant is available.
In Alingsås: *Stads* (Bankgatan 1, Tel. [0322] 14000). A good, comfortable hotel, open all year. Rooms from $6 to $7 for best single, $10 to $11 for best double; private baths, central heating, full pension from $8.50/day, taxes and services included; fully licensed for liquor, wine, beer.
In Göteborg: See the section for accommodations under *Göteborg Golf Club,* pp. 238-239 and *Delsjö Golf Club,* p. 237.

Swedish National Travel Office

The Båstad Golf Links, one of the fine seaside courses in southern Sweden.

TOURIST ATTRACTIONS: There are typical Swedish amusements, including folk dancing, walking tours, as well as visits to castles, cotton and woolen mills, local museums.

FOR FURTHER INFORMATION: Write to: Secretary, Öijared Golf-klubb, P. O. Box 69, Floda, Sweden. Telephone: (0302) 30230.

Båstad Golf Club

The Båstad Golf Club is located in one of the most beautiful summer resorts in Scandinavia, and the town has come to be known in northern Europe as the "Sorrento of the North." The course has a stunning view of Laholm Bay and is one of the most picturesque in Sweden. It is hilly but not tiring and of moderate length. This is an excellent place for the average golfer to begin in Sweden—a course with good fairways and some interesting holes but nothing extraordinary or too challenging. Only the roughs may need especially careful play.

LOCATION: The course is about 4 miles from Båstad, 35 miles N of Hälsingborg, 68 miles N of Malmö, 115 miles S of Göteborg, 342 miles SW of Stockholm and about 70 miles N of Copenhagen (drive from Copenhagen to Helsingør, take the ferry to Hälsingborg and then drive north to Båstad. Whole trip shouldn't take more than 3 hours). It is accessible by car.

OTHER INFORMATION: The course is open to nonmembers (but golfer must be a member of a golf club), unlimited, the entire season (April 15 through October); a professional is always on hand. The most crowded months are June, July, August, with the weather best in May and September. Practice ground is available.

Number of holes: 18. Par: 71. Length: 5583 yards.
Green fees: weekdays, $3; weekends, $4/day. Lessons: $2/half hour. Caddies: usually not available. Golfing equipment and caddie carts: only carts for rent at $.75/day.

OTHER SPORTS FACILITIES: Tennis, swimming, riding, boating.

ACCOMMODATIONS: No living space at the club house, but restaurant and bar are available.

In Båstad: Skånegården (Båstad, Tel. [0431] 71000). A first-class hotel, open June-August. Rooms from $10 to $11 for best single, $12 to $16 for best double; private baths, central heating, full pension from $12/day, taxes and services included; fully licensed for liquor, wine, beer. Båstad (Båstad, Tel. [0431] 71020). A very good, comfortable hotel, open all year. Rooms from $7 to $8 for best single, $10 to $11 for best double; private baths, central heating, full pension from $8/day, taxes and services not included; fully licensed for liquor, wine, beer.

TOURIST ATTRACTIONS: Davis Cup and other international tennis tournaments are held here. See the lovely gardens and take the walking tours. Don't miss "The Viking's Tomb" on the outskirts of Båstad. The inside of the tomb resembles a Viking ship.

FOR FURTHER INFORMATION: Write to: Secretary, Båstad Golf-klubb, Box 37, Båstad, Sweden. Telephone: Båstad 73136.

Falkenbergs Golf Club

On the western coast of Sweden, a few minutes from the Kattegat and the fashionable seaside spa of Falkenbergs Havsbad, the Falkenbergs Golf Club offers the average golfer an attractive course and one that he will enjoy. Both short and long drivers will find it to their liking. However, it also demands an accurate, straight game. The lengthened course (before 1967 it was a 9-holer) has added many interesting features, mostly in the bunkering and the roughs. And if you wish to mix golf with other activities, try the salmon fishing in the immediate region.

LOCATION: The course is 3 miles S of Falkenberg, 70 miles S of Göteborg, 25 miles N of Halmstad, 55 miles N of Hälsingborg, 95 miles N of Malmö and 345 miles SW of Stockholm. It is accessible by car.

OTHER INFORMATION: Falkenbergs is open to nonmembers, un-limited, for the entire year; there is no professional on hand. The most crowded months are July and August; the weather is best in May, August and September.

Number of holes: 18 holes (by 1967). *Par:* 72. *Length:* 6032 yards. *Green fees:* weekdays, $2; weekends, $3/day. *Lessons:* none. *Caddies:* $1.25/18 holes when available. *Golfing equipment and caddie carts:* a few clubs and carts on request.

OTHER SPORTS FACILITIES: Tennis, swimming, motor-boating, salmon fishing.

ACCOMMODATIONS: No living space in the club house, but restaurant is available.

In Falkenberg: *Grand* (Falkenberg, Tel. [0346] 14450). A very good, comfortable hotel, open all year. Rooms from $6 to $7 for best single, $10 to $11 for best double; private baths, central heating, full pension from $9.50/day, taxes and services included; fully licensed for liquor, wine, beer. *Strandbaden* (Falkenberg, Tel. [0346] 14320). A very good, comfortable hotel, open June 19–August 22. Rooms from $5 to $6 for single, $8.50 to $9.50 for double; central heating, baths and toilets available for general use, full pension from $9.50/day; taxes and services included; fully licensed for liquor, wine, beer.

TOURIST ATTRACTIONS: Falkenberg is a small, pleasant town with narrow winding streets and an old castle. The surrounding area is famous for its fishing. About 25 miles north along the coast is the Varberg fortress, which has one of the most important museums in Sweden. Don't miss the *Bocksten,* the only fully preserved medieval soldier in complete armor in the world.

FOR FURTHER INFORMATION: Write to: Secretary, Falkenbergs Golfklubb, Box 122, Falkenberg, Sweden. Telephone: (0346) 10333.

Halmstad Golf Club at Tylösand

Surrounded by dense forests (with every hole literally cut out of the woods) and close to one of the best beaches on the western coast of Sweden, the Halmstad Golf Club is a championship course and one of the best in northern Europe. With its considerable length it favors the long hitter, but the short, accurate driver has plenty of opportunity here to display his game. Many of the fairways are narrow, and several sharp doglegs require precision. This is a course for everyone, with balance the chief quality.

LOCATION: The course is in Tylösand, about 6 miles W of Halmstad, 99 miles S of Göteborg, 58 miles N of Hälsingborg, 97 miles N of Malmö, 329 miles SW of Stockholm, and 90 miles N of Copenhagen (drive north from Copenhagen to Helsingør, take the ferry to Hälsingborg, and then drive north to Halmstad). It is accessible by car.

OTHER INFORMATION: Halmstad is open to nonmembers (but golfer must be a member of a golf club), unlimited, for the entire year; two professionals are on hand for the entire season (May-October). The weather is best from June through September. Practice ground is available. *Number of holes:* 18. *Par:* 72. *Length:* 6511 yards. *Green fees:* daily, $5/day. *Lessons:* $3/50 minutes. *Caddies:* $1.75/18 holes. *Golfing equipment and caddie carts:* clubs $2/day, carts $1/day.

OTHER SPORTS FACILITIES: Tennis, boating, water-skiing, fishing.

ACCOMMODATIONS: No living space in the club house, but restaurant and bar are available.

In Tylösand: *Tylösands Havsbad* (Tylösand, Tel. [035] 30500). A very good, comfortable hotel, open April 1–September 15. Rooms from $10 to $11 for best single, $10 to 18 for best double; private baths, central heating, full pension from $10/day, taxes and services included; fully licensed for liquor, wine, beer. In Halmstad: *Mårtenson* (Storgatan 52, Tel. [035] 18070). A very good, comfortable hotel, open all year. Rooms from $8 to $10 for best single, $14 to $16 for best double; private baths, central heating, full pension for $10/day, taxes and services included; fully licensed for liquor, wine, beer. *Svea-Gillet* (Hamngatan 3, Tel. [035] 18800). A good, comfortable hotel, open all year. Rooms from $6 to $7 for best single, $9 to $11 for best double; private baths, central heating, taxes and services included; fully licensed for liquor, wine, beer.

TOURIST ATTRACTIONS: Recommended are Halmstad Castle, built in the early sixteenth century; a famous fountain representing the *Rape of Europa* by Sweden's best sculptor, Carl Milles; an open-air island of Tylö, famous for its Viking tombs and birds.

FOR FURTHER INFORMATION: Write to: Secretary, Halmstad Golfklubb, Tylösand, Halmstad, Sweden. Telephone: Halmstad 30077.

SPAIN

For your trip south, I have chosen five of the best courses in Spain. There are several others, but most are 9 or 12 holes, while these are 18. At these five you can expect first-rate golf, lovely surroundings, and all the amenities that make the game so pleasurable.

Nearly all visitors to Spain pass through Madrid, and nothing is easier than a stop at the Club Campo. It is barely outside of the city, yet the location is attractive. The golf itself is stupendous. If you're coming up from the south, you'll find that *Campo* plays better after some practice at *Guadalmina* and *Málaga* on the "Costa del Sol." Those two leisurely southern links provide the utmost in comfort and beauty and will be good preparation for the more difficult northern courses. But *Campo* in Madrid will be an experience, any way you play it.

Barcelona is another "must" stop on your trip to Spain for both its own attractions and the fine golf awaiting you. Both *El Prat* and *San Cugat* are good, knotty courses, a fine test for the experienced golfer and an excellent workout for the average player.

Ideally, start with *Málaga*, the easiest of the courses: then move on to *Guadalmina*, of average difficulty. Then come up the east coast of Spain, perhaps with stops at Valencia (Golf del Aero Club de Manises, 9 holes) and Castellon (Club de Golf "Costa de Azahar," 9 holes), continuing up to Barcelona for *El Prat* and *San Cugat*. Then circle around Barcelona to Madrid and close out your trip with *Campo*. This will make a golfing holiday to remember.

Real Sociedad Hípica Española Club de Campo

Campo is only two miles from the center of Madrid, giving you a full championship course by day and all the advantages of a lively city by night. The location of the course is particularly attractive—just off the right bank of the Manzanares River. The drive out from Madrid is also appealing—an old Castilian road with the river on your left. Campo is one of the longest courses in Europe and certainly the longest in Spain; at 7150 yards, it is a strong driver's paradise. But this course has also been the site of several championship matches, so you know that length isn't everything. Clever bunkering, roughs that are really rough, tricky doglegs, deceptive hazards, immense greens—all of these add to the difficulties—and the pleasures—of the course. Campo is for the above-average, more expert player. But for the less experienced golfer who is willing to accept a high score, the course will provide a taste of championship golf in fine surroundings. And there is always Madrid for consolation.

LOCATION: The club is 2 miles to the west of Madrid, going out by way of the Casa de Campo. It is accessible by bus or car, but a car is your best bet.

OTHER INFORMATION: The course is open to nonmembers all year with some limitations on weekend play. Reserve the green on weekends. Also carry proof of membership in a local club. Several professionals are always on hand. The best weather is in the spring and autumn; summers are very hot and therefore least crowded. Practice ground is available (driving range).
Number of holes: 18 (with an additional 9). Par: 72 (S.S.S.). Length: 7150 yards.
Green fees: weekdays, $1; weekends, $2/day. Lessons: $1.50/hour.

Real Sociedad Hípica Española Club de Campo golf course, a pleasant two-mile drive from Madrid, offers lush landscaping.

Shell's Wonderful World of Golf

Caddies: $1.50/18 holes. *Golfing equipment and caddie carts:* available by arrangement, nominal cost.

OTHER SPORTS FACILITIES: Tennis, riding, indoor swimming, bull fighting (spectator sport), numerous excursions.

ACCOMMODATIONS: No living space in the club house, but bar and restaurant are available.
In Madrid: Luxury accommodations: *Palace* (pl. de las Cortes 7, Tel. 221.11.00). Center of city, pension $15 to $20/day; *Plaza* (pl. España 8, Tel. 247.12.00). Center of city; *Ritz* (pl. de la Lealtad, Tel. 221.28.57). Center of city; *Castellana-Hilton* (paseo de la Castellana 57, Tel. 257.22.00). North of city; *Wellington* (Velázquez 8, Tel. 275.44.00). Center of city. Prices of all: Singles $9 to $10, doubles $15 to $20. Comfortable, centrally located hotels: *Madrid* (Carretas 10, Tel. 221.65.20), *Rex* (av. José Antonio 43 dpl., Tel. 247.48.00), *Montesol* (Montera 25, Tel. 231.76.00). All are open the year round. All have private baths, central heating, garage; singles $4 to $6, doubles $8 to $9.

TOURIST ATTRACTIONS: Madrid is the geographical center of Spain and, besides its own attractions, makes an excellent base for tours and trips. Within two hours by car are Toledo, Segovia, El Escorial, Valley of the Chiefs and several other attractive sites. In Madrid there is the Prado, one of the world's great museums; El Retiro, a park; Palacio Real (Royal Palace); Casa de Campo and many others. You can expect exciting night life here, with fine clubs that feature flamenco—among the best in Spain. And, of course, the bull fighting is plentiful throughout the area.

FOR FURTHER INFORMATION: Write to: Club Secretary, Real Sociedad Hípica Española Club de Campo, Madrid, Spain.

Real Club de Golf "El Prat"

This is a seaside links, with many of the holes bordering on the sea, while others lie between pines and palm trees. The water hazard is a natural lagoon. The greens are big and nearly all differentiated, creating a variety of holes and approaches. El Prat is a modern course in that all shots must be placed in a determined area; you can't just swing away. The course favors the precise hitter, although it does not penalize the long driver who is careful about his position. El Prat has length, tight fairways and roughs that are to be reckoned with. It is a challenging course in surroundings that should please everyone.

LOCATION: The club is reached best by car from Barcelona, 10 miles away, or from Castelldefels, 5 miles. It is only 1¼ miles from the El Prat del Llobregat Airport.

OTHER INFORMATION: The course welcomes nonmembers if they

can show proof of membership in another golf club or if they are invited to play by a member. The only restrictions against visitors may occur on tournament days; it is a good idea to check this out ahead of time by reserving your hour. El Prat is open all year. A professional is in daily attendance. The most crowded seasons are autumn and spring, with good weather a reasonable expectation at all times. Practice ground is available.

Number of holes: 18 (plus a 9-hole course ready by 1967). *Par:* 72 (S.S.S., 74). *Length:* 6517 yards (5350 yards for women).

Green fees: weekdays, $5; weekends and holidays, $10/day, $33.50/ week, $50/15 days, $75/month. *Lessons:* $3/lesson. *Caddies:* $1.35/round. *Golfing equipment and caddie carts:* clubs $1/round, carts $.35/round.

OTHER SPORTS FACILITIES: The club has a swimming pool, and the nearby beaches are very fine. In the Barcelona area: water sports, tennis, riding.

ACCOMMODATIONS: No living space in the club house, but a bar and a restaurant in the club house and a snack bar next to the swimming pool.

In Casteldefels: *Rey Don Jaime* (Torre Barona, Tel. 55), *Playafels* (Ribera San Pedro, Tel. 50), *Vilumar* (paseo Marítimo, Tel. 153, open only from April to October 15). Comfortable lodgings, private baths, central heating, excellent views of the beach; $5 to $6/person; full pension $9 to $10/day and up. *Santillana* (Torre le Guardia, Tel. 174, open from May 15 to October), *Riviera* (carret. Barcelona, Tel. 87, open from March 20 to December), *Flora Parc* (via Triumfal, Tel. 355). Some rooms with private baths, lower rates than above.

In Barcelona: The *Ritz* (av. José Antonio 668, Tel. 2 214 701), *Presidente* (av. Generalísimo 574, Tel. 2 541 829), *Avenida Palace* (av. José Antonio 605, Tel. 2 226 440). Only a few of the many luxury hotels, with prices $7 to $8/person; full pension from $12/day; all comforts; private baths, central heating, experienced staffs.

TOURIST ATTRACTIONS: Barcelona offers everything the tourist could want, from cultural attractions to excellent shopping for leather goods, handmade articles, laces, dresses, suits, and so on. Worth seeing: the Pueblo Espanol (Spanish Village), Gothic quarter, the cathedral, the museum of Catalán art, the town hall.

FOR FURTHER INFORMATION: Write to: Club Secretary, Real Club de Golf "El Prat," Prat de Llobregat, Barcelona, Spain. Telephone: 2 225 190 Barcelona.

Golf Club San Cugat

This is a pleasantly situated inland course, agreeable and untaxing in nearly every respect. Without great length and without too many demanding holes, it is excellent for the experienced holiday golfer. It is not as difficult as El Prat, also in the Barcelona area, and therefore more suitable if your game is average or if you have time for only a round or two. San Cugat is "open," with all holes visible from the tees and no deceptive doglegs. Still, the fairways are lined with pines, creating a lovely country-side effect against a panorama of hills and woods behind. This is a course for the medium hitter, with only two par-5 long holes, both near 500 yards. For the careful, less powerful player, there are 6 short holes that are really short (140 to 160 yards), many others in the 200-to-300-yard range. San Cugat will also prove not too tiring, for it is mostly flat. Generally, the above-average golfer should find it to his taste, with the added flavor of Barcelona, a very lively city, close at hand.

LOCATION: The course is in San Cugat, 11 miles NW of Barcelona, accessible by car in about 20 minutes; there is regular bus and electric train service from Barcelona to San Cugat every 20 to 30 minutes.

OTHER INFORMATION: The club is open all year with nonmembers most welcome; they should, however, carry proof of membership in another golf club. A professional is in daily attendance. The best time for golf is during the spring and autumn, the worst during July and August, when it becomes very hot. Practice ground is available.
Number of holes: 18. Par: 68. Length: 5258 yards.
Green fees: weekdays, $3.25; weekends and holidays, $6.50/day. Lessons: $2.25/hour. Caddies: $1.25/18 holes. Golfing equipment and caddie carts: clubs $2/day, carts at nominal cost.

OTHER SPORTS FACILITIES: None in the immediate area; near Barcelona, all water sports, tennis, riding.

ACCOMMODATIONS: No living space in the club house, but bar and restaurant are available. There are several fine restaurants in San Cugat, all very reasonable.
For hotels in Barcelona, see this section for Real Club de Golf "El Prat," p. 247, and the listings below.
Cristina (av. Generalísimo Franco 458, Tel. 2 282 301), Astoria (Paris 203, Tel. 2 300 600), Resid. Telstar (vía Layetana 93, Tel. 2 312 197), Condado (Aribau 201, Tel. 2 172 500), Continental (rambla Canaletas 140, Tel. 2 228 770). Full pension, from $6/day; all amenities; English and French spoken; private baths, central heating, experienced staffs; singles from $3.50, doubles $7 to $8.

TOURIST ATTRACTIONS: San Cugat is a charming little town, with the Romanesque Monastery of some interest and popular with visitors. For details of Barcelona, see this section for Real Club de Golf "El Prat," p. 247.

FOR FURTHER INFORMATION: Write to: Club Secretary, Golf Club San Cugat, San Cugat del Valles, Barcelona, Spain. Telephone: 69.

Golf Club Guadalmina

One could hardly imagine a golf course in more lovely surroundings than the Guadalmina. Situated on the southern coast of Spain (the "Costa del Sol"), only 46 miles from Málaga (with an international airport) and on the main road to Gibraltar, this beautiful green course is resplendent with sun, trees (more than 10,000), flowers and other lovely features of terrain and view. The first hole starts at the hotel and runs parallel to the sea; the rest of the course runs parallel to the Guadalmina River. Guadalmina itself is very long, but that should not discourage the weaker hitter. There are 4 holes under or around 200 yards, and only 3 over 500. The rest are in the high-middle range of 350 to 450 yards. The greens are large and beautifully tailored, the fairways tight but negotiable, the roughs not too difficult. Any golfer who comes here will want to play the course again and again to enjoy the rest and serenity of the surroundings.

LOCATION: The course is 8 miles from Marbella and accessible by bus or car. Marbella is itself 46 miles SW of Málaga and about 50 miles NE of Gibraltar. Madrid is 275 miles N.

OTHER INFORMATION: The course is open all year to visitors and nonmembers. The professional is in daily attendance. Every season except winter is crowded, with the weather almost always excellent; there is a little rain in the winter. Practice ground is available.
Number of holes: 18. *Par:* 74. *Length:* 6849 yards.
Green fees: $6.50/day ($1.25 for guests of the Hotel Guadalmina). *Lessons:* $1.25/½ hour, $2.10/hour. *Caddies:* $.85/9 holes, $1.25/18 holes. *Golfing equipment and caddie carts:* clubs $1.25/day.

OTHER SPORTS FACILITIES: This immediate locale is a sports paradise. On the hotel grounds are three swimming pools, miniature golf, tennis courts. Nearby is a lovely beach, with safe swimming, as well as boating, water skiing, sailing; fishing and hunting excursions.

ACCOMMODATIONS: The course is located on the grounds of the *Hotel Guadalmina,* which provides luxurious living quarters as well as a restaurant and bar. One may rent rooms in the hotel or rent, or even buy, apartments adjoining. The rooms are as follows: double room with bath, $8; with terrace also, $8.50; with sitting room also, $15; bungalow with two double rooms, bath and sitting room, $25; with an extra bath, $30; full pension, from $5.25/day. All meals available, all comforts.
In Marbella: (on the road to Cádiz): *Don Pepe* (Tel. 823 978 Marbella). Luxury hotel, singles from $8.50, doubles from $14; full pension from $15/day. All comforts. *Marbella Club, Guadalpin, Chapas* (on road to Málaga), *Rancho Wellington* (on road to Málaga). Singles from $4 to $9, doubles $7 up; pension from $9/day. All comforts; private bath, central heating.

TOURIST ATTRACTIONS: Near Marbella the visitor will find walking and car excursions—fine scenery, old villages, local products. Málaga (46 miles) is a fine shopping area; recommended are the cathedral as well as the fortresses of Alcazaba and Gibralfaro. In the opposite direction is Gibraltar, always a popular spot. Granada, Seville, and Cordoba are 4 or 5 hours away by car or bus.

FOR FURTHER INFORMATION: Write to: Hotel Manager, Golf Hotel Guadalmina, Marbella (Málaga), Spain. Telephone: 82 73 90.

Club de Campo Málaga Golf

Not excessively long as Spanish courses go, the Málaga Course offers diversity—a wide variety of testing holes that should appeal to every type of game. The course and its surroundings should certainly appeal to the eye, with views of the "Costa del Sol" from many tees. For the long driver the course offers several holes over 400 yards, particularly on the second nine. The grass fairways are tight but generous, the greens of good size; altogether, this is a good vacation course. If you want a place to start, begin with Málaga and then tackle some of the tougher links around Barcelona.

LOCATION: The club is 5 miles from Málaga and 3 from Torremolinos. The local train stops at a station about 600 yards from the club; the bus stops about ½-mile from the course. It is best to arrive by car. Madrid is 250 miles N.

OTHER INFORMATION: The course is open to nonmembers all year upon payment of the green fees. The visitor can also become a member if he wishes by paying the entrance fee of $85 and yearly dues of $10. The professional is available except on Sundays and holidays. The most crowded time is during the winter, when the weather is generally milder than in the middle of the summer. Practice ground is available.
Number of holes: 18. Par: 72. Length: 6113 yards.
Green fees: $1.65/round, $12.50/15 days. Lessons: $1.25/hour. Caddies: $.75/18 holes. Golfing equipment and caddie carts: available by arrangement, at nominal cost.

OTHER SPORTS FACILITIES: The "Costa del Sol" offers all types of water sports: swimming, boating, yachting, fishing; also tennis, riding and hunting (excursions).

ACCOMMODATIONS: Living quarters right at the course are available. The hotel, the Parador del Golf, belong to the tourist bureau; it has all modern conveniences, including air conditioning; reasonable prices, from $6/person. Write to Sr. Administrador del Parador Nacional de Golf, Málaga, Spain. The hotel has a restaurant and bar.
In and around Málaga: Miramar (paseo de Reding 8, Tel. 2 105 01). Lovely view of the sea from its large terrace; prices upon application. All

comforts. *Emperatrix* (paseo de Sancha 34, Tel. 2 115 51), a very comfortable hotel facing the sea, with a garden; singles from $3, doubles from $6; full pension $6.50 to $7.25/day. Private baths, experienced staff.

In and around Torremolinos (8 miles): *Torremora* (Tel. 881 525). Faces the sea; singles from $4.50, doubles from $6.50; full pension $7 to $8/day. All comforts, private bath, central heating when necessary.

TOURIST ATTRACTIONS: See this section for the *Golf Club Guadalmina,* p. 250.

FOR FURTHER INFORMATION: Write to: Spanish Tourist Bureau in Málaga or Madrid; or to: Club Secretary, Club de Campo Málaga Golf, Málaga, Spain.

SWITZERLAND

Like most things in Switzerland, golf is well developed and well organized. From mountains, lakes and thick forests, the Swiss have carved out a number of excellent courses, many with the highest standards of the continent. And for views of the Alps or the deep valleys between, of blue lakes and green foliage, you would have to go far to see better. Golf in Switzerland is very pleasant indeed.

One great advantage of golfing in Switzerland—aside from the game itself —is the relative smallness of the country. Once you are based in or near a city, you can find a good course within an hour's drive. Every major city has its own clubs within a radius of 30 to 40 miles.

The visitor coming in from Italy through the Lake Country around Como and Lugano can make a little tour of six Italian and Swiss courses. *Menaggio e Cadenabbia, Lanzo* and *Villa d'Este* (all Italian) and *Patriziale* (Swiss) are good average courses, recommended as a starter, while *Varese*

(Italian) and *Lugano* (Swiss) are tougher, more demanding in nearly every respect.

Four other Swiss courses besides *Lugano* that you shouldn't miss are *Engadine, Crans, Lausanne* and *Basel*. They are possibly the best in the country, almost on a par with championship courses in the British Isles. They are all in excellent locations. *Engadine* is near St. Moritz and can be combined with *Kulm* and *Lenzerheide-Valbella* to make up a little tour. *Crans* is in an attractive part of southwestern Switzerland, the well-known Valais Alps. Lausanne, with its proximity to Geneva and the beautiful lake, is a must for most visitors. And Basel is a modern city that has still retained its old flavor.

Two good courses near Zürich provide the variety and general excellence every visitor will be looking for. Both courses are recommended for the average golfer.

Whatever the standard of your game, Switzerland has courses to suit you. And for your other comforts, you know from experience or the experiences of your friends that Switzerland seems set up solely to make your stay enjoyable.

Golf and Country Club Blumisberg

Set against the background of the Bernese Alps, the Golf and Country Club Blumisberg is one of the loveliest in Europe. It offers the golfer a championship course with some spectacular holes and favors the long, accurate driver. But its length should by no means discourage the short driver; there is sufficient variety of approaches and of hazards to keep every type of golfer alert. And the testing quality of the tees will make the precise, accurate player happy. The fairways and approaches to the greens are excellent.

LOCATION: The course is in Wünnewil, about 11 miles W of Bern and 9 from Fribourg, 70 miles NE of Lausanne, 108 miles NE of Geneva, 71 miles SW of Basel, 88 miles SW of Zürich. It is accessible by car.

OTHER INFORMATION: The course is open to nonmembers, unlimited; for the entire season (March 15 to November 30); two professionals are always on hand. The weather is best from May to September. Practice ground is available.

Number of holes: 18. *Par:* 72. *Length:* 6697 yards (6381 yards for front tees).

Green fees: weekdays, $4; weekends, $5/day. *Lessons:* $2/half hour; $3.50/hour. *Caddies:* limited number available at $2/18 holes. *Golfing equipment and caddie carts:* limited number of clubs and carts. Each $.75/day.

OTHER SPORTS FACILITIES: Swimming pool at the clubhouse. Tennis and fishing in Fribourg and riding in Bern.

ACCOMMODATIONS: No living space in the club house, but restaurant and bar available.

In Bern: *Hotel Schweizerhof* (Schweizerhoflaube, Tel. [031] 224501). A very good, comfortable hotel, open all year. Rooms from $9.50 to $14 for best single, $19 to $28 for best double; private baths, central heating; taxes and services included, continental breakfast. *City-Hôtel* (Bubenbergerplatz 7, Tel. [031] 225377). A good, comfortable hotel, open all year. Rooms from $7 to $10 for best single, $14 to $20 for best double. Private baths, central heating; taxes and services included, continental breakfast.

In Fribourg: *Terminus* (Av. de la Gare 30, Tel. [037] 24037). A good, comfortable hotel, open all year. Rooms from $5 to $7 for best single, $10 to $14 for best double; private baths, central heating; taxes and services included, continental breakfast. *City-Hôtel*, rue Pillettes 1, Tel. [037] 26733). A good, comfortable hotel, open all year. Rooms from $5.75 to $7 for best single, $11.50 to $14 for best double; private baths, central heating; taxes and services included, continental breakfast.

TOURIST ATTRACTIONS: From the tower of the Cathedral of St. Vincent you get a panoramic view of Bern and the Alps beyond. Be sure to see old Bern with its arcaded streets and flower-decked fountains. And don't miss the fine historical museum, the Museum of Fine Arts, the zoo and botanical gardens. Painted pottery is a specialty of the area. In Fribourg, don't miss the Cathedral of St. Nicholas, one of the oldest in Europe. There is also a good art and history museum devoted to the history of Fribourg. And, of course, as in all of Switzerland, there are breathtaking views.

FOR FURTHER INFORMATION: Write to: Secretary, 3184-Wünnewil, Switzerland. Telephone: (037) 36380.

Bad Ragaz

Surrounded by forests and mountains with peaks over 10,000 feet, the course at Bad Ragaz is one of the most beautiful and breathtaking in all Europe. It is flat, easy on the feet and a sheer delight to play, with cool, comfortable weather most of the time. Short as well as long drivers should do well here, although the good length and several holes over 400 yards give the nod to the power hitter. Particularly recommended is the 578-yard 12th. Five par 3s contribute to the overall balance. The course has the added advantage of being a few miles from Liechtenstein, should you want to combine golf with a visit to that fabulous tiny principality.

LOCATION: Bad Ragaz is 73 miles SE of Zürich, about the same N of St. Moritz; 68 S of St. Gallen, 122 SE of Basel, 161 E of Bern, 119 NE of Lugano, 162 N of Milan, Italy. It is accessible by train and car.

OTHER INFORMATION: The course is open to all guests, unlimited,

for the entire season (April-October), with three professionals always on hand. The weather is best during the summer; the most crowded month is October. Practice ground is available.
Number of holes: 18. *Par:* 70 (S.S.S., 71). *Length:* 6408 yards.
Green fees: weekdays, $3; weekends, $4.25/day. *Lessons:* $4.50/hour. *Caddies:* $1.50/18 holes, tip included. *Golfing equipment and caddie carts:* clubs and cart for $1.25/day.

OTHER SPORTS FACILITIES: Swimming, tennis, riding, miniature golf, fishing.

ACCOMMODATIONS: None in the club house, but restaurant and bar are available.
In Bad Ragaz: *Quellenhof* (Tel. [085] 91803). A first-class hotel, open April-October. Rooms from $9 to $16.75 for best single, $18 to $33.50 for best double; private baths, central heating, continental breakfast; taxes and services included. *Grand Hôtel Hofragaz* (Tel. [085] 91505). A very good, comfortable hotel, open April-October. Rooms from $7.50 to $13.50 for best single, $15 to $27 for best double; private baths, central heating, continental breakfast; taxes and services included. *Lattmann* (Tel. [085] 91315). A good, comfortable hotel, open all year. Rooms from $6.50 to $9.50 for best single, $13 to $19 for best double; private baths, central heating, continental breakfast; taxes and services included. *Bad Hôtel Tamina* (Tel. [085] 91644). A good, comfortable hotel, open April-October. Rooms from $6.50 to $9.50 for best single, $13 to $19 for best double; private baths, central heating, continental breakfast; taxes and services included.

TOURIST ATTRACTIONS: Recommended are excursions into the Alps by cable car, mountain walks, dancing and a visit to the Tamina Gorge with its hot water springs.

FOR FURTHER INFORMATION: Write to: Secretary, Golf Club Bad Ragaz, Bad Ragaz, Switzerland. Telephone: (085) 91556.

Basel Golf and Country Club

Here is one of the best and most challenging Swiss courses, only a few miles from one of Switzerland's most attractive cities. Although Basel is an important international business center, it still has all the characteristics of an old Rhenish town built of limestone, a town in which the great humanist Erasmus once lived. The course calls for careful and accurate play and strongly favors the long driver, since many of the holes are well over 400 yards and a few are over 500. The fairways and greens are in excellent shape, an expectation that is always fulfilled in Switzerland. This is not a beginner's 18 holes, not at 6800 yards and with clever bunkering and narrow fairways. Work up to Basel at some of the shorter Swiss courses, and then this should prove a challenging experience.

LOCATION: The course is about 10 miles from downtown Basel, 4 from Basel airport, 18 miles S of Mulhouse, 160 miles NE of Geneva, 72 miles NE of Bern, 62 miles W of Zürich. It is accessible by car.

OTHER INFORMATION: The course is open to nonmembers, unlimited, for the entire season (April-October); a professional is always on hand. The weather is best from June through September. Practice ground is available.
Number of holes: 18. *Par:* 72. *Length:* 6813 yards.
Green fees: weekdays, $4; weekends, $5/day. *Lessons:* $3.50/hour.
Caddies: $2/18 holes. *Golfing equipment and caddie carts:* clubs $5/day, carts $1/day.

SPORTS FACILITIES: Riding, hunting, swimming, and tennis.

ACCOMMODATIONS: No living space in the club house, but restaurant and bar are available.
In Basel: *Hotel Euler* (Centralbahnplatz 14, Tel. [061] 244500). A first-class hotel, open all year. Rooms from $10 to $16.50 for best single, $20 to $33 for best double; private baths, central heating, continental breakfast; taxes and services included. *Trois Rois au Rhin* (Blumenrain 8, Tel. [061] 241850). A first-class hotel, open all year. Rooms from $10 to $16.50 for best single, $20 to $33 for best double; private baths, central heating, continental breakfast; taxes and services included. *Bernina Garni* (Innere Margarethenstrasse 14, Tel. [061] 247316). A very good, comfortable hotel, open all year. Rooms from $6.50 to $9.50 for best single, $13 to $19 for best double; private baths, central heating, continental breakfast; taxes and services included.

TOURIST ATTRACTIONS: Basel is the second city of Switzerland and has been one of its art and culture centers since the Renaissance. Try not to miss the Fine Arts Museum, one of the best in Europe; the Cathedral (Münster), from whose top you can see the Rhine, the Black Forest and the Vosges Mountains; and the Zoological Gardens.

FOR FURTHER INFORMATION: Write to: Secretary, Golf & Country Club Basel, Basel, Switzerland. Telephone: 380837.

Lausanne Golf Club

The Lausanne Golf Club is on the outskirts of Lausanne, a lively, cosmopolitan city with attractive boulevards, sophisticated shops and interesting nightlife. It also has a great literary heritage; Voltaire lived and wrote there, and André Gide adapted his *Caves of the Vatican* as a play for the university students. The course is about 2800 feet high, surrounded by hills and forests, with a panoramic view of Lake Léman and the Alps. It is of championship standard and favors the long, accurate driver. The fairways and greens are always in excellent condition. A good challenging course to play, possibly the best in Switzerland, but it is not easy. Perhaps you should not begin your European play with this course—it may be too demanding.

LOCATION: The course is about 7 miles from the center of Lausanne, 117 miles SW of Basel, 58 miles SW of Berne, 38 miles NE of Geneva, 138 miles SW of Zürich, 211 miles NW of Milan (Italy), 320 miles SE of Paris. It is accessible by car.

OTHER INFORMATION: The course is open to nonmembers (but the golfer must be a member of some golf club), unlimited, for the entire season (April-November); two professionals are always on hand. The most crowded months are June through September, with the weather best May through September. Practice ground is available.
Number of holes: 18. *Par:* 71. *Length:* 6760 yards.
Green fees: weekdays, $5; weekends, $7/day. *Lessons:* $5/hour. *Caddies:* $2/18 holes. *Golfing equipment and caddie carts:* clubs $2.75/day, carts $.75/day.

OTHER SPORTS FACILITIES: Swimming, tennis, boating, water-skiing.

ACCOMMODATIONS: No living space in the club house, but restaurant and bar are available.
In Lausanne: *Beau-Rivage* (Chemin-de-Beau-Rivage, Tel. [021] 263831). A luxury hotel of international standing, open all year. Rooms from $10 to $19 for best single, $20 to $38 for best double; private baths, central heating, continental breakfast; taxes and services included. *Mirabeau* (Av. de la Gare 31, Tel. [021] 226234). A first-class hotel, open all year. Rooms from $7 to $12 for best single, $14 to $24 for best double; private baths, central heating, continental breakfast; taxes and services included. *Montana* (Chemin de Pré-Fleuri 6, Tel. [021] 264444). A very good, comfortable hotel, open all year. Rooms from $6.75 to $11.25 for best single, $13.50 to $22.50 for best double; private baths, central heating, continental breakfast; taxes and services included.

TOURIST ATTRACTIONS: Lausanne possesses probably the finest Gothic cathedral in Switzerland, dating back to the twelfth century; a fifteenth-century castle; the old town built around the cathedral; four museums; boat excursions; and walking tours with superb scenery.

FOR FURTHER INFORMATION: Write to: Secretary, The Golf Club of Lausanne, Marin-sur-Lausanne, Switzerland. Telephone: (021) 916316.

Golf-Club Montreux

Montreux is the most popular resort on Lake Geneva and one of the most beautiful in Switzerland. Hills and mountains covered with woods and vineyards shelter it from the cold north and east winds, and keep the temperature at an average of about 50° all year. It has often been called the "Riviera of Switzerland," and you can see vines, walnut trees and fig trees on the shores of the lake and on the hills overlooking the city. The course is new, flat, almost without roughs, and made for all categories of players. Its 6500-yard length, however, favors the power hitter, while its well-bunkered tees give the precise golfer the advantage.

LOCATION: The course is just outside of Aigle, about 9 miles from Montreux, 26 miles SE of Lausanne, 143 miles SW of Basel, 58 miles NE of Geneva, 164 miles SW of Zürich, 181 miles NW of Milan (Italy), 346 miles SE of Paris. It is accessible by car.

OTHER INFORMATION: The course is open to nonmembers, unlimited, for the entire year; three professionals are always on hand. The weather is best from May through October; the most crowded months are May, June, September. Practice ground is available.
Number of holes: 18. Par: 71. Length: 6500 yards.
Green fees: weekdays, $3; weekends, $3.50/day. Lessons: $3/half hour. Caddies: $2/18 holes. Golfing equipment and caddie carts: clubs $3/day, carts $.50/day.

OTHER SPORTS FACILITIES: Tennis, mountain climbing, riding, water-skiing, flying.

ACCOMMODATIONS: No living space in the club house, but restaurant and bar are available.
In Montreux: Montreux-Palace (Av. des Alpes, Tel. [021] 613231). A luxury hotel of international standing, open all year. Rooms from $8.50 to $16.50 for best single, $17 to $33 for best double; private baths, central heating, continental breakfast; taxes and services included. Excelsior (rue Bon Port 21, Tel. [021] 613305). A first-class hotel, open all year. Rooms from $7.50 to $11.50 for best single, $15 to $23 for best double; private baths, central heating, continental breakfast; taxes and services included. Parc (Grand Rue 38, Tel. [021] 623738). A very good, comfortable hotel, open all year. Rooms from $5 to $7.50 for best single, $10 to $15 for best double; private baths, central heating, continental breakfast; taxes and services included.

TOURIST ATTRACTIONS: Main attractions here are the Naye Rocks, from which you get a great view of Lake Geneva and the surrounding Alps; the old quarter of Montreux and the castle of Chillon. Of literary interest is the suburb of Clarens, the setting for Rousseau's The New Héloïse.

FOR FURTHER INFORMATION: Write to: Secretary, Golf Club of Montreux, Montreux, Switzerland. Telephone: (021) 613384.

Lugano Golf Club

The Lugano Golf Club is just outside of Lugano, in the Italian section of Switzerland. The town, known throughout Europe for centuries as an ideal tourist spot, lies at the end of a beautiful bay surrounded by hills and woods. Innumerable festivities and excursions to Lakes Maggiore, Lugano and Como are arranged for the visitor to make his stay an absolute delight. The course is of average difficulty, flat, made for long as well as short drivers, but it does require accurate play. Its considerable length—6500 yards—places it with Lausanne and Crans as a demanding course requiring some practice before it can be seriously challenged.

LOCATION: The course is about 3 miles from Lugano, 19 miles S of Bellinzona, 142 miles S of Zürich, 190 miles SE of Basel, 165 miles SE of Bern, 245 miles E of Geneva, 46 miles N of Milan (Italy). It is accessible by car.

OTHER INFORMATION: The course is open to nonmembers, unlimited, for the entire year; a professional is always on hand. The weather is best April through October, and spring and autumn are the most crowded seasons. Practice ground is available.
Number of holes: 9. *Par:* 73 (for twice around). *Length:* 6492 yards.
Green fees: weekdays, $2.50; weekends, $3.50/day. *Lessons:* $3.50/an hour. *Caddies:* $1.75/18 holes. *Golfing equipment and caddie carts:* clubs $2.50/day, carts $.50/day.

OTHER SPORTS FACILITIES: Swimming, tennis, riding, sailing, water-skiing.

ACCOMMODATIONS: No living space in the club house, but restaurant and bar are available.
In Lugano: *Splendide-Royal* (via Riva A. Caccia 7, Tel. [091] 27101). A first-class hotel, open March-November. Rooms from $8.50 to $15 for best single, $17 to $30 for best double; private baths, central heating, continental breakfast; taxes and services included. *Bristol* (via Maraini 11, Tel. [091] 21945). A very good, comfortable hotel, open all year. Rooms from $5.75 to $10 for best single, $11.50 to $20 for best double; private baths, central heating, continental breakfast; taxes and services included. *International au Lac* (via Nassa 68, Tel. [091] 21304). A very good, comfortable hotel, open March-November. Rooms $5.75 to $8.50 for best single, $11.50 to $17 for best double; private baths, central heating, continental breakfast; taxes and services included.

TOURIST ATTRACTIONS: Lugano features excursions to Lakes Maggiore, Lugano and Como; a beautiful municipal park with tame deer and open-air concerts every morning; Villa Favorita with its private art gallery containing some remarkable paintings by Dürer, Holbein, Van Eyck, Rubens and Van Dyck; the Church of St. Mary of the Angels, with its two famous frescoes of Luini.

FOR FURTHER INFORMATION: Write to: Secretary, Golf Club Lugano, Magliaso, Lugano, Switzerland. Telephone: (091) 96557.

Golf Club Patriziale Ascona

In the heart of the Ticino Riviera, on the shore of Lake Maggiore, this course is one of the most picturesque in Switzerland. It is rather flat with sandy soil·and favors the long driver (many of the holes are well over 400 yards) but should not really discourage the short one. There is plenty of variety, including several par-3 holes of medium difficulty and much clever bunkering—something for everybody. Just beyond the course lies Ascona, a charming, colorful fishing village, long a favorite resort of artists from all over Europe. September is devoted to music festivals.

LOCATION: The course is in southern Switzerland, about 2 miles from the center of Ascona, 3 from Locarno, 132 miles S of Zürich, 179 miles SE of Basel, 117 miles S of Lucerne, 154 miles SE of Bern, 221 miles E of Geneva, 72 miles N of Milan (Italy). It is accessible by car.

OTHER INFORMATION: The course is open to nonmembers, unlimited, for the entire year; three or four professionals are always on hand. The weather is best from April to October; the most crowded seasons are Easter and September to the middle of October. Practice ground is available.
Number of holes: 18. *Par:* 71. *Length:* 6262 yards.
Green fees: weekdays, $3; weekends, $4/day. *Lessons:* $2/half hour. *Caddies:* $3/18 holes. *Golfing equipment and caddie carts:* clubs $.75 a day. Caddie carts if caddies not available.

OTHER SPORTS FACILITIES: Swimming, tennis, sailing, flying, water-skiing, mountain climbing, riding and fishing.

ACCOMMODATIONS: No living space in the club house, but restaurant and bar are available.
In Ascona: *Acapulco* (Ascona, Tel. [093] 81151). A first-class hotel, open March-November. Rooms from $6 to $13 for best single, $12 to $26 for best double; private baths, central heating, continental breakfast; taxes and services included. *Ascona* (Ascona, Tel. [093] 21135). A very good, comfortable hotel, open March-November. Rooms from $8 to $11.50 for best single, $16 to $23 for best double; private baths, central heating, continental breakfast; taxes and services included.
In Locarno: *La Palma au Lac* (Locarno, Tel. [093] 73771). A luxury hotel of the highest international standing, open all year. Rooms from $9 to $15 for best single, $18 to $30 for best double; private baths, central heating, continental breakfast; taxes and services included. *Esplanade*

Swiss National Tourist Office
Good form at the Engadine golf links near St. Moritz, Switzerland, with the Alps as backdrop.

(Locarno, Tel. [093] 72121). A first-class hotel, open all year. Rooms from $7.50 to $14.50 for best single, $15 to $29 for best double; private baths, central heating, continental breakfast; taxes and services included.

TOURIST ATTRACTIONS: Ascona is a colorful fishing village on the shore of Lake Maggiore, with a famous international music festival in September. There are various excursions by boat. Don't miss the one to the Brissago Islands, with its lovely park, exotic plants, and art exhibition.

Locarno is one of the most beautiful little towns in Europe. The climate is so exceptional here that magnolias and camellias blossom in midwinter. If possible, see the fifteenth-century castle of the Visconti, and take advantage of the numerous excursions by car or boat.

FOR FURTHER INFORMATION: Write to: Secretary, Golf Club Patriziale Ascona, Ascona, Switzerland. Telephone: (093) 72532.

Engadine Golf Club

In the heart of the great ski resorts of southeast Switzerland, the Engadine Golf Club offers the golfer a magnificent panoramic view of the Alps surrounding St. Moritz. And the climate here is as fantastic as the view: clear, blue skies, dry, cool breezes and an intense sunshine because of the rarified air. This is almost a championship course, made for both long and short drivers, with a variety of testing shots. Definitely a course worth going out of your way to play, although it is not easy. Its proximity to the international resort of St. Moritz gives it additional excitement. For a brief description of St. Moritz, see Kulm Golf and Country Club.

LOCATION: The course is just outside Samedan, 5 miles NE of St. Moritz, 81 miles NE of Lugano, 125 miles SE of Zürich, 178 miles SE of Basel, 198 miles E of Bern, 298 miles E of Geneva, 112 miles N of Milan (Italy). It is accessible by car.

OTHER INFORMATION: Engadine is open to nonmembers, unlimited; the season is from July 1 to September 15; the most crowded period is from July 15 to the end of August. A professional is always on hand. Practice ground is available.

Number of holes: 18. *Par:* 70. *Length:* 6289 yards.

Green fees: weekdays, $3; weekends, $4/day. *Lessons:* $6/half hour. *Caddies:* $1.50/18 holes. *Golfing equipment and caddie carts:* clubs $2.50/ day.

OTHER SPORTS FACILITIES: Tennis, swimming, skiing, sailing, boating, riding, flying, gliding, rock and mountain climbing.

ACCOMMODATIONS: No living space at the club house, but restaurant and bar are available.

In St. Moritz-Dorf: *Carlton* (St. Moritz, Tel. [082] 33721). A luxury hotel, open June-September and December-April. Rooms from $9 to $23 for best single, $18 to $46 for best double; private baths, central heating, continental breakfast; taxes and services included. *Caspar Badrutt* (St. Moritz, Tel. [082] 34012). A very good, comfortable hotel, open June-September and December-April. Rooms from $6 to $14 for best single, $12 to $28 for best double; private baths, central heating, continental breakfast; taxes and services included. *Calonder* (St. Moritz, Tel. [082] 33651). A very good, comfortable hotel, open June-September and December-April. Rooms from $6 to $14 for best single, $12 to $28 for best double; private baths, central heating, continental breakfast; taxes and services included.

In Pontresina: *Saratz* (Pontresina, Tel. [082] 66321). A first-class hotel, open June-September. Rooms from $9 to $18 for best single, $18 to $36 for best double; private baths, central heating, continental breakfast; taxes and services included. *Parkhotel* (Pontresina, Tel. [082] 66231). A very good, comfortable hotel, open June-September and December-April. Rooms from $7 to $13 for best single, $14 to $26 for best double; private baths, central heating, continental breakfast; taxes and services included.

In Samedan: *Sporthotel* (Samedan, Tel. [082] 65333). A good, comfortable hotel, open May-September and December-April. Rooms from $5 to $6.50 for best single, $10 to $13 for best double; private baths, central heating, continental breakfast; taxes and services included.

TOURIST ATTRACTIONS: Here is a made-to-order area for mountain climbers (check on the well-known Diavolezza Tour for glacier climbers) and walkers (the last foothills of the Piz Languard). There is also the famous spa area of St. Moritz-Bad, for the sick and the well. And, of course, St. Moritz-Dorf itself is one of the great international skiing centers of the world.

FOR FURTHER INFORMATION: Write to: Secretary of the Engadine Golf Club, Samedan (St. Moritz), Switzerland. Telephone: (082) 65226.

Kulm Golf and Country Club

Here is a small, hilly Alpine course made for the short driver since almost all the holes are under 200 yards. It should present no difficulties to the average golfer. It is, in fact, a good place to start if you are in this part of Switzerland; then you can work up to the tougher courses. The surroundings are certainly congenial. The setting is picturesque, with the mountains surrounding St. Moritz visible everywhere. St. Moritz, of course, needs no introduction, for it is the most famous ski resort in Switzerland and one of the best known in the world. It has an international clientele, and any day you may see a visiting king, prince, head of state, movie star, painter or writer walking in the village or eating at one of the restaurants. If you want a glamorous and fashionable resort where the famous come to see and to be seen, then this or the Engadine is your course.

LOCATION: The course is about 2 miles from St. Moritz, 78 miles NE of Lugano, 128 miles SE of Zürich, 181 miles SE of Basel, 194 miles E of Bern, 294 miles E of Geneva, 108 miles N of Milan (Italy). It is accessible by car.

OTHER INFORMATION: The course is open to nonmembers, unlimited, for the entire season (July 1-August 31); a professional is always on hand. The most crowded month is August. Practice ground is available. Number of holes: 9. Par: 58 (for twice around). Length: 1550 yards. Green fees: 9 holes, $1.25; 18 holes, $2/day. Lessons: $3.50/half hour. Caddies: $1/18 holes. Golfing equipment and caddie carts: none for rent.

OTHER SPORTS FACILITIES: Riding, swimming, sailing, tennis, mountain climbing, flying and gliding.

ACCOMMODATIONS: No living space in the club house, but restaurant and bar are available.
For accommodations see this section under Engadine Golf Club, p. 262.

TOURIST ATTRACTIONS: See this section under Engadine Golf Club, pp. 262-263.

FOR FURTHER INFORMATION: Write to: Kulm Hotel, St. Moritz, Switzerland. Telephone: (082) 33931.

Golf Club Lenzerheide-Valbella

Tucked away in the southeast corner of the Alps, Lenzerheide-Valbella is a picturesque resort at an altitude of 5000 feet with a panoramic view of the surrounding Alps, which protect it from the winds of the north and the east. The weather is usually sunny, dry and cool. The course itself, one of Switzerland's newest, favors the short, accurate driver. Nevertheless, it has good length for a mountain course and is full of variety for every type of player. A good course to play if you are on a mountain holiday.

LOCATION: The course, between Chur and St. Moritz, is 94 miles SE of Zürich, 147 SE of Basel, 153 E of Bern, 262 NE of Geneva, 106 NE of Lugano, 129 N of Milan, Italy. It is accessible by bus and car.

OTHER INFORMATION: Lenzerheide is open to all guests, unlimited, for the entire season (June-September); two to three professionals are always on hand. The weather is best from mid-June to September 15, with August the most crowded month. Practice ground is available.
Number of holes: 18. *Par:* 69. *Length:* 6020 yards.
Green fees: weekdays, $2.50; weekends, $3.50/day. *Lessons:* $4.50/hour. *Caddies:* $1.15/18 holes. *Golfing equipment and caddie carts:* carts available at nominal cost.

OTHER SPORTS FACILITIES: Tennis, swimming, fishing, mountain climbing.

ACCOMMODATIONS: None at the club house, but restaurant and bar are available.
In Lenzerheide: *Grand Hotel Kurhaus* (Tel. [081] 42134). A very good, comfortable hotel, open June-October and December-May. Rooms from $6 to $13.75 for best single, $12 to $27.50 for best double; private baths, central heating, continental breakfast; taxes and services included. *Lenzerhorn* (Tel. [081] 42105). A good, comfortable hotel, open all year. Rooms from $4.75 to $8.50 for best single, $9.50 to $17 for best double; private baths, central heating, continental breakfast; taxes and services included.
In Lenzerheide-Valbella: *Post-Hôtel Valbella* (Tel. [081] 42212). A very good, comfortable hotel, open May-October and December-April. Rooms from $5 to $11.25 for best single, $10 to $22.50 for best double; private baths, central heating, continental breakfast; taxes and services included.

TOURIST ATTRACTIONS: Highly recommended are the mountain passes, beautiful Alpine walks, some old churches and the great and fashionable resort of St. Moritz, about 22 miles SE of the course.

FOR FURTHER INFORMATION: Write to: Secretary (Tel. [081] 42316), Golf Club Lenzerheide-Valbella, Lenzerheide, Switzerland. Telephone of Tourist Office: 341588.

Swiss National Tourist Office

*Picturesque Lenzerheide-Valbella, one of Switzerland's newest courses, at
5000 feet.*

Crans Golf Club

In southwest Switzerland facing the Valais Alps, the Crans Golf Club has one of the best Alpine courses in Europe. Hilly, challenging and tough on the feet, it is laid out for the long driver and demands careful, accurate play. The fairways and greens are always in excellent condition. The length of the course, as well as its difficulty, compares favorably with the top championship courses in the British Isles. Crans-sur-Sierre is one of the most famous mountain resorts in Switzerland with modern hotels, lovely panoramic views and delightful walks. If you want to combine a unique mountain vacation with first-rate golf, this is your course.

LOCATION: The course is in Crans-sur-Sierre, 13 miles E of Sion, 73 miles SE of Lausanne, 112 miles E of Geneva, 91 miles S of Bern, 139 miles S of Basel, 106 miles SW of Zürich, 134 miles NW of Milan (Italy).

OTHER INFORMATION: Crans is open to nonmembers, unlimited, for the entire season (May-October), with a professional always on hand. The most crowded month is August; the weather is best in July and the first two weeks in September. Practice ground is available.
Number of holes: 18, 9. *Par:* 74, 36. *Length:* 6932 yards, 3275 yards. *Green fees:* weekdays, $5; weekends, $7/day. *Lessons:* $6/hour. *Caddies:* $2.50/18 holes. *Golfing equipment and caddie carts:* clubs $3/day, carts $.50/day.

OTHER SPORTS FACILITIES: Sailing, fishing, tennis, riding, mountain climbing.

ACCOMMODATIONS: No living space in the club house, but restaurant and bar are available.
In Crans-sur-Sierre: *Golf & Sports* (Crans-sur-Sierre, Tel. [027] 52282). A first-class hotel, open December-October. Rooms from $8 to $16.50 for best single, $16 to $33 for best double; private baths, central heating, continental breakfast; taxes and services included. *Royal* (Crans-sur-Sierre, Tel. [027] 23287). A very good, comfortable hotel, open June-October and December-April. Rooms from $6.50 to $12.50 for best single, $13 to $25 for best double; private baths, central heating, continental breakfast; taxes and services included. *Rhodania* (Crans-sur-Sierre, Tel. [027] 52389). A very good, comfortable hotel, open June-October and December-April. Rooms from $6.50 to $12.50 for best single, $13 to $25 for best double; private baths, central heating, continental breakfast; taxes and services included.

TOURIST ATTRACTIONS: Walking tours and excursions into the Alps. In nearby Sion there is an interesting church (Nôtre Dame-de-Valère), as well as great views of the Rhône Valley from the hills of Valère. The Valère Museum contains many specimens of fine furniture and embroidery and lace.

FOR FURTHER INFORMATION: Write to: Secretary, Crans Golf Club, Crans-sur-Sierre, Switzerland. Telephone: 72168.

Lucerne (Luzern) Golf Club

This is a hilly course with a magnificent view of Lake Lucerne and the Alps in the distance. The fairways, bordered by woods and trees, are excellent for the visitor and not too difficult the first time around. Short and long drivers should do well here, with an edge for the former. The course is short but with a diversity of testing shots, such as the par-five 5th, 11th and 13th. Lucerne can also be recommended for those interested in music, for the great International Music Festival in August and September is an event no music lover should miss.

LOCATION: The course is in Dietschiberg, about 1 mile from Lucerne, 32 miles S of Zürich, 63 miles SE of Basel, 56 miles E of Bern, 117 miles NE of Lausanne, 155 miles NE of Geneva. It is accessible by car.

OTHER INFORMATION: The course is open to nonmembers, unlimited, for the entire season (April-October); a professional is always on hand. It is hardly ever crowded, and the best weather is from May to September. Practice ground is available.

Number of holes: 18. *Par:* 70. *Length:* 5480 yards.

Green fees: weekdays and Saturdays, $4; Sundays, $5. *Lessons:* $3/half hour, $5 hour. *Caddies:* $2/18 holes. *Golfing equipment and caddie carts:* clubs $2/day, carts $.75/day.

OTHER SPORTS FACILITIES: Tennis, swimming, sailing, mountain climbing and riding.

ACCOMMODATIONS: The club house has simple, comfortable rooms; $4 for double with running water, two bathrooms on a floor, and breakfast. Full board $8.50. Restaurant and bar available.

In Lucerne: *Schweizerhof* (Schweizerhofquai 3, Tel. [041] 25801). A luxury hotel, open all year. Rooms from $9 to $16 for best single, $18 to $32 for best double; private baths, central heating, continental breakfast; taxes and services included. *Astoria* (Pilatusstrasse 27, Tel. [041] 26226). A pleasant, first-class hotel, open all year. Rooms from $7 to $11 for best single, $14 to $22 for best double; private baths, central heating, continental breakfast; taxes and services included. *Carlton Tivoli* (Haldenstrasse 57, Tel. [041] 32333). A first-class hotel, open from April-October. Rooms from $8 to $14 for best single, $16 to $28 for best double; private baths, central heating, continental breakfast; taxes and services included.

TOURIST ATTRACTIONS: Take advantage of the numerous excursions by boat, bus or mountain railway for some breathtaking views, especially of the Alps. There is also a famous music festival and the Richard Wagner Museum. The walker shouldn't miss a stroll along the lakeshore and through the old town.

FOR FURTHER INFORMATION: Write to: Secretary, Lucerne Golf Club, Lucerne, Switzerland. Telephone: (041) 21932.

Golf and Country Club Zürich

Golf at Zürich gives the visitor a twofold experience—a good game deep in the lovely countryside and proximity to a sophisticated city. Zürich is now the most important industrial and commercial center in Switzerland as well as a traditional hub of artistic festivals and intellectual life. The Zürich Country Club provides a pleasant, undulating course in fine surroundings, suitable for both long and short drivers. This course should present no great difficulties to the average golfer, although its good length requires solid hitting. The fairways and approaches to greens are good, and all hazards are clearly defined. This is a course of medium difficulty and should prove attractive to the visiting player.

LOCATION: The course is in Zumikon, about 6 miles from Zürich, 50 miles E of Basel, 30 miles NE of Lucerne, 74 miles NE of Bern, 135 miles NE of Lausanne, 172 miles NE of Geneva. It is accessible by car.

OTHER INFORMATION: The course is open to nonmembers on weekdays only; the season is from April 1 to October 31; a professional is always on hand. The weather is best from May to September. Practice ground is available.
Number of holes: 18. *Par:* 72. *Length:* 6300 yards.
Green fees: $5/day. *Lessons:* $2.50/half hour. *Caddies:* $3.50/18 holes. *Golfing equipment and caddie carts:* clubs $1.50/day, carts $.50/day.

OTHER SPORTS FACILITIES: Tennis, fishing, riding and swimming.

ACCOMMODATIONS: No living space in the club house, but restaurant and bar are available.
In Zürich: *Dolder Grand Hotel* (Kurhausstrasse 65, Tel. [051] 241700). One of the finest hotels in Zürich, open all year. Rooms from $8 to $15 for best single, $16 to $30 for best double; private baths, central heating; taxes, services, and continental breakfast not included. *Carlton-Elite* (Bahnhofstrasse 41, Tel. [051] 236636). A very good, comfortable hotel, open all year. Rooms from $8 to $11.50 for best single, $16 to $23 for best double; private baths, central heating; continental breakfast; taxes and services not included. *Bellerive au Lac* (Utoquai 47, Tel. [051] 327010). A very good, comfortable hotel, open all year. Rooms from $7.50 to $11 for best single, $15 to $22 for best double; private baths, central heating; continental breakfast; taxes and services not included.

TOURIST ATTRACTIONS: Zürich is possibly the most vital and exciting city in Switzerland. During the summer months there are many concerts, operas, dramatic and film festivals. The old town, with its narrow streets, ancient houses and wrought-iron signs, should not be missed. Toys, painted pottery, cut crystal and jewelry are specialties of the area—and, of course, watches. Of special interest is the Odeon Cafe, where Lenin spent almost all his time during the First World War. The Fine Arts Museum and the Swiss National Museum are especially recommended.

FOR FURTHER INFORMATION: Write to: Secretary, 8126 Zumikon, Switzerland. Telephone: 903167 and 903639.

WEST GERMANY

West German clubs are located in very fine surroundings, possibly not as spectacular as some in Scandinavia or Scotland but with a different kind of arrangement. Plenty of gardens, deep and varied woods and pleasant streams mark the limits of the fairways or provide the chief obstacles.

For those who find themselves in the most popular parts of Germany— Berlin, Hamburg, Bavaria, Cologne, Wiesbaden, Frankfurt, or in the north near the Baltic—there are always courses within driving distance. It should not be too difficult to combine good golf with a tour of the country. For the history buffs, several courses are in areas that figured prominently in World War II.

If you are near Hamburg, always a popular spot with visitors for its cultural attractions and bizarre night life, three courses give you a range from relatively easy to more difficult. Start with *Hamburger Land-und-Golf Club,* move on to *Hamburger* and finish with *Hamburg Walddörfer.* If you plan to make a real swing around West Germany, then try the Düsseldorf courses last. They are tough by anyone's standard, of excellent length, well bunkered, with narrow fairways. Particularly recommended are a long driver's course like *Bremen,* an especially well-balanced 18 like *Lubeck-*

Travemünder and a knotty links like *Augsburg*. All should provide pleasure and satisfaction and add immeasurably to your trip.

Golf-und-Land Club Berlin-Wannsee

Prosperous and still an important cultural and artistic center in Europe, West Berlin has retained some of its prewar excitement. And if you enjoy classical and modern theater, cabaret life and good music, you might include it on your European holiday. Right in the center of an attractive public garden near the western outskirts of Berlin, Berlin-Wannsee strikes a good balance for the wild-swinging power hitter and the less strong careful player. This is a diversified course, with good balance, neither difficult nor easy. It is good for the average player and for the visitor, especially if you later want to try the more difficult 18-holers that run close to 7000 yards.

LOCATION: The course is about 10 miles W of the heart of the city, 237 miles SE of Hamburg, 167 miles E of Hanover, 366 miles NE of Frankfurt, 368 miles E of Bonn, 348 miles E of Cologne, 375 miles N of Munich, 275 miles NE of Nürnberg. It is accessible by car.

OTHER INFORMATION: The course is open to guests of members of the club and to visitors who belong to a local club at home. It is open all year except January, and a professional is always on hand. The weather is best from June to September; the most crowded season is May through September. Practice ground is available.
Number of holes: 9. *Par:* 70 (twice around). *Length:* 5980 yards (2 x 2990).
Green fees: weekdays, $2.50; weekends, $3.50/day. *Lessons:* $3/hour. *Caddies:* $1/9 holes. *Golfing equipment and caddie carts:* none available.

OTHER SPORTS FACILITIES: Tennis.

ACCOMMODATIONS: None in the club house, but restaurant and bar are available.
In West Berlin: *Berlin Hilton* (Budapester Strasse 2, Tel. 130381). A luxury hotel of international standing, open all year. Rooms from $11.50 to $14 for best single, $23 to $30 for best double; private baths, central heating; taxes and services not included. *Savoy* (Fasanenstrasse 9, Tel. 325055). A first-class hotel of international standing, open all year. Rooms from $7.50 to $10 for best single, $15 to $20 for best double; private baths, central heating; taxes and services not included. *Tusculum* (Kurfürstendamm 68, Tel. 32.50.96). A very good and very comfortable hotel, open all year. Rooms from $5.50 to $8 for best single, $11 to $16 for best double; private baths, central heating; taxes and services not included. *Roxy* (Kurfürstendamm 34, Tel. 91.03.21). A good, comfortable hotel, open all year. Rooms from $3.25 to $5 for best single, $6.50 to $10 for best double; private baths, central heating; taxes and services not included.

TOURIST ATTRACTIONS: West Berlin is a tourist's paradise with just about everything you may want or need to make your stay comfortable and enjoyable: modern, sophisticated shopping centers, new theaters and movie houses, international hotels, first-class restaurants, smart off-beat night-clubs, dozens of museums (especially the Dahlem) and historical monuments and one of the best zoos in the world.

FOR FURTHER INFORMATION: Write to: Golf-und-Land Club Berlin-Wannsee, 1 Berlin 39, Am Stölpchenweg. Telephone: 805955.

Golf-Club Augsburg

Located in the outskirts of Augsburg, within touring range of some of the finest lake, forest and hill country in southeast Germany, this course should prove more rewarding to the long than to the short driver; but the rather narrow fairways and clever bunkering call also for straight, accurate play. For the less powerful player, there are several holes, like the 4th and 6th, that will be rewarding. This should be a pleasant, enjoyable course for the average golfer. There is also a women's course of 2795 yards.

Augsburg is over 2000 years old and is probably the best preserved large medieval city in Germany. It has had a turbulent history and has always attracted artists of international renown; Dürer, Titian and Licinio lived and worked in Augsburg, and Hans Holbein the Younger was born there.

LOCATION: The course is in Burgwalden, about 10 miles SW of Augsburg, 46 miles W of Munich, 94 miles S of Nürnberg, 306 miles SW of Berlin, 90 miles E of Stuttgart, 131 miles W of Salzburg, Austria. It is accessible by car.

OTHER INFORMATION: The course is open to nonmembers, unlimited, for the entire season (April-October), with a professional always on hand. The weather is best from July through September. Practice ground is available.

Number of holes: 9. *Par:* 36. *Length:* 3164 yards.

Green fees: weekdays, $2.50; weekends, $4/day. *Lessons:* $3/hour. *Caddies:* $1/9 holes. *Golfing equipment and caddie carts:* clubs $2/day, carts $.50/day.

OTHER SPORTS FACILITIES: Tennis, swimming and riding.

ACCOMMODATIONS: No living space in the club house, but restaurant and bar are available.

In Augsburg: *Palasthotel Drei Mohren* (Maximilianstrasse 40, Tel. 20321). A first-class hotel of international standing, open all year. Rooms from $7.50 to $9 for best single, $15 to $18 for best double; private baths, central heating; taxes and services not included. *Parkhotel Weisses Lamm* (Ludwigstrasse 36, Tel. 22705). A very good, comfortable hotel, open all year. Rooms from $5 to $7 for best single, $10 to $12 for best double; private baths, central heating, continental breakfast; taxes and services included.

TOURIST ATTRACTIONS: You should see the Cathedral of Augsburg, over a thousand years old, with famous eleventh-century bronze doors and paintings by Holbein the Elder; Mozarthaus, where Mozart's father was born; some good medieval and Renaissance churches; a very good art museum with works by Holbein, Dürer, Titian, Rubens and Rembrandt; an opera house; a puppet theater.

FOR FURTHER INFORMATION: Write to: Secretary, Golf-Club Augsburg e.V., Hofer Strasse 10, 89 Augsburg, Germany. Telephone: 42731-36.

Club zur Vahr Bremen

Probably the oldest port in Germany, Bremen dates back to the eighth-century, when it was one of the northern outposts of Charlemagne's empire. Today it is one of Germany's most important cities and its second biggest port. The course, on the flat, open countryside north of Bremen, is stiff and challenging and requires endurance as well as careful, accurate play; full of clever hazards and difficult bunkering, it strongly favors the long driver, many of the holes being well over 500 yards. Its length and difficulty remind one of the toughest Scottish courses. Don't begin here or in Düsseldorf unless you are somewhat experienced.

LOCATION: The course is in Garlstedt, about 20 miles N of Bremen, 15 miles S of Bremerhaven, 97 miles W of Hamburg, 93 miles NW of Hanover, 266 miles NW of Berlin. It is accessible by car.

OTHER INFORMATION: The course is open to nonmembers, unlimited, for the entire year, and a professional is always on hand. The weather is best from May to September. Practice ground is available.
Number of holes: 9. *Par:* 75. *Length:* 6866 yards.
Green fees: $3/day. *Lessons:* $2.50/hour. *Caddies:* $1.25/18 holes. *Golfing equipment and caddie carts:* clubs $1.50/day, carts $.50/day.

OTHER SPORTS FACILITIES: Hockey, tennis, swimming.

ACCOMMODATIONS: No living space in the club house, but restaurant and bar are available.
In Bremen: *Columbus* (Bahnhofsplatz 5, Tel. 314161). A very good, comfortable hotel, open all year. Rooms from $6.75 to $8 for best single, $13.50 to $16 for best double; private baths, central heating; taxes and services not included. *Übersee Hotel* (Watchtstrasse 27, Tel. 320197). A good, comfortable hotel, open all year. Rooms from $4 to $5.50 for best single, $8 to $11 for best double; private baths, central heating; taxes and services included.

In Bremerhaven: *Nordsee-Hotel Naber* (Theodor-Heuss-Platz 1, Tel. 47001). A very good, comfortable hotel, open all year. Rooms from $6 to $8.50 for best single, $12 to $17 for best double; private baths, central heating; taxes and services not included.

TOURIST ATTRACTIONS: Bremen is a good place for you to get the feel of port life in northern Germany. Especially recommended are some interesting old restaurants and bars, a twelfth-century church, the Liebfrauenkirche (the Church of our Lady), a few historic buildings in the center of town, where you can see one of the few statues of Roland in Europe, and the Overseas Museum (Überseemuseum), devoted to nationalities and cultures from all over the world.

FOR FURTHER INFORMATION: Write to: Secretary, Club zur Vahr, 28 Bremen, Germany. Telephone: Bremen 321671.

Land-und-Golf Club Düsseldorf

The course is one of the longest and also one of the toughest in Germany. It is made for the power hitter (several of the holes are between 400 and 500 yards) and demands careful, accurate play as well. It has variety and surprises, including plenty of detail in the bunkering, the hazards and approaches. This is not a course to start your European tour with; it is, frankly, tough. Work up to Düsseldorf with some of the 9-holers in Lübeck, Augsburg and Wiesbaden.

LOCATION: The course is in Hubbelrath bei Düsseldorf, about 9 miles from Düsseldorf, 33 miles N of Cologne, 49 miles N of Bonn, 150 miles NW of Frankfurt, 256 miles SW of Hamburg, 354 miles W of Berlin, 169 miles SW of Hanover. It is accessible by car.

OTHER INFORMATION: The course is open to nonmembers for the entire year, but golfer must be a member of a home club; a professional is on hand from March through October. The weather is best from June to August, with June and July the most crowded months. Practice ground is available.
Number of holes: 18. *Par:* 73. *Length:* 6864 yards.
Green fees: weekdays, $2.75; weekends, $4/day. *Lessons:* $3/hour. *Caddies:* $1.50/18 holes. *Golfing equipment and caddie carts:* none available.

OTHER SPORTS FACILITIES: Riding, swimming and tennis.

ACCOMMODATIONS: No living space in the club house, but restaurant and bar are available. See accommodations section under *Düsseldorfer Golf Club,* p. 275.

TOURIST ATTRACTIONS: See this section under *Düsseldorfer Golf Club,* pp. 275-276.

FOR FURTHER INFORMATION: Write to: Secretary, Land und Golf Club Düsseldorf, Düsseldorf, Germany. Telephone: Mettmann 22422 or 24548.

Düsseldorfer Golf-Club

Designed by the English architect Hawtree, this course, along with Land und Golf Düsseldorf, is one of the most challenging and rewarding in Germany. It is laid out for both long and short drivers and calls for accurate play. Both Düsseldorf courses are carefully designed, and the careless player will find himself wincing. Like the other course, this one is tough. Don't start with it. Its length alone requires experience.

Düsseldorf is worth visiting. It is the economic and cultural center of the Rhineland (the artist quarter with its outdoor cafes will immediately remind you of Paris), the center of West Germany's new fashion industry, and an excellent place to try the regional cuisine associated with the Rhineland.

LOCATION: The course is in Ratingen in NW Germany, 8 miles N of Düsseldorf, 32 miles N of Cologne, 48 miles N of Bonn, 149 miles NW of Frankfurt, 356 miles W of Berlin, 170 miles SW of Hanover, 257 miles SW of Hamburg. It is accessible by car.

OTHER INFORMATION: The course is open to nonmembers, unlimited, for the entire year; a professional is always on hand. The weather is best from August to September. Practice ground is available. *Number of holes:* 18. *Par:* 72. *Length:* 6600 yards. *Green fees:* weekdays $2.50; weekends $5/day. *Lessons:* $3/half hour. *Caddies:* available at $1.50/18 holes. *Golfing equipment and caddie carts:* clubs $1.50/day, no carts.

OTHER SPORTS FACILITIES: Tennis and boating.

ACCOMMODATIONS: No living space in the club house, but restaurant and bar are available.

In Düsseldorf: *Breidenbacher Hof* (Heinrich-Heine-Allee 36, Tel. 8601). A luxury hotel of international standing, open all year. Rooms from $8.75 to $13 for best single, $17.50 to $26 for best double; private baths, central heating; taxes and services not included. *Savoy* (Breite Strasse 2, Tel. 20541). A very good, comfortable hotel, open all year. Rooms from $8 to $10 for best single, $14 to $20 for best double; private baths, central heating; taxes and services not included. *Prinz Anton* (Karl-Anton-Strasse 11, Tel. 352055). A very good, comfortable hotel, open all year. Rooms from $5 to $9 for best single, $10 to $18 for best double; private baths, central heating; taxes and services included.

TOURIST ATTRACTIONS: Recommended for the visitor are some famous museums, including the Goethe Museum and a good art museum, libraries, churches, a zoo, an aquarium, a castle and many lovely parks and gardens; there are some splendid walking tours along the Rhine. Don't miss the boat trips up and down the Rhine.

FOR FURTHER INFORMATION: Write to: Secretary, Düsseldorfer Golf Club, 403 Ratingen Golfplatz, Ratingen, Germany.

Hamburger Land-und-Golf Club

The Hamburg Land-und-Golf Club is in the southern outskirts of Hamburg in flat industrial country. Cut out of a dense wood, the course, although rather short by championship standards, is tough and challenging. The fairways are lined with trees and are very narrow, especially for the first 11 holes, with many doglegs. The fact that several of the greens cannot be seen from the tees adds to the difficulty. The course is made for both the long and the short driver and calls for very careful, accurate play. With this course, the visitor to Hamburg has three links of excellent golf, and this might be the one to begin with.

LOCATION: The course is about 2 miles from Hittfeld, 8 miles S of Harburg, 20 miles S of Hamburg, 160 miles SW of Lübeck, 65 miles NE of Bremen, 72 miles N of Hanover, 259 miles NW of Berlin, 300 miles NE of Frankfurt, 280 miles NE of Bonn. Best way to get there from Hamburg is to take the autobahn to Bremen and turn off at Hittfeld.

OTHER INFORMATION: The course is open to nonmembers, limited, for the entire year; a professional is always on hand. The weather is best in May, June, August and September. Practice ground is available.
Number of holes: 18. Par: 74. Length: 5245 yards.
Green fees: weekdays, $2.50; weekends, $4/day. Lessons: $3/hour. Caddies: $1.50/18 holes. Golfing equipment and caddie carts: none available.

OTHER SPORTS FACILITIES: Swimming, tennis, riding.

ACCOMMODATIONS: No living space in the club house, but restaurant and bar are available. For accommodations see this section under Hamburger Golf Club, p. 279, and Hamburg Walddörfer, p. 277.

TOURIST ATTRACTIONS: See this section under Hamburger Golf Club, p. 279.

FOR FURTHER INFORMATION: Write to: Secretary, Hamburger Land-und-Golf Club in der Lüneburger Heide, Hamburg, Germany. Telephone: Hittfield 04105/2331.

Golf Club Hamburg-Walddörfer E.V.

The course, one of the best in northern Germany, is in the Walddörfer, a fine old residential area in rural surroundings a few miles outside Hamburg. It favors the long, accurate driver, since many of the holes are well over 450 yards, with 7 par-5 holes. But as with so many other German courses, both length and precision are necessary. A course of medium difficulty, Hamburg-Walddörfer, along with Hamburger in the same area, is a good place to begin, unless, of course, you can first work out of a 9-holer in Lübeck or Augsburg. There is also a woman's course of 5710 yards.

LOCATION: In Hoisbüttel, about 12 miles N of Hamburg, 28 miles SW of Lübeck, 62 miles NE of Bremen, 82 miles N of Hanover, 254 miles NW of Berlin, 323 miles NE of Frankfurt, 303 miles NE of Bonn. It is accessible by car.

OTHER INFORMATION: The course is open to nonmembers, unlimited, for the entire season (May-November), but the player must be a member of a golf club; two professionals are always on hand. The most crowded months are September and October, with the weather best from May to October. Practice ground is available.
Number of holes: 18. *Par:* 73. *Length:* 6298 yards.
Green fees: weekdays, $2.50; weekends, $4.50/day. *Lessons:* $3/hour. *Caddies:* $1.50/18 holes. *Golfing equipment and caddie carts:* clubs $1.50/day, carts $.50/day.

OTHER SPORTS FACILITIES: Tennis and riding.

ACCOMMODATIONS: No living space in the club house, but restaurant and bar are available.
In Hamburg: *Atlantic* (An der Alster 73, Tel. 248001). A first-class hotel of international standing, open all year: rooms from $12 to $15 for the best single, $24 to $30 for the best double; private baths, central heating; taxes and services not included. *Alsterhof* (Esplanade 12, Tel. 341781). A very good, comfortable hotel, open all year. Rooms from $7.50 to $10 for best single, $15 to $20 for best double; private baths, central heating; taxes and services not included. *Reichshof* (Kirchenallee 34, Tel. 241212). A very good, comfortable hotel, open all year. Rooms from $6.25 to $7.50 for the best single, $13.50 to $15 for best double; private baths, central heating; taxes and services included.

TOURIST ATTRACTIONS: See this section under *Hamburger Golf Club*, p. 279.

FOR FURTHER INFORMATION: Write to: Secretary, Golfclub Hamburg-Walddörfer, 2071 Hoisbüttel über Ahrensburg, Germany.

Shell's Wonderful World of Golf

Hamburger Golf Club, one of three excellent courses near the city of Hamburg in northern Germany.

The Hamburger Golf Club offers the visitor the delights of beautiful countryside by day and the facilities of a large and sophisticated city by night. Located only 10 miles from the center of Hamburg, the club is surrounded by woods, heath and hillocks. It is a challenging course, possibly favoring the long driver but not discouraging to the shorter driver who favors precision over power. Although many of the holes are over 450 yards, sheer strength will never get you through the narrow fairways. For the golfer interested in a pleasant course, not too difficult but demanding enough to give his game a workout, the Hamburger Golf Course is to be recommended.

LOCATION: About 10 miles from the center of Hamburg, 30 miles SW of Lübeck, 60 miles NE of Bremen, 80 miles N of Hanover, 252 miles NW of Berlin, 321 miles NE of Frankfurt, 301 miles NE of Bonn.

OTHER INFORMATION: The course is limited and closed to non-members, but if a golfer is a member of another club, he can qualify as a guest member. Hamburger is open the entire year, and a professional is always on hand. The weather is best from June to August. Practice ground is available.

Number of holes: 18. *Par:* 73. *Length:* 6533 yards.

Green fees: weekdays, $2.50; weekends,, $4.50/day. *Lessons:* $3/hour. *Caddies:* $1.50/18 holes. *Golfing equipment and caddie carts:* clubs $1.50/day, carts $.50/day.

OTHER SPORTS FACILITIES: Swimming, tennis and riding.

ACCOMMODATIONS: No living space in the club house, but restaurant and bar are available.

In Hamburg: *Vier Jahreszeiten* (Neuer Jungfernstieg 9, Tel. 341014). A very pleasant, first-class hotel of international standing, open all year. Rooms from $10 to $15 for best single, $20 to $30 for best double; private baths, central heating; taxes and services not included. *Berlin* (Borgfelder Strasse 1-9, Tel. 264351). A very good, comfortable and pleasant hotel, open all year. Rooms from $7.50 to $9.50 for best single, $15 to $19 for best double; private baths, central heating; taxes and services not included. *Bellevue* (An der Alster 14, Tel. 242746). A good, comfortable hotel, open all year. Rooms from $6.50 to $7.75 for best single, $13 to $15.50 for best double; private baths, central heating; taxes and services not included.

TOURIST ATTRACTIONS: Hamburg has many attractions of which it has reason to be proud—its lovely Alster Lake, its broad acres of parks, its bustling port, its theaters and superb orchestras, its historic sites, its old picturesque cafes and restaurants. And if you are looking for wild night life, don't miss a visit to the justly famous St. Pauli district.

FOR FURTHER INFORMATION: Write to: Mrs. Lore Schrader, Hamburger Golf Club, Hamburg 55, Germany. Telephone: 812177.

Lübeck-Travemünder Golf Klub

The Lübeck-Travemünder Golf Klub is in northeast Germany on the outskirts of Travemünde, a lovely Baltic resort with old houses, a good sandy beach, small shipyards and a large fleet of fishing boats. The Casino, specializing in roulette and baccarat, is known throughout Europe and has made Travemünde the most popular resort in Northern Germany.

The course should present no difficulties to the average golfer and is a good place to begin, to get the feel of a European links. There is overall balance, with the holes distributed for the long and short hitter—two 5s, two 3s, the rest 4s. There are no special difficulties or unique features.

LOCATION: The course is about 2 miles from Travemünde, 18 miles NE of Lübeck, 85 miles NE of Hamburg, 330 miles NW of Berlin, 200 miles NE of Bremen, 565 miles NE of Bonn. It is accessible by car.

OTHER INFORMATION: The course is open to nonmembers, unlimited, for the entire year, and a professional is always on hand. The most crowded months are July and August, with the weather best from June to September. Practice ground is available.

Number of holes: 9. *Par:* 72 (for twice around). *Length:* 6240 yards. *Green fees:* weekdays, $4; weekends, $5.50/day. *Lessons:* $2/half hour. *Caddies:* $1/9 holes. *Golfing equipment and caddie carts:* clubs $2/9 holes, carts $.50/9 holes.

OTHER SPORTS FACILITIES: Tennis, riding, fishing, hunting and bathing.

ACCOMMODATIONS: No living space in the club house, but restaurant is available.

In Travemünde: *Kurhaus-Hotel* (Aussenallee 10, Tel. 2821). A first-class hotel of international standing, open May-September. Rooms from $6.50 to $8.75 for best single, $13 to $18 for best double; private baths, central heating; taxes and services not included. *Strand-Hotel* (Kaiserallee 2B, Tel. 2652). A very good, comfortable hotel, open all year. Rooms from $4.50 to $8 for best single, $9 to $16 for best double; private baths and showers, central heating; taxes and services not included.

In Lübeck: *Parkhotel am Holstentor* (Holstentorplatz 7, Tel. 76057). A very good, comfortable hotel, open all year. Rooms from $4.50 to $7.50 for best single, $9 to $13.50 for best double; private baths, central heating; taxes and services included.

TOURIST ATTRACTIONS: The area has some very old churches, with walking tours along the sea, a gambling casino, deep-sea fishing and historic sites. In the Salzepeicher, an old section, the visitor will see many medieval merchant residences. For the literary-minded, its is the native city of Thomas Mann and the setting for many of his novels.

FOR FURTHER INFORMATION: Write to: Lübeck-Travemünder Golf Klub, 2407 Travemünde, Germany, Telephone: Lübeck-Travemünde 2939.

Wiesbadener Golf Club

Wiesbaden, the capital of Hesse, is a modern, cosmopolitan city with a long historical past. It was founded about 10 B.C. by Roman legions, who were attracted by the warm springs and mild climate. To this day, Wiesbaden is known throughout Europe as a famous spa. The course, on the outskirts of Wiesbaden, is sheltered from winds and cold by the Taunus Mountains. It is hilly and picturesque and has a winding creek through its center. Lovely to look at and not too difficult to play, the Wiesbadener Course should appeal to both the power hitter and the short, accurate player. It is good place to begin your golf if you are touring Germany.

LOCATION: The course is about 8 miles NE of Wiesbaden, 22 miles W of Frankfurt, 88 miles SE of Bonn, 101 miles SE of Cologne, 369 miles SW of Berlin. It is accessible by car.

OTHER INFORMATION: The course is open to nonmembers, unlimited, for the entire season (April-October), and a professional is always on hand. June, July and August are the most crowded months, with the best weather in August and September. Practice ground is available. *Number of holes:* 9. *Par:* 70 (for twice around). *Length:* 5124 yards (2 x 2562). *Green fees:* weekdays, $2; weekends, $3/day. *Lessons:* $1.50/half hour. *Caddies:* available only on Sundays at $2/18 holes. *Golfing equipment and caddie carts:* clubs $2.50/day, carts $.50/day.

OTHER SPORTS FACILITIES: Riding, sailing, shooting and tennis.

ACCOMMODATIONS: No living space in the club house, but restaurant and bar are available.

In Wiesbaden: *Rose* (Kranzplatz 8, Tel. 39591). A first-class hotel of international standing, open all year. Rooms from $6.75 to $10.50 for best single, $13.50 to $21 for best double; private baths, central heating; taxes and services not included. *Blum* (Wilhelmstrasse 44, Tel. 39611). A very good, comfortable hotel, open all year. Rooms from $5 to $7 for best single, $10 to $14 for best double; private baths, central heating; taxes and services not included.

TOURIST ATTRACTIONS: Recommended are excursions on the Rhine, where there are many castles dating back to the Middle Ages, an international opera and drama festival in May, museums specializing in German, Dutch and Italian masters and possibly the best champagne in Germany. There is also a well-established casino.

FOR FURTHER INFORMATION: Write to: Secretary, Wiesbadener Golf-Club, Wiesbaden, Germany. Telephone: Wiesbaden 41038.

THE AUTHOR AND HIS BOOK

SAUL GALIN is a sportsman, a seasoned traveler, and a free-lance writer with a broad range of interests. A New Yorker, born in 1926, Mr. Galin has at various times been a teacher and the editor of a literary magazine. He is co-author of *The Complete Puppy and Dog Book* (Atheneum, 1965). His love of travel has taken him far and wide, but most often to Europe, where his fluency in French and German is a decided asset. Sports in which Mr. Galin excels (and those he likes best) are fishing, hunting, skiing, camping, mountain climbing, sports car racing—and, of course, golf. Mr. and Mrs. Galin and their two children live in New York City between trips to Europe.

GOLF IN EUROPE was set in type by the Pyramid Composition Company, Inc., of New York. The text type is Caledonia, which was designed by William Addison Dwiggins and was cut by the Mergenthaler Linotype Company in 1938. Its name (which is the ancient Roman name for what is now called Scotland) denotes that the face was intended to have a Scottish-Roman character.

A HAWTHORN BOOK